D0228621

YOUTH IN TRANSITION

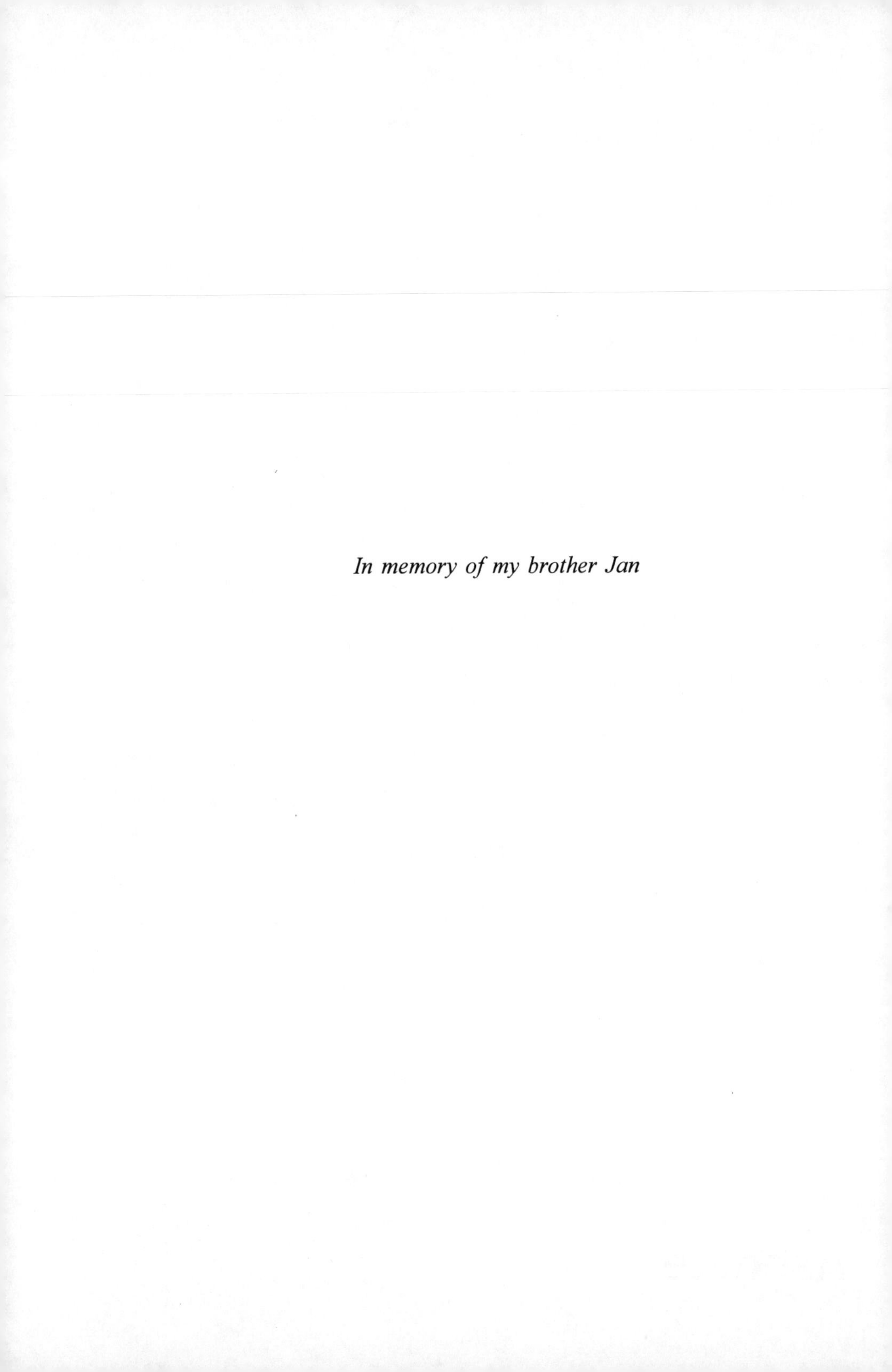

In memory of my brother Jan

Youth in Transition

Housing, employment, social policies and families in France and Spain

TERESA JURADO GUERRERO
Universidad Nacional de Educación a Distancia, Madrid

Ashgate

Published by
Ashgate Publishing Limited
Gower House
Croft Road
Aldershot
Hampshire GU11 3HR
England

Ashgate Publishing Company
131 Main Street
Burlington, VT 05401-5600 USA

Ashgate website: http://www.ashgate.com

British Library Cataloguing in Publication Data
Jurado Guerrero, Teresa
Youth in transition : housing, employment, social policies and families in France and Spain
1. Youth - Spain - Social conditions 2. Youth - France - Social conditions 3. Youth - Employment - Spain 4. Youth - Employment - France
I. Title
305.2'355'0944

Library of Congress Control Number: 2001094284

ISBN 0 7546 1816 1

Printed and bound in Great Britain by MPG Books Ltd, Bodmin, Cornwall

Contents

List of Figures

List of Tables

Appendix Tables

Preface

This study is one of the first in-depth cross-national comparisons of living arrangements of young people in Europe. It compares two countries and proposes a theoretical framework for understanding international variations in young people's living conditions and transitions to adulthood. For this scope it asks a very concrete question 'Why do some young people stay longer at home than others?' The answer to this question leads to a sociological interpretation of differences in the opportunity structures of young people and of their respective strategies in the transition to social independence. The particularity of the research is that it links micro and macro-level analysis, it matches two national large-scale surveys and it treats a topic which is of relevance for many people and for social policy reforms.

This book poses the question why Spanish young people leave home later than French youth and it answers it from a socio-economic perspective. In 1992, three quarters of French young people had already left home by age 29, while in Spain not even the majority of their counterparts were socially independent. Besides late nest-leaving, most Spanish young people connect departure from home with marriage. By contrast, in France young people leave home very frequently also in order to live in a residence hall for students, to live in a one-person household or to cohabit with a partner.

The study of two large national surveys with logistic regression techniques and the institutional analysis of French and Spanish social policies reveal the existence of different individual strategies for becoming socially independent in the two countries. French young people have to enter a labour market with high unemployment and short-term employment rates. Yet, active employment policy, extensive public housing supply and housing allowances, frequent support from parents and comparatively high wage levels allow them to set up their own households early. Spanish young people face a labour market with even higher unemployment and short-term employment rates, and the difficult integration into stable employment is not mitigated by a supply of public housing nor by extensive and generous public allowances, but must coexist with a very crowded housing market with high prices and rents. Spanish young people obtain subsistence-level wages comparatively late and they have to rely mainly on parental help not only whilst in education but also during the phase of entering the labour market and of acquiring a home. Unlike their French contemporaries, Spanish women have much more difficulties in pursuing an individual strategy of household formation, since they depend more frequently on marriage and on a spouse with a stable job when leaving home.

Teresa Jurado Guerrero
U.N.E.D.
Department of Social Structure
Madrid, April 2001.

Acknowledgements

A PhD thesis is a personal challenge and it needs much support from different sides. It would have been impossible to go through the last years without the unconditional support of my parents, María and Juan who have transmitted to me so many abilities. My partners have been very important; in particular Benno, who for so many years contributed to my happiness and Ivan who transmits to me his optimism and good humour. My friends and flat-mates of the last years made sure that I did not loose contact with real life. I thank all my friends in Germany for not forgetting me during my absence: Hava who is always on my side when I need her, and María, Ibo, Hüseyin, Mario, Bärbel and Dieter. I thank my friends in Italy and France who accompanied me during difficult moments: Maria José, Elena, Catherine, Manuela, Guido, Franca, Anne, Josep, Gerben, Davide, Guglielmo and Ciaran. The last months of my work in Spain were very nice thanks to Nacho, Kattya and Josu who really took care of me and thanks to Ana, María, Daniel, Loli, Susanna, Wili and Fabian, and my family in Madrid.

Much of the content of this work is the result of very useful advice from Peter Flora, Manuela Naldini, Lluis Flaquer, Elisabet Almeda, Birgit Fix, Colin Crouch, María José González, Pau Miret, Catherine Marry, Richard Breen, Antonio Villanacci, Guido Legnante, Luis Garrido, Miguel Requena and Juan Jesús González. Elmar Rieger taught me how to become a sociologist and he always increased my self-confidence. Colin Crouch was like a good father during the years in Florence. Richard Breen helped me a great deal with doing multivariate statistical analysis without losing substance. I thank all my colleagues of the Mannheim Centre for European Social Research, and in particular Franz Kraus and Marlene Alle for their help with questions related to data acquisition and transformation. José Saturnino Martínez helped me a lot with the Spanish data. I have to underline the cordial reception and the support received from the researchers of IRESCO/LASMAS in Paris, Catherine Marry, Annick Kieffer, Irène Mearelli Fournier and Jaël Brinbaum. My time in the Juan March Institute in Madrid also was very nice thanks to the friendly researchers and librarians.

I have received grants and logistic support from many different institutions in Europe. In Germany: *Deutsche Forschungsgemeinschaft,*

Mannheimer Graduiertenkolleg, *Deutscher Akademischer Austauschdienst,* and *Robert Bosch Stiftung*. The EURODATA archive of the *Mannheimer Zentrum für Europäische Sozialforschung* provided me with the Spanish survey "Encuesta Sociodemográfica, 1991" conducted by the INE. The completion of the thesis was supported by the *Freudenberg Stiftung*. In France help came from the *Institut de Recherche sur les Sociétés Contemporaines* and the *CNRS*. The use of the survey "Enquête Jeunes, 1992" conducted by the INSEE was possible thanks to a collaboration with Catherine Marry of LASMAS-IDL. In Spain I received support from the *Instituto de Estudios Sociales Avanzados*, the *Centro de Estudios Sociales Avanzados*, the *Ministerio de Educación y Ciencia, Diputació de Barcelona,* and the *Generalitat de Catalunya*. At the transnational level the *European Science Foundation*, and, last but not least, the *European University Institute* have to be mentioned. The EUI was a good place to write the dissertation in freedom. I thank Nicki Hargreaves and Nicky Owtram for their help and encouragement with the English language, Cecilia Picchi for her very motivating introduction into the Italian language and Eva Breivik for helping with the completion of the thesis. Last, the preparation of the publication was supported by the Department of Sociology II of the *Universidad Nacional de Educación a Distancia* and by Juan with great patience.

1 Comparison of Young People's Living Arrangements

Introduction

This research deals with an extended current social phenomenon in Europe: the difficult transition of young people into adulthood. Particularly, in Southern Europe young people have difficulty in finding stable employment and in creating their own independent households; thus the family formation process is delayed and for some young people it will not be possible to create a family at all. For most young people, to reach the legal recognition of adulthood does not mean reaching the social status of adulthood. In 1994, 60% of Spanish employed people between the ages of 25 and 30 still lived in their parents' households. This is an issue which also appeared on the first page of the Spanish newspaper 'El País' (28.4.1997) and which has been discussed in a commission of the Spanish parliament. A similar article appeared at the same time in an Italian newspaper (Corriere della Sera 22.4.97). Of all of the Italians between the ages of 25 and 34, 33% still lived with their parents.

Late Nest-Leaving: Social Problem or Social Resource?

The definition of a social problem is often ambiguous and can change rapidly over time. Often the deviant behaviour of social groups, for example, youth riots in French cities, changes the perception of a situation, and consequently gives rise to the perception of a social problem until then not amply recognised as such. As long as the situation of long-lasting intergenerational co-residence is not seen in connection with any other social phenomena that most citizens or experts might classify as a social or political problem, these family patterns do not constitute a social problem in itself or, at least, not a widely recognised social problem.

Delayed emancipation of young people from their family of origin is seen as a problem especially because of its consequences for the demography of the societies affected. The gross marriage rate has fallen sharply since the 1960s in all member states of the European Union and it is particularly low in Italy and Spain (Jurado/Naldini 1996). As a consequence, the total fertility rate has also decreased strongly in the last decades. Since the mid 1980s, Spain and Italy have had the lowest birth rates in the European Union (Delgado Pérez/Livi-Bacci 1992). In conclusion, the reproduction of families is in crisis, and it is still not clear what the final results will be.

A totally different perspective of the effects of long-lasting cohabitation with parents results from the idea that a late transition from the family of origin to the family of destination without a phase of independent non-family living contributes to the reproduction of traditional marriage and family patterns. Goldscheider and Waite (1987) have found some first evidence that women living independently during their youth delay their marriages and that these experiences reduce their orientation towards traditional family roles. If the contrary is also true, then it could be argued that an important element in the reproduction of the Southern family model is the delayed nest-leaving pattern of women. Scholars who have analysed the role of strong family solidarity and family networks among different generations argue in a similar way. Strong family networks are supposed to favour gender-specific roles within couples (Bruckner et al. 1993).

Delayed home-leaving patterns have demographic and social consequences, but they can also affect the well being of families in terms of conflicts and frustration. Some survey data give an approximate picture of the perception of the long lasting cohabitation of young people with their parents by the general public.[1] In 1993, Europeans were asked: 'Compared to ten years ago, grown-up children tend to stay in their parent's homes longer. In your opinion is it quite a good thing or quite a bad thing?' Most Europeans said that it is quite a good thing (52%), while 20% answered that it is quite a bad thing and 22% said that it is neither one nor the other. The divergences between countries are not very pronounced, with the exception of Spain and Greece. Only around 30% of Spaniards think that it is 'quite a good thing', while about 70% of Greeks do so. Nearly 40% of Spaniards say that it is neither the one nor the other and about 30% say that it is quite a bad thing. Contrary to Spaniards, Italians and the French express opinions that are in line with the European average (Eurobarometer 1993), i.e. these answers show that a great majority of the general public in the European Union does not see this as a social problem.

Things change if the opinions of people directly affected are surveyed. In Spain, in 1985 and in 1997, more than half of the single young people aged 15 to 29 and living with their parents wished to leave the parental home, a proportion which increases with age. Young people said that the largest obstacle to leaving was that of economic problems (Valles 1992, Cruz/Santiago 1999). In a survey conducted among young Basques (1990), the age group between 25 and 29 years showed the highest degree of dissatisfaction with living in the parental home, and of those living in the family of origin 48% wished to leave (Elzo 1990). In 1993, 72% of the Spanish young people aged 21 to 24 lived with their parents, and of these 42% stated that they were satisfied, while 58% expressed dissatisfaction (Elzo Ímaz et al. 1994). Thus, at least half of the Spanish young people who live with their parents are not satisfied with this situation. One could even argue that some of the young people who declare themselves to be satisfied say so because they have adapted psychologically to this situation. This would mean that it is the result of a process of cognitive consonance with an objective situation which does not permit emancipation from the family of origin for economic reasons. Some young people also seem to feel that dependence on their parents is a restriction on their freedom, especially if they seek social independence. In qualitative research in the United Kingdom, Wallace (1988) found that young unemployed people who were more dependent upon parental subsidy were also more subject to parental moral control.

Up to this point it has been assumed that if there is a social problem it stems from the excessive length of intergenerational co-residence. Not everybody thinks in this way. In the United Kingdom, for example, voices have been raised in the last few years which find leaving the parental home prematurely to be just as much of a problem, because it is seen in connection with the increasing homelessness of young people. In consequence, appeals are made to prevent young people from leaving home 'too early' (Jones 1995). Other research also suggests that some young people living outside a family setting risk loneliness, depression, and illness (Riesman and Gerstel 1985 in: Goldscheider/Goldscheider 1993).

The fact that parents accept young adults at home and even favour their long permanence should be seen as a social resource, in particular when young people live with parents who are able and willing to support their children financially and emotionally. Emotional help during the difficult and often frustrating transition from school to work, during phases of unemployment or of precarious employment can be very important. The family can also protect its members from the pressures of the labour market, so that young people can exit from very bad jobs and find help at home (Wallerstein 1984). The family can be especially important for women who do not want to repeat the role of their mothers and therefore intend to stay in education for a long time with the aim of entering a highly qualified job. Staying in their parents' home for a long period can thus represent an adequate strategy in a context of difficult employment situations (Flaquer 1995). One last important function of parents is well-known: the possibility of living in the family of origin allows young people to save a good part of their income in order to start a family with a relatively high standard of living. It is important to notice that parents can only fulfil these protective and support functions if they have enough emotional and financial resources to do so; otherwise they might present more difficulties than solutions for their children.

Long-lasting intergenerational co-residence can also represent a social resource for society as a whole. A high rate of resource-pooling households lowers the overall costs of social reproduction and partially prevents the reduction of consumption standards. Consequently, extended co-residence also has to be seen as a societal resource for competition in global markets.

Staying in the parental home for a long time and depending financially on one's parents might well cause tension, frustration, and drug abuse, just as leaving early can increase certain risks such as poverty, homelessness, deviant behaviour, and illness. There is no biological or natural law which appoints the right moment for leaving the family of origin, even if the majority of human beings leave their parents in their process of becoming adults and autonomous individuals. The right moment is socially constructed and varies in time and in geographical space. A social problem emerges in two cases within a given time and geographical space: first, if leaving the family of origin is not possible at the time it is socially expected, and, second, if the creation of a new family at the socially expected time becomes difficult and ends in a failure. In those cases societies can adapt in two ways to the lack of fit. First, by changing the social definition of the right time of leaving the parental home, and, second, by helping young people to create new families through the specific regulation of markets and families. Does a common definition of the right time exist within Europe?

In general, for Western Europe since World War II some socially legitimised definitions about the right time to leave the family of origin can be found. The most legitimate mode of family emancipation, in particular for men, is to first find a job and then to marry in order to create a new family. It is possible to marry and still stay on with the parents for some time, but in Western Europe this is always a minority phenomenon because the norm of neolocality is highly valued. A young person who is financially independent can also live in the parental home, but in these cases legitimacy problems may begin to emerge. These general norms explain why research results about young people who are employed but still live with their parents were given a particular attention in the newspapers cited before. These young people are beginning to go beyond the limits of legitimised and thus unproblematic behaviour. In consequence, this behaviour is discussed as a social problem. If the young person has no partner, staying at home is probably more legitimate than if he or she has a partner. If the child helps to finance household expenditure, his or her permanence might also be more legitimate. However, in some societies to reach a certain age in conditions of financial independence seems to be more strongly linked with leaving the parental home than in others. In general, there is a strong relationship between being financially dependent on the parents and living in the parents' household. On the other hand, the link between financial dependence and staying at home is weakened in some societies for young students. Often parents consider migration to another living place in order to pursue studies as a legitimate departure and they finance it. Thus, in those cases, young people create their own household, being totally or partially financially dependent on parents.

Macrosociological Frame and Research Questions

The phenomenon of the transition into adulthood, in particular, the transition from the family of origin to the family of destination, displays important cross-national and regional variations. These variations have their origin in the way in which the family is institutionalised across societies, i.e. the social construction of the division of labour between three societal institutions: the family, the market, and the state. The theoretical aim of this research is to contribute to the theory on Welfare States by focusing on the family in one southern European and one north-western European country, and on the construction of citizenship for young people. The point is that in Southern Europe we find a particular model of social division of labour between the market, the state, and the family, and a specific social construction of youth.

The market structure of Southern Europe, in particular Italy and Spain, is different from that in other West European societies and it is characterised by:

1. the generally subordinated role of these economies in the international division of work;
2. the more intensive economic crisis, that is, higher and structural unemployment (characterised by a higher percentage of unemployed women, young people and long-term unemployed people);
3. a labour market with many precarious jobs that affect young people and women in particular, high employment in agriculture, a high rate of self-employed people as well as a higher rate of workers working in small enterprises and last but not least, a high propensity toward informal jobs (OECD 1994, European Commission 2000);
4. few opportunities for part-time employment in the formal sector; and
5. the concentration of economic and social disadvantages in some areas and regions.

At the same time social policies are also institutionalised in a peculiar way. In Italy and Spain, the entitlement and the level of public social benefits and social services are often related to the family unit and to family income. Social assistance, support for agricultural workers, family allowances, help for handicapped persons, scholarships, services for the aged, etc. are not institutionalised as individual social rights, but as social rights related to family income and family situation. Unemployment benefits for young people seeking first employment are non-existent, as they are supposed to be supported by their families (Jurado Guerrero 1995). This is also frequently the case in Western European Welfare States, but in Italy and Spain it is more frequent and is based on a different Welfare State model (Naldini 2001, Neubauer 1993). In particular, support for children is 'poor' in comparison with other Western European countries.

The family and kin culture in the south is dominated by the relevance of children and family-oriented values, by the importance of obligations, by the solidarity between generations, and by the relative importance of religious norms (cf. p.45). Despite secularisation processes, southern family culture maintains many traditional elements because it adapts well to a context of a long-term employment shortage and a scarce availability of social services for families.

The research questions are the following:

1. Which configuration of labour market, housing market, social policies, and family norms is related to early nest-leaving in France and which to late nest-leaving in Spain?
2. How far can these cross-national differences in young people's living arrangements be explained with a socio-economic model, which does not consider family norms and other cultural particularities?
3. Through which mechanisms does the specific institutionalisation of the state-family relation influence young people's living arrangements?

This work is divided into ten chapters. In Chapter 1, figures on cross-national differences in living arrangements of youth are presented and the dependent variable is defined. In Chapter 2 current research results about the process of becoming adult are reviewed. In Chapter 3 a theoretical model is developed and the empirical application of it is presented. Chapter 4 shows relevant context differences between France and Spain, and Chapter 5 discusses the results of individual-level statistical analysis. In Chapter 6 regional variations within France and Spain are presented and an explanation for Spanish regional differences in intergenerational co-residence is proposed. Chapters 7 to 9 offer an explanation of the mechanisms through which young people's nest-leaving is facilitated by public benefits and compares systematically cross-national differences in entitlements, coverage, and generosity of state benefits. Finally, Chapter 10 presents the conclusions of the work, i.e. the two societal configurations in relation to their respective nest-leaving patterns and discusses alternatives for the future.

The aim of the first two chapters is twofold. First, the chosen definition of what has to be explained is presented. Second, the variation of the explanandum across time and place, and the relation between young people's living arrangements and modernisation, current labour market changes, housing market characteristics, Welfare State institutions, and dominating family values are discussed. This discussion includes a review of existing literature at every step.

Why Do Some Young People Share Households with Parents More than Others?

The research project consists of a comparative cross-sectional analysis of young people's living arrangements within the European Union and in particular in Spain and France. The comparison is made for the years 1991 and 1992, because two comparable surveys exist for this time for Spain and France. In this chapter, the dependent variable is specified and its historical and cross-national variance is explored.

When persons share a household with each other it means that they share at least the house as a physical unit and the equipment of the house. Not always, but very often, they also share services (housework) and earnings (symmetrically or asymmetrically). From a societal perspective, the consequence of sharing households is economies of scale in the cost of social reproduction. This means that the labour force can be paid less than if all individuals lived in one-person households.

The interest of this analysis lies in the sharing of households between different generations as opposed to one-generation households. Two elements seem to be responsible for the theoretical difference between these households: the financial and the social dependence of young people on their parents. Table 1.1 shows the four logical combinations of the two dimensions of dependence and their relation to household patterns. This conceptualisation is based on Wallace's work (1988) but it has been partially changed. A financially dependent person is one whose own resources (from labour market and/or state) cannot assure the personal reproduction process, while a financially independent person can assure her reproduction and probably even that of a partner and of children. A person who has some income but who additionally needs parental financial help is considered a financially dependent person. The concept of social dependence refers in this analysis only to the fact of sharing or not sharing a household with somebody of an older generation. This conceptualisation is justified by the fact that most of the time the state and society relate this type of young people's living arrangements with immaturity or, equivalently, with the non-attainment of adulthood status. A young person in a two-generation household is also socially dependent because she or he has to accept parental authority in the last instance.

Most of the empirical cases are contained in the classification shown in Table 1.1, with the exception of young people sharing households with other relatives of an older generation, here ignored for reasons of clarity and of the low number of empirical cases. Again, for the sake of greater clarity, I have also excluded the dimension of young people's contributions to the household income through the pay of board money, help in family firm, etc. This dimension is important in some societies (e.g. in the United Kingdom) and in some social classes (e.g. agricultural workers in southern Spain) (Jones/Wallace 1992, Talego 1995).

Table 1.1 Types of Households of Young People

	Financial Dependence	Financial Independence
Social Dependence	Young people without sufficient personal resources living with parents Two-generation dependent household	Young people with sufficient personal resources living with parents Two-generation independent household
Social Independence	Young people without sufficient personal resources living away from parents One-generation dependent household	Young people with sufficient personal resources living in own household One-generation independent household

What does living in a two-generation household mean in comparison to living in a one-generation household? First of all, this household type consists of an asymmetric sharing of resources, because parents normally contribute with income, services, and a completely furnished dwelling, while their children either do not contribute at all or, if they do, they normally have fewer resources (e.g. no savings). This situation is due to the fact that parents and children find themselves at different stages of the family cycle and at different moments in the life cycle. Similar asymmetric relations can also exist in living arrangements where a young person (normally the woman) lives with a partner of the same generation who has more resources or a more stable income.

It is, however, important to notice that there is a difference between asymmetry among different generations and asymmetry within the same generation and that this is due to the phase of the family cycle. A young couple where the husband has an income and who wants to create a new household has to accumulate resources in the form of personal property and real estate, which the older generation has already been accumulating for decades. In many countries this has to be added to the fact that there is, in general, a systematic variance between the earnings of the current parent generation, which are more stable, accompanied by extended social security arrangements; most frequently these are higher than those of the current generation of youth (OECD 1996).

The first task of this research is to determine the empirical relevance of each of the four household types in Italy, Spain and France. For Spain, it can be estimated for 1992 by using a survey conducted among 5000 young people aged 15 to 29 and for France the *Enquête Jeune* 1992 was used (youth aged 20 to 29) (Table 1.2).

Table 1.2 Frequency of Household Types of Youth in Spain and France, 1992

Type of household (Column %)	France (aged 20-29)	Spain (aged 15-29)
Two-generation **dependent** household	20.5	40
Two-generation **independent** household	21.0	35
Two-generation household	41.5	75
One-generation **dependent** household	23.4	3
One-generation **independent** household	42.7	22
One-generation household	66.1	25

Source: for Spain: Navarro/Mateo 1993, 76, 106; for France: author's elaboration with Enquête Jeunes 1992.[2]

This table allows only for an approximate comparison due to the given age differences of the available samples of young people. The Spanish figures of two-generation households will all be overestimated, since younger people are included than in France. The greatest cross-national difference we find is the small number of dependent one-generation households in Spain, which means that French parents are more likely to maintain their children in spite of being in a different household. Even if the real difference were smaller, if one compared youths of the same age, leaving home in Spain seems much more connected to financial independence than it is in France. This corresponds with the fact that young Spanish people leave more frequently when they marry and very rarely when they start university studies or when they move to a non-family setting as is shown throughout this work.

One-generation independent households can take four different forms: one-person household, married couple, cohabiting couple, and peer household. From an economic point of view, there is a difference between the first type and the other three types, because of differences in the degree of resources shared (cf. Figure 1.1). The last three types, on the contrary, fulfil economically similar functions while they vary in their social dimensions. In France and Spain we find great differences not only in the degree of resource sharing but also in the social forms of living arrangements of young people, as shown below in Figure 1.1.

Figure 1.1 Degrees of Resource-Sharing

High	Middle			Low
Two-generation household	**One-generation household**			**One-generation household**
with parents	married couple	cohabi-tation	with peers	one-person household

The degree of institutionalisation is normally the highest for married couples, lower for cohabiting couples, and even lower for peer households, even if the degree of institutionalisation varies significantly among countries. In Scandinavian countries, marriage and cohabitation, in particular, have reached similar degrees of institutionalisation.

For the concept of institutionalisation I follow the ideas of Jepperson (1991) and Lepsius (1995). By degree of institutionalisation they understand how far a social pattern is reproduced by routine, is associated with a system of sanctions, is taken for granted, and how far it structures behaviour. An institution is highly institutionalised if it takes a great effort in collective action to change the reproductive process of the given institution. The interruption of reproduction is more difficult if the institution is strongly embedded in a framework of institutions and follows common principles and rules or if it has been in place for long time. If the institution is seen as the result of a socially exogenous authority or as a product of natural laws, it will be more stable. Also, a strong taken-for-grantedness of the institution prevents its change, because individuals do not even think about alternatives, or if they think about them these appear as unrealistic or as taboo. Referring to types of households one has to answer five questions:

1. How stable over time was the two-generation household for young people? When did changes occur and did they diminish the degree of institutionalisation of such living arrangements? (p.13.)

2. Does the institutionalisation of the two-generation household differ across nations? (p.18.)
3. Is this form of household sustained by the specific institutionalisation of the family-state relationship? (p.38.)
4. Is the two-generation household in line with the specific institutionalisation of the youth labour market and of the youth housing market? (p.32 and 42.)
5. To what degree is this living-arrangement disputed by given social groups?

This chapter will answer the first two questions, but first the operationalisation of the dependent variable for the historical and cross-national description has to be discussed. There are several possibilities for operationalising the living arrangements of young people. The first possibility is to construct two *staying home rates*, i.e. the proportion of young people in the age group from 20 to 24 years living with at least one parent and the proportion of young people doing so in the group of the 25 to 29 year-olds. These staying home rates would be justified for three reasons: first, each of them captures different social realities of young people. The age group from 20 to 24 years includes young people who have finished their compulsory education and are ready to go into the labour market or to a tertiary education institution. The older age group (25 to 29 years) is composed of people who have mainly finished their formal education and who are already on the labour market or are entering it and who have also arrived at the average age in which a new family is created. The second reason is based on the pragmatic reflection that it is convenient to use the same age groups as are usually used in official statistics so that comparison with them becomes possible. Thirdly, this is a way of controlling to some extent for age effects, which is very important in the case of a dependent variable which is strongly related to age, as is the case in this analysis.

The second way to operationalise the living arrangements of young people is to compute single-year, age-specific net rates of leaving home, as many demographers do (Yi et al. 1994, Desplanques 1994). This method is less synthetic than the first operationalisation, but it can be transferred without any problems to the first one. The advantages of single-year, age-specific net rates is that the variance within a wider age group can be known and this permits us not only to know the average timing of the event, but also the pattern within the whole youth population. A more differentiated and richer interpretation of the data is therefore possible. The problem with this construction is that most published data exist only for age groups and do not differentiate for each single year. This implies that a method of interpolation has to be used to estimate the lacking data. The problem does not exist when using individual data, as will be the case for Spain and France for the 1990s. At this stage the first operationalisation has been used but later on the more detailed second operationalisation also will be added.

Historical Variations

The existing data on types of households for young people over time are scarce, because they are not standard demographic indicators. It is possible to describe the historical development for every ten years by using census data, but for this description only data reported in the existing research will be presented and discussed. In Spain, specific surveys for young people have been conducted since 1960 on an average five-year interval. Unfortunately, the same age groups have not always been interviewed: older young people, i.e. over 25, have only been interviewed since 1977 and afterwards not always (Navarro/Mateo 1993).

Table 1.3 Young People by Type of Household in % of Age Group, Spain 1960-1993

<table>
<tr><th rowspan="2">Year of study</th><th rowspan="2">Two-generation household</th><th colspan="4">One-generation household</th></tr>
<tr><th>Total</th><th>Married couple</th><th>Cohabiting couple</th><th>Other</th></tr>
<tr><td>1960 (aged 16-20)</td><td>95</td><td>5</td><td>-</td><td>-</td><td>-</td></tr>
<tr><td>1975 (aged 15-25)</td><td>84</td><td>16</td><td>-</td><td>-</td><td>-</td></tr>
<tr><td>1980 (aged 15-20)</td><td>92</td><td>9</td><td>3</td><td>0.5</td><td>5</td></tr>
<tr><td>1984 (aged 16-29)</td><td>70</td><td>29</td><td>-</td><td>-</td><td>-</td></tr>
<tr><td>1988 (aged 16-29)</td><td>73</td><td>25</td><td>-</td><td>-</td><td>-</td></tr>
<tr><td>1992 (aged 15-29)</td><td>75</td><td>25</td><td colspan="2">18</td><td>7</td></tr>
<tr><td>1993 (aged 17-21)</td><td>95</td><td>6</td><td>2</td><td>1</td><td>3</td></tr>
<tr><td>1996 (aged 15-29)</td><td>77</td><td>24</td><td colspan="2">19</td><td>5</td></tr>
<tr><td>1999 (aged 15-24)</td><td>92.5</td><td>7.5</td><td>2.4</td><td>1.6</td><td>3.5</td></tr>
</table>

Sources: Beltrán Villalba et al. 1984, Conde 1985, Navarro López/Mateo Rivas 1993, Elzo et al. 1994, Encuesta Juventud 1988 in: Casal Bataller 1993, Martín Serrano/Velarde Hermida 1997, Elzo et al. 1999.

The published data are only partially comparable (Table 1.3). The figure for 1960 can be more or less compared with those of 1980 and 1993. In 1960, 95% of very young people were living with their parents, while in 1980 fewer were doing so (92%), while in 1993 they showed a similar percentage as in 1960 (95%). We do not know which part of the rate is explained by the difference in the denominator, but because leaving the parental home is positively correlated with age it can be checked if the rate is over- or under-estimated. If we take the age group of 1960 as a reference group (16-20) it can be estimated that the percentage of 1980 for the same age group would be somewhat lower than 92 per cent, the figure shown in Table 3.1, and for 1993 it would be somewhat higher than 95 per cent. In conclusion, it might be that in 1960 very young people remained with their parents longer than in 1980 but less time compared to 1993, but the differences are rather small. Figures for the more recent period are clearer, since up to 1999 they show an increase in two-generation households.

Data coming from the sociodemographic survey show a trend towards a delayed home leaving and show an increase in the proportion of young people living with their parents for the period of the 1980s (16-29 year-old) (Garrido/Requena 1996). This is also confirmed by an analysis of labour force surveys of different years. Among young men aged 25 to 29, family heads represented 47 per cent of this age group in 1976. This percentage fell to 43 per cent in 1981, to 39 per cent in 1986, to 30 per cent in 1991 and to 26 per cent in 1995 (Garrido/Requena 1996).

At the same time there is some evidence for a slow pluralisation of one-generation households, even if the figures are scarce and some of these living arrangements are difficult to capture statistically. Garrido and Requena, in the same study (1996), found an increasing rate of young non-married household heads since 1976. In 1976, 4 per cent of young socially independent people aged 25 to 29 were in such households, while in 1995, 15 per cent were.

The same tendency towards a delayed leaving home process is shown by three retrospective Catalan surveys among young people (Table 1.4). The increase is stronger between 1981 and 1987 and affects women somewhat more than men. All four sources show that the delay in the emancipation from the family of origin became especially relevant from the beginning of the 1980s. These are the years when unemployment rates of young people and also general unemployment rates began to increase dramatically (Jurado Guerrero 1995).

Table 1.4 Living Arrangements at Age 19/20 (in % of respective age), Catalonia 1977-87

Year	Men		Women	
	Two-generation household	One-generation household	Two-generation household	One-generation household
1977	90	10	81	20
1981	87	14	82	19
1987	98	2	98	2

Source: Casal Bataller 1993.

The last Spanish labour force survey data show that the average age at leaving home began to fall somewhat in 1998 and 1999, while rising again in 2000 (Requena 2001). In the Spanish case, figures on the development of first marriage rates can be used as a proxy for leaving the family of origin, because consensual unions, living on one's own, and living with persons of the same generation are minority phenomena. These data are more easily available in the literature and permit a more accurate description of the evolution of the last decades. In recent research Miret (1996) describes the development of Spanish marriage patterns and proposes some possible explanations. The mean age at first marriage for men began to increase in 1979 when it reached 26,1 years of age and 28,7 years of age in 1992. The development of the mean age at first marriage for women is similar: in 1979, it was 23,7 years of age, reaching 26,4 years of age in 1992. This trend can be interpreted as the reaction of the marriage patterns to the economic crisis which began in the mid-1970s. If this interpretation is right, than there should be a recovery of the marriage rate after the middle of the 1980s, when there was a rapid growth in the employed population and unemployment rates began to decrease. The analysis of the probabilities of marrying for every single age shows that, in fact, there was a significant recovery in adult nuptiality. Men over 26 years old and women over 23 experienced higher probabilities of marrying than before. This positive trend lasted a few years only, because in 1987 the increase in the probabilities of marrying in these age groups diminished or even became totally absent. Only women over 27 years of age and men over 29 years of age continued the tendency initiated in 1985. This disruption cannot be explained with the development of the labour market because unemployment was still diminishing and employment growing.

Miret points to the housing market as a possible explaining variable of this phenomenon. During the 1980s, the Spanish housing market was transformed into one of the least regulated housing systems of Western Europe. In addition, with the entrance of Spain into the European Union (1986) massive speculation occurred on the housing market and, as a consequence, housing prices increased strongly. The increases in housing prices even overlapped increases in wages. 'Many young people could no longer afford either to buy or to rent an accommodation, and the weak Spanish Welfare State did not have as a priority in the political agenda to help them' (Miret 1996, 8).

In conclusion, in Spain there are variations in the presence of two-generation households over time even if they are not very spectacular. This means that two-generation households are not very strongly institutionalised, in the sense that they are related to socio-economic phenomena and vary with time, and are thus not a very stable 'cultural' institution. This does not exclude the idea that, from a comparative perspective, two-generation households are more institutionalised in Spain than in other societies. We can imagine that French two-generation households vary accordingly also with socio-economic development, but that differences between the prevalence of these types of households in Spain and France remain stable over time. Table 1.5 shows that in France also the deterioration of the employment situation was accompanied by an increase of the proportion of two-generation households. The question whether the differences between the Spanish and the French rates remain stable can only be answered using similar data sources such as census information and constructing the probabilities of staying at home for each age for different calendar years.

Table 1.5 Living Arrangements at Age 20/24 (in % of respective age), France 1982, 1990

	Men		Women	
	Two-generation household		Two-generation household	
Year	age 20	age 24	age 20	age 24
1982	81	38	62	19
1990	81	47	69	28

Source: Desplanques 1994.

In contrast to Spain, it can be stated that in the French case more substantial changes occurred. In France, a clear pluralisation of one-generation households can be observed since the 1970s with the spread of consensual unions and one-person households among young persons (Leridon/Toulemon 1995, Villeneuve-Gokalp 1990, Lefranc/Thave 1994). This does not affect the degree of institutionalisation of two-generation households, but only the institutionalisation of marriage as the prevalent one-generation household among young people. In short, in Spain and France two-generation households have a degree of institutionalisation which seems to permit some short-term changes in order to adapt to changes in the socio-economic context. But how important are the international differences in the proportions of two-generation households? At this point, some international and regional variations for 1987 and 1991/92 can be presented.

International and Regional Variations

Until some time ago, international variations in living arrangements could only be studied through either national census data or information from international surveys such as Eurobarometer surveys. Both data sources present problems of comparability and reliability, as will be seen, and thus figures obtained from them have to be taken as rough approximations. Since 1994 a European Household Panel organised by EUROSTAT has been set up and in 1997 the first results dealing with European living arrangements of young people were published.

Yi et al. (1994) have used census data to compare parental home-leaving patterns across eight countries and over a time period. They have taken the proportion of people who are children of adults by single years of age and include grandchildren, daughters-in-law and sons-in-law from different censuses. The three western countries of the sample, the United States, Sweden, and France, show permanence and even a decrease in the proportion of young persons living with parents over the decades from 1960 to 1980. In the United States, the median age for leaving home for men and for women remained quite stable from 1950 to 1980,[3] while in Sweden it decreased during the 1960s and the 1970s. In France too, young people left their family of origin earlier in the mid-1960s, compared to the period from the end of the 1960s to the mid 1970s.

The French trend observed by Yi et al. was also observed by Blöss et al. (1990) in a study of two cohorts of French women in southern France. The cohort born in 1959 left the parental home on average earlier than the cohort of women born in 1947. A study of different German cohorts confirms these trends, because they show that the average age of leaving home decreased for the cohorts born in 1929-31, 1939-41 and 1949-51 (Wagner/Huinink 1991). If these trends are representative of the other European countries, we can affirm that during the period of economic affluence in the 1960s and 1970s, young people became independent from their parents earlier. This hypothesis would need more data and a deeper time series analysis to be tested.

For the time of the increasing employment crisis of the 1980s, data is available from European Youth surveys conducted by Eurobarometer. The published data allow a comparison for the years 1982, 1987 and 1990 as shown in Table 1.6. As in Spain, we can observe for most European countries a slight increase in the staying home rates of young people during the 1980s. The only exception is France, but interpretations have to be made very cautiously because the French census data is quite different from the Eurobarometer data. Following Desplanques (1994), in 1982 around 68 per cent of young people aged 16 to 24 years were living with their parents compared to 75 per cent of the 15 to 25 year-olds in 1990. In addition, figures from the French Labour Force Surveys of 1982, 1985 and 1988 show an increase in the proportion of young people (20-24 years) living with their parents. The German study mentioned above also shows an increase of the average age of leaving home for men since the cohort of 1953-57 and for women for the cohort of 1958-1962 (Wagner/Huinink 1991). In short, there is evidence of a delay in leaving home in the 1980s in most European countries, which suggests once again a correlation between the development of unemployment and the living arrangements of young people.

Table 1.6 Youth (16-24 years) Living with Parents, EU 1982, 1987, 1990

in % of age group	1982	1987	1990
Denmark	48	48	55
France	65	-	62
United Kingdom	64	-	67
West Germany	65	-	70
Netherlands	70	-	74
Greece	-	-	79
Belgium	-	-	80
Portugal	-	-	80
Ireland	80	84	83
Spain	-	85	86
Italy	-	92	94
Standard deviation	-	-	11,2

Sources: Kiernan 1986, Commission of the European Communities 1989, 1991.
Note: The survey of 1982 includes also people aged 15.

For the period between 1980 and 1990, we can classify European countries into different clusters on the basis of their staying home rates. For 1982/87 Table 1.6 shows three groups:

1. A first cluster includes Denmark and probably other Scandinavian countries with the lowest staying home rate (< 50%);
2. a second cluster is constituted by central European countries, West Germany, the United Kingdom, the Netherlands, and France, with rates oscillating from around 65 per cent to 70 per cent;
3. third, there are Southern Europe and Ireland with rates going from 80 to 90 per cent.

In 1990, we can distinguish four groups.

1. The first group is represented by Denmark (<60%);
2. the second by Central Europe without the Netherlands and Belgium (60-70%);
3. the third group by the Netherlands (74%);
4. and the fourth group by the Mediterranean countries, Belgium and Ireland (>=80%).

This classification is based on young people aged 16 to 24, but what happens if we take other age groups as a measure?

In Table 1.7, the age group of young people from 20 to 24 years of age for 1990 and 1995 is shown. First, it can be observed that the standard deviation increases (16,8) compared to the rates of younger people aged 16 to 20 (11,2). This is the result of the greater homogeneity of living arrangements of very young people across countries due to the fact that most of them still live in their families of origin. Thus, the classification for more adult young people is more accurate if we divide the European Union countries of 1990 into five groups:

1. first, once again, Denmark (<30%);
2. second, France (40-50%);
3. third, Central Europe formed by the United Kingdom, West Germany, and the Netherlands (50-60%);
4. fourth, Belgium and Portugal (60-70%) and,
5. in final position, once again, the Mediterranean group and Ireland (>=70%).

In 1995, nearly all countries display higher staying home rates. France moves into the Central European group and Portugal and Belgium move into the Mediterranean group. These classifications can be summarised into three types in 1995 - Northern Europe (<40%), Central Europe (40-60%) and Southern Europe (60-90%), including the Catholic countries Belgium and Ireland. A similar classification is made by Cavalli and Galland (1993) as a result of six national studies. Fernández Cordón (1997) analyses six European Union countries with EUROSTAT Labour Force Survey statistics, excluding Denmark for technical reasons, and he also finds two distinct patterns: a Central European and a Southern European pattern.

Table 1.7 Youth (20-24 years) Living with Parents in EU, 1990 and 1995

in % of age group	1990	1995
Denmark	27.9	-
France	42.2	52
United Kingdom	49.1	47
West Germany	53.3	55
Netherlands	57.7	47
Belgium	65.9	68
Portugal	68.9	82
Ireland	72.4	64
Spain	75.2	89
Italy	88.3	87
Standard deviation	16.8	16.9

Source: for 1990: author's elaboration with survey of Commission of the European Communities 1991; for 1995: EUROSTAT 1997.

Fernández Cordón points to the fact that it is in the 25-29 year age group that the largest international variations are found and that the gap between Southern European countries and the Central European ones has grown. Table 1.8 reveals that cross-national differences in this age group are smaller among women than among men and that they have increased from 1986 to 1994.

Table 1.8 Youth Aged 25-29 Living with Parents by Gender, EU Countries, 1986/1994

Countries	Women (% of age group)		Men (% of age group)	
	1986	1994	1986	1994
United Kingdom	8.6	10.8	21.9	20.8
Germany	11.0	12.7	27.4	28.8
France	8.4	10.3	19.3	22.5
Spain	35.3	47.6	53.2	64.8
Italy	25.5	44.1	49.6	66.0
Greece	23.8	32.1	53.8	62.6
Standard deviation	11.1	17.2	16.3	22.3

Source: Fernández Cordón 1997 (Labour Force Survey statistics).

All previous figures show that the degree of institutionalisation of two-generation households differs across countries, i.e. that these cross-national differences are relatively immune to changes in the economic context and are not clearly related to differences in national economic wealth as shown by differences between Germany and Denmark for instance. Since the 1980s the figures for young people aged 25 to 29 even demonstrate an increasing divergence across Europe, which could be the result of diverging answers to the same problem of rising unemployment and employment precariousness. Consequently, the modernisation perspective which would foresee a convergence of different national family patterns to one European pattern does not help understand persisting differences. These have to be related to the specific societal configuration of each country if they are to be understood. A more detailed cross-sectional comparison would also help understand the international differences in one-generation households, as for instance the respective importance of cohabitation among young people. Iacovou (1998) shows for 1994 that the proportion of women aged 25 to 29 who live without children in cohabitation with a partner numbers 27.3% of all childless women in this age group in France and only 3.8% in Spain. Among women with children, the respective rates are 23.6% in France and 5.8% in Spain.

At another level, similar conclusions about the importance of differences in the institutionalisation of two-generation households can be made independently of socio-economic variations. Figure 1.2 shows Spanish regional differences in the staying home rates of 25 to 29 year-olds. Contrary to the idea of a correlation between levels of income, degree of modernisation, unemployment rates, and living arrangements of young people, the regional staying home rates show a complex picture. Catalonia and the Basque Country, regions which from the modernisation perspective and also in terms of economic wealth are the most similar, show the most diverging staying home rates. At the same time, Andalusia, a "backward" and "poor" region, displays average rates, while Galicia -which also has an important agricultural sector and great economic problems- displays high staying home rates (cf. Chapter 6). A macrosociological model able to explain international and regional differences has still to be constructed.

In the next chapter a review of existing studies on leaving the parental home and becoming adult will show the possibilities of using existing models and their shortcomings.

Figure 1.2 Staying Home Rates by *Comunidades Autónomas* (age group 25 to 29 years), 1991

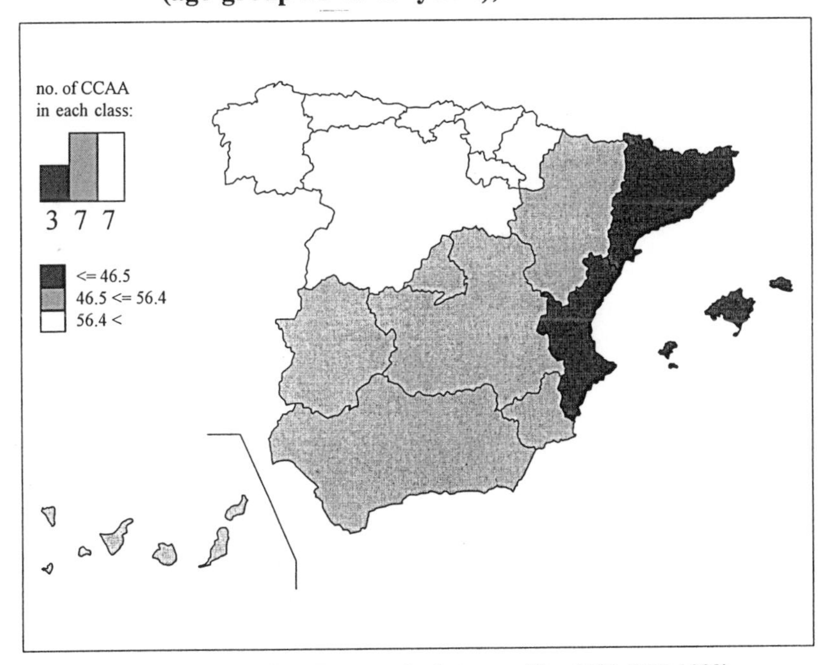

Source: Author's elaboration, Encuesta Sociodemográfica 1991 (INE 1993).
Note: Ceuta and Melilla were excluded. Minimum rate: 40,5, Maximum rate: 68,1.

Notes

[1] Opinion data of the affected persons would only give a more accurate picture of the problem.

[2] The Spanish information is based on the self-report of young people when asked to state which of the following four statements described their situation: 1. they lived exclusively from their own income or from the income of the spouse, 2. lived mainly from own income but received family help, 3. lived mainly from the money received from parents with some own income, or 4. lived exclusively from their parents' money. The French variables takes the income amount of 3000 FF per month and the type of income source as objective criteria to asses their household type instead (cf.Appendix).

[3] This affirmation is based on U.S. censuses (1960, 70, 80) which exclude people living in college dormitories from the category of "living with parents". If these college students are included in the category of staying at home because they return home very often (for holidays, on weekends), then a slight increase in the proportion of young people living with their parents can be observed since the 1970's. Glick and Lin (1986) interpret existing U.S. census data in this way, showing an increase in the proportions of young adults living with their parents after 1960.

2 Becoming Adult in Europe

Emancipation from the family of origin is a relatively new field of enquiry in European sociology, which is at present dominated by quantitative studies referring to one national context. There are only a few theories about the phenomenon, especially concerning the macrosociological determinants such as the labour market, social policies, housing market, or other features of the regional or national context. This part will address the question of the theoretical frame of the research and what existing studies can contribute to understanding the international differences in the institutionalisation of two-generation households.

Becoming an adult is a process during which a person has to climb different steps of a ladder to arrive at the top. The status of adulthood is reached after passing through a range of transitions which are connected with each other. Galland (1993) divides the transition into adulthood into two. First, the transition from school to work and second, the transition from living with the family of origin to living with a partner as a couple. Wallace (1988) conceptualises three layers of transition, those from school to work (the school-to-work transition), from the parental home to one's own accommodation (the housing transition), and from the family of origin to the family of destination (the domestic transition). Jones and Wallace (1992) also emphasise the importance of the acquisition of citizenship rights and duties to reach adult status. Alternatively, Zárraga (1985) differentiates between four transitions: 1. from economic dependence to economic independence; 2. from the administration of resources by parents to self-administration; 3. from parental control to personal autonomy; and 4. from living in the parental home to the creation of one's own household.

Probably, the school-to-work transition should be better re-conceptualised as a transition from economic dependence on the family of origin to financial independence from it, going through a stage of half-dependence and half-independence (financial transition). In this way, employment with wages below the existence minimum, the increasing importance of reincorporation into formal education after an employment break, the diffusion of private formation offers, and the increasing combination of employment and studies can more accurately be taken into account. The empirical study can then focus on the entry into the labour market because better data is available, but theoretically it seems more useful to conceptualise it in terms of economic dependence. A further advantage of this transition concept is that it permits the incorporation of the dimension of social rights, which can result in a higher degree of independence from parents but also dependence on the Welfare State.

The second layer of transition, the housing transition following Wallace, can be seen as related to the transition from parental control to personal autonomy insofar as it is valid to say that living in the parental home always restricts the autonomy of children even if they have reached an adult age. It is often argued that since the end of the 1960s young people have acquired autonomy within the parental home due to the change in authority structures within the family, especially related to the increase of tolerance on the parents' side (Cavalli 1993, Iglesias de Ussel 1989).[1] These changes probably only reflect an evolution of social control exerted in an open and authoritarian way to more subtle and psychological ways of exerting power. Whatever the case may be, where there is conflict the family control is higher if a young person lives in the parental home than if she or he lives in an independent dwelling and is also economically independent.

Most of the time the domestic transition, i.e. the creation of a new family, coincides with the housing transition, but there is one exception. A young person can marry or cohabit with a partner without leaving the family of origin, but creating a new family within the household of her or his parents (patrilocality). Nevertheless, neolocality is still a norm followed by the great majority of European young people when they start out life as a couple.

To conclude, it seems adequate to conceptualise the transition from youth to adulthood as two separate transitions, as mentioned already in the discussion of the explanandum:

1. The transition from financial dependence to financial independence, which is related to the school-to-work transition and to the transition of indirect citizenship rights to direct citizenship entitlements (**financial transition**).
2. The transition from social dependence to social independence, which is mainly described by the housing transition and most of the time also by the domestic transition (**social independence transition**).

In short, youth has to be conceptualised as a "series of processes of transition to adult life" which take place in different areas of society: mainly the education system, the family, the labour market and the housing market. Furthermore, youth means the gradual acquisition of citizenship rights and duties (Jones/Wallace 1992). Patterns of young people's living arrangements are a reflection of young people's transition into adulthood. In the next part, changes in these transitions will be discussed in relation to current changes and characteristics of general modernisation, the employment situation, social rights, housing markets, and family values.

Increasing Individualisation of the Life Course?

The changes in family structures and life-courses which have occurred since the 1960s have been described by family sociologists as a pluralisation of family types and as an individualisation of biographies. The decline in fertility and marriage rates, the increase in divorce rates, the birth of children out of wedlock, consensual unions, and one-person households have all been labelled as the pluralisation of the family (Roussel 1988). These trends have spread from northern to southern Europe but without reaching a convergence- or at least, in the 1990s great differences in family structures and behaviour still persist between southern and northern Europe (Requena 2001). The pluralisation of the family is seen as a result of the economic boom, cultural liberalisation, and the expansion of education during the 1960/70s which have particularly changed the role and life of women. The constraints of former times which pushed women to have a larger number of children, to continue in unhappy marriages, and to accept an unequal division of labour in the private sphere have diminished. Contraceptive methods, the liberalisation of abortion and divorce, and the increasing education and employment participation of women have changed their position in society (Kaufmann 1990).

The other side of pluralisation, or even its cause, is seen in the increasing individualisation of the family. The state and the market have weakened intermediary instances of social control, such as kinship groups, the church, and the neighbourhood, as a consequence of the general differentiation process of modern societies. This has resulted in a privatised small family with changed functions (loss of production and education functions) and a higher autonomy and self-control. Family members have become more independent of each other and their individual life options have increased. Marriage and family are less important for the economic and social security of individuals, because they depend more on a complex net of institutions. If students, wives, and grandparents receive public benefits directly instead of via the family head, they can decide to leave households and families and be independent (Mayer/Müller 1989). In modern societies individuals acquire citizenship rights which create special ties between them and the state. The increasing involvement of most citizens in market mechanisms also enables them to become more independent of social identifications and identity constructions based on membership in status groups and local communities (Buchmann 1989).

What are the consequences of these trends for life courses? Have these become more individualised? Buchmann further argues that the life course has become less regulated by the family and the community and is instead largely subjected to state regulation. Nowadays, traditions and customs constrain an individual's action orientation less, but individual choices have to be made within the context of standardised life patterns. In this view the modern standardisation of life courses is the result of the growth of the Welfare State.

For over a century now, national Welfare States have emerged and have begun to provide mechanisms to insure citizens against the risks of invalidity, unemployment, illness, old age, homelessness, and poverty, as well as creating a comprehensive education system. The importance of state intervention in relation to individuals' lives increases the more social groups are included in a uniform social insurance system (Mayer/Müller 1989). The state defines the entrances and exists of transitions in people's lives, for example, exit from school, entrance into employment, breaks because of illness or family work. This results in some predictability of life courses and in public help to secure its continuity. At the same time, the state increases the age segmentation, because it offers services and allowances for specific life phases such as child-care services, care services and old age pensions for the elderly, and scholarships for students. Nevertheless, the most important consequence of the Welfare State is the reduction of economic restrictions so that chances for individual action and social mobility increase. This individualisation of the life course finds its limits in the standardisation imposed by the state, but it is felt to have reached a high degree if looked at from a historical perspective.

For the last two decades this trend towards a strong standardisation and individualisation of the life course has been changing. The Welfare State, the employment system and the education system are in crisis so that transitions from one life sequence to another are becoming more difficult and less predictable. Also, the family is becoming a more unstable institution with fewer life-long commitments. The tensions inherent in the dynamics of standardisation and individualisation are producing a partial de-standardisation of the life course regime of modern societies (Buchmann 1989, Mayer 1997). Does this mean that individualisation is reaching its highest levels and that social class differences are again becoming more important?

Buchmann compared two cohorts of American high school leavers. The cohort of 1960 showed much more rapid role transitions and a lower variety in transition patterns compared to the cohort of 1980. For the 1980s, she found a greater complexity and diversity in transition patterns into adulthood than twenty years before. The transition from school to work, for example, has become more gradual and less clear cut. At the same time sex differences in the passage to adulthood have diminished because women's transition patterns have changed so much. In general, Buchmann found a greater determination of biographical orientations and transition behaviours by social status for the early cohort, while the youngest cohort displayed more individually stratified patterns. The socio-economic position seems to have become less influential on value and action orientations. In her opinion, this can be partly explained by the mediation of the education system in social reproduction. However, it must, of course, be taken into account that Buchmann's research refers to a relatively homogenous social group of high school leavers and to the American reality, which differs in many aspects from European societies.

In contrast, other scholars emphasise that social class still strongly determines the probability of a young person attending high school, university, or college and the position she reaches on the labour market (Breen 1998, Jones/Wallace 1992, Bourdieu/Passeron 1970). In this sociological tradition education is seen as a mechanism to reproduce social classes and status groups in modern societies without really changing the social structure. At the same time, social rights for young people have been cut back in the United Kingdom, and this is reinforcing, once again, old social class differences. Furthermore, for Southern Europe it can be stated that a wide range of risks (unemployment, informal work, lack of public transfers) are higher for women and young people than for male family heads in their forties. In these countries the Welfare State had not fully developed by the time it went into crisis. Hence, a general individualisation of life courses cannot be spoken of and even less of an individualisation or pluralisation of the transition into adulthood, because social class and gender still strongly determine the probabilities of experiencing particular life course patterns, especially in Southern Europe.

Expansion of Education: Prolongation of Youth?

The expansion of the participation of young people in education, especially of young women, is one of the most important developments of the last few decades, and has had a great deal of influence on young people's expectations, life styles, and form of transition into adulthood. However, the effect of young people's enrolment in formal education on their household and family formation pattern is contradictory. On the one hand, it delays leaving home and family formation because of prolonged financial dependence on the parents (**delay hypothesis**), but, on the other, it has given rise to new living arrangements such as consensual unions, sharing households with peers and living in student residences. As a consequence, this has even precipitated young people's nest-leaving in some countries (**acceleration hypothesis**). The first relationship is more likely to be observed in countries where financial dependence from parents is seen as a reason not to leave the parental home, where the state provides little income support for young people, and where leaving home is strongly connected to marriage. Other value orientations will instead favour leaving home to study in spite of financial dependence on parents.

Evidence confirming the first relationship comes from different national and cross-national studies. In a recent international study of changes in family formation in eight European countries and the United States, it was found that in seven of the countries the enrolment rate in the educational system has a strong and significant negative effect on the rate of entry into marriage (Blossfeld 1995). This means that postponement of family formation is due to a longer transition from youth to adulthood. In countries where leaving the parental home is strongly connected to marriage, the increasing participation of young people in education might thus be delaying the domestic transition. Desplanques also (1994) argues that the delay in leaving the parental home from 1982 to 1990 in France is partly due to the expansion of the educational participation of young people. Wagner and Huinink (1991) come to a similar conclusion for German cohorts born between 1953 and 1965.

On the micro level, however, some studies have shown that students do leave the parental home earlier than other young people or that young people with higher educational levels leave earlier than those with lower levels. Both relationships would confirm the idea that these behaviours aggregated on the macro level, other things being equal, would suppose that educational expansion has lowered the staying home rates. Mayer and Wagner (1989) analysed three German cohorts (born in 1929-31, 1939-41 and 1949-51) and found that, especially in the older cohorts, young people with high educational levels left the family of origin earlier than those with lower levels.

Jones and Wallace (1992) describe for the United Kingdom a trend, where students increasingly lived away from their family of origin from 1920/21 until 1979/80. They argue that these student living patterns were possible because of the introduction of maintenance grants in the 1960s and because of the construction of campus universities. This analysis refers to transitions into adulthood from 1920 to 1980 and, hence, does not describe more recent trends. A study of a panel survey of German "Gymnasiasten" (high school students) who were 30 years old in 1984/85 found that university studies precipitate leaving the parental home independently of the location of the university (Ziegler/Schadt 1993). These results cannot confirm the acceleration hypothesis because the first study refers only to the decades before 1980 and the second result is based on an analysis of the specific population of high school students without taking other young people into account.

In contrast, a French study of the cohort born between 1963 and 1966 interviewed in 1992 shows an interesting phenomenon: 64% of young people with a high education level (tertiary education) left the parental home before beginning their studies or in the same year. On the contrary, only 13% of young people with the lowest education level (without any professional education) left the parental home before finishing their education or in the same year. This means that many students left their family of origin to live independently. It was further found that persons with a university degree have a higher probability of leaving the parental home at an earlier point than the median age. If students leave home before completing their education, they leave while being financially dependent on parents or the Welfare State. In France, it is quite usual for parents to finance their children even if they have left home. A strikingly high percentage of young people live in a dwelling paid for by their parents and this living arrangement has increased from 1983 (10%) to 1992 (18%) by 80% (Galland 1995). Young (1989) found similar patterns using an Australian survey from 1982: over one half of the men and nearly one-third of the women left their family of origin before they completed their education. Hence, students have very specific transition patterns and this surely has an effect on the macro level, especially in comparison to societies where these student specific transition patterns are less frequent.

However, there is also evidence which falsifies the hypothesis of students' early-leaving patterns. For Germany, it was found that in the cohorts born after 1953 young persons with a high education level left the parental home later than those with a low level, and in addition a survey conducted among German students shows that the number of students living with their parents has increased between 1982 and 1986, while before it had continuously fallen (Wagner/Huinink 1991). For Italy, scholars have found that the lower the educational level the earlier young people marry (Menniti et al. 1994). A French analysis of census data of 1982 and 1990 shows that among young people aged 24, students lived more often with their parents than the average and than employed persons (Desplanques 1994). Comparative studies done in different countries, with different data sources, definitions and methods do not really permit us to draw clear conclusions. The contradicting French results of Desplanques and Galland may be due to differences in survey methods. The problem of census data, like those used by Desplanques, is that they often underestimate children's temporary and informal living away. Another problem is the different concepts used: Desplanques uses the rate of young people aged 24 as a dependent variable, comparing students with average young people, while Galland uses the median age and the quartiles of the cohort born between 1963 and 1966, comparing persons with different levels of education.

To conclude, for a cross-national comparison, two alternative conceptualisations and tests seem interesting to follow up.

1. A comparison of a group of people during the period of enrolment in university (i.e. 20 to 24 years) by their activity status (studying, employed, unemployed, inactive) and their living arrangements.
2. A comparison of a group of people who have already passed the transitions of finishing education and leaving home, e.g. those aged 30, to see if they left home before finishing their studies. This allows conclusions to be drawn about the dominant norms with respect to legitimate reasons to leave the family of origin, which then can also be related to social policies.

The cross-national question to be answered is whether the fact of studying accelerates or delays leaving home in all countries in the same way. Figures on effects of enrolment in education on living arrangement probabilities in Spain and France are presented in chapter 5.

Employment Crisis and Labour Market Risks

The employment crisis which began in the mid 1970s is affecting the possibilities and forms by which young people enter the labour market in all European countries. In some countries specific labour market segmentations following age lines have emerged so that we can even speak of “youth labour markets”. Young people are increasingly performing jobs in the periphery of the secondary and tertiary labour markets and seem to have problems in entering stable jobs on the primary labour market segment. This is to an important degree the product of state regulation in order to solve the problem of youth unemployment. The aim here is to describe at a general level young people's employment problems and labour market risks in Spain and France, the main trends in active employment policy towards young people, and then to ask how different activity situations relate to differences in living arrangements.

Young people in Spain have decreased their participation in the labour force over the last decades. In 1976, 55% of young people between 16 and 19 years of age were active while this dropped to 32% in 1990. In contrast, the group aged 20 to 24 years increased its percentage from 60% to 67% because of an increase of young women in the labour force. French young people (15 to 19 years old) followed the same trend as Spanish youth, but at lower levels. In 1975, 27% of the age group between 15 and 19 were in the labour force and the rate fell to 11% in 1990. In contrast to Spain, the evolution of the activity rate of the older age group (20-24) increased from 45% in 1975 to 52% in 1990. In the same year, more young people in Spain were in the labour force than in France (Meron/Minni 1995). In both countries the incorporation of these young persons into the labour market was strongly affected by high unemployment.

From 1976 to 1990, young Spanish people aged 20 to 24 had much higher unemployment rates than the adult group of 25 to 54 years. In 1976, those aged 20 to 24 had an unemployment rate of 9%, four times higher than that of the adults. At the moment of the highest unemployment rates in 1986, this rate reached 44% and it was three times higher than the adult rate. Finally, in 1990 it fell to 30% but was still two and a half times higher than the rate of those aged 25 to 54. For France, if we compare those aged 15 to 24 with those aged 25 to 49, we can also observe over time a higher unemployment risk for young people. In 1974, young people had an unemployment rate of 7%, i.e. three and a half times higher than the adult group, and in 1990 the rate reached 18%, two and a quarter times higher (Dumartin 1994).

French data for 1990, comparable to the Spanish figures, show that the 20 to 24 year-olds had an unemployment rate of 19%, which meant that it was nearly two and a half times higher than the unemployment rate of those aged 25 to 54 (8%). Thus, the differences between the unemployment rates of young compared to older people were very similar for Spain and France in 1990, but in 1991 the unemployment rate of Spanish youth in the age group from20 to 24 was one and a half times higher. In the same year, the unemployment rate of Spanish youth between 25 and 29 years of age (22%) was two times higher than the French rate (11%) (INSEE 1992, Ministerio de Trabajo y Seguridad Social 1993). More recent figures show that the unemployment rate differences by age were still very large in 1996 (EUROSTAT 1997).

For Spain the risk of being employed in irregular jobs, i.e. without social security, with inadequate social security, or receiving unemployment benefits while doing a job, can be estimated using data from a survey conducted in 1985. Over 40 per cent of employed young people (20-24) were in irregular employment compared to 20 per cent of the adult group

(25 to 54). Another risk which affected young people more than adults is the risk of being in temporary employment. In 1987, over 30 per cent of the young had such a job compared to nearly 20 per cent of adults. In France too, the risk of young people having a short-term contract is higher than for older people. Three-quarters of the French youth employed between 15 and 24 years of age had temporary contracts in 1989 (Dumartin 1994).

An analysis of cohorts of young Spanish people since 1976 show that over successive generations the numbers of unemployed with employment experience have increased, suggesting the existence of a strong job rotation which could mean that less qualified young people lose their jobs in favour of people who were studying before and then entered the labour market with higher qualifications (Toharia Cortés 1994). Similar trends can be observed on the French labour market, where the entrance of young people into an employment situation is increasingly accompanied by an alternation of periods of unemployment and short-term employment (Dumartin 1994).

Spanish governments since 1978 have tried to solve youth unemployment via the regulation of special contracts for young people. First, with the "Pactos de la Moncloa", temporary contracts for young people aged 16 to 26 years searching for employment were implemented. In 1980, the age limit was expanded to 28 years for people with a university degree. The duration of the contracts could oscillate between 16 months and two years and the employer received a subsidy of 75 per cent of the employer's social security contribution if the young person was entering his first job. This program ended in July 1981 and was substituted by norms which made it possible to conclude contracts for part-time work, for practical training, and for vocational training (Lorente 1986, cf. p.225).

The general employment policy in Spain is based on the worker's statute of 1980 which regulates the possibilities of temporary contracts. Over the 1980s, the possibilities for employers to use short-term contracts were expanded. Four types of temporary contracts for specific types of work were enacted in 1984. In addition, other forms were prolonged or changed, such as temporary contracts as a measure for employment for the unemployed, part-time contracts, contracts for practical training, for formation, long-term contracts for young people, and measures for increasing employment in the public sector, etc. (Ministerio de Trabajo y Seguridad Social 1988). In 1989 employers could choose between 14 different ways of establishing an employment contract, of which the most popular were the temporary contracts for specific jobs ("de obra o servicio") for one year, and the contracts for temporarily increased need of labour force (a person can only work for six months a year in a particular job or he has to be taken on long-term). Most subsidies are given for the employment of young people between 16 and 25 years of age (El País

11.2.1990, Segura et al. 1991). The results of this employment policy are very high rates of temporary employment among young people. In 1992, 85 per cent of the employees in the age group between 16 and 19 years had temporary contracts, 70 per cent of those aged 20 to 24 and 47 per cent of those aged 25 to 29 years, while the adult age group of 30 to 59 years had a rate of 21 per cent (Ministerio de Trabajo y Seguridad Social 1993). These percentages have actually increased in recent years and a clear segmentation by family situation also appears. Dependent young people display the highest rates of temporary employment (Garrido Medina 1996).

In France, special measures to combat youth unemployment have been in force since the mid-1970s. As in Spain, the first measures subsidised employers who employed young people by diminishing or even eliminating their social security contribution. At the beginning the government introduced alternating vocational training programs which enabled young people to gain professional qualification at school and in the workplace. Special programs for low-qualified young people were also enacted and later special labour market entrance measures for young people were created. In 1986, a special emergency plan for youth employment was made which consisted mainly of subsidising the employment of young people with contracts of alternating vocational training. Since 1988 local measures have been implemented and the contracts of public interest jobs have been reorganised (cf. p.225).

Besides these specific measures, the general flexibilisation of the labour market has increased over the last decades, even if in 1988 the government re-regulated the labour market after a phase of deregulation (Meron/Minni 1994, Lochet 1994, Steinhilber 1995). In 1994, 5 per cent of the young people from 16 to 25 years of age in the labour force had government-subsidised employment (emplois aidés), 3 per cent were in vocational training (apprentis), and 27 per cent were normally employed (Balan/Minni 1994). The percentage of young people (15-29 years) in subsidised employment, short-term employment, and vocational training increased from 9 per cent in 1982 to 19 per cent in 1994, while for the older labour force (30-40 years) the increase was from 1 to 4 per cent only (Meron/Minni 1994).

There is some empirical evidence for OECD countries that young people's wages have decreased proportionally to adult's wages and remain considerably lower (OECD 1996). In France, two-thirds of the labour force aged 18 to 29 earn less than the median wage of the total employed population and the difference is higher for those aged 18 to 25 years (Moncel/Rose 1995).

How do higher unemployment rates and increasing temporary employment affect the living arrangements of young people in Spain and

France? If people's jobs become more precarious, they will clearly be less independent financially. This may result in an increased dependence of young people on their parents or on the Welfare State. It is thus probable that precarious labour market conditions are positively related to high staying home rates or at least to higher financial dependence. The Spanish 1991 sociodemographic survey permits us to analyse the situation of young people aged 25 to 29 years. Figure 2.1 shows the rate of young people living with their parents or parents-in-law by their activity status and by gender.

Figure 2.1 Spanish Staying Home Rates by Gender and Activity Status, 1991 (in % of 25-29-year-olds)

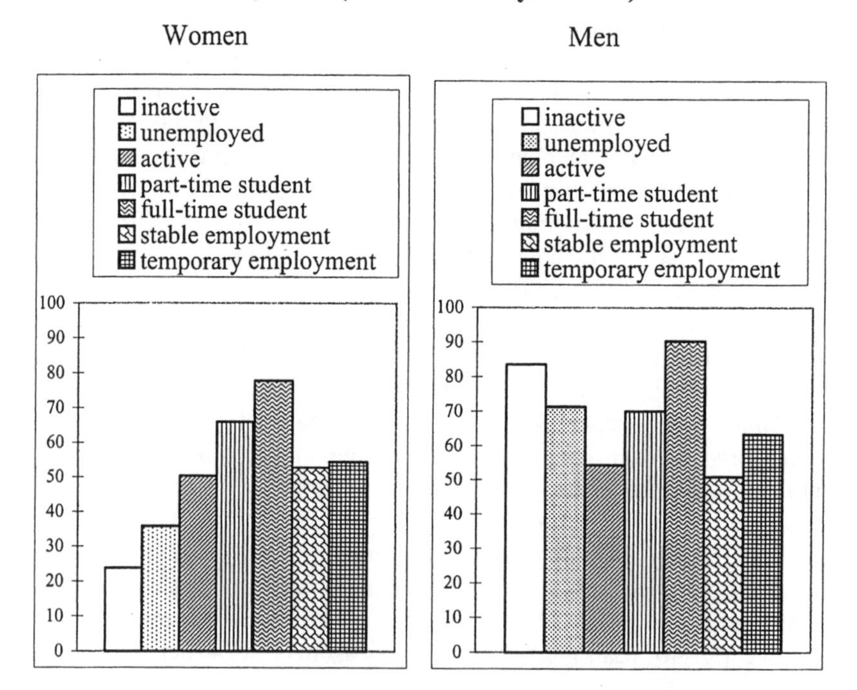

Source: Author's elaboration, Encuesta Sociodemográfica 1991 (INE 1993).

Unemployed women often stay in their family of origin a shorter time than employed women and there is hardly any difference between women in a long-term employment and those in short-term employment. This means that the difficulties young women find on the labour market are not related in the presumed way to the high staying home rates of Spanish women (44%). In contrast, there is a positive relation between unemployment, temporary employment, and living in the parental home for Spanish men. Sixty one percent of Spanish men aged 25 to 29 live with their parents, while 71% of the unemployed, 63% of the short-term employed and 51% of the long-term employed do so. Another approach which allows us to relate employment and unemployment to living arrangements is to correlate changes in youth employment with changes in staying rates. For Spain, Requena (2001) compares for the years 1988 to 2000 employment rates of youth aged 16 to 29 with the rates of youth aged 16 to 34 living independently. He observes that employment recovery since 1996 correlates with a small increase in the rate of independent youth.

For 1987, Galland (1993) analysed French young people aged between 16 and 29 according to social origin and activity situation and found that in general the highest staying home rates were shown by those who were students, those temporarily employed or those unemployed. A more differentiated analysis according to gender shows similar results to the Spanish ones. In France, being unemployed (for at least one year) delays - independently of social or habitat origin and for all education levels- the time of leaving the family of origin, but only for young men.[2] Unemployed women do not necessarily leave the parental home early. Their probability of leaving early is related to the level of education, i.e. women with the lowest education level have a high probability of being among those who leave the parental home the earliest (Galland 1995). Another study with a sample of persons between 20 and 34 years of age interviewed in 1986/87 confirms the difficulties that men who are only temporarily employed have to leave their family of origin. They leave later, go back more often to the family of origin and some of them live with their parents after the age of 30 (Battagliola et al. 1994).

Two important questions emerge for this research.

1. What does the fact that women's leaving home is not delayed by unemployment and temporary employment conditions mean? Does it mean that unemployed and short-term employed women leave their parents' home because they can rely on a spouse or partner, thus making no difference if they leave home with or without a job? There is some French evidence that leaving the parent's home in order to marry, instead of for other reasons, is related to a weak relationship with employment and is more often followed by a strong occupational discontinuity, even if factors related to the family of origin are also important (Marry et al. 1995). It seems to be important to differentiate between women who leave their parent's home to become independent from their parents without depending on a partner and those who

become independent of their parents to become dependent on a male partner.

2. How can the activity situation of young people be operationalised in the best way to take into consideration not only the current activity situation, but also the activity career since the end of formal education. Degrees of instability in their activity career should be distinguished in looking at the incidence and duration of phases of unemployment and of short-term employment, as well as combining this with the dimension of the educational credentials the young person is able to exchange on the labour market. The educational level strongly influences employment trajectories of young people and thus connects social origin with school to work transition and other transitions to adulthood (Jones/Wallace 1992, Marry et al. 1995, Galland 1993). The comparative perspective of this work and the insufficient quality of the Spanish retrospective data have forced us to take the activity and employment situation at one point in time instead of activity and employment trajectories as independent variables (cf. p.72).

Social Rights for Young People

The existing Welfare State literature neglects the question of social rights for young people. This is probably due to two reasons: first, young people have not been seen as a special risk group because the traditional risks which social security covers are those of illness, invalidity, old age, unemployment and poverty, which do, or rather did not especially affect young people (Schultheis 1993). Second, the theory of the Welfare State was developed by American and North European scholars who live in countries where the demographic pressure of young people was the highest when the employment crisis was not very deep and where the unemployment rates of young people were not very high. However, in the last few years English scholars have increasingly analysed the topic of social rights for young people (Stewart/Stewart 1988, Jones/Wallace 1992, Coles 1995). Coles argues that young people constitute a distinctive social group because of the transitions through which they have to pass and that therefore they need special rights.

Youth can be regarded as a state of half-dependence or mixed dependence which reaches its end when the individual reaches the typical independence and autonomy of an adult. The concept of dependence has a great number of meanings and is charged with many ideological assumptions. The dichotomy between independence and dependence which is often used in Welfare State research is problematic because it hides the fact that modern societies are characterised by relations of interdependence as a result of the high degree of division of labour (Fraser/Gordon 1994). Youth is a good field to study the relations of interdependence in a given society and the institutionalisation of the division of labour between the market, the state, and the family.

From a comparative perspective it seems useful to create a concept which can be labelled as dependence-diversification degree. The lowest degree would be reached when an individual depends financially on only one institution - the family, the state, or the market. This situation is empirically not very relevant in modern Welfare States, because even a male adult with a stable full-time job depends normally not only on the market but also on the public social security system. The highest degree of dependence diversification would be reached by an individual in employment, with extensive social rights to protect her or him against the loss of market income, and with the possibility of receiving financial support from other family members in case of need. This perspective implies the study of employment possibilities and situations taking into account the level of market income which can be received and the stability of that market income (cf. p.32). Furthermore, the willingness and the possibilities of family members to help other family members has to be considered (cf. p.45). Finally, the entitlements to public benefits, their realisation in practice, and their generosity have to be analysed.

Young people can have direct social rights which entitle them to receive state benefits of different types and they can have indirect rights or social rights by proxy which they receive through their parents because of their dependence on them (Jones/Wallace 1992). The social rights situation of young people depends on the social division of family tasks between the state and the parents, and on the financial dependence of the children on the family or on the family and the state. This division of labour influences the living conditions and arrangements of young people. I hypothesise that the more the state takes care of children and the more children do not depend solely on their parents, the more the early independence of young people from their parents is promoted. Children can leave the parental home earlier if they receive generous public benefits in their own right and they will also have higher probabilities of living in a one-person household or financially independent from a spouse or partner. There are three areas in which the parents/relatives and the state share the tasks of socialisation and maintenance of children.

1. Who socialises and educates children?
2. Who maintains children?

3. Who provides social security?

From the perspective of the children one can ask: On whom are they financially dependent and how do these dependence relations change during youth? Three ideal typical State-Family-Dependence models can be distinguished (Figure 2.2).

Figure 2.2 State-Family Dependence Models

1. No Division of Labour and Complete Dependence on Parents

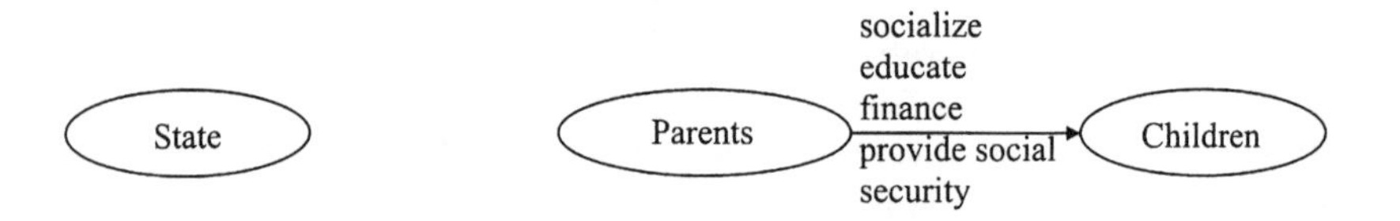

2. Partial Division of Labour and Relative Dependence on Parents

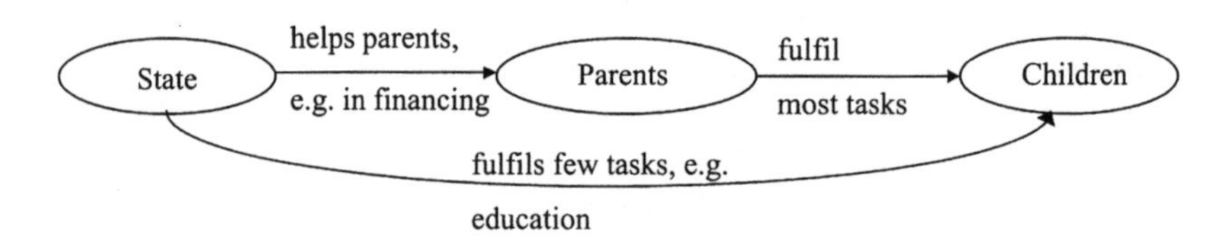

3. Strong Division of Labour and Diversified Dependence

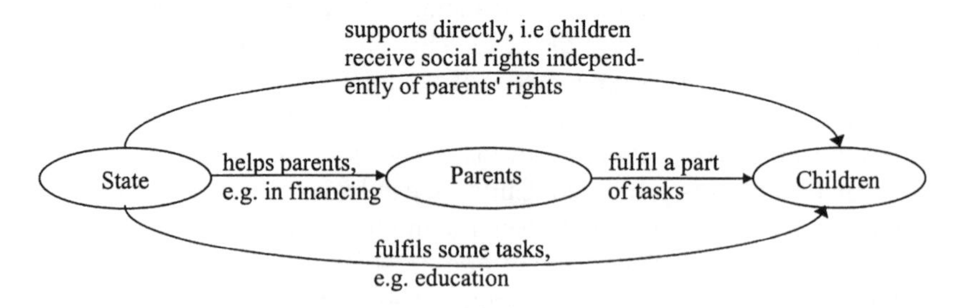

I hypothesise that a strong division of labour between the State and the family and diversified dependence (Model 3) favour an early independence of children from parents and also an early home leaving.

Like family policy, social policy for young people is a fragmented field of very different public allowances and services, which makes it necessary to analyse different public benefits. First, young people's indirect benefits have to be considered:

1. child allowances
2. tax benefits for dependent family members
3. entitlement of dependent family members to health services (in non-universal health systems)
4. consideration of dependent children in unemployment, housing benefits, and social assistance

Second, young people's direct entitlements to public benefits have to be analysed:

1. active employment policy and vocational training measures
2. education benefits (public services like universities, residences, and benefits such as scholarships, students' health insurance, subsidies for transport)
3. entitlement to social security allowances for young workers (unemployment, health, old-age)
4. entitlement to health services (in non-universal health systems)
5. housing benefits
6. benefits for special groups such as allowances for orphans, services for disabled, drug addicts, etc.

The cross-national comparison of these different social policy measures for young people has to follow three questions. First, how do Welfare Sates define entitlements for young people, i.e. direct versus indirect entitlement, age limits, and cohabitation in same household as a condition for entitlement? Second, which benefits exist in one society but are lacking in others? Third, how much does the state spend on these measures or how generous are the benefit rates? Ideally, all these questions have to be answered in the frame of a cross-sectional analysis of direct and indirect social benefits for young people. The possibility of answering the third question is determined by the availability of official statistics for the different measures, but this question is only relevant when comparing very similar configurations. In chapter V social policies for young people in France and Spain are compared and the above-mentioned questions are answered.

Housing Market Structure and Offer

The housing transition is the basis for the creation of a new household, which can be a new household in the family-home of origin or in a different house. Leaving the parents' home does not necessarily mean that a young person creates a new independent household (Jones 1995).

This is so, first, because the child can continue to depend financially on the parents while living in a separate place and, second, because a dwelling can be intermediate and for a given time period after which the young person returns to the family of origin. Thus, an independent household is only attained if a young person is predominantly financially independent and if the household is conceived by this person as the first step into a housing career. Statistically, it is often only ex-post possible to know if the household was intermediate or if instead it was an independent household. Theoretically, an intermediate household can be defined as a young person's dwelling separate from the parents' home whose tenant depends mainly financially on the family of origin or who is temporarily independent and conceive this accommodation only as a short break from living at home. The intermediate household is from the transition perspective equivalent to the one-generation dependent household as defined in chapter 1.

Do the characteristics of the housing market influence young people's living arrangement choices? They would not influence young people if these took the decision to leave home first and then, in a second step, searched for a dwelling, adapting to the market offer and reducing their expectations to realistic possibilities. Chew (1990) assumes such behaviour for migrants arriving in cities, because once they have chosen to move, they have to pay sellers' prices for housing. Nonetheless, in most cases and especially at the beginning of housing careers, deciding to create a household while simultaneously taking information about housing supply into account is likely to be the way the decision making process works. Consequently, household formation will depend on housing affordability (which is determined by income level and housing price) and on the vacancy rate. American researchers have found that abundant supply facilitates the formation of households in general (Smith et al. 1984). In addition, a relation seems to exist between housing costs and living alone, so that areas with high incomes and easily affordable housing supply should show the highest probabilities of non-sharing households. For Spain, Leal Maldonado (1997) points to the importance of the housing market in leaving home by a comparison of the four Catalan provinces. In all these provinces excepting the province of Barcelona the rates of young people living independently are among the highest in Spain. He sees the lower rate in Barcelona as related to high housing prices. Also Serrano Secanella (1997) considers the housing market a basic factor in explaining regional variations in living arrangements in Spain.

Another way in which housing markets influence household formation might be the characteristics of housing tenure, i.e. rented versus owned housing. If for one moment we assume that the relation between both forms of tenure is not determined by demand, then it might be supposed that a market with a high supply of owned dwellings might make it more difficult to create non-family or informal households (with peers, alone, cohabiting) and by contrast might favour only the options of staying with parents or marrying and buying a dwelling. This assumption has two problems. First, the supply of housing also reacts to demand through public regulation and normal market forces; consequently, a high demand for rented housing from people who are ready to pay high rents can provoke new offers and change the supply structure. Second, the decision to create informal households is surely not only determined by economic possibilities but also by preferences. It is difficult to analyse to what extent a low rate of informal households is due to economic restrictions and to what extent it can be explained by a lack of interest in creating such living arrangements (or social pressure against them), but in chapter 4 this is discussed further.

Castles and Ferrera (1996) argue that high rates of home ownership in Southern Europe might be a cause of delayed home leaving and family formation of young people, and of the strong imperative for both partners in a young couple to have a job. This would be due to the fact that the acquisition of a dwelling is a front-end loaded investment in comparison to renting a dwelling. The high rate of home ownership in Southern Europe, in its turn, is seen as a consequence of four factors:

1. high saving rates due to the pooling of resources and needs in families;
2. a scarcity of alternative investment opportunities;
3. the high rate of income coming from the informal labour market favouring saving for old age through home acquisition instead of through social security contributions;
4. a housing policy directed towards incentives for acquisition of dwellings, failing to promote an adequate supply of social housing and establishing rigid systems of rent control, which caused a shrinkage in the housing stock available for renting.

These authors, thus, suggest that the tenure structure is related to the long-lasting family in Southern Europe. This high property-delayed leaving mechanism is supposed to be valid not only in Southern Europe but in general.

Existing urban research also points to the importance of the type of cities for the distribution of young people's living arrangements. An American analysis of 145 American metropolitan areas with census data of 1980 and 1970 has shown that in information-processing cities (state capitals, centres of higher education, etc.) high non-family household rates (living alone, with peers, or in consensual unions) were very common. Conversely, cities engaged in manufacturing, resource extraction, or similar activities displayed low non-family household rates (Chew 1990). The urban-rural divide will also probably influence young people's living arrangements due to migration and immigration, differences in education offer and in social control. The transition from living at parents' homes to living independently will probably occur earlier in rural areas and will be dominated by leaving for marriage with low proportions of informal living arrangements. In chapter 5 some evidence for this as well as some contradicting facts are presented.

To unravel the effects of housing affordability and tenure structure on young people's staying home rates, different intervening factors such as type of habitat (rural versus urban, tertiary dominated versus secondary dominated cities) and preferences should ideally be taken into account. For a cross-national comparison this implies a careful choice of the units of analysis, which should probably be towns instead of regions or nations. A necessary step before engaging in such a comparison is that it has to be tested if in a given society these variables are to have explanatory power on the individual level.

In 1991, Spain was one of the European countries with the lowest rate of rented dwellings: 15% of the principal residences were rented as opposed to 35% in the European Community and 39% in France (Cortés Alcalá 1995). Another difference which has to be taken into account is the low proportion of public rented dwellings in Spain in comparison to northern European countries. At first sight these differences confirm the idea that there is some relation between leaving home patterns and housing market structure, even if this explanation has to be seen in relation to other context characteristics of a country. A simple descriptive cross-national comparison between national home-ownership rates and young people's staying home rates shows that most frequently high home-ownership rates correlate with high staying home rates, but there are some countries with high rates of owned dwelling and low staying home rates, as for instance, Belgium, the United Kingdom and the United States (Taffin 1991, Fernández Cordón 1997).

In addition to the specific Spanish tenure structure, the Spanish housing market is also characterised by how difficult it is for people to afford a dwelling. First, the interest rates for mortgages in Spain exceeded the Union average in 1991: they were almost at 13 per cent in Spain, 10 per cent in France, and 10 per cent in the European Community (Rodríguez López 1994). From a chronological point of view, the Spanish housing market has also made access to first dwellings very difficult. From 1985 until 1991, the selling prices for apartments rose in Spain, and then from 1987 to 1991 the increase of prices exceeded by far the rise of wages and in 1991 the monetary effort related to the family income (one income) necessary to buy a dwelling was 72 per cent before taxes and 60 per cent after taxation (Rodríguez López 1994). More details on similarities and differences of the Spanish and French housing markets are presented in Chapter 4.

Cross-National Differences in Family Values

Differences in norms across countries can, theoretically, be due to differences in the socio-economic contexts or to differences in worldviews, which themselves originate from religious or other ideological constructs. In the last instance it can be argued that even ideologies have their roots in socio-economic contexts, or, at least, this is suggested by a materialist way of conceiving the social world. Without entering into this discussion it can be stated that norms and values as part of ideologies are to some extent independent of the socio-economic context, because they have a proper development dynamic and change only slowly. Thus, theoretically, it should be possible to find very similar socio-economic contexts with different norms and values, at least during a certain period which would last as long as the existing time lag between socio-economic change and cultural change. If these ideas are correct, it means that values and norms have to be taken into account to explain differences in family patterns among countries. Some international and national studies on solidarity norms among generations and the connection between leaving home and getting married are reviewed in this part.

Variations in Norms about Family Solidarity

Within European societies divergences in values about inter-generation solidarity seem to exist, or, at least, expressed opinions in international surveys suggest the existence of cross-national differences. Ideas about duties between generations can be deduced from two questions of the World Values Survey in 1990-93 (Table 2.1). First, a question about duties towards parents: over three-quarters of the Spaniards and Italians asked feel attached to their parents, independently of their behaviour and attitudes, whereas only about half of the Danes and West Germans asked do. Forty to 50 per cent of the latter tend to support a more differentiated vision. Italy and Spain and, with some distance, France seem to cluster into one group of high inter-generation solidarity. This is similar in the values related to children.

Table 2.1 Love and Respect Parents and Parents' Duties Related to Children, 1990-1993

Column %. How many people mentioned	Italy	Spain	Denmark	France	United Kingdom	West Germany	Group-average
'Regardless of what the qualities and faults of one's parents are, one must always love and respect them'	82.8	80.8	47.0	76.9	68.8	61.8	69.7
'One does not have the duty to respect and love parents who have not earned it by their behaviour and attitudes'	17.2	19.2	53.0	23.1	31.2	38.2	30.3
'Parents' duty is to do their best for their children even at the expense of their own well-being'	78.0	75.7	51.9	80.5	75.4	53.3	69.1
'Parents have a life of their own and should not be asked to sacrifice their own well-being for the sake of their children'	11.5	15.4	39.0	19.5	18.8	33.7	23.0
Neither	10.5	8.9	9.1	0.0	5.8	12.9	7.8

Source: author's elaboration with World Values Survey, 1990–1993. Var. 224.

With respect to the duties of parents in relation to children, three-quarters of the Spaniards and Italians and even more French people expressed a family-oriented opinion.[3] The group-average of the Central/Northern European is still different. The two questions are not easily comparable, because the question of parents' duties related to children includes the possibility of a neutral answer, while the questionnaire did not offer this possibility for the first question. Only for

France is it possible, because both questions were asked in comparable ways. In France, inter-generation solidarity seems to be highly institutionalised in both directions, i.e. from parents to children as well as from children to parents. These indicators from 1990–91 point to a higher institutionalisation of inter-generation solidarity in Southern Europe and France compared to Central/Northern Europe. The situation of the United Kingdom is contradictory and has to be clarified with further indicators.

It should be mentioned that in this survey different generations were asked and important age differences have to be assumed. The same question asked to young people in the Basque Country in Spain in 1990 show very different results from the general Spanish results of the World Value Survey. Of those aged 15 to 29 years, only 63 per cent said that one has always to love one's parents regardless of their qualities and faults and only 40 per cent answered that parents' duty is to do their best for their children. Opposite opinions were subscribed to by 36 per cent and 26 per cent respectively. For the first question 1 per cent gave a neutral answer and 33 per cent for the second question. Very similar answers were given by a general sample of Spanish young people, only with somewhat higher approval of strong inter-generation obligations (Elzo 1990). Even if the answers are not totally comparable to the general Spanish figures of the World Value Survey, a lower degree of support for strong inter-generation obligations can be observed among Spanish young people compared to all Spanish people.

Another more indirect indicator of the importance of inter-generation solidarity is the opinion about the importance of children for life and for a couple. Europeans were asked how important it was for them to have a child. The findings show the central and fundamental role of children in most countries but with important differences. The percentage of people aged 15 to 24 who consider having a child as essential and very important number around 60 per cent in Spain, Italy, France, and Belgium; in Portugal and Greece the rate reaches even more than 70 per cent, while it is under 50 per cent in the United Kingdom, the Netherlands, Ireland, and West Germany (Eurobarometer 1993 in: EUROSTAT 1997). In addition, in Spain, Italy, and France, people answered that it was important for them to have children for their marriage to be successful (World Values Survey 1990-1993). One possible conclusion is that the Italians, Spaniards, and the French are more child-oriented than Germans, the English, and Danes. One could also say that Italian and Spanish people attribute to children an important role in increasing solidarity within the couple, as shown by the higher percentage of Italians and Spaniards who consider having a young child as a good reason for not getting divorced.

Are these differences in values about family obligations related to differences in religious denomination and degree of secularisation? If this was so Spain, Italy and France should cluster into one religious group in contrast with the to other European countries. I present here a simple ranking list of indicators of religiosity and of the importance of family solidarity (Table 2.2).

Table 2.2 Ranking of Religiosity and Family Duties, 1990-93

Raised religiously	Children encouraged in religious faith	Religious service once a week	Church answer to family life is adequate	Love and respect parents always	Parents' duty is to do best for children	Essential to have a child
Italy	Italy	Italy	Italy	Italy	Italy	Spain
Spain	Spain	Spain	Spain	Spain	Spain	Italy
France	United Kingdom	West Germany	United Kingdom	France	France	France
West Germany	West Germany	United Kingdom	West Germany	United Kingdom	United Kingdom	Denmark
United Kingdom	France	France	France	West Germany	West Germany	United Kingdom
Denmark	Denmark	Denmark	Denmark	Denmark	Denmark	West Germany

Sources: World Values Survey 1990-93, Eurobarometer 1993.

With the exception of the first indicator, France always appears as a strongly secularised society in a comparative perspective, while Italy and Spain are representative of weakly secularised societies. The higher secularisation degree of French society is also shown in other comparative research (Crouch 1998). This suggests that the similarity of Italy, Spain, and France in family values cannot be explained by a similar degree of secularisation. It could only be argued that the Catholic denomination as a tradition present in all three countries influences family values, There is some further evidence that Catholicism is positively related to strong family kinship obligations.

Greeley (1989), using the International Social Survey Project data of 1986, found, for seven countries (United Kingdom, United Sates, Australia, Hungary, Germany, Austria and Italy), that Catholics do form more intense family networks (frequency of visits and living close/far from relatives) than do other Christians. His results suggest that denominational background independent of social class and education level predict quite good value orientations. For West Germany, Szydlik (1995) found differences among people of Catholic denomination and those of no religious denomination, the first showing stronger inter-generation relationships than the last. However, following an American study by Rossi and Rossi (1990), race and religious affiliation had no effect on kinship obligations in a sample of Americans living in Boston. Similarly, Goldscheider and Goldscheider (1993) found relatively small overall differences in nonfamily living arrangements of American young people among Jews, Catholics, and others in the non-Hispanic, non-Asian, and non-black population. A differentiation of Catholics by southern European origin versus other origins showed differences in the proportions expecting nonfamily living but not in the proportions of those actually having left home for nonfamily settings. Those results reinforce other American research which suggested that secularisation had led to a homogenisation of religious denominations with respect to a variety of family-related behaviours. To sum up, Catholicism or a secularised Catholic tradition probably favour strong kinship obligations, but this is a question which still has to be investigated in more detail, in particular for Europe.

Immigration societies are an interesting case to use in studying the persistence and thus importance of specific cultural traditions among social groups. The above-mentioned study of people living in Boston found that differences in the ethnic origin of the Americans of the sample did not show great influence on kinship obligations. East and West Europeans, Germans and Italians show kinship obligation patterns very similar to the British ones. Only Americans of Irish origin display stronger obligations towards kin than British Americans (Rossi/Rossi 1990). On the contrary, Clausen (1993) found that family solidarity in the United States was stronger among Latin-American and Asiatic than Anglo-Saxon white people. Like Clausen, many other American scholars have found that differences among ethnic groups on family norms are often as great as those of income or education. Unmarried Hispanics, for instance, are less likely than white non-Hispanics to live independently of their parents (Goldscheider/Goldscheider 1993). Again, national studies show a contradictory picture due to the complexity of interactions between ethnic origin, religiosity, and familism.

A good indicator of norms of inter-generation solidarity are monetary transfer flows among different generations, but it is difficult to find comparable international figures on this. The Luxembourg Income Study provides information of within family transfer payments only for family members living in separate households, but not for those sharing households. In the European Household Panel in the individual questionnaire, the information is elicited in an ambiguous way, but in principle it should be available. For the moment, however, the comparative information is not yet available. Some national figures on this question for the United Kingdom, Germany, Spain, and France can give at least a first idea about cross-national differences.

Jones and Wallace (1992) found that when children reach 17 years of age in the United Kingdom the general flow of cash payments is from parents to children, but by the age of 19 the general flow is inverted and children pay more board money than they receive pocket money, at least among those who are living at home and are not in full-time education. Furthermore, in the United Kingdom young people in employment and living with their parents seem to pay board money in the form of a fixed amount for their board, while in the United States this is only the case when the parents' financial situation is very precarious. In addition, British young people in poor families pay higher amounts for their board than in wealthier families so that their contribution to the family income is very important.

A survey of young people in the region of Aragon in Spain conducted in 1985 offers some information about the financial contribution of young people to their families. From young people aged 14 to 25 years in employment, 56 per cent gave all or most of their income to the family of origin, 13 per cent gave a minor part of it, and 30 per cent kept it all for themselves. As in the British study, the results show that the lower the professional category of the young person the more he or she contributes to the family income. Young agricultural self-employed workers, family helps, and agricultural workers contributed more often, i.e. in nearly 80 per cent of the cases, to the household income. In addition, men contribute more often to the family income than do young women, who in turn earn less than their male counterparts (López Jiménez 1987). A more recent Spanish survey (1992) of young people aged 15 to 29 years show that of those young people who said they lived exclusively or primarily from their own income, i.e. described themselves as self-sufficient, 28 per cent gave their income or the majority of it to the family and 57 per cent conserved most or the whole amount for themselves.[4] Self-sufficient young people represented only 45 per cent of the general sample, while the others lived mainly or exclusively from the money received from home (Instituto de la Juventud 1994). These Spanish figures suggest a lower general contribution of young people to their family of origin than that of British young people. If this is confirmed by more comparable figures, it would explain the greater interest of young people in the United Kingdom in leaving home earlier than in Spain and of those from lower social origin compared to those of higher origin.

A German survey of 300 families in Bamberg, where young people aged 18 to 28 and their parents were interviewed, gives some insights into inter-generation solidarity in Germany. Half of the parents supported their children regularly with money transfers, which is quite similar to the Spanish percentage, although the Spanish percentage is higher because it also includes young persons between 15 and 17 years of age. The amount German parents spend to help their children varies according to social class. In the case of parents earning low incomes, only 12 per cent supported their children, while this figure jumped to 72 per cent if they had high incomes. Nearly 40 per cent of the young people aged 25 to 28 were not yet financially independent, of whom 80 per cent were not yet employed, while 20 per cent were employed but their earnings were under the minimum existence level. Of all the young people who were financially dependent, only 67 per cent were still living with their parents, which also meant that parents were supporting children when they were not at home. Most of the independent young people came from families with a good income position and less often from families with many siblings. The results of two other longitudinal surveys conducted among cohabiting couples in the federal state of Bavaria (900) and among married couples in West Germany (1,500) show that 47 per cent of the cohabiting couples and 61 per cent of the married couples had received large presents and financial support from their parents and other relatives when the couple set up house together. The most common support was in form of cash presents and of furniture (Vaskovics 1993).

A French survey at the beginning of the 1990s asked young people (25 to 34 years) if they had received help from their parents during the year that followed their leaving home. If they left to study they received, in 35 per cent of the cases, help to cover all their costs and in 24 per cent of the cases monthly help to cover a part of their expenditures. If they had left for reasons of employment or to live with a partner as a couple they received very little financial help, but received more help in kind: 33 per cent of those leaving to live with a partner as a couple had received such help (Bozon/Villeneuve-Gokalp 1995). Similar figures are shown by another French survey of 1992: 23 per cent of the students living in their own household received financial help from their parents (Caussat 1995).

The European Household Panel wave of 1994 provides cross-national data on the rate of young householders who said that they had received economic help from parents or friends. Around 18 to 22 per cent of young householders in Germany, Denmark, and Greece affirmed that they had received support, while in Spain, Italy, Portugal, and Ireland only 2 to 9 per cent had benefited from help. In France and the Netherlands 13 and 12 per cent respectively had been supported by parents and friends (EUROSTAT 1997).

The German and French studies and the European Household Panel figures suggest a weaker connection between the financial and social dependence of young people on their parents in northern and central European countries compared to most southern European countries. In the latter people leave home late, but once they have created their own households they seem to be less dependent on economic support from the older generation. Therefore, the Spanish situation, in which one-generation households are good proxies for the financial and social independence of young people, is a specific Spanish and southern feature. In this case the question is: Why don't young people in Spain live in one-generation dependent households very often? Is it due to a lack of desire for independence, to the lower resources of Spanish parents, to difficulties on the housing market, or the lack of adequate public allowances which reduce parents' financial efforts in the case of dependent one-generation households? These questions will be answered in the successive parts of this work.

Leaving Home in Order to Get Married?

The assumption that most young people leave home when they marry is in many cases not correct. Historians found that in the European past many young single people left their family of origin to live as servants or lodgers in other households. There is some evidence that in Europe the closest link between marriage and leaving home was a phenomenon of the short period of time of the 1960s. Already during the 1970s, young people began to leave their family of origin more often to cohabit before marriage, to live on their own and for educational reasons. This weakening of the link between marriage and leaving home can be observed for Europe in general, but important differences still remain across European societies and among social groups (Kiernan 1989).

German studies often point to the importance of getting married as a reason for leaving the parental home. The already-mentioned study of Mayer and Wagner (1989) found that marriage was significantly related to the leaving rate of young German people from 1944 to 1980. Weick also (1993) found that marriage was the most influential factor on the leaving age, even if this influence has diminished among the younger cohorts.

An Australian survey of 1982 shows differences within the country. The young Australian adults who were most likely to leave the family of origin in order to marry were those with a strong attachment to religion, with southern European parents, with strong traditional family values, coming from a large family, and who had left school young (Young 1989). These results suggest that there could be a connection between Catholicism and a low degree of secularisation in Spain and Italy and the norm of leaving home to marry. Another possibility to follow up is the differences in the proportion of young people with low educational levels and from large families, which is also higher in Spain and Italy compared to France.

Two French studies analyse the connection between leaving home and marriage. The first is based on a longitudinal survey among 3,000 French people aged 25 to 34. Of those men who left their parents' home before age 28, 18 per cent did so for educational reasons, 19 per cent for employment reasons, 38 per cent to live in a couple, 8 per cent because of conflicts with their parents, and 9 per cent because they wished to be independent. Women showed a similar behaviour pattern and left only a little more often to live with a partner as a couple and less often for employment reasons (Bozon/Villeneuve-Gokalp 1995). Galland (1995) shows, with data from the French Youth Survey of 1992, that two-thirds of young French people (26 to 29 years) followed the transition into adulthood in the following way: they finished their studies, entered their first employment, created their independent household, and then formed a couple. This transition sequence is more frequent among men (72 per cent) than among women (59 per cent).

The Spanish sociodemographic survey of 1991 allows for a rough hypothesis on the reasons why young people who lived with their parents in 1981 subsequently left this household.[5] The codification does not account for employment but only for family, education, and housing. Approximately 25 per cent of the young people aged 20 to 29 in 1991 had left their parents' home at least once and they first left in 90 per cent of the cases, to form a stable couple (marrying or cohabiting) and in 5 per cent to become independent of the family of origin. This longitudinal information confirms the cross-sectional figures of young people's arrangements in Spain, which are dominated by living in the family of origin or with a spouse. Unlike in France, the connection between leaving home and marrying is very strong in Spain. Holdsworth (2000) shows, in her comparative analysis of leaving home in the United Kingdom and in Spain, that very few Spaniards leave home in order to study compared to the British. Contrary to this, the probability of leaving home to live with a partner is nearly the same for both countries only with a different timing.

Norms about legitimate reasons for leaving home, especially the strong link between marriage and leaving home, may explain differences in young people's household patterns in Europe. This is the conclusion of Holdsworth's comparison (2000) on leaving home in the United Kingdom and in Spain. Yet, it is not clear if these norms are explaining variables or, more probably, intervening variables. If young people in Spain normally leave home in order to get married it could be a result of their preferences, but it could also be related to the difficulties of leaving home for educational reasons, to share accommodation with others, or to live in a one-person household. If the possibilities of receiving public allowances are low, if the offer of students' residences is scarce and if the housing market is dominated by an offer of dwellings for ownership instead of rental, then these variables could explain to a large extent the strong connection between leaving home and marriage and the high rate of young people staying in their parents' households.

In addition, the formation of more formal partnership relations among young unmarried people is related to income. An analysis of Spanish data from 1995 shows that young people with high income have more chances to have a regular or formal relationship with a partner than those with low income, after controlling for gender, age, and educational level (Garrido/Requena 1996).[6]

Conclusion: Lack of a Comparative Theoretical Framework

The review of the international literature on young people's leaving home patterns has shown that nearly all studies focus on one national setting and there is thus almost no theoretical framework for understanding cross-national differences in young people's living arrangements. The individual-level theoretical propositions relate leaving home to other status transitions: access of employment, end of secondary schooling, and family formation. Leaving home is differentiated according to destinations of social independence, whereby family formation (marriage and consensual union) is distinguished from nonfamily autonomy. National differences result from differences in the timing of nest-leaving and in the destination upon leaving. In addition, it was shown that social independence does not mean financial independence everywhere.

Analysts agree on the importance of the employment/unemployment situation of the young person for her likelihood to live independently. The effect of long-lasting enrolment in education on the timing of leaving home is sometimes seen as delaying nest-leaving and sometimes as accelerating it. American analysts relate family norms and family formation to religiosity, religious denomination, and ethnic origin, but this perspective is almost absent in studies about European societies. The role of housing markets and social policies for leaving home is addressed less frequently, the former mainly by analysts studying Southern Europe and the latter mainly by British scholars, but again no comparative studies were found.

This research wants to explain cross-national differences in two-generation households without differentiating along the dimension of financial dependence/independence. Thus, the dependent variable is residential, or in the term chosen here, social dependence versus independence. The comparative perspective of the present study allows for the analysis of the role of labour markets, housing markets, social policies, and family norms at once. It aims to develop an analytic framework for a macro-sociological theory on leaving home. The great challenge of this work is the application of this theoretical perspective to an empirical case study of cross-national differences in household patterns of young people in France and Spain. In the next chapter the theoretical model is developed.

Notes

[1] Findings of the Spanish Youth Survey of 1988 contradict this idea of increasing tolerance, since 78 per cent of the young people aged 15 to 29, when asked if they had freedom to "make love at home" answered that they did not, they would not be allowed to (Zárraga 1989).

[2] This is the result of a logistic regression with a sample of young people born between 1963 to 1966 and interviewed in 1992.

[3] French answers are not really comparable to answers from other nationals, because the questions were not formulated in an identical way. Only the French had no possibility of giving a neutral answer ("neither").

[4] Unfortunately, the report of this study has not excluded married persons (16%) from the sample to compute the percentages of young people contributing to the family. This means that a number of the young people who give their money to the family are married and are thus not contributing to the family of origin but to the new family. An older Spanish youth survey (1988) also found that the majority of young people aged 15 to 29 gave some of their earning to their parents, but that this contribution did not compensate the costs produced by nest-staying (Zárraga 1989).

[5] The problem with this survey is that a change of dwelling is only classified as such if the new dwelling became the usual residence for more than three months. Residences for more than three months are not accounted for if the individual still conserved their permanent residence in another place. Therefore an underestimation of students and young employees living away for some time has to be expected.

[6] Compared to the group which has more informal relationships and taking only young people who do not live with a partner.

3 Leaving Home: A Macro-Micro Model

A study of comparative living conditions makes cross-national conceptualisation necessary. In cases of applied empirical studies, this task presents two challenges: first, a theoretical challenge consisting of finding concepts which mean the same thing in different social contexts or that at least specify the context to which they can be applied. Second, there is the challenge of operationalising these concepts in such a way that existing information and data can be used to test hypotheses containing these concepts. At the end of the day there is always the danger of studying what the data permits us to and not what we were really interested in. To be aware of this danger it is therefore very useful to start from an abstract theoretical level and only then pass to the concrete empirical method to be used.

A theoretical model has to be found which can explain cross-national and cross-regional differences in the diffusion of two-generation households in comparison to one-generation households. This question is asked at the macrosociological level and to prevent an ecological fallacy (Flora 1974) it has also to be answered on the same level. Models on a macrosociological level always assume given social mechanisms at the micro-sociological level, so that a complete model should include both levels. In this case, this means that the explanation of differences in household structures has to include and analyse differences in household creation behaviour within each macrosociological unit and then determine how the micro-sociological logic of action is aggregated to these macrosociological structures.

There are two main causes which can explain international differences in social structures. Mayer (1997) calls the first causes "proximal" causes; they refer to explanatory factors on the individual and group level. The second causes he calls "distal" causes; these are explanatory factors at the national level and mostly of an institutional nature. He argues that in some instances micro-conditions will be translated into macro-variables by aggregation and in those cases international differences are the result of pure composition effects. Most of the time, this sort of macro-micro link is insufficient, because institutional differences also account for international differences. In those mixed cases, more historical and contextual interpretations of national configurations of institutions have to be added. In the following chapter two theoretical models linking the micro and macro level are constructed as a base for cross-national comparison (tertium comparationis).

Macro-level Model

For Western societies after World War II, the following family formation behaviour for young people is assumed to represent a good ideal type to compare with empirical data. Since gender differences are basic for the home leaving process, two different ideal types need to be considered.[1]

A young man will leave the parental household and create a new one or go into another already existent one under three main conditions:

1. He has a sufficiently high and stable income to support himself and, if he wants to create a male breadwinner family also to maintain his spouse and eventually children, which means financing living in an independent household and covering his (their) needs.[2] The income can be a pure market income, a public allowance, and/or an allowance given by other family members or a mix of different income sources.
2. Another basic condition for leaving is to have found a dwelling to go to. Thus income and housing are necessary conditions for leaving, although not sufficient ones.
3. Additional conditions are the wish to marry or cohabit, the desire for independence or the beginning of an activity or study which makes geographical mobility necessary.

Transition into adulthood will follow the order of, first, finishing education, second, becoming financially independent, and, third, finding a dwelling to live alone, with a partner, or with peers.

The first two sets of conditions refer to means and the third set to preferences. The relation between means and preferences can be formulated in the following way: "Whilst increasing affluence provides the young person with the opportunity to leave his or her parental home, the decision whether and when to use this opportunity depends on values and preferences" (Mayer/Schwarz 1989). Hence, every analysis should draw its attention first to the opportunity structures and in a second step to dominating preferences.

On the macrosociological level this means that there are three conditions which facilitate young people forming independent households and which might explain a low rate of two-generation households:

1. The labour market for young men should ideally offer stable jobs with earnings at least at a minimum subsistence level, while the state should help young men who are not on the labour market or whose earnings are too low to allow economic independence. Parents should support young men's household formation by more or less regular gifts to facilitate the first expensive investments. Each of the three social institutions can serve as a functional equivalent of the others, but the labour market remains the basis on which the state and the family intervene.
2. The housing market has to offer dwellings which can be paid for by young men, regardless of whether they are owned or rented.
3. Dominant values should not connect household formation only with marriage, but include alternative reasons for creating a new household, such as beginning a consensual union, desire for independence, and so on.

A young woman can follow the same logic as a man. This could be called an **independent household formation** and in this case the same conditions as above are relevant. A woman, however, can also follow a second logic, which is to marry or cohabit with a man fulfilling the conditions described above. Thus, if a woman creates a household with a financially independent man, without herself being economically independent of him, one can speak of **dependent household formation**. In this case the following conditions have ideally to be fulfilled:

1. The women has bad prospects on the labour market and low hopes of being able to enter employment which permits her to be economically independent. She has to find a man willing to create a new family with her and with an income which permits the satisfaction of the needs of two people.
2. The income of the male partner has to be high enough to allow for a dwelling for two persons to be rented or bought.
3. The female partner has to be willing to enter an asymmetric relationship (in terms of economic dependence).

On the macro level, the same for men is true for women if an independent household formation is aimed at. In contrast, **dependent household formation** will occur more probably under the following conditions:

1. The female labour market is characterised by high unemployment rates and unstable employment conditions.
2. The educational structure of women is dominated by low levels of formal education.
3. Dominant values connect female household formation with marriage; this means that most women prefer marriage to a consensual union and do not want to live alone or with peers.

The more the dependent household formation dominates, the stronger the connection between leaving home and getting married will be, at least for women. At the same time the socio-economic situation of young men will be very important, so that difficult labour and housing market conditions will strongly influence the timing and possibilities of leaving home in order to create a new family. This might also explain the strong connection between household formation and marriage, since women with few employment chances will search for an alternative in marriage. In theory they could also search for an alternative in a consensual union, but only if social pressure against it is not too strong because consensual unions have already reached the critical number to be seen as a normal and acceptable social fact. However, marriage is more convenient for couples where the woman depends economically on the man, since it protects the weaker part to some extent. Assuming similar educational structures, more two-generation households will be found if dependent household formation is widespread because for young women legitimate reasons for creating a one-generation household are restricted to marriage and they leave only for this reason.

These ideal types serve as heuristic instruments to make the social mechanisms which are assumed explicit, especially those at the micro level. It is obvious that social reality is more complex, but these ideal types permit us to explore the relations between different institutions specifying precisely the micro and the macro level. In addition, the micro-level mechanisms will be looked at in more detail below. The macrosociological model, as illustrated in Figure 3.1, follows from the individual-level ideal types and from the given macrosociological perspective.

Figure 3.1 Macro Model

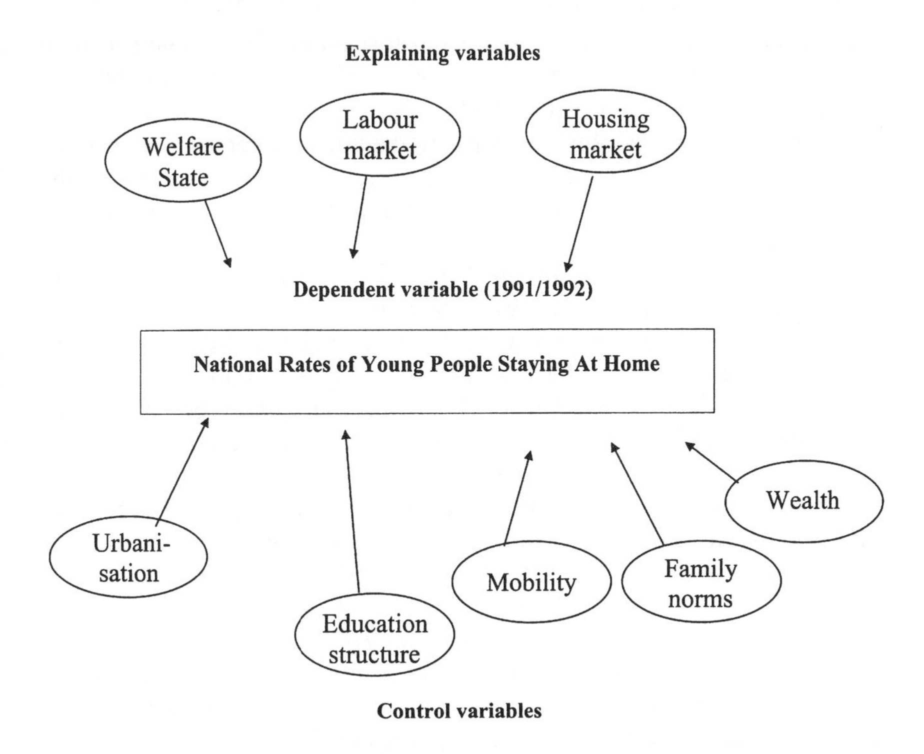

Three macro level hypotheses will be tested to explain national (regional) differences in two-generation households. Their micro level assumptions have to be analysed before testing the hypotheses on the macro level itself. The hypotheses are presented in monocausal forms but these will later be linked.

1. Dependence-diversification hypothesis In cases with a strong division of labour between the Welfare State and the family in the fulfilment of family tasks and a high degree of diversification of the economic dependence of children, low rates of two-generation households and a high diversity of young people's living arrangements will be found with a high frequency of one-generation dependent households. By diversification of economic dependence the source of income is intended: market income, family support, public benefit (cf. p.38). The individual-level test has to be restricted to France, since the French survey is the only one to contain information on public benefits. This is done in Chapter 2.

2. Precariousness hypothesis A high occurrence of precarious employment trajectories and low earnings result in high male staying home rates and in high rates of dependent female household formation. Taken together, both phenomena will make two-generation households more probable and one-generation households less diversified (fewer consensual unions and single households) (cf. p.32). Relationships at the micro-level can be studied through national surveys with the exception, in the Spanish case, of the earning variable, for which data has to be estimated using other sources.

3. High property-low affordability hypothesis In housing markets with high prices, low vacancy rates, and a low supply of rented housing, two-generation households will be more frequent and the diversity of one-generation households will be low (cf. p.42). These variables are context variables at the level of cities or regions, which can partly be constructed using national data sets and have to be taken partly from published sources.

These hypotheses can only be tested by controlling for intervening variables. The list of possible intervening variables is long, but an attempt has been made to choose the most significant and directly related ones.

1. Young People's Consumption Preferences Hypothesis If young people live in a context of low average income levels, but they spend similar absolute amounts for transport, communication, and leisure as young people in contexts with higher average income levels, then in the first context the prevalence of two-generation households will be high. It is assumed that living in the parental home is a strategy to prevent a low consumption capacity.

2. Urbanisation The influence of the context of one's residence in terms of it being rural or urban, gauged through the measuring of the size of the municipality where one lives, can work in two ways. First, it can be supposed that in regions with a high degree of small and middle-sized towns, rates of two-generation households will be low, because of more favourable housing markets. Second, areas with a high presence of rural municipalities will show a high occurrence of two-generation households due to more traditional social norms.

3. Education structure High university enrolment rates in contexts of restricted social rights will relate to high rates of two-generation households, while in contexts of more extended social rights the rate of two-generation households will be lower, because one-generation dependent households will be more common. High rates of low education will result in low levels of two-generation households, all other things being equal.

4. Mobility Areas of immigration of young people for reasons of study or work will present lower rates of two-generation households and more one-generation households, especially in the form of peer and single-person households.

5. Family norms Areas where consensual unions are more widespread will present lower rates of two-generation households, since informal living arrangements favour young people's early nest-leaving. In addition, territorial units where neolocal and early marriage was important in the past will show lower rates of two-generation households, while areas where in the past stem-families and late and patrilocal marriage predominated will display higher rates of two-generation households. These historical patterns are closely related to the agricultural production mode in the respective regions and are relevant here only in those areas where agriculture is still important.

Some other intervening variables have not been included in this list, because it is assumed that their effect is mainly transmitted through the controlling variables listed above. This is the case of age structure as a measure of the demographic pressure of young people which is, however, likely to be already reflected in unemployment rates and in dwelling vacancies.

The theoretical model consists of three explaining variables and five controlling variables, which have been presented with the hypothetical assumption of statistical independence from each other. Nevertheless, in the empirical test of the model, the interaction among all the eight independent variables has to be taken into account. This has to be done at least for those variables which presumably correlate in such a way that a particular independent variable modifies the effect of another, outweighing it instead of reinforcing it. This will surely be the case for the variables of education structure and labour market uncertainty. In the following part the right methodology to link micro and macro level and to account for interaction effects will be discussed.

Individual Choice Model

In this chapter an individual choice model for describing the leaving-home process of young people in two countries will be developed. In the previous sections some individual action ideas were already presented. It is the aim of this chapter to formalise them and to make the selection mechanism of young people facing the choice to stay versus to leave the parental home explicit. People's decisions to leave the parental home will depend on unconscious norms and values deriving from reference groups, about which they may not reflect at all. In addition, they will also depend on a personal evaluation of perceived alternatives. I assume that young people perceive a choice at given life course moments and these can be identified in general as events of status transitions.

Status Transitions and Leaving Home

I will distinguish three important decision-taking moments or status transitions:

1. on becoming financially independent from parents;
2. on moving from secondary school to vocational training or university;
3. on converting unstable relationships into relatively stable partnerships, through celebration of a marriage and/or birth of a child.

At these moments individuals might - or might not- consider the possibility and feasibility of leaving the parental home. The extent to which a choice is perceived and analysed in a rational manner at a given moment will depend on the norms of the reference group and on the *habitus* of the young person. For example, let us imagine a society in which the only reason young people leave their parents is in order to marry, and this fact appears to people to be a natural law and is thus not questioned. In this case individuals will think about leaving home only in the third status transition. Thus, it can be stated that two general conditions have to be fulfilled for a choice mechanism to become operative:

1. The individual is not under constraint, for example, because a previous decision has eliminated the possibility of making a choice in the present. This might be the case of young people who decide to study and who have to migrate because the nearest university is too far away for them to remain in the parental home.
2. A choice is perceived by the individual. In this case it means that a choice is perceived at the status transition moments mentioned above.

It could be that because of social norms young people do not realise that they would have the choice of leaving the parental home, for example, when they finish secondary education.

In some European contexts, for instance in Southern Europe, marriage, i.e. the third transition, is strongly related to the leaving home process, while in other societies financial independence, university attendance, and marriage together form a mixed pattern influencing home-leaving. For the Netherlands, Baanders (1998) found that in families where either or both parents had pursued higher education, their adult children expect more often the concurrence of home-leaving and the educational career, and they link home-leaving less to the precondition of financial independence. For most West European societies it is, however, assumed that all three of the above-mentioned moments represent transition moments at which at least some young people perceive the choice of leaving home, and that outside these transitions few people reflect on leaving home. Only a minority of young people will decide to leave home, for instance, when they feel that it is no longer possible for them to share the household with their parents independently of other transitions. In addition, there are certain universal conditions that have to be fulfilled in order to become independent. A young person in the process of choosing between the alternative of staying in the parental home or leaving it will, in order to be able to select the alternative of leaving home, have to fulfil two economic conditions. The individual has to have access to an income, at least at a low subsistence level, and she or he has to find a dwelling.

Individual Choice through Comparison of Standards of Life

The new situation, which results from a transition or from the expectation of a transition which the individual predicts will take place, pushes the young person to evaluate the possibility and desirability of leaving home. The hypothesis is that in this situation the person will reflect upon the quality of life she will reach if she leaves, and will compare it to the quality of life she could have by remaining in the parental home. Quality of life is determined by material resources (constraints) and emotional well being (preferences). It is not a given that a young person who earns a subsistence income, who could have access to a dwelling, and who thus has no material constraints to becoming independent, sets up an independent household. Leaving the parental home under such economically "constraint-free" conditions will depend on norms and on the personal definition of a life of quality.

The quality of living in the parental home ($ST_{parents}$) can be seen as the result of the income of the parents minus the expenditures of the household plus the young person's own income plus the non-material well-being in the parental home. Income includes market income, public allowances, rent income from property, and family transfers. Expenditures refer to the costs for housing, food, and leisure, and to the saving capacity of parents and child. The non-material well-being at home is the result of the emotional support parents give to their children, the extent of a possible generation conflict, and the possible social stigmatisation of living with parents at a certain age.

$$(1)\ ST_{parents} = \underbrace{I_{parents} - EXP_{parents} + I_{own}}_{\text{economic constraints}} + \underbrace{NQUAL_{parents}}_{\text{preferences}}$$

Culture and social norms (SN) may affect a rational choice in a twofold way. First, they might, for instance, influence the relationship between one explanatory factor of economic nature and the standard of life. People can prefer to buy a dwelling instead of renting it, so that expenditures for housing mean the costs of a mortgage and not the costs of a rent. Second, social norms might give greater weight to some preferences rather than to others. Social norms may encourage early independence by rewarding young people with strong preferences for independence, while stigmatising young people with other preferences. In this analysis the second view about the mechanism of norms has been taken and, thus, an additive relationship between individual level variables and social norms was chosen.[3]

$$(2)\ ST_{parents} = \underbrace{(I_{parents} - EXP_{parents} + I_{own} + NQUAL_{parents})}_{\text{economic constraints and preferences}} + \underbrace{(SN_1 + SN_2 + SN_3..)}_{\text{in a cultural context}}$$

This equation will be developed later on in Chapter 5; for the moment let us concentrate on the situation without taking the context into account.

The quality of living in an independent household is the opposite of the quality of living in the parental home. It is the result of the income of the young person and sometimes of the income of a partner or spouse minus the expenditures of the household and plus the non-material well being, which is the personal and social evaluation of some independence from parents and of a life on one's own, with peers or with a partner. With regard to income two aspects are important: the level of income and the expectation that the job will be long lasting. An aspect which is not taken into consideration in this individual-level equation is the availability of accommodation, since it is a feature of the context.

$$(3)\ ST_{indep} = \underbrace{(I_{own} + I_{partner} - EXP_{indep} + NQUAL_{indep})}_{\text{economic constraints}} + \underbrace{(SN_1 + SN_2 + SN_3..)}_{\text{and preferences in a cultural context}}$$

The outcome of the evaluation of possible alternatives is believed to influence young people's decision to set up their own households.

If $ST_{parents} <= ST_{independent}$ the individual will set up an independent household

If $ST_{parents} > ST_{independent}$ the individual will not set up an independent household

The model posits that, if a young person thinks about the possibility of leaving home, the decision to leave will be taken if the quality of living in the independent household is as high or higher than the current quality of living in the parents' home. This model is similar to that of Baanders (1998) in her study for the Netherlands, except that it does not separate between the intention to leave and the home-leaving behaviour. In addition, the role of subjective considerations is less theorised in my model, because I use demographic data and not opinion data. In the model here it is assumed that the decision process of leaving home is guided by a rational selection procedure within a given cultural context and thus shaped by norms. An individual's decision is not seen as the outcome of an unreflected action according to tradition, passion, or anxiety. It is further assumed that even if some people do not act in a rational choice manner, the aggregation of all individual choices at the macro-level will be dominated by rational choice-oriented individual actions within a context. In addition, it has to be remembered that this theoretical approach implies rational actors who perceive a choice and think about the short-term future at the moment of a status transition, who are not constrained by previous decisions and who are capable of sensibly evaluating the real chances of their expectations being fulfilled.

In the next sections of the chapter methodological questions and choices are presented and discussed. First, the selection of cases is described, then the choice of the surveys is discussed and finally the statistical method and its application is presented.

Individuals, Regions, and Nations as Cases

I have chosen a two country comparison, because this work aims to develop a comparative theoretical framework by analysing in detail the micro-level phenomena and their relations to national contexts. A large-N study of home-leaving would have necessitated a large number of analyses with individual data, as many as contextual units had been chosen. Clearly, this could not be the scope of a PhD thesis.

The cases of France and Spain were chosen because at the macro level they have different dependent variables, while displaying some similarities in the independent context variables, which reduces to some extent the typical problem of small-N studies. It is well known that a high number of diverging independent variables which could be candidates for the explanation of the difference in the dependent variable makes small-N comparisons a difficult task. The solution to this problem can be sought through two methods. First, one should try to choose two cases with different values on the dependent variable, which at the same time show the smallest possible variation in the values of the independent variables. Second, a strategy of using so-called macro-variables which do not permit testing for one causal condition but which argue in terms of causal configurations can be pursued (Ragin 1987, Ragin/Hein 1993).[4] The primary interest of this work is to explain the long-lasting intergenerational co-residence in Spain from a comparative perspective, for which I follow a case-oriented and variation-finding comparative method (Tilly 1984). Thus, a country with early home-leaving behaviour and some similarities with Spain was selected. In Chapter 1, international variations were presented. The candidates for comparison with Spain were the United Kingdom, West-Germany, the Netherlands and France. The decision to use France is based on the following similarities with Spain:

1. similar norms about family solidarity as shown in Chapter 2;
2. similar age at first marriage (cf. Chapter 4);
3. the dominance of the Catholic denomination;
4. a vocational training system based on school-training with low significance of dual vocational training;
5. similar enrolment rates of young people in universities (cf. Chapters 4 and 7);
6. a relatively high youth unemployment rate in the second half of the eighties and perception of youth unemployment as social problem at this time (cf. Chapter 4);
7. a particularly high increase of short-term employment among young people (cf. Chapter 4);
8. agricultural production still has an important weight in the economy and social structure (cf. Chapter 4).

However, the variance in the independent variables is still important and difficult to control in a two-country comparison. For further analysis of the importance of the contexts of labour, housing markets, and family patterns, the cases are changed. Instead of comparing France and Spain, Spanish regions are compared to each other. This does not allow us to draw conclusions on Spanish-French differences, but it gives an idea of the role of different societal institutions in shaping young people's behaviour. The analysis of the macrosociological Spanish-French difference will follow an interpretative and descriptive path based on causal configurations. The individual-level French-Spanish analysis will highlight the respective difficulties of different groups of young people in becoming socially independent in each country. Based on these results the interpretative part will focus on how far differences in young people's social rights might explain the national differences in living arrangements and the different micro-sociological patterns.

The cases change throughout this work. The research question is based on countries as units of analysis, but it makes a recurrence to individuals as units of analysis necessary. This is achieved through a statistical multivariate analysis of two large samples of French and Spanish young people. This is necessary in order to compare the logic of the selection of individuals in both countries. As already mentioned, the logic of aggregation will be studied for France and Spain through the use of regions as cases. Multi-level statistical analysis with individual characteristics and context characteristics as independent variables will take into account interactions between individual level and context level variables (cf. Chapter 5).

I will use two surveys, a Spanish survey from 1991 (Encuesta Sociodemográfica) and a French survey from 1992 (Enquête Jeunes), both conducted by their respective national statistics offices. The French survey covers 9,344 young people between the ages of 18 and 29 and the Spanish survey 25,555 young people between 20 and 29 years of age. For Spain, three large and representative surveys of young people were available in 1995, the date when this research project began. First, there was the Spanish labour force survey with a sample of 60,000 households. The problems with this survey for this research are twofold: 1. one person of the household answers for all other household members and very frequently it is the housewife/mother who answers. Since youth researchers have noticed that parents tend to state that their children are living at home while in reality they are living away, e.g. in residence halls, with peers, etc., surveys where the young person herself answers are more adequate. 2. No information on the first time of leaving home and the first dwelling, on dwelling tenure, nor on consensual unions is provided. Second, there is the Spanish Youth Survey of 1992 with a sample of 5,000 young people aged 15 to 29 years. This survey has the advantage of providing income information, but it also lacks information on the point of time and the destination of the young person's leaving. Thus, it was decided to choose the third possible survey, namely the Encuesta Sociodemográfica of 1991, which has, nonetheless, one problem, namely the lack of information on income. Apart from this problem it presents the advantages of having a large sample with retrospective information on many different areas of life. The choice of the Spanish survey constrained the French choice insofar as the French survey had to be from about the same year. This made the choice of the Enquête Jeunes the most appropriate one, because of the year, the fact that the young person answered herself, and because of the retrospective information. The European Household Panel data became available at a point in time when this research project was already very advanced and thus a change of surveys presented costs that were too high. In addition, the sample of young people who had left home during survey time is very small and information at the regional level is not available for reasons of data protection.

Statistical Possibilities for Testing the Individual Choice Model

The test of such a theoretical model requires very rich statistical information, since, firstly, data on preferences and values have to be available and, secondly, detailed retrospective or panel data are also essential. The surveys used in this research do not include information on preferences nor do they include retrospective measures on income and expenditures. These problems will be discussed below and the decision in favour of a cross-sectional statistical model and against a longitudinal model will be justified.

Missing: Preferences, Expectations, and Time-Varying Variables

The first problem could be solved by testing only the economic part of the model, which means assuming that if somebody leaves home and, in the process, accepts a deterioration in her material quality of life, it is because she gains a high reward in her emotional well-being ($NQUAL_{independent}$). The problem of lack of data on the emotional side is serious, because it leads us to a situation whereby this hypothesis cannot be falsified, for if evidence against the economic side of the model is found, it is not clear if the unexplained variance is due to the lack of non-material variables in the reduced "economic model" or to the incorrectness of the "general model". Nevertheless, it might be worth applying the model in a reduced form. This application will not aim to test the validity of the model but rather will use it as a heuristic instrument. If it is assumed that different groups of persons have different preferences, then it can be stated for which groups the economic model has greater predictive power. In this way the general model per se cannot be tested, but the reduced model could serve as an ideal-type to which different realities are compared in order to see how they differ from each other. If, for example, the reduced model makes better predictions in one country than in another, then it can be affirmed that in the country where the model has a greater predictive power, the socio-economic factors measured at individual level are more important in leaving home than in the other country. The Spanish and French models employed in this work have similar predictive capacities, there only being differences between the models for men and women (cf. Chapter 4).

The available data not only lack information on preferences but the data set to be used for Spain does not provide information on income and expenditures. If the theoretical model in its reduced economic form is to be translated into a statistical model, income and expenditures have to be approximated with the available information. To find the best corollaries to test the theoretical action model two steps were necessary: first, the most exact indicator of the theoretical variable was found in each survey; separately and, second, the most adequate common variable was constructed at the level of the survey with the poorest information. Income can be approximated with information on the activity and employment situation and expenditures of parents can be partially approximated by knowledge of the number of children. More details on the operationalisation of the theoretical variables will be provided later on.

At first sight, the general theoretical model would suggest the use of an event history model, because two points in time have to be observed - the moment when still living with parents and after having left - and these occur at different moments for different individuals. The probability of the event of moving out of the parental home has to be estimated by observing young people over the period in which they are likely to leave the parents' home. Obviously the two moments can only be observed for those who have already left home, which in the Spanish survey were 42 per cent and in the French survey 66 per cent at the time of the interview. For those who did not make the transition at a given moment some expectations about their quality of life in the near future have to be known. Unfortunately, the interviewers did not pose questions about expectations but only about behaviour, and as a consequence one has to deduce young people's expectations from their behaviour.

This can be done by assuming that a young person's expectation of her situation in the near future, e.g. in the year 1990, coincides more or less with the situation they finally attained in that year. If this assumption is correct, then we would define the income situation in 1990 of a person who, in 1990, for instance, lived for the first time in an independent household, as equal to her income expectations in 1989, when she was still living in the parental home. At this point the problem that some expectations cannot be estimated in this way emerges. The data to be used does not provide information about an individual's expectations with regard to expenditure in an independent household while she was in her parents' home nor if the individual expected to have a partner or a spouse.

There is another important problem, which is only inherent in an event history approach. The Spanish data set that is available for this study does not provide exact information on the activity situation for every retrospective year, for it is not possible to know when somebody entered unemployment and which type of job she had in a given year. It is only possible to know if, for instance, somebody was economically inactive, searching for her first employment, in a first activity period with unemployment and short-term employment periods, or in a first activity period with long-term employment and without unemployment periods. This is not very satisfying, particularly because youth is characterised by many changes in the activity situation. Taking into account that the activity and employment situation is taken as a proxy for income, this is a serious problem, because types of activity careers would have to be taken as proxies for the activity situation at the crucial moment of the transition out of the parental home, which in its turn is a proxy for income.

To sum up, there is the general problem of scarce information on preferences, on retrospective information on income and expenditures and on expectations. In addition, the retrospective information of the Spanish data was not collected with sufficient detail. These problems of applicability of the theoretical model cannot be solved for the moment, because there are no surveys that could provide the necessary information. In the future the European Household Panel conducted by EUROSTAT might help to solve some of the problems mentioned. It is therefore necessary to reformulate the model and to deduct some new hypotheses, which can then be more easily tested with the current information.

Reformulating the Model by Starting from Context Differences

The problem of missing information on preferences can be tackled by assuming that national contexts and social groups provide dominant cultural norms and that to some extent these influence personal preferences. If this is true, then some testable hypotheses can be deduced from the quality-of-life hypothesis. The basic idea is that in Spain there is a dominant cultural pattern in home leaving, while in France there are at least two alternative patterns. In Spain leaving home is strongly connected to marriage, while in France it is connected to studying and to forming a family. Thus, two different models for each country have been created. In addition, women and men might have different rationales towards leaving home depending on their household formation strategy as discussed in chapter 2.

It is also assumed that young people who are at school or at university follow a different rationale than those who have finished their education. Students' leaving is not connected to a full-time and long-term job, but most of the time to transfers from the state and/or the family and/or income from a part-time job. The rationale of some of the students might be similar to that of non-students, in particular when leaving home is related to the formation of a couple with a partner who has a stable income, something which occurs more often to women. However, the fundamental difference is that for students, stability and security is not decisive in opting for an independent household, since by definition their future is rather unsure. It means that when they compare standards of living at the parental home and outside of it, the non-material aspects of the quality of life might weigh more. As a consequence the reduced economic model should have a lower predictive power for students than for non-students. Different models for students and non-students are run to control for these differences.

The group of non-students is less homogeneous with regard to preferences, because some non-students will follow the rationale of leaving home only after having attained a stable income independently of having a partner or not, while others will connect setting up their own household with the creation of a new family, and still others may prefer to leave home like students do, i.e. accepting income instability as the necessary cost of social independence. Non-students might be a more homogeneous group in Spain than in France, since leaving home and creating a new family are culturally more strongly connected in the first country.

The problem of missing and inadequate time-varying variables will be approached by comparing differences in quality of living among groups of persons at a given moment and not by comparing the situation of one person at two points in time. In this sense it can be assumed that students (especially ones without public benefits), first-employment seekers, and people with short-term employment have the same or a lower and more uncertain income than people with long-term employment. Unemployed people without public benefits can also be expected to have low and uncertain income. If a low social origin, low educational level, and high housing costs are added, it can surely be assumed that this group of persons will have the lowest comparative quality of living. The problem is that not every social group has the same expectations of quality of living necessary to leave home. Thus educational level should be controlled for as a measure of expectations and of timing of the school-to-work transition. By introducing social origin, the original idea of the influence of the parental resources on the decision to leave home can be adapted to a cross-sectional perspective.

A different rationale for students and non-students is assumed and two equations have to be defined. The probability of leaving home for non-students will depend on possible income sources of the individual and potential partner, on the amount and stability of this income ($I_{own} + I_{partner}$);[5] on expenditures of the household (especially rent or mortgage) (EXP_{indep}); on educational level and social origin; and on a stable partner to create a family (PART). Social origin is not taken as a proxy for the financial capacity of parents to help their children in becoming independent, because parental transfers are assumed to be of minor relevance for young people leaving home for non-study reasons (cf. Chapter 3). Instead, it is taken as a proxy for expectations about the minimum standard of life to leave home.

(4) $ProbNOSTU_{leaving} = I_{own} + I_{partner} + EXP_{indep} + EDU + CLASS + PART$

The probability for students leaving is slightly different, because it can be assumed that parents play a crucial role in helping the individual financially. A student's probability of leaving will thus depend again on her income, potentially on her partner's income, but especially on her parents' income after subtraction of their expenses. In this equation social origin is not taken as a proxy for preferences about the adequate standard of life for creating one's own household, but as a proxy for the parents' financial capacity to support a dependent one-generation household. This different use of social origin is justified by the assumption that students form a social group whose members have similar cultural preferences, at least if compared with non-students, and that for this reason social class will not indicate differences in preferences but instead differences in financial resources. In addition, those students whose parents live so far away from the university that they cannot commute, have no choice about the timing of leaving home. They have to leave when they begin to study.

(5) $ProbSTU_{leaving} = I_{own} + I_{partner} + Exp_{indep} + CLASS$

If young people under the same socio-economic conditions have the same probabilities of living in a two-generation household irrespective of their country, then the macro level differences will be due only to composition effects. If, on the contrary, the national context changes the effects of the independent variables, then context variables can be said to have their own independent explanatory power. In reality, it will be a mix of both. The comparative cross-sectional model will help to exclude explanations due to composition effects, but it cannot answer the macro-sociological question about national differences in staying home rates. It can only help to see which groups of young people behave most differently in both countries.

All the above-mentioned relationships can be formulated as six micro-level hypotheses, which are to be tested with logistic regression models.

1. All young people with stable employment should show a higher likelihood to be socially independent than those studying and those being unemployed (**market-income hypothesis**).
2. In a society where setting up an independent household is culturally connected to family formation through marriage, most people will perceive the choice of leaving home only at the transition moment of having formed a stable partnership and not when entering university or entering their first stable job. At the same time they are more likely to marry when they can afford it, except for cases when marriage is advanced due to pregnancy. Hence, young people in Spain will tend to leave home under two conditions: 1. if they decide to marry and 2. if they have a long-term job (men) or if they marry a partner in a long-term employment without having such a job themselves (women) (**stability hypothesis**). This hypothesis should have the following corollaries for people in the labour market: a) in Spain men's long-term employment is more important for leaving home than in France, since it is not only essential for them but also for a potential spouse who has chosen a dependent household formation strategy; b) women in Spain are less dependent on long-term employment compared to their French counterparts, since they follow a dependent household formation strategy more frequently and do not need to rely (completely) on a job.
3. In Spain and in France, young people on the labour market from lower social classes face a low economic quality of living in their parents' home, which makes the attainment of a similar or higher economic quality of living outside the parental home easier than for young people of higher social classes (**low-quality-of-life hypothesis**).
4. In Spain and in France, non-students with low educational levels have a higher probability of living outside of the parental home, since they entered the labour market relatively early, may be able to afford an earlier marriage, and they have relatively low expectations with regard to the economic standard of life they expect to reach when living independently (**low-expectation and early school-to-work transition hypothesis**).

5. In a society like the French one, where a more diversified pattern of setting up one's own household is found, i.e. as a student in a residence hall, in an informal co-residence arrangement, and in a single-person household, all the above-mentioned transition moments are important. Some people will think about leaving home when they enter long-term employment independently of marrying, many will think about leaving when entering university, and others again when forming a new family through marriage. Hence, in France to have a first long-term job will predict leaving home less than in Spain, and French students will show a higher probability of leaving home than Spanish students (**pluralisation hypothesis**).
6. If after controlling for social origin, educational level, and activity, age-differences are still strong, then it can be argued that youth-adult cleavages are as important or even more important than class cleavages. This means that the distribution of economic resources is strongly linked to age and less to social class (**age-cleavage hypothesis**).

These six hypotheses require eight different models according to national context and social group of reference:

Figure 3.2 Logistic Regression Models for France and Spain

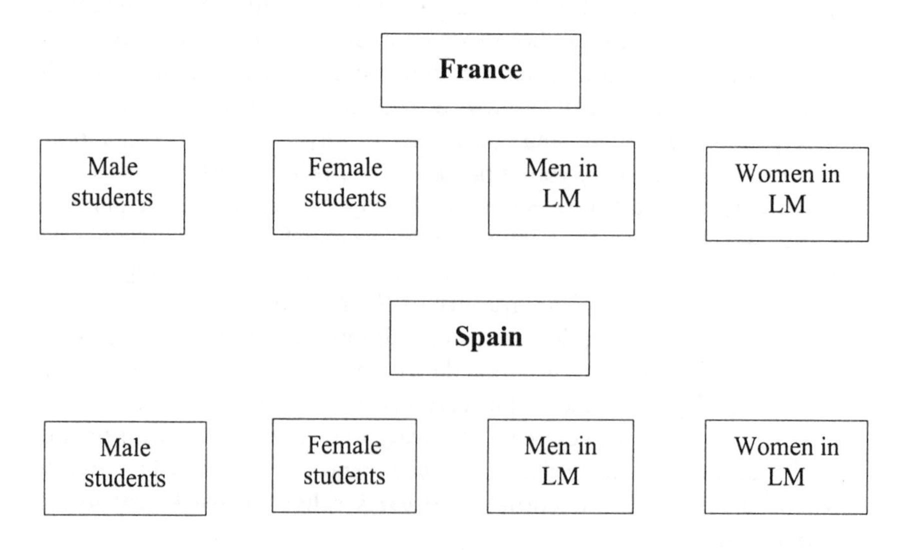

Note: LM = labour market.

Cross-sectional Logistic Regression Model at the Individual Level

The alternative to an event history approach is a traditional cross-sectional multivariate analysis. Here the problems of the application of a cross-sectional model will be discussed, the choice of a cross-sectional model as opposed to a longitudinal model will be justified, and the construction of the variables for the logistic regression will be described.

A cross-sectional analysis of transitions out of the parental home presents the problem of analysing individuals in the survey year, and thus young people who left home in the survey year are analysed together with those who left home one or more years before. It means that we must assume that their situation in 1991 is similar to the situation at the non-identified time of leaving home. In reality it might be that somebody left home in 1987 when she was unemployed and now she lives independently and is employed. Her leaving home might be related to unemployment but in the model it will appear to be related to employment. To be sure, these are correlations and do not inform us about causality because this person could have been expecting to get a job in the near future, even if she left home when she was unemployed and perhaps receiving unemployment benefits. Thus, in reality becoming independent is in fact caused by the expectation of employment and not by the unemployment situation at the moment of leaving. For this reason an event history analysis based on one year periods can sometimes be as misleading as a cross-sectional analysis with persons who are observed at a distance from one to five years after the event occurred. This is the problem related to a lack of information on expectations as mentioned above.

This problem of a cross-sectional analysis has to be contrasted with the problem of incomplete retrospective information in the case of applying an event-history approach. The most important factor in deciding the method, however, is the research question which has to be answered. The interest of this research lies in analysing the role of national configurations of the labour market, the housing market and, in particular, the Welfare State. There are two possible research designs for the study of this question: 1. a historical approach based on the question of how changes in social policies, for instance, in one society affect changes in the home-leaving process of young people; 2. a cross-national comparison of one historical moment in order to explain cross-national differences in home-leaving rates between two or more countries. This research has opted for the second alternative, which means that an event-history analysis taking account of changes in the historical context is not that useful. Contextual variables, such as the labour market, the housing market, and the educational structure, and social policy measures should be held constant as much as possible in order to assess the importance of given cross-national context differences without being disturbed by within-country changes. As a consequence the ideal design would be to compare two years for Spain and France. This is not possible, since the sample size would then be too small, but a solution would be to reduce the observation period to five years in each country respectively. By doing this an event history approach loses its strength, which consists in controlling for changes in the context. The research question instead requires a parameterisation of context in order to be able to relate the results to a given historical country context.

Clearly, the choice of a cross-sectional method rather than an event-history analysis can be criticised. However, the poor quality of some of the crucial retrospective data and the necessity of keeping the historical context as constant as possible have been the main reasons for selecting a cross-sectional approach. At this point the construction of the samples and the definition of variables for the cross-sectional model is described.

A specific feature of the leaving home process is that it is best described as a survivor function, which means that nearly everybody passes the transition from the parental home to an independent household and that this process is strongly related to age. By age 40 very few people have "survived" in their parents' home. The samples used include only young people from 20 to 29 years and thus not all of them have already passed the transition, but they will pass it in the future. As a consequence we have a group of right-censored individuals, that is, individuals who will probably leave the parental home, but our samples do not allow us to know the moment when this happens. Hence, no general statements about home leaving patterns can be made, as it is only possible to interpret the patterns of young people until age 29.

The decision process is conceived of as a choice between staying at home or leaving home and is not thought of as a choice between staying at home or getting married, living as a single person, living with peers, living with a partner, living in a residence hall, or living otherwise. Thus, a binary logistic regression model has been chosen.

Figure 3.3 Possible Forms of Young People's Choices

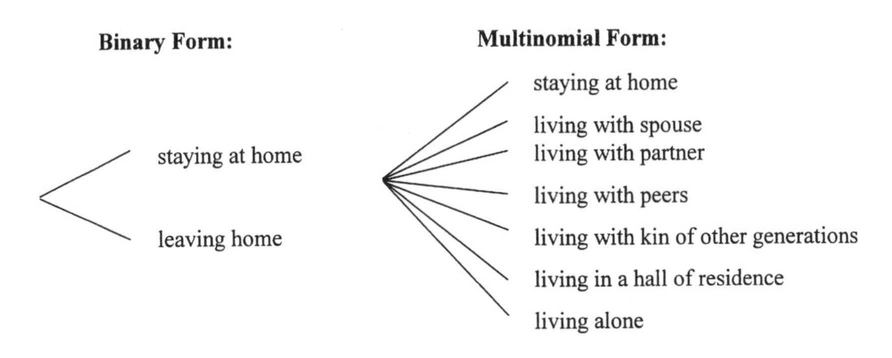

It is assumed that a person will think about concrete alternatives, i.e. she will reflect on staying with her parents as opposed to marrying a partner and setting up a household with him or staying with the parents as opposed to living in a one-person household; it is not probable at all, however, that a person has eight alternatives in mind, as shown in the second tree. I could have taken account of the different destinations - partnership or other reason - by dividing the sample according to type of destination like Holdsworth and Miret (1997) have done in a comparison between the United Kingdom and Spain. For the reasons mentioned above, I preferred to distinguish people according to their activity situation and to focus on the difference between one-generation and two-generation households (cf. chapter 1) ignoring the differences within the former. The fact that more people in Spain than in France leave home to form a formal family is an important difference, but I want to analyse how far the cross-national differences can be explained without recurring to a cultural explanation of the type, "young Spanish people prefer to leave home only when they marry". Or better, the question of interest in this research is to see how far a socio-economic approach is able to explain why in Spain people marry late and why they form informal one-generation households less frequently, phenomena indicated by the high rates of staying in the parental home.

The dependent variable is the logit of living in an independent household for the first time (IND91/92), which means a household occupied for more than three months. It can be a one-person household, a household shared with a spouse, with a partner, with non-kin, and with other kin. Having left home in order to go to live with parents-in-law is considered as living independently, but staying with one's own parents and the partner/spouse having joined this household is considered as staying with parents.

Leaving home is a complex process, which for some people means living away from parents in a residence hall without creating one's own household, for others it means having an independent household that is paid for or owned by the parents and, thus, being, at least partly, financially dependent on their parents, and again for others it is a progressive process with a first leaving, a return to living in the parental home, and a final leaving home. Different meanings of nest-leaving have obviously to be distinguished (Villeneuve-Gokalp 1997). In Chapter 1 the concept of social independence was introduced as the phenomenon to be explained by this research; in consequence people living outside of the parental home being financially dependent on their parents are nonetheless considered as living independently. Young people living in a residence hall are considered as living independently insofar they were recorded by the surveys. Both surveys have samples which exclude most people living in residence halls. Due to the fact that these young people are frequently officially residing with their parents, they have sometimes been interviewed if they were at home at the moment of the interview, but in general they are underrepresented in both samples. Thanks to retrospective information it is, however, possible to study some aspects related to residence halls for those people who passed through such a living arrangement but are now living in a private household.

The last problem, concerning young people who return to the parental home, is solved by taking the current state of the young person, independently of what she did before. Thus, people who left home and came back are counted as living with parents, those who left and in the future will probably come back are counted as living independently, and those who left, went back, and left again are considered as living independently.

Eight logistic regression models with the same five independent variables will be run in order to test the two theoretical models (cf. Figure 3.2). Not all persons of the sample will be used, but only those staying at home in France in 1986 and in Spain in 1985. French individuals were between 14 and 23 years old at this time, and they were observed until 1992 when they were 20 to 29 years old. In Spain the people were, like the French, between 14 and 23 years old, and they were observed until 1991, the year of the interview. Thus, individuals will be observed for a time period of six years, during which they all faced the same economic and political context of the second half of the eighties in France and Spain. Figure 4.1 shows in which years most of the individuals in both samples left home.

In order to distinguish students from non-students, the sample is divided into two groups: on one hand, individuals who have finished primary, secondary, and/or tertiary education and who are employed, searching for a job, or economically inactive (except for study reasons), and, on the other hand, individuals who are in vocational training or tertiary education as full or as part-time students. Technically it means that I first select young people who were at home in 1985/86; second, those who during this period of observation finished their formal education and entered the labour force (employed/unemployed) or started housework and thus in 1991/92 were in the labour market; third, those who during this period were enrolled in formal education (including 1991/92). In addition, both groups are again divided by sex to run a model for men and another for women.

The variables refer only to the situation in 1991/92, which is not necessarily the year when the person left home. The perspective is not longitudinal, but one of comparing young people who had the same starting point in 1985/86, i.e. they lived with their parents, and who passed through the same biographic cycle. One group is characterised by the event of having begun vocational training or tertiary education and of continuing it until 1991/92 and the other group has passed the event of entering the labour force or housework at the latest by 1991/92. The question is therefore, how do people who have passed the same biographic transitions behave in terms of home-leaving in two different national contexts?

The results of a cross-sectional model have to be interpreted in cross-sectional terms, which is to compare people who left in a five-year period with those who did not leave. For instance, if it is found that people employed in long-term jobs live independently more often than those employed in short-term jobs, then it will not be possible to assert that those long-term employed young people who are in an independent living-arrangement left home when they entered this job.

The students' model (5) posited above requires five independent variables:

$$(5)\ \text{ProbSTU}_{\text{leaving}} = \text{I}_{\text{own}} + \text{I}_{\text{partner}} + \text{Exp}_{\text{indep}} + \text{CLASS}$$

The sample of students is formed by those people who in 1991/92 were full-time or part-time students, independently of the moment they began to study. It means that the sample might contain individuals who have been studying for 4 years and others studying only for one year. To approximate income I rely on information about employment parallel to studies (ACTIVEST),[6] but this variable can only partially be used as a proxy for income for students. Student's activity situation allows only for two variations: full-time student and part-time student, which means that the first are supposed to have no or less income than the latter. This assumption is problematic, for it ignores the possible existence of scholarships. We know the income only of the people in the French surveys, and if a student receives public benefits or family help. For French people we will, thus, be able to test the extent to which ACTIVEST is a good corollary of market income and how public benefits can constitute an incentive to leave home (cf. Chapter 5).

Social origin is operationalised by the social class of the father (FACLASS) and together with the number of siblings (SIBL) these variables can provide an idea of the income and the expenditure of the parents, and in consequence can inform us of the probability of receiving financial help.

Tenure of the dwelling could be taken as a rough indicator of expenditure, but this information is available only for those who live independently. Again the problem of missing information on expectations emerges. At this stage of the research the problem is avoided by dropping these variables from the statistical analysis. These variables will have to be dealt with at context level and in a descriptive bivariate way.

Age (AGE) and educational level (EDUC) are added to the model, in order to control for the age heterogeneity of the group and in order to have the same variables as in the non-students' model. The educational level of students should not be significantly related to their living arrangement.

$$\text{(6) logit (IND91/92)} = \alpha + \beta_1(\text{ACTIVEST}) + \beta_2(\text{FACLASS}) - \beta_3(\text{SIBL}) + \beta_4(\text{EDUC}) + \beta_5(\text{AGE})$$

The theoretical model for non-students, compared to the theoretical model for non-students, includes two supplementary variables: educational level and existence of a partner.

$$\text{(4) ProbNOSTU}_{leaving} = I_{own} + I_{partner} + EXP_{indep} + EDU + CLASS + PART$$

Unlike in the students' model, activity is a better proxy for income and the educational level of the individual is introduced as a proxy for time spent in education and for expectations about the standard of life to be obtained. The existence of an employed partner can be assessed for those who live independently, but no information exists about partners of people living in the parental home. Social origin is introduced as for students, but as a proxy for expectations and not as a proxy for economic resources. Formally the equation is the same as above equation (6).

Conclusion

In this chapter, the research strategy which will allow this investigation to answer the main research question, namely why there are national differences in the rate of two-generation households in France and Spain, was explained and discussed. Three main explanative macro-level hypotheses were elaborated: the dependence-diversification hypothesis, the precariousness hypothesis and the high property-low affordability hypothesis. The micro-sociological foundation of the problem was treated with a rational choice model, which formalises the selection process through which individuals pass when they think about leaving home. The methodological procedure will consist in changing the units of analysis in order to grasp the relationships at each different level and the interactions between different levels. Two large samples will provide the information for the logistic regression analysis of young people's behaviour in France and Spain. The control of individual characteristics will help to recognise where the main differences between the behaviour of Spanish and French young people lies (Chapter 4). A multi-level logistic regression analysis with regions and regional variables as context variables will show the relative importance of regional labour markets, housing markets and family patterns in Spain (Chapter 6). Finally, we come back to the initial cross-national research question by a comparative institutional analysis of social rights for different groups of young people (Chapters 7-9). The procedure and hypotheses are summarised in Figure 3.4; some parts of the research strategy have not yet been presented in detail, but will be discussed below.

Figure 3.4 Research Strategy and Hypotheses

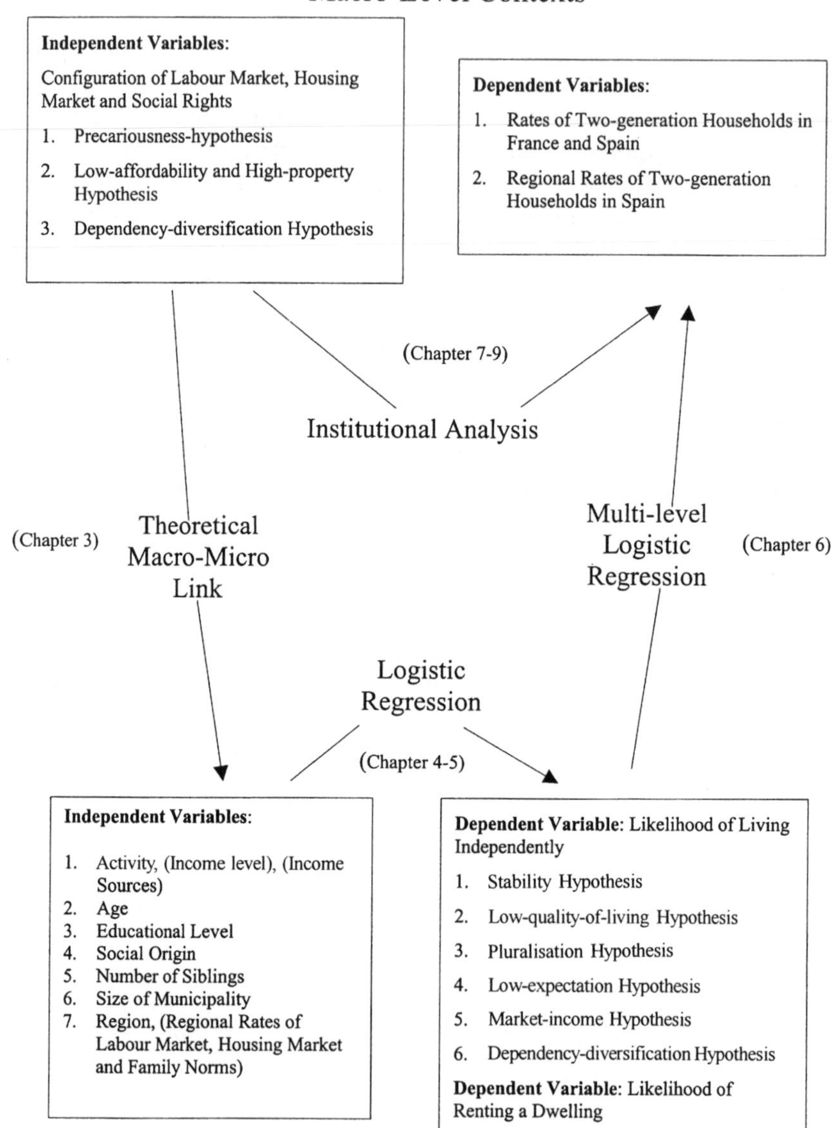
Macro-Level Contexts
Independent Variables:
Configuration of Labour Market, Housing Market and Social Rights
1. Precariousness-hypothesis
2. Low-affordability and High-property Hypothesis
3. Dependency-diversification Hypothesis
Dependent Variables:
1. Rates of Two-generation Households in France and Spain
2. Regional Rates of Two-generation Households in Spain
(Chapter 7-9)
Institutional Analysis
(Chapter 3)
Theoretical Macro-Micro Link
Multi-level Logistic Regression
(Chapter 6)
Logistic Regression
(Chapter 4-5)
Independent Variables:
1. Activity, (Income level), (Income Sources)
2. Age
3. Educational Level
4. Social Origin
5. Number of Siblings
6. Size of Municipality
7. Region, (Regional Rates of Labour Market, Housing Market and Family Norms)
Dependent Variable: Likelihood of Living Independently
1. Stability Hypothesis
2. Low-quality-of-living Hypothesis
3. Pluralisation Hypothesis
4. Low-expectation Hypothesis
5. Market-income Hypothesis
6. Dependency-diversification Hypothesis
Dependent Variable: Likelihood of Renting a Dwelling
1. High-property Hypothesis
Individuals

Notes

[1] These ideal-types do not account for all the possibilities but only the empirically more relevant or theoretically more clear-cut situations. The exceptions and more mixed forms of the home leaving process will be confronted with the ideal-types at the empirical analysis stage.

[2] The concept of needs is to some extent subjective and socially constructed and thus expectations have to be assumed. The expectations are supposed to be related to the educational level attained and to the standard of living of the parents.

[3] The first view on norms would have required the transformation of the equation by aggregating norms in a multiplicative way.

[4] I have followed this strategy in a first explorative regional analysis of living arrangements of young people in Spain (Jurado Guerrero 1997).

[5] I could have used the Treiman prestige scale to estimate income in both samples in order to solve the lack of Spanish income data. Then employed young people could have been distinguished according to low and high earnings. Unfortunately, this idea was suggested to me by Luis Garrido, Miguel Requena and Juan Jesús González at a late phase of my thesis, so that I decided to postpone the realisation of this idea to future work.

[6] The exact operationalisation of all variables used throughout this work is documented in the Appendix.

4 Timing of Transitions and Context Differences

The ideal situation for a comparative case study would be to have differences in the phenomenon to be explained and in only one of the independent variables, since then it could be argued that the difference in the dependent variable most probably is due to the one difference in the factors which determine the form of the dependent variable. This is very unlikely to occur in a cross-national study and for this reason the individual characteristics of young people in France and Spain have been controlled for in the multivariate analyses performed below. Yet, it is important to show how large or small cross-national contextual differences are and this is one of the aims of this part. The first sections of this chapter describe context differences and in the last sections the empirical results of the cross-sectional logistic regression models will be presented. The presentation's aim is to discuss in how far the results confirm or falsify the theoretical hypotheses presented previously.

In this paragraph the retrospective information of the French and Spanish samples is used to compare patterns of timing in the leaving-home process. In addition, the cross-sectional information was used to construct some comparative indicators on the timing of the exit from the education system and entrance into employment in order to better understand timing differences in the process of integration into societies in both countries. First, the retrospective information is presented and, second, transversal indicators will show current timing patterns.

High Speed and Nonfamily Destination of Leaving Home in France

Figure 4.1 presents survival rates in the parental home of young people aged 20 to 29 in 1991 in Spain and in 1992 in France. Survival rates have been calculated for thirteen years, which means from 1978 until 1991 for Spain and from 1979 until 1992 for France. In these years the interviewees were 7 to 16 years old and accordingly nearly all lived with their parents. Then, little by little, young people begin to leave the parental home with important timing differences in both countries. In France people leave home at a much higher velocity than in Spain. It was found that little more than one third of the French young people had survived at home in 1992, whereas three quarters of their Spanish contemporaries were still found in the family of origin in 1991. In 1990, the majority of the French sample had left home, that is when the observed cohort was between 18 and 27 years old, while their Spanish counterparts had not nearly arrived at this point in 1991, when they were 20 to 29 years old.

Figure 4.1 Survival Rate in Parental Home in France and Spain, 1978-1992 (% of people staying home every year out of total of people aged 20-29 in 1991-92)[1]

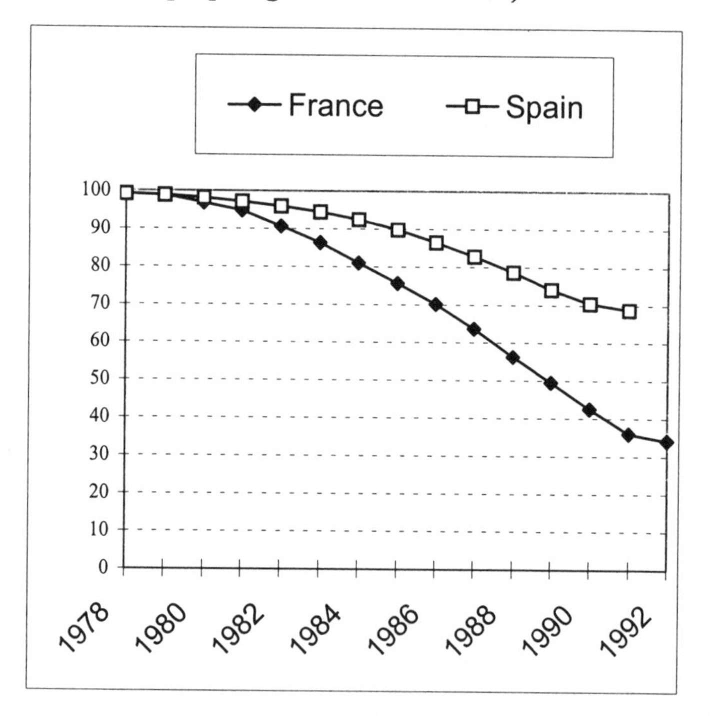

Source: author's elaboration with *Spainall* (PAR78-PAR91) and with *Franceall* (IND79 to IND92).

Figure 4.2 shows the hazard rates and confirms the previous description; in addition, it reveals that the pace of leaving home increases strongly from 1987 to 1990 in France, while in Spain the slope is much flatter and does not show any period of particular increase as in France.

Figure 4.2 Hazard Rate of Leaving Home in France and Spain, 1978-1992 (those leaving every year divided by those at risk of leaving every year)

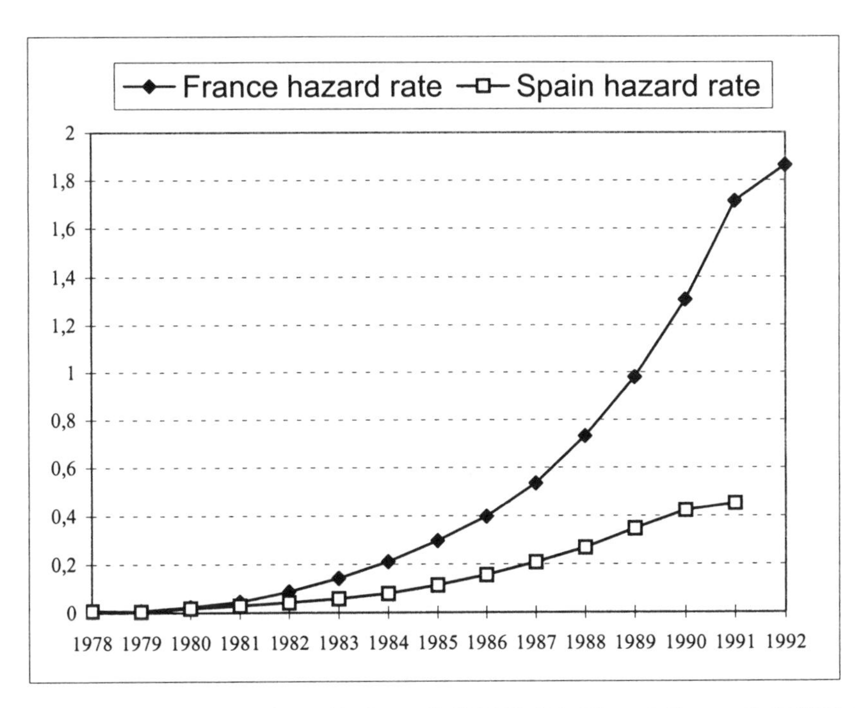

Source: author's elaboration with *Spainall* (PAR78-PAR91) and *Franceall* (IND79 to IND92).

Figure 4.3 shows the age of leaving home of all those young people who in 1991/92 had left home. Unlike the previous figures, information on first leavers was used for France, which means that some of those who left will have come back home later. Spanish figures, instead, reveal the age of the last exit of those who left home between 1978 and 1991. The age with the highest rate of leavers is 19 in France and 24 in Spain. These figures suggest that some French young people leave home after having finished their compulsory education at age 16 and 17 and many of them leave after having reached legal and educational maturity. This might be because young people who begin to study, leave their parents' home in France, whereas in Spain this is less important. In Spain the peak of age 24 is near to the average age of first marriage, namely 26 (cf. Table 4.2). The majority of French people had left by age 20 or before and three quarters of them had left by age 29 or before, while in Spain not even the majority had left home when they were 29 years old.

Figure 4.3 Age at First Time of Leaving, Young People Aged 20-29 in Spain 1991/France 1992 (% of first-time leavers out of total of those living independently in 1991/92)[2]

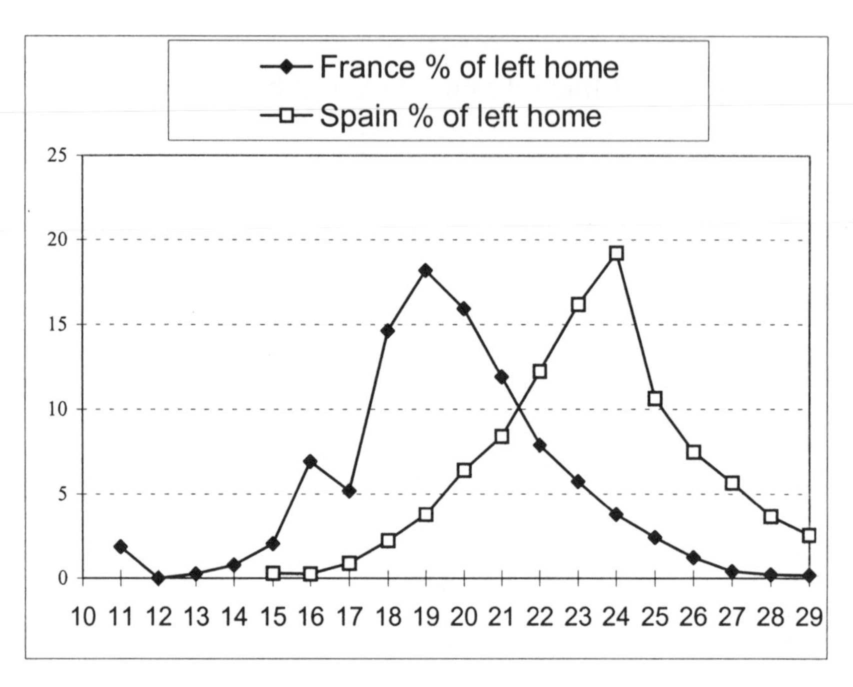

Source: author's elaboration with *Spainall* and *Franceall* and QLAGE.

Both surveys permit a comparison of the type of first dwelling young people went to when they left home. This last retrospective finding will help to imagine the process of leaving home before a cross-sectional analysis is made. This corresponds with the previous suggestion that many French young people may leave home not to form a new family but in order to study or work in another place. Figure 4.3 demonstrates that nearly one third of all first dwellings for French young people were residence halls; by "residence hall" a residence of students or young workers is meant. Unlike the French, only 2 per cent of Spanish youth had passed through this experience. It has to be recalled that the Spanish survey considered residence halls only if they were the official s and if the person lived there for at least three months. An idea about the underestimation of young people leaving for residence halls or for dwellings shared with flatmates can be obtained through the calculation of the number of informal leavers. The data discrepancy in the Spanish survey between the part with information on parents and the part on dwellings was used to estimate the number of informal leavers, i.e. young people who officially lived with their parents in their dwelling in 1991 but who said they had left the parental home in 1991 or before.[3] After this calculation a figure of 2.2 per cent of young people having left informally was obtained, which is a rather small proportion. Official statistics published by education authorities show that there are large cross-national differences in the number of young students living in residence halls in both countries (cf. chapter 7).

Figure 4.4 First Dwellings of Leavers (% of total independent youth), France 1992/Spain 1991

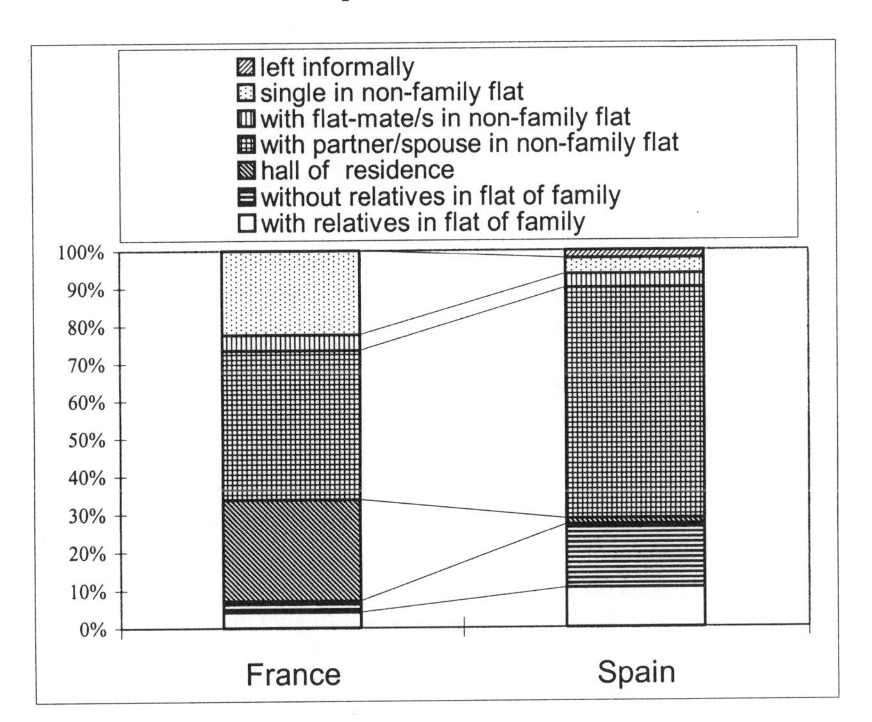

Source: author's elaboration with *Spainall* and *Franceall* and FIRDWELL.

The type of first dwelling of French young people differs largely from Spanish ones too for other reasons. Figure 4.4 reveals that of those living independently in Spain in 1991 nearly all had set up their first dwelling:

1. with a partner/spouse in a nonfamily flat,
2. without relatives in a family-owned flat, or
3. with relatives.

Thus, the family plays a crucial role in the provision of a dwelling for young people.

In France, on the contrary, most young people left home in order to live in a nonfamily arrangement and without the direct provision of the flat by the family. It is the state and the market which basically enable young people's social independence, as will also be shown further on. Those setting up a household with a partner or spouse number 40 per cent, that is 20 per cent less than in Spain and young people in one-person non family-owned flats reach 22 per cent of those socially independent.

The way in which French young people leave home has consequences for the form of the process. People who leave home in order to create a new family, and in particular those who do so in a formal way, are less likely to return to the parental home after they have left, while people who left for military service, for reasons of education or work are more likely to return home after first leaving. In fact, French young people return home relatively frequently after a first leaving, and the probability of returning home depends mainly on the reason for which they first left. According to a multivariate analysis performed by Villeneuve-Gokalp (1997), age at first leaving, educational certificate, and parental economic help do not have an effect on returning home in France. Instead, young people who left home in order to carry out their military service or those who left to go to a residence hall are those who have a high probability of returning to the parental home. Nearly three quarters of the men who left home for their military service went back home afterwards and more than half of all young people, women and men, who went to a residence hall returned home. Young people who left home before finishing their education had a higher probability of returning home (27%) than those who left after having finished their education (13%).

Leaving home has different social meanings in France and Spain, since French people leave frequently without being financially independent. In France, frequently social and economic independence do not go together, while Spanish young people tend to combine social independence with economic independence. The question becomes thus why young people in Spain do not leave home during periods in which they are financially dependent on parents and/or the state. If Spanish students with upper class origins leave home more often than those with lower class origins, then it could be a question of the economic resources of the family, but if they do not, then, to not leave under precarious economic conditions might be a social norm. This question is dealt with in Chapter 5. Next, cross-national similarities and differences of young people out of the parental home are described.

Degrees of Resource-Sharing and Types of Living Arrangements

In Chapter 1 the concept of resource sharing was introduced in order to classify young people's living arrangements according to the economic aspect of sharing resources (dwelling and maintenance costs) with each other. Figure 4.5, which deals with first destinations of those who have left home, has already shown that in Spain the majority of living arrangements of the leavers are where a young person shares resources with a partner or a spouse. In France, sharing resources with others, be it with a partner/spouse or with peers in a residence hall, constitutes the majority of living arrangements as well, but there is a large minority (20%) of young people who live in one-person households and thus do not share resources.

Why do young people in France live more frequently in non-resource sharing living arrangements? Is it because they have higher earnings than in Spain, or because they receive more economic help from their parents or from the state while living alone, or because they accept lower standards of life? A mix of all these factors produces this specific French situation as demonstrated in Table 4.1.

Table 4.1 Average Income, Diversification, Activity, Age, and Gender of Independent Youth in France According to Resource Sharing Degree, 1992

	Type of Household of Independent Youth (RESOUR)		
		Column % of one-person household	Column % of other*
Age group	20-24	44.1	29.4
	25-29	55.9	70.6
Sex	Men	48.0	40.3
	Women	52.0	59.7
Activity	Full-time student	22.1	7.1
(ACTIVEST)	Part-time student	13.1	5.5
	Long-term employment	47.1	51.4
	Short-term employment	8.0	5.8
	Economically inactive	0.6	10.7
	Unemployed	6.8	13.8
	Other	2.3	5.7
Income	no income	2.3	8.8
(INCOSUM)	<=2500	15.2	14.1
(FF/month)	<=5000	23.8	24.2
	<=7500	32.8	31.3
	<=46000	23.9	18.8
	no answer	1.9	2.7
Diversification	market income	37.4	4.3
(DIVERS)	public benefits	5.8	3.3
	family help	1.4	5.4
	market & state	27.3	6.2
	market & family	6.9	31
	state & family	16.4	19.9
	market, state, & family	4.8	30
Sample (N)		872	3680

Note: * "other" does not include young people in residence halls and "family help" includes help from parents and from spouse. Source: author's elaboration with *Franceall*. More information on variables cf. appendix.

Table 4.1 shows that French young people in one-person households are more frequently aged 25 to 29 than younger and to a degree are more often women than men. It is mainly a living arrangement of people with a long-term employment and of young people enrolled in education. Interestingly, the income distribution of young people in one-person households is not very different from other independent young people: the former are less frequently without income and more frequently they earn more than 7,500 FF, i.e. 1081 PPS (1992).[4] Most young people living alone might have a similar or a lower standard of life, for most of them have similar income levels as their counterparts in resource-sharing households. Yet, this depends on the existence of a formal partnership relationship, which does not decrease the costs of maintaining a one-person dwelling but might decrease other maintenance costs. The most curious finding refers to the diversification of dependencies (cf. p.147 for definition of variable). Compared to young people, who share resources, young people living alone more frequently depend totally on market income or on market income and state benefits. The family plays a comparatively minor role for these young people.

Figure 4.5 Types of Living Arrangements of Independent Youth, Spain 1991/France 1992 (% of independent youth aged 20-29)

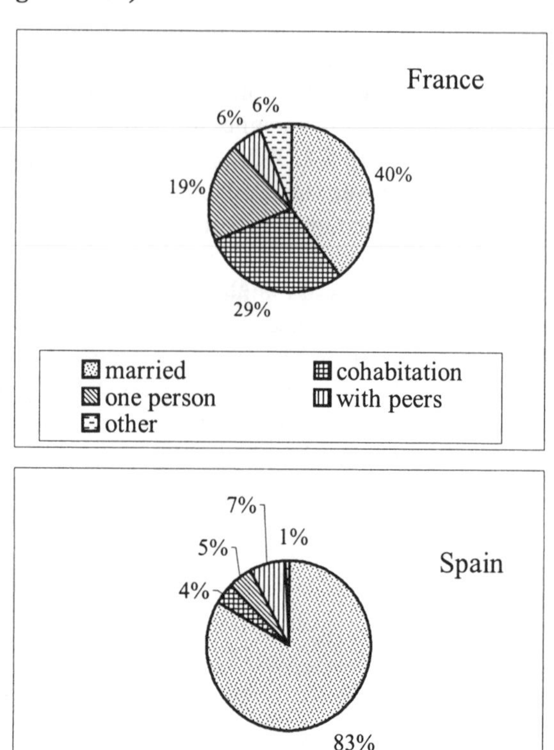

Sources: author's elaboration with *Franceall* and *Spainall* and LIVARR.

There are not only differences in resource-sharing degrees, but also in the types of resource-sharing one-generation households. Living with peers has a similar diffusion in both countries, but cohabitation with a partner is much less prevalent in Spain than in France.[5] It is not possible to explain the low proportion of consensual unions in the framework of this investigation, but some ideas can be offered for reflection. Young people aged 15 to 24 who were asked about their opinion on "living together without being married" answered in most European countries that this is something not to be judged by others (Eurobarometer 1993 in: EUROSTAT 1997). In Spain and in France the proportions who answered in this way are very similar, as are also the rates of people stating that it is a good thing (around 23%) and a bad thing (2%). The proportion of Spanish young people approving consensual unions is by far higher than those exercising it, while in France the rate of those living in consensual unions is higher than the proportion of those approving it explicitly. Some Spanish youth surveys asked people if they would like to live in a consensual union and around 15% would like to do so (Elzo et al. 1994, Orizo et al 1985). Thus, the low rate of consensual unions in Spain seems not to be a result of a low approval, but the reasons have to be sought elsewhere. It might be related to three socio-economic factors:

1. the low Spanish rate of accessible dwellings to rent;
2. social pressure from the older generation in favour of marriage. Since young people in Spain depend very frequently on the support of their parents, they may also have taken into account their parents values and preferences more seriously than French young people; and
3. the convenience of a marriage contract for women who follow the dependent household formation strategy.

Most likely, the low rates of consensual unions and the strong preference for owner-occupied dwellings contribute to the delayed home-leaving pattern in Spain. In fact, further on (p.154), it is shown that young people living in a rented dwelling, a living arrangement requiring a lower investment than an owner-occupied dwelling, are younger and more frequently cohabiting partners than young people in dwellings they own. The regional analysis in Chapter 6 shows that people in regions with a high rate of consensual unions and of rented dwellings are less likely to be in an intergenerational co-residence setting. Since in Spain we find a very small housing sector with rented dwellings, it can be argued that, if the supply of rented dwellings were more accessible to young people, they would leave earlier and they would cohabit more. It can be objected that the low supply of rented accommodation is not the cause of low rates of consensual unions and of early home leaving but its consequence. This question depends on the strength of social norms and preferences for marriage as a way of leaving home, independently of the tenure structure of the housing market. Since more Spanish young people affirm they would like to cohabit with a partner than actually do, some objective conditions influence the low rate of Spanish cohabitants and of early leavers. Let us put it the following way: housing and labour market structures do not determine consensual union patterns and early leaving, but they influence both and probably prevent the creation of a significant minority of innovators (Prinz 1995). Villeneuve-Gokalp (1990) shows for France that consensual unions were a rather diffused living arrangement among working class men in the 1960s and 1970s because they could not afford an early marriage. This contradicts the argument of this work, which sees in the worse employment situation a condition favouring marriage. However, French working class women were less likely to cohabit than their male counterparts. The author does not explain this contradiction. It is not clear how working class men cohabited relatively frequently, while their female counterparts did not, given that couples tend to be homogamous with respect to social class. Besides, the author shows that practising Catholics and Protestants were less likely to begin a consensual union. The fact that religious practice hinders the starting of a consensual union is something which occurs in Spain too, as discussed in Chapter 6, but religious practice is somewhat less related to consensual unions than is the housing market structure.

Another fact that indirectly indicates the importance of consensual unions for early social independence in France is the similarity of the age at first marriage in Spain and France. Thus, early nest-leaving in France is not related to early marriage. Male mean age at first marriage was in both countries 27 in 1988. Women also marry at similar ages, Spanish women on average at age 24.8 and French women at age 25.2 (cf. Table 4.2). Yet even if French and Spanish people marry at similar moments, it does not mean that the forms of formal family formation are similar.

Table 4.2 Mean Age at First Marriage in Some European Countries, 1988

	Males	Females
Denmark	29,6	27,1
West Germany	28	25,5
Italy	28	25,1
France	27,2	25,2
Spain	27	24,8
UK	26,4	24,2
Standard deviation	1,12	0,98

Source: EUROSTAT 1992.

In fact, in Spain we find more women who depend economically on their spouses compared to France. In the theoretical part it was argued that France and Spain may differ in the proportion of women who follow a dependent family formation path, i.e. need to be (partly) maintained by their husbands in order to be able to leave the parental home. A detailed test of these French-Spanish differences cannot be performed, but there is cross-sectional evidence which shows that of those women who are living outside of the parental home a higher proportion are economically inactive in Spain than in France. Figure 4.6 reveals that in 1991, 33 per cent of all socially independent women in Spain were economically inactive, while in France the same rate numbers only 14 per cent. These figures cannot tell us if these women left home while being economically inactive, if they became so just after marriage, for instance, or if they quit the labour market after a child was born. Yet, if we define family formation as a process which happens from age 20 to 29 and comprises partnership formation and eventually child birth, then it can be stated that in France in this life phase there are many fewer economically inactive women among those who are living out of the parental home than in Spain. Thus, in Spain we find more male-breadwinner families among young people than in France, even if from 1976 to 1991 the rate of young married women (25-34) with employment has increased in Spain, which points to some changes in female employment and family biographies (Garrido/Requena 1996).

Figure 4.6 Socially Independent Women (aged 20-29) by Activity, France 1992/Spain 1991

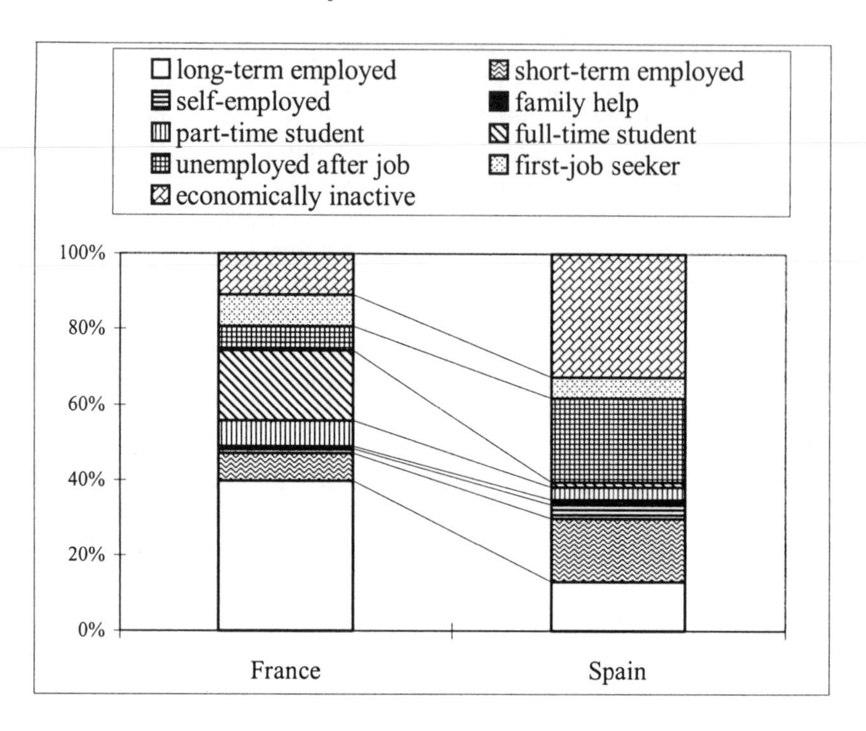

Source: author's elaboration with *Franceall* and *Spainall* and ACTIVEST.

Economically inactive women who do not live with their parents have to rely on their partner's income or on public benefits. Since in Spain there are fewer types of public benefits and the existing ones are less generous than in France, it is to be expected that most of these economically inactive women rely mainly on their husband's income. As a consequence this means that their husbands have to receive a sufficiently high and stable income in order to be able to maintain at least two adults. Long-term employment is of great significance for Spanish family formation. This is confirmed by recent findings of a longitudinal analysis on the determinants of partnership formation in Spain which shows that long-term employment has become more relevant for male partnership formation in the last decades (Luxán/Miret/Treviño 1999).

Early Exit from Education and Late Employment Stability in Spain

Young people in Spain enter the labour market on average earlier than French young people. In 1987 half of all Spanish young people had entered the market at age 19, while half of all French young people had entered at age 20. In 1995 the age difference was 21 to 22 respectively (EUROSTAT 1997). Besides, employment conditions young people face on the labour market vary from one country to the other. The cross-sectional information of 1991 for Spain and 1992 for France permits the analysis of some timing differences related to education and employment in both countries in these years. Unlike in the previous paragraphs, the figures presented here do not originate from the retrospective answers of the interviewees, but refer to the situation of the surveyed young people of different ages at the moment of the interviews.

Figure 4.7 Male Integration into Adulthood, Spain 1991/France 1992 (transversal in % of age group)

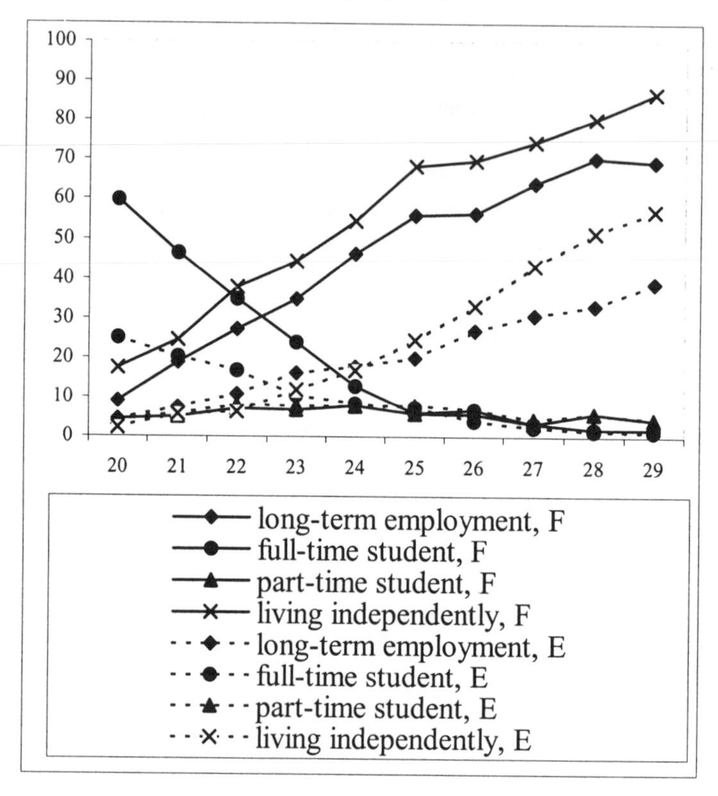

Source: author's elaboration with *Franceall* and *Spainall* and with ACTIVEST, IND91/92.

Figure 4.8 Female Integration into Adulthood, Spain 1991/France 1992 (transversal in % of age group)

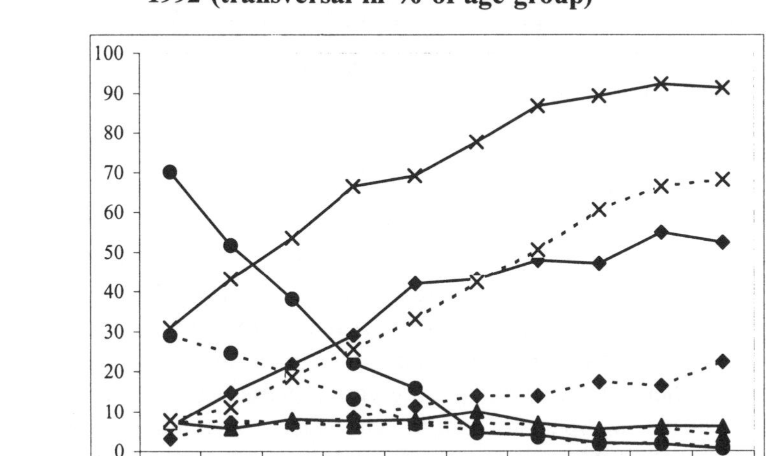

Source: author's elaboration with *Franceall* and *Spainall* and with ACTIVEST, IND91/92.

Figure 4.7 and Figure 4.8 display some indicators for men and women of different ages in Spain and France. In France more than half of the young men aged 20 follow some formal education programme, while only around 30 per cent of their Spanish counterparts do.[6] For women the percentages of enrolment are higher in both countries, but the differences between the two countries are very similar to those of the men. In general, young people in Spain leave education earlier than in France and only at age 25 do the two national patterns become similar, since in both countries only a minority of young people are enrolled in education after age 25. Young people who combine education with work represent in both countries less than 10 per cent of their age group in all ages, but in this case there are nearly no cross-national differences. These differences in enrolment are also confirmed for 1995 by labour force statistics. Of the 18 year-olds, 66 per cent of the Spaniards and 84 per cent of the French were enrolled in education, which yields a difference of 18 per cent between the two rates. On the other hand, enrolment rates of those aged 24 are very similar in both countries, namely around 15 per cent (EUROSTAT 1997).[7]

The interesting fact is that Spanish people leave education earlier than in France, but that they do not acquire a long-term employment earlier than in France, as it could be expected due to their earlier entrance into their labour force and their potentially longer work-experience. Seventy per cent of men aged 29 in 1991/92 had a long-term job in France, while in Spain they did not even reach 40 per cent, i.e. a difference of 30 per cent between both countries. This is exactly the same percentage of difference between French socially independent and Spanish socially independent men. The same differences exist for female long-term employment in France and Spain, but the difference between the rates of social independence are somewhat smaller (23%). By comparing young people aged 29 in 1991/92 we have chosen a Spanish cohort who faced a relatively friendly employment context when they entered employment at the end of the 80s, as was also the case in France. Yet unlike in France, these Spanish young people were offered more short-term jobs and they had to face a very difficult housing situation, with a small supply of rented accommodation and very high rents and prices for the purchase of accommodation.

To sum up, in Spain young people do not stay longer in education than in France, but this does not mean that they enter long-term employment earlier. It means that young people in Spain pass more time searching for employment and changing jobs than in France. To leave home in such circumstances would mean to leave home with uncertainty in order to search for a job somewhere else or to share a dwelling with peers or with a partner, and less in order to form a new family. It is not a context where young people can afford to get a mortgage under their own responsibility, but where they need some support from the family or the state and an easier access to rented accommodation. The next section completes the cross-national contexts description with additional cross-sectional information.

Main Labour Market Features from 1985 to 1992 in Spain and France

The aim here is to give an overview of the main characteristics of the labour market situation in the period from 1985 to 1992 in France and Spain. This allows one to get an impression about the economic cycle during which the young people under analysis were likely to leave home and about the possibilities of young people to accede to a stable employment situation.

In the first half of the 1980s the labour market situation in Spain was very difficult for young people, much more than it was for French young people, but in the second half of the 1980s the unemployment problem diminished (Figure 4.9). Yet Spanish-French differences in youth unemployment persisted. These differences are partly due to a higher demographic pressure of young people in Spain, but also due to variations in the employment creation capacity of both economies. In 1990 the demographic pressure as measured by the rate of young people aged 15 to 24 in relation to the population aged 25 to 54 was around 37 per cent in France, while in Spain it reached 43 per cent (OECD 1996).

Figure 4.9 Unemployment of Young People (aged 15-24), in France/Spain 1985-1992 (in thousands)

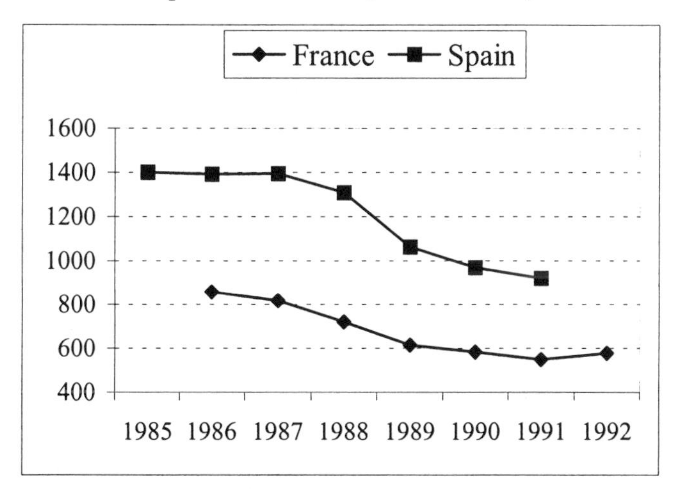

Note: Unemployed people aged 15 to 24 in France and 16 to 24 in Spain.
Sources: BEL 1994, INSEE 1992.

In both countries the number of unemployed people in the youngest age group fell in the period of this study, which means that in both countries the labour market situation was rather favourable to leaving home. In Spain this employment boom was related both to economic and institutional factors, since many young people found their first employment in regulated short-term jobs (cf. Chapter 8). The employment boom should have been accompanied by a decrease of young people's staying home rates, but this was not the case in either country. Spanish employment rates for young people increased strongly from 1986 to 1991, but young people's staying home rates increased, too. This paradox disappears if one looks at the employment rates of young men (25 to 29) who had had their job for three or more years, because the rates fall in a very similar way compared to the rates of young male family heads (Garrido/Requena 1996). Thus, there was expansion in employment in France and Spain, but most new jobs where fixed-term ones, especially in Spain. EUROSTAT labour force statistics show the impressive increase of fixed-term employment in the last decade in two out of 15 European countries, namely Spain and France. In 1987, 29 per cent of the Spanish employees aged 15 to 29 had a temporary work contract, while in France only 18 per cent were in this situation. Eight years later the Spanish rate had more than doubled (64%), while the French rate increased by less than double and stood at 29 per cent in 1995 (Freysson 1996). Thus, waiting queues to obtain a long-term employment are longer in Spain than in France and this also has consequences for earning levels, which are lower in Spain than in France as shown in Chapter 8.

Despite employment growth in both countries, from a comparative perspective unemployment in Spain was much higher than in France. This means that young people in Spain faced a very crowded labour market, which surely influenced their perceptions of employment possibilities and clearly also their actual employment chances. Not only were the expectations of finding employment much worse in Spain, but in particular the expectations of finding long-term employment. This is illustrated for 1991/92 in Figure 4.10, where one can see that more French young people were in long-term employment than Spanish ones. This is especially true for men, since more than 40 per cent of French men had a long-term contract, whereas only 20 per cent of their Spanish counterparts were in the same situation. The higher employment instability of the Spanish youth labour market is further indicated by the lower Spanish rate of first-employment seekers and the higher rate of unemployed who previously had had a job, compared to their French counterparts.

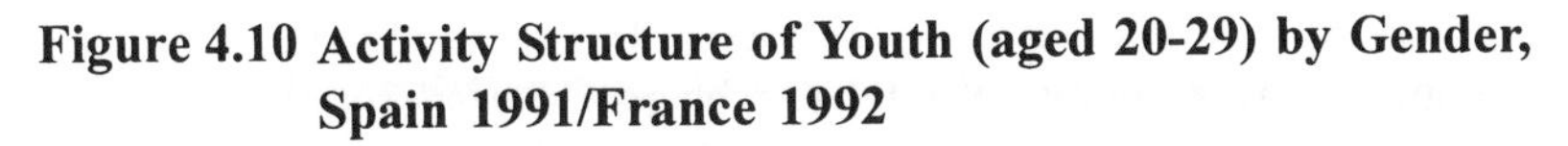

Figure 4.10 Activity Structure of Youth (aged 20-29) by Gender, Spain 1991/France 1992

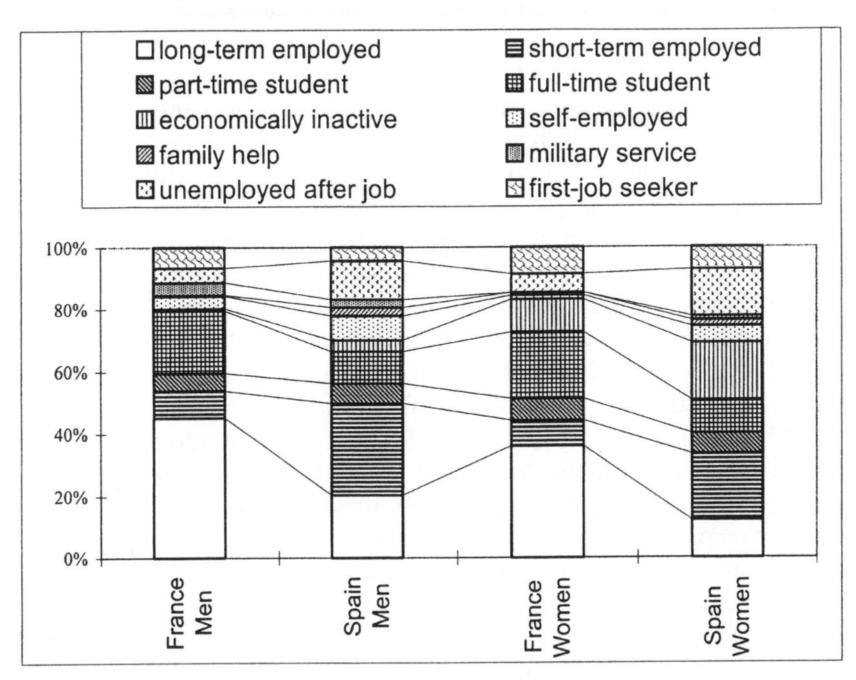

Source: author's elaboration with *Franceall* y *Spainall* and with ACTIVEST.

Another two important Spanish-French variations are the higher female unemployment and economical inactivity rates in Spain compared to France. Spanish women were twice as likely to be unemployed and economically inactive than French women.

The problem with regard to the Spanish labour market is not just of finding a first employment, but in particular, keeping a job. The high levels of unemployed people aged 30 to 34 who had a job before, show the difficulty of keeping a job during a life-phase where family formation usually takes place (Garrido/Requena 1996). The same authors interpret the development of the Spanish labour market towards a market with a very high rate of short-term jobs as the solution to an important intergenerational inequality problem. Young Spanish people are much more qualified than their parents who spent their infancy and youth in the post-war dictatorship and acquired relatively low levels of education. One possibility for compensating for this disadvantage of the older population was to maintain the legal protection of the employment stability of older people, in order to prevent a substitution of older people by more flexible and better qualified young people. This solution might have been accepted by the younger generation thanks to the family support they receive (Garrido Medina 1996).

A recent study supports the idea of short-term contracts as measures favouring the integration of young people into employment, but it also shows that the diffusion of short-term contracts produces high job rotation, produces specific risks of becoming unemployed independently of social class, and has effects on the level of earnings. García Polavieja (1998) reports that in the period from 1987 to 1995 few short-term workers became long-term workers, and when this did happen, it occurred mainly in highly qualified occupations. Thus, in general, short-term employment means increasing job-rotation as shown by data from the Spanish labour force survey. In 1987, 21.4 per cent of the short-term workers had been employed in a different job one year before. This rate constantly increased until 1995, when it reached 50.9 per cent. These trends lead to high rates of unemployment, since many temporary workers pass through phases of unemployment until they enter a new job. Interestingly, the fact of having short-term employment is the most determinant factor of the probability of being unemployed, even if one controls for age, sex, occupational category, activity sector, place of residence and social class.[8]

In Spain, apart from the wide diffusion of unemployment and short-term employment there is an additional problem, which is the high incidence of irregular jobs. To give an idea of this phenomenon two figures should suffice. The survey on life and work conditions of 1985 (ECVT) estimated the number of irregularly employed people, who were defined as those who had a job without social security, with incorrect social security, or who were receiving unemployment benefits although they had a job. In 1985 they estimated that 27 per cent of the population in paid work was irregular, with estimations of 73 per cent of those aged 16 to 19 and 45 per cent of people aged 20 to 24 (CIS 1986, Muro et al. 1988). In the Catalan youth survey of 1991, people were asked if their job was without social security, a sporadic job, or employment without a contract. These jobs were classified as irregular. Around 18 per cent of those aged 22 to 29 years who were working or had worked, said that their jobs were irregular (Martínez/Berney 1991).

Lower Educational Levels in Spain As Compared to France

Figure 4.10 shows that the number of students who work and study is very similar in both countries, while the proportions of young people who only study is different. More French (21%) than Spanish (11%) young people are enrolled in formal education in the group of those aged 20 to 29. This is due to differences in the age group from 20 to 24, where many more French youth are in education than Spaniards, while in the older age group (25-29) French and Spanish youth display the same enrolment rates (cf. Figure 4.7 and Figure 4.8) These different educational participation patterns lead to different levels of completed education in both countries.

Figure 4.11 Completed Educational Level (aged 20-24 and 25-29), Spain 1991/France 1992

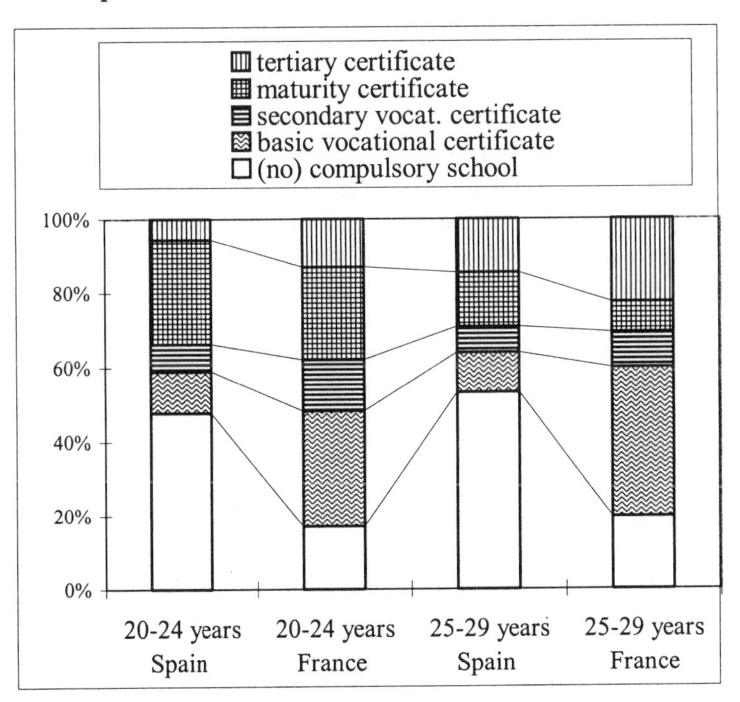

Source: author's elaboration with *Franceall* y *Spainall* and with EDUC.

As can be seen from Figure 4.11 many more Spanish than French young people have only a primary certificate or a lower educational level. In the age group 25 to 29 they number 53 per cent in Spain and 20 per cent in France. These large cross-national differences are not due to the fact that many more French people complete secondary and tertiary education, but are related to the very small proportion of Spanish young people with a basic vocational qualification. Only 11 per cent of those aged 25 to 29 have such qualifications, whereas their French contemporaries represent 40 per cent of their age group.[9] EUROSTAT figures on enrolment rates of young people in vocational training show that in 1993/94 41 per cent of Spanish students enrolled in secondary education were undergoing vocational training, while 53 per cent of their French contemporaries were (EUROSTAT 1997). These figures correspond to the higher Spanish rate of people with a non-vocational secondary certificate among those aged 25 to 29 compared to the French rate in 1991/92, as shown in Figure 4.11. In addition, all Spanish young people aged 15 to 29 enrolled in basic vocational training courses are mainly in school (more than 75% of the hours), while 22 per cent of their French counterparts combine school training with training on the job (EUROSTAT 1997).

At the other end of the educational ladder, a higher proportion of people with a completed tertiary certificate can be found in France than in Spain. This is not due to timing differences, since cross-national differences are found for those aged 20 to 24 and those aged 25 to 29. If one looks at Spanish young people from 30 to 34, a very similar proportion of people with a tertiary certificate is found (Rivière in Garrido/Requena 1996).[10]

For the explanation of the cross-national differences in leaving home in France and in Spain, it is very important to have a closer look at students in tertiary education. In 1990/91 in France there were 74 universities, where 1,698,700 students were studying, while in Spain in 1991 there were 36 public universities, 5 private universities and around 1,137,228 students were enrolled (Consejo de Universidades 1992, INSEE 1993). Unlike France, Spain does not have elite universities. This is probably one reason for the less centralised character of the Spanish university panorama. In France, 33 per cent of all students were studying in the Ile-de-France region, in other words in the area of Paris, while in Spain 20 per cent of all students were studying in the region of Madrid and 14 per cent in Catalonia (Schäferbarthold 1992, Consejo de Universidades 1993).

In France in 1990, 8 per cent[11] of the new entrances into universities were young people coming from another administrative region (académie). The migration balance of students leaving and students coming to a region varies significantly from one region to another. The *académies* of Montpellier, Lyon, Strasbourg, Aix-Marseille, Toulouse, Bordeaux and Ile de France show a positive balance, these universities traditionally attract many students. In 1990 fewer migrations of students than ten years before could be observed (MEN 1993).

French tertiary education includes not only universities, but also Higher Technical Colleges (STS), University Institutes of Technology (IUT), and Preparatory Classes for the Grandes Ecoles (CPGE). The length of study in these institutes lasts from two to three years and ends with a Technological University Diploma (DUT). At university, students obtain a first degree after two years (DEUG). If they continue they obtain a second degree (Licence) after another year, and if they add a supplementary year, they can reach a third degree (DEA or DSS). After these diplomas, students can continue with doctoral studies. This means that, in general, French young people obtain their maturity certificate at age 18, their DEUG or DUT at age 20/21, the Licence at age 21, the maîtrise at age 22 and the DEA or DESS at age 23. Engineering Diplomas should be obtained at age 23, too (Jallade et. al 1993).

In Spain, tertiary education can be divided into two types: courses of one cycle lasting three years and courses of three cycles, whereby the first lasts three years, the second two to three years and the third as long as it takes to complete the doctoral thesis. The first type of tertiary courses are offered by the University faculties (*facultades universitarias*) and the Higher Technical Schools (*Escuelas Técnicas Superiores*). In the university schools (*Escuelas Universitarias*) short cycle courses can be followed. In another type of institution (*Colegios Universitarios*) students can enrol for the first cycle and then they have to change to another tertiary institution in order to obtain a degree. Last, there is a university where students can study without having to attend, i.e. long-distance (*Universidad Nacional de Educación a Distancia*). In the last few years, special postgraduate courses are becoming very important in Spain. These courses aim to provide students with a master degree. They are offered by universities, as well a by private institutions. After short-cycle studies students obtain a degree of *Diplomado, Arquitecto Técnico* or *Ingeniero Técnico*, while long-term studies finish with a certificate of *Licenciado, Arquitecto* or *Ingeniero* (MEC 1988).

In France students in tertiary education can decide almost year by year if they want to carry on tertiary education or if they want to try their luck on the labour market with a university certificate of a lower level than the DEA or DESS.[12] In Spain people have to study at least until age 21, that is, until they can obtain the *diplomatura* or an equivalent, and if they decide to continue they have do so until age 23, when they obtain the *licenciatura* or an equivalent.

Social Class Structures

Social class and occupation structures vary greatly within Europe according to a north-south divide, where Germany and the Netherlands show the highest rates of professionals and technicians compared to agricultural and non-skilled workers and Portugal and Greece the lowest ones (Garrido Medina 2001). Here, French and Spanish social class structures are analysed for the group of parents of young people aged 20 to 29 in 1991/92. Thus, Figure 4.12 does not show the current social structure as a whole, but only the structure of a specific generation of people, namely adults who at the end of the 1980s had adult children. The French social class structure shows more people in higher levels, since the French service class is nearly twice as large as the Spanish one and the group of French skilled workers is about one third larger than the group of Spanish skilled workers. Correspondingly, we find many more non-skilled and agricultural workers in Spain than in France. Interestingly, the rate of young people from a farming background is very similar in both societies. This social class structure is also reflected in the lower average net earnings of Spanish people compared to French. According to data of the European Household Panel of 1994, average net earnings were 144,065 PTAs per month in Spain and 9,790 FF in France, which converted to the Power Purchasing Standard results into 1,110 and 1,402 monthly PPS respectively (Barailler 1997).

Figure 4.12 Social Origin of Youth (aged 20-29), Spain 1991/ France 1992

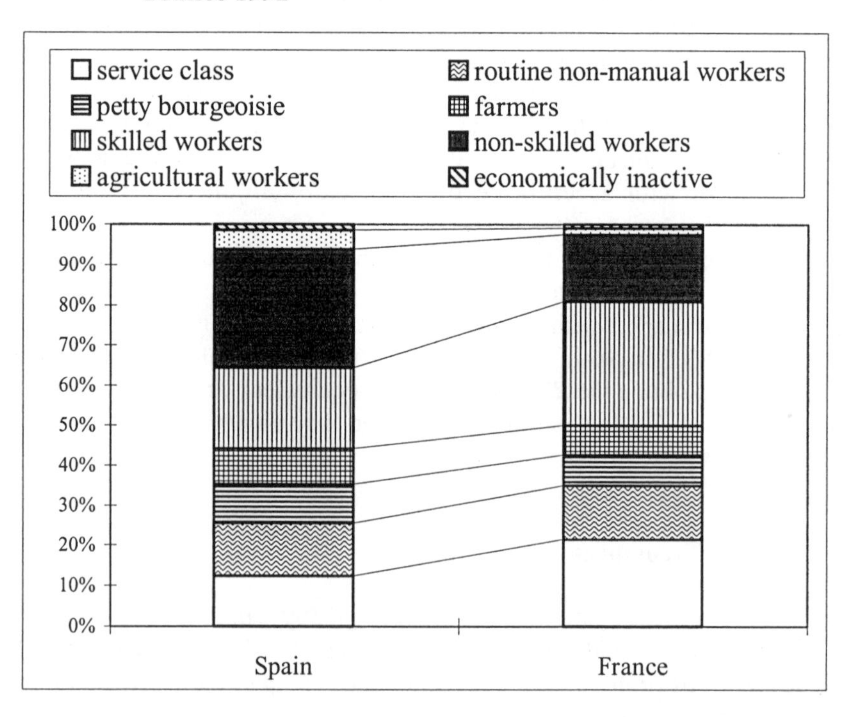

Source: author's elaboration with *Franceall* and *Spainall* and with FACLASS.

For 1994/95 there are some comparative figures on cross-national differences in young people's family background. Very similar proportions of those young people living with their parents and aged 15 to 29 did live in a household where at least one parent was unemployed: 14 per cent in Spain and 12 per cent in France. Yet 42 per cent of the socially dependent Spanish young people said that the household experienced major difficulties in making ends meet, while in France only 23 per cent of those living in the parental home stated the same thing (EUROSTAT 1997). There are also some differences in the number of siblings young people have in both countries. In France young people have a high number of siblings less frequently than in Spain. In particular, in Spain 5 per cent of the young people aged 20 to 29 have no siblings, while their French counterparts without any siblings number 9 per cent (Figure 4.13). Thus, young people in Spain have to share their parents' welfare more often with some sibling than happens in France.

Figure 4.13 Number of Siblings of Youth (aged 20-29), Spain 1991/France 1992

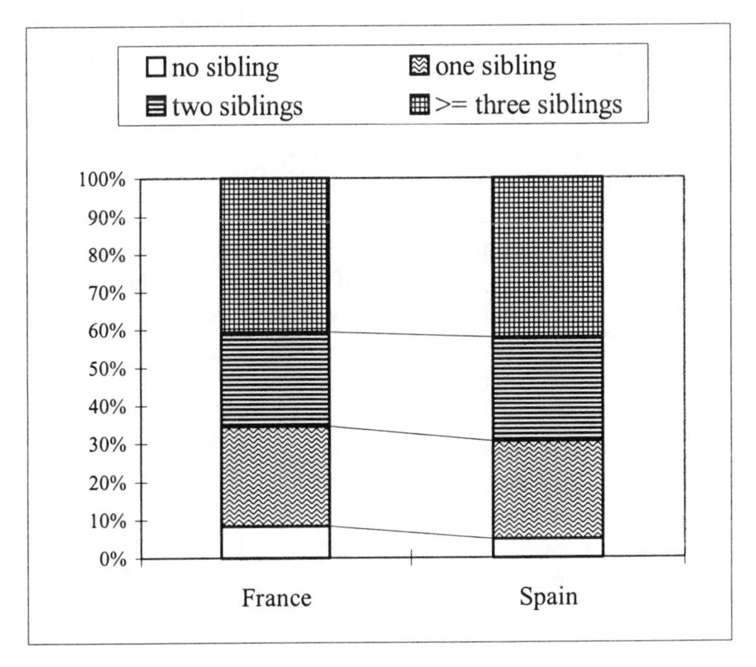

Source: author's elaboration with *Franceall* and *Spainall* and SIBLI.

Thus, compared to France, young people in Spain have a family background which has more frequently lower economic and social resources. Since young people need their parental home in the phase of becoming adults, it is evident that in Spain they have less chances of being supported by their parents in the way French young people do. Very probably, Spanish young people have to support their parents more frequently than their French neighbours, but no comparative figures on this are available.

Housing Market Structures: Differences and Similarities

Housing markets in Spain and France are very different, for they display opposite tenure structures and because they faced country-specific problems in the second half of the 1980s. Spain has a very high proportion of people living in owner-occupied accommodations, and it is the European Union country with the highest proportion of empty dwellings and of secondary residences. Also, Spain has a very high rate of new dwellings, namely dwellings constructed after 1945, since in the last decades many houses had to be constructed due to large internal migration processes and high fertility rates in the 1960/70s.

At the beginning of the 1990s, Spain had one of the lowest rates of rented accommodation in Europe: in 1991, 15 per cent of the main residences were rented as against 35 per cent in the European Community and 39 per cent in France (Cortés Alcalá 1995, EUROSTAT 1997). Another difference which has to be taken into account is the low proportion of state-owned rented accommodation in Spain in comparison to northern European countries. Only 7.6 per cent of all rented dwellings consisted of state-subsidised public housing, while this percentage was nearly five times higher in France in 1988 (Leal 1992).

In addition to the specific Spanish housing tenure structure, the Spanish housing market is also characterised by a difficult affordability of property. First, interest rates for mortgages in Spain exceeded the Union average in 1989, 1990 and 1991: they oscillated around 15 per cent in Spain and 10.5 per cent in France (Banco Hipotecario Argentaria 1992). From 1985 to 1991, selling prices for apartments rose in Spain, and then from 1987 to 1991 the increase of prices exceeded the rise of wages by far. In 1985 the financial effort related to the family income (one income) necessary to buy a dwelling was 47 per cent before taxes and 34 per cent after taxation; then it increased constantly until 1991 when the effort after taxation reached 57 per cent of the family income. By 1991, it was estimated that the cost of a dwelling in one of the large towns had risen fivefold in the previous seven years (Rodríguez López 1994, Valenzuela Rubio 1994). Yet price increases were not homogenous, since they particularly affected large towns such as Madrid and Barcelona. Data from the respective national household budget surveys permit a comparison of the average expenditures of households on housing. In 1985 an average French household directed 17.5 per cent of its expenditures towards housing, while the Spanish part of housing expenditure stood at 19.5 per cent. In 1989 the respective rates were 20.5 in France and 22.5 per cent in Spain (Geindre 1994, INE 1993, EUROSTAT 1990).[13]

The enormous Spanish price increases were a consequence of increasing demand due to the improvement of the employment situation, and the high number of young people at home-leaving age; but most importantly, they originated in the attractiveness of the Spanish housing sector to national and foreign speculative investment, since Spain's entering of the European Union in 1986. Investing in housing was considered an ideal way to launder money from informal activities and to obtain income tax deductions (Leal 1992, Gómez 1989, Naredo 1996). House construction was directed mainly to high-income groups, to people demanding secondary residences and it was concentrated in touristic areas. From the total increase of dwellings constructed between 1981 and 1992, only 56 were main residences, while the remaining ones became secondary or unoccupied residences (Leal 1992). This period, from 1986 to 1991 was also characterised by a fall of state-subsidised housing construction and a clear dominance of non-subsidised construction. This means that in the second half of the 1980s neither rented accommodation nor property were accessible to a large part of the population (Valenzuela Rubio 1994).

In France, on the other hand, mortgage interest rates diminished in real terms from 1981 to 1986 and were then stable until 1991 (Geindre 1994). State expenditure for the subsidised rented sector decreased from 1985 to 1990 and then increased somewhat until 1992, while expenditure for subsidised home-ownership decreased during this period. As a consequence, the social-rental housing (HLM) part of the housing stock increased from 16.4 per cent in 1984 to 17.1 per cent in 1993 (Blanc/Bertrand 1996). Added to this, the proportion of personal housing allowances in the total public housing budget constantly increased between 1985 and 1992 (Geindre 1994).

In Spain, the cost of renting had risen at almost the same rate as the cost of buying. This was partly because of a 'spill-over' effect, but it was also a result of the implementation of a new rent act, which made rents of newly rented accommodation increase well above the rate of inflation. In 1992 the average national monthly rent for a dwelling was estimated to have reached 67,000 Ptas for an average flat of 88 m^2, which represented nearly half of the average national wage. By this time renting was as expensive as paying a monthly mortgage (Valenzuela Rubio 1994/Cortés Alcalá 1995). In France the average national monthly rent of a dwelling was 1,793 FF and 27.5 FF per square metre in October 1992 (Blazévic/Detour/Martinez 1997). If we take as reference an 88-m^2 dwelling the average French rent would be 2,420 FF. The Purchasing Power Standard permits a comparison of both average rents: 349 PPS for a French dwelling and 540 PPS for a Spanish dwelling. Thus, on average to rent a dwelling was more expensive in Spain than in France.

Figure 4.14 shows the tenure structure of the dwellings of those young people who in 1991/92 were living on their own. There are very large differences between both countries, for in France nearly three quarters of the socially independent young people were renting their dwelling, while in Spain only one quarter was doing so. Most Spanish young people living out of the parental home have bought their dwelling (67%). In addition, Spaniards receive help somewhat more frequently in the form of a dwelling that has been given to them, i.e. a dwelling not rented or owned but given by the family or the employer for cost-free use.

Figure 4.14 Dwelling Tenure of Independent Youth (aged 20-29), Spain 1991/France 1992

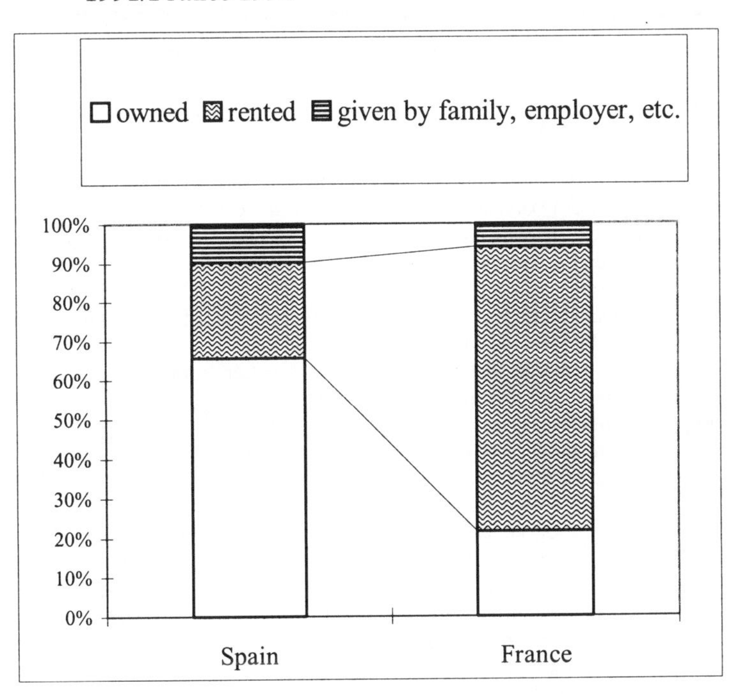

Source: author's elaboration with *Franceall* y *Spainall* and DWELL.

The figures of Figure 4.14 can be compared to other official statistics. A survey of the Spanish Housing Ministry in 1991 shows that, in fact, young people live more frequently than older people in rented accommodation and that rented accommodation is more significant in large towns than in rural communities, with the exception of towns between 500,000 and 1,000,000 inhabitants, where property dwellings are more diffused than in larger towns (Valenzuela Rubio 1994). French literature shows also that young people are more likely to rent than to own a dwelling. Curci and Taffin (1991), for instance, report that at the end of the 1980s in France, tenants of rented housing were most frequently aged 30 or less, while most owners were aged 50 to 64 years. Besides, the first wave of the European Household panel of 1994 shows nearly the same distribution of rented dwellings among all young people's households as that obtained from my own elaboration (EUROSTAT 1997).

Notes

[1] This figure is based on the retrospective information of Spainall and Franceall and it measures, in the French case, the stock of young people according to their living arrangement in each single year and in the Spanish case the "last" separation of parents and child in each single year.

[2] As in Figure 4.1 retrospective information of the French and Spanish surveys is used. The French survey allows to know the time of first time of leaving, while the Spanish survey only allows to know the "last" separation of parents and child. However, since in Spain departure from parents' home is more definitive than in France, the difference between first time of leaving and last time of leaving should be rather small.

[3] It was checked that young people did not leave the parental home and return later, so that this would be the reason for the incongruency.

[4] In 1992 the exchange rate was 1 Purchasing Power Standard for 6.94 FF and for 124.13 Ptas. Thus, 1081 PPS are the equivalent of 134,185 Ptas.

[5] It has to be remembered that consensual unions suffer from underreporting in most surveys and census, and this might be a greater problem in countries where it is still a minority phenomenon (Prinz 1995). The European Household Panel reports similar figures for Spain and France for 1994. Of those aged 25 to 29, 4 per cent live in consensual unions in Spain, whereas in France they number 25 per cent (EUROSTAT 1997).

[6] The Spanish figures on educational enrolment presented here are lower than those of Rivière (1996) who uses also the socio-demographic survey. This is probably because he used the retrospective information on education, while the figures here come from the cross-sectional part on activity. The figures of the Spanish Labour Force Survey give a similar number of young people aged 20 to 29 enrolled in education as the results of my own elaboration with *Spainall* (cf.Appendix).

[7] OECD statistics show that young men's (aged 20-24) labour force participation rates have decreased from 1979 to 1994, but that they were always higher in Spain than in France. In addition, the cross-national difference has increased in the last decade (OECD 1996).

[8] García Polavieja used two surveys, one for 1991 and one for 1997, and he performed a logistic regression analysis.

[9] The results for Spain are very similar to the results Jaime Rivière obtained in his analysis of the Sociodemographic Survey (Garrido/Requena 1996).

[10] However, EUROSTAT labour force figures of those aged 30 to 34 in 1995 show a higher percentage of Spanish people with a tertiary certificate, namely 22 per cent compared to the 15 per cent obtained here for 25 to 29 year old people (EUROSTAT 1997).

[11] The rate is calculated by dividing the number of new entrances into a university by the number of young people who have obtained their maturity certificate in the same academic year (MEN 1994).

[12] But, in practice, the DEUG certificate only has academic significance (Jallade et al. 1993).

[13] The figures for 1989 are taken from their respective national surveys. Housing expenditure in France includes rent, payment of mortgage, maintenance, energy, heating, taxes, and insurance. In Spain it includes rent, mortgage, heating, and energy. If in Spain one includes maintenance, furniture, and domestics, good the proportion of all these expenditures increases to 28 per cent. The figures for 1985 come from a EUROSTAT publication using standardised results of national household budget surveys. They include gross rents, rents of tenants, imputed rents of owner-occupiers, expenditure on repairs and maintenance of housing, and water charges.

5 Different Strategies of French and Spanish Youth

The results of this section refer to model (6) presented previously in chapter 3. with two differences. For reasons of sampling and to avoid weighting of the samples used for the logistic regression (*France86* and *Spain85*) two context variables were introduced. The model used for all logistic regressions of this section is as follows:

$$(7)\ \text{logit}(\text{IND91/92}) = \alpha + \beta_1(\text{ACTIVEST}) + \beta_2(\text{FACLASS}) - \beta_3(\text{SIBL}) + \beta_4(\text{EDUC}) + \beta_5(\text{AGE}) + \beta_6(\text{RURURBAN}) + \beta_7(\text{REGION})$$

This equation was applied separately by country, gender and activity situation. At this point it is useful to recapitulate, in a summarised form, what the variables are thought to be measuring and which hypotheses are to be tested.

Table 5.1 Micro-level Variables and Hypotheses

Variables	Proxy for	Related hypotheses
ACTIVEST	1. own resources (men+women) 2. family formation strategy (women)	1. market-income hypothesis 2. pluralisation hypothesis 3. stability hypothesis
EDUC	1. expectations of standard of life 2. timing school to work transition (non-students)	1. low-expectation hypothesis/early transition
FACLASS	1. expectations of standard of life (non-students) 2. resources of parents (students)	1. low-expectation hypothesis 2. low-quality-of-life hypothesis
SIBL	1. standard of life at home (non-students) 2. resources of parents (students)	1. low-quality-of-life hypothesis
AGE	1. age differences	1. Age-cleavage hypothesis

The detailed results of the models are all in the appendix and the most important findings are presented here in a more illustrative way. First, the predictive capacities of the models are compared to each other. Second, the probabilities of the reference categories of the models are shown to allow for an appreciation of the cross-national differences that persist after controlling for many socio-economic variables. In a third step, the results are interpreted for each single group.

The predictive capacity of the models is indicated by the –2 Log Likelihood, which is a measure of how the prediction of the dependent variable becomes more accurate once one introduces the independent variables. Since this measure is sensitive to the sample size, it was decided to compare different models through the comparison of the proportions by which the inclusion of all independent variables increase the –2LL with respect to the –2LL without independent variables. Contrary to what was assumed, the models for students have a higher predictive power than those for non-students. It means that the reduced model, i.e. the socio-economic model, explains nest-leaving probabilities better for students.[1] This could mean two things: first, non-material aspects of leaving home are more important for young people on the labour market than for students or second, activity situation as a proxy of income level and income stability is more appropriate to differentiate among students and less among non-students. Within the group of students, the best fit is found for French men, followed by Spanish men, Spanish women and French women. The best prediction for non-students is obtained for Spanish men, followed by French men, Spanish women and French women. This reveals that the male models always show a better fit than the female models, which suggests that in the female cases non-measured variables such as the availability of economic help from a male partner or/and non-material aspects of the quality of life have a high relevance for their nest-leaving probabilities. The socio-economic models predict somewhat better for Spaniards than for the French with the exception of Spanish male students. This does not necessarily suggest that non-material aspects of the quality of life are more important in France than in Spain, but it might mean, for instance, that in the former model, the activity situation is not as good a proxy for income as in the latter model. It will be shown later that there is some important income heterogeneity among French long-term employed young people, while Spanish research suggests that long-term employed people in Spain always earn more than short-term employed.

High Individual Resources Do Not Always Encourage Young People to Live Independently

The models allow the estimation of the probabilities of living independently in 1991/92 according to given individual characteristics. The estimated probability of living out of the parental home of a person with the characteristics of the reference category of each independent variable can be computed through the transformation of the coefficient of the intercept into the estimated probability.[2] According to the model of young people enrolled in education, a French women who combines studies and work, is between 25 and 29 years old, has already obtained a tertiary certificate, whose father belongs to the service class, has no siblings, and lives in a large town in the Ile-de France region has a 79 per cent probability of living independently of, while her Spanish counterpart in a large town in the region of Madrid reaches a 33 per cent probability. Of the French sample of women enrolled in formal education, 42 per cent are living independently (Figure 5.1), which clearly shows that this reference category is more likely to be found among the independent than the average female student.[3] The average Spanish student has a rate of independence of 12 per cent. This means that the fact of belonging to the reference category increases the chances of young Spanish women to be socially independent by 64 per cent, while in France by 53 per cent only. These figures show three important things.

1. First, the difference between the Spanish and French average female independence rates cannot be explained as a mere composition effect of the variables included in Model7. There are other individual or context variables which are not included in the model and which make French and Spanish students who display the same socio-economic conditions behave differently.
2. Second, the fact of belonging to the "privileged" group increases the chances of a Spanish female student living independently more than that of her French counterpart.
3. Third, people with the characteristics of the reference category are supposed to have a high standard of life in the parental home, since they belong to the service class, have no siblings and live in a context with many resources. Their standard of life outside the parental home is relatively high in terms of human capital, since they already have a tertiary qualification and in terms of economic capital, since they have a job. Yet it is only in France that the relatively high standard of life that such people reach, when they live independently, makes most of them leave home, while in Spain the majority of these people stay at home. In

Spain, "privileged" young people estimate the relative high standard of life they could reach away from home as too low to make nest-leaving attractive, because non-measured features such as income levels, housing market, social benefits, and family formation norms make the standard of life of living independently lower than in France. Unfortunately, the logistic regression models do not permit us to disentangle the exact significance of each of these unmeasured features. The institutional analysis and the cross-regional analysis explore these aspects further on.

Figure 5.1 Estimated Probabilities of Being Socially Independent and Independence Rates (Youth Enrolled in Education, Spain 1991/France 1992)

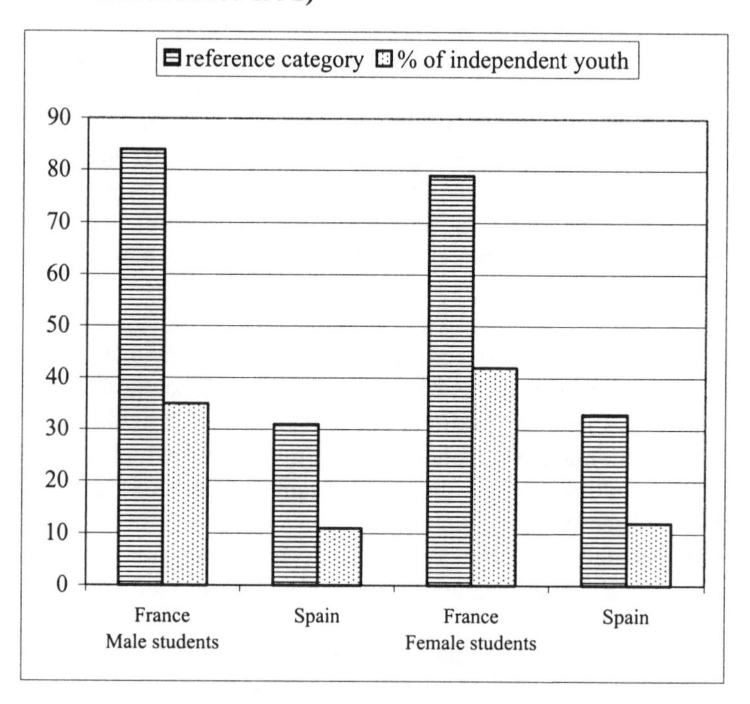

Source: author's elaboration with figures from Appendix, Tables 1 and 2.

"Privileged" male students in France have a very high likelihood of living independently (84%), whereas their Spanish counterparts have a small probability (31%). As in the female case, the reference categories in both countries have higher probabilities of living outside of the parental home than the average student (35% and 11% respectively in each country). Again like women, the Spanish reference category increases its chance of living independently by 63% compared to the average student, while his French counterpart only does so by 58%. This means that, though the models control for different socio-economic variables, national differences persist. Male students in France might follow a different rational choice logic than Spanish male students or the model has to be changed by including better variables in order to discover the same logic.

These figures show that differences between the average probability of living on one's own and the estimated probability of the reference group are larger in Spain than in France, which suggests that the influence of social inequalities with respect to parents' and one's own resources on the chances of being a socially independent student are greater in Spain than in France.

The analysis of women in the labour market gives very interesting results, since we find here the greatest differences between French and Spanish living arrangement patterns (Figure 5.2). Of the French sample, 67 per cent of the women live independently, while for the Spanish sample the figure is 45 per cent. This shows that French and Spanish women not enrolled in education are found more frequently outside of the parental home than their respective counterparts who are still enrolled in formal education. The delay hypothesis (cf. Chapter 2) which affirms that longer enrolment in education delays leaving home is supported by these individual-level findings. The French reference category, a women with long-term employment, aged between 25 and 29, with tertiary qualification, from service class origins, without siblings, in a large town in the Ile-de France has an estimated probability of 82 per cent of living independently. This means a higher probability than the average women of the sample. Interestingly, the Spanish reference category, a woman with the same characteristics living in a large town in the region of Madrid, has a lower likelihood of living outside the parental home (28%) than the average women of the sample (45%).

Figure 5.2 Estimated Probabilities of Being Socially Independent and Independence Rates (Youth in the Labour Market, Spain 1991/France 1992)

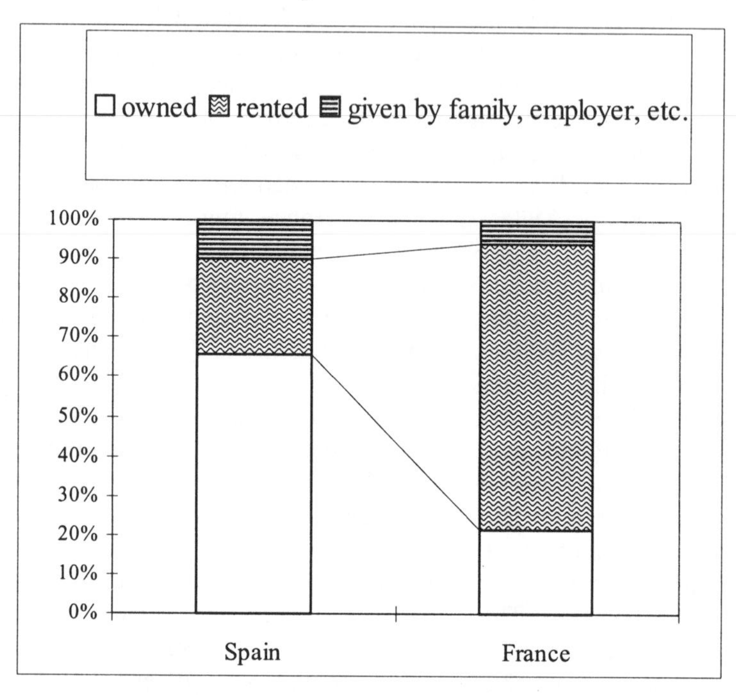

Source: author's elaboration with figures of four models, cf.Appendix, Tables 1 and 2.

These figures dealing with people on the labour market show again, as in the case of students, that French and Spanish women with the same socio-economic characteristics follow different strategies. Unlike in the students' case, Spanish "privileged" women do not show a higher probability of living independently than the average women of the sample. Thus high resources do not encourage early social independence or, in other words, low resources encourage youth to leave home early. This confirms the prediction for women that was deduced from the **stability hypothesis** in Chapter 3, which stated that Spanish women are less dependent on a long-term employment than French women, since they choose more frequently a dependent family-formation. Yet from a comparative macro-sociological perspective this specific Spanish pattern does not support early home leaving in Spain, since only 45 per cent of the women in the Spanish sample are living independently, compared to 67 per cent of the French women.

Patterns for men are similar to those of women with one difference. "Privileged" Spanish men have a slightly higher estimated probability of living outside of the parental home than the average rate of the sample. However, compared to French men the difference between the reference category and the average is much smaller. French men with high resources have a 36 per cent higher chance of living independently than the average, while Spanish men with high resources increase their chance only by 11 per cent. This contrasts with the figures of young people enrolled in education. It means that in both countries high resources are much more important in facilitating leaving home for male students than for men in the labour market.

It is very striking that young Spanish men with long-term employment, aged 25 to 29, with tertiary qualifications, from service class origins, without siblings, living in a large town in the region of Madrid display an estimated probability of social independence of only 36 per cent. It means that the great majority of these young men are still living with their parents, despite their high level of personal resources. On the other hand, 78 per cent of their French counterparts are living on their own. This shows clearly that long-lasting cohabitation in Spain is not a problem mainly confined to young people without long-term employment, but must relate to housing accessibility and/or specific family-formation norms such as the link between leaving home and becoming married, and leaving home and buying a dwelling. In the next section the analysis of the activity situation's role in living arrangements will shed more light on these French-Spanish differences.

Unemployment, Full-time Education, and Short-term Jobs Delay Leaving Home Everywhere

In the following sections, the results of the regression models are presented in figures showing the net unstandardised logistic regression coefficients. Each independent variable of the model, which estimates the logit of living outside of the parental home, has one omitted or reference category. The influence of the independent variable "activity" on living independently is measured by comparing the relationship of different categories of "activity", for instance "short-term employment", "unemployed", "family help", with the dependent variable relative to the omitted category "long-term employment". Figure 5.3 shows that French men who have short-term employment reduce their logit (or likelihood) of living independently by a net coefficient of "–1" compared to French men with long-term employment, or in other words, they have a lower probability of living independently. The figures show the net effects, which means that the influence of activity is the estimated net of the influence of the other independent variables: education, social origin, etc. A French man with short-term employment has a lower chance of living independently compared to a French man with long-term employment, independently of whether he has a low or a high educational level, independently of coming from a service class or a working class origin, and so on. In the figures, the omitted or reference category of an independent variable is represented by the horizontal axis and the coefficients of the other categories are shown by the bars. Thus, figures show only relative differences within each country and within each gender group. Detailed results can be found in the Appendix.

The **market-income hypothesis** states that receiving a stable market income is the most important condition to allow nest-leaving. Thus, it has to be expected that people without a job have the lowest likelihood of being socially independent, those with a short-term job have higher chances and those with long-term employment have the highest probabilities. Figure 5.3 demonstrates that this applies to Spanish men, but not really to French men. Spanish men with some income are more probably living outside of the parental home than full-time students, first-job seekers, unemployed men, and economically inactive men. By contrast, French male family helps have the lowest probability of living independently compared to long-term employed men; next come first job-seekers and these are followed by full-time students, short-term employees, and last by unemployed people who previously had a job. Thus, the hypothesis has to be falsified for French men. The fact that short-term employed French men are less likely to be socially independent than unemployed ones has to be seen in relation to the low earnings of young people in fixed-term employment measures. The market-income hypothesis is also not valid for women, since women who are economically inactive have more probability of living independently than women with a long-term job. However, these female patterns are in line with the theoretical assumptions, since for women it was stated that the role of the resources of the partner can be as or even more important than the resources of the women herself. However, for technical reasons it was not possible to include the information about the presence or absence of a partner.[4]

Young women in full-time education show the lowest likelihood of living outside of the parental home compared to ones with long-term employment, while young male full-time students also have a low likelihood of living independently, but they do not belong to the group with the lowest chances. In Spain, male first-job seekers have an even lower probability of living outside of the parental home than students if both are compared to long-term employed men. French full-time students are more likely to live independently than first-job seekers and family helps. In both countries part-time students are more likely to live outside of the parental home than full-time students with the exception of French men, for whom the estimated coefficient is statistically not significant. Short-term employed people have everywhere a relatively low likelihood to be living outside of the parental home, but their likelihood to do so is always higher than that of first-employment seekers with the exception of French women.

Figure 5.3 Net Effects of Activity Situation on the Likelihood of Social Independence (All Young People, France 1992/Spain 1991)

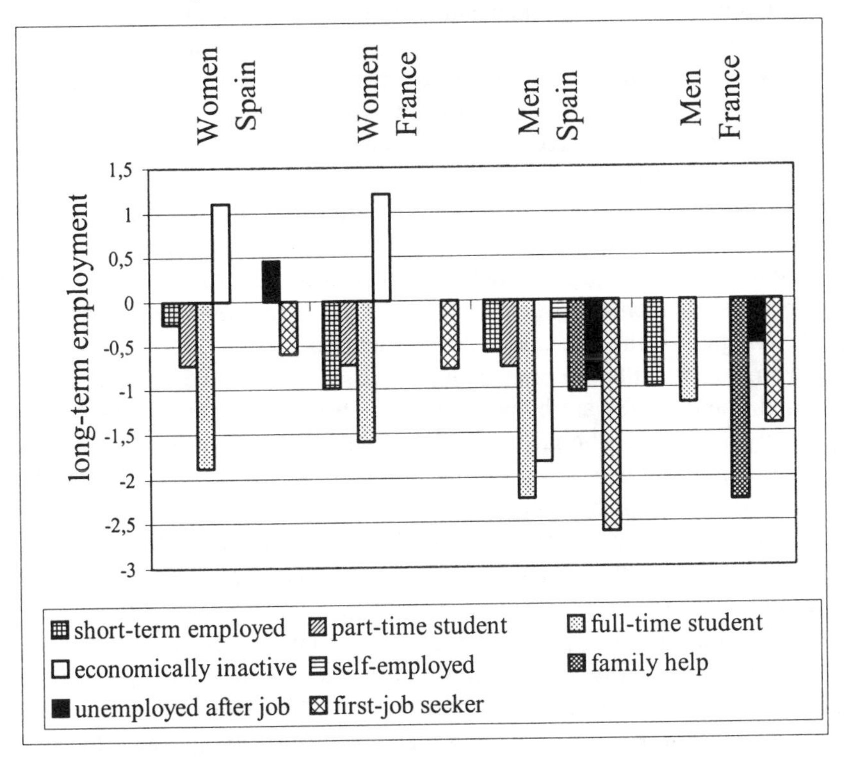

Source: logistic regression with *France86* and *Spain85*.
Notes: statistically significant at <=0.05. No table in Appendix.

The **pluralisation hypothesis** predicts that French students will show a higher probability of leaving home than Spanish students, which corresponds with the results of the logistic regressions. In the female case part-time students in both countries have the same likelihood of living independently, but French full-time students have a significantly higher chance of being socially independent than their Spanish counterparts.[5]

In the next two sections students' and non-students' living arrangement patterns will be analysed separately and cross-national differences will be interpreted.

Social Class Affects Students' Living Arrangements in France

If students are analysed separately, the activity effects confirm the previous findings.[6] In both countries, students who combine a job with education are more likely to be living independently and the strength of the effect is equally strong for French and for Spanish people, although in both countries it is somewhat stronger for men than for women.[7] Again, the latter finding might be related to the possibility female students have of depending on the resources of their spouse/partner. As shown above in Figure 4.10 nearly as many French as Spanish men and women combine work with studies, so that in this case of similar individual strategies in both countries, composition effects cannot help to explain the overall differences in the intergenerational co-residence patterns between French and Spanish students. It means also that there are no contextual effects influencing part-time students in both countries.

Female students in France are more likely to live outside of the parental home if they are between 25 and 29 years old, and if they have a relatively high educational level. This means that nest-leaving is more diffused among university students than among students of secondary vocational training for example. Interestingly, students from petty bourgeoisie and farming backgrounds show higher probabilities of living independently than those of service class origin. On the other hand, those of working class origin have low probabilities of living out of the parental home (Figure 5.4). The petty bourgeoisie and farmer effects might be due to the fact that young women from these family backgrounds are more frequently forced to emigrate for study reasons. Yet, even if this is the case it means that these young people are able to afford living away for study reasons, because of the relatively high resources of these families, and/or because of the fact that students from these origins are more likely to receive scholarships than those of working class origin. This might be due to the phenomenon that the parents' income in the former case is more difficult to estimate correctly by the state bureaucracy than that of dependent workers. Findings presented later on show that all these social origin effects persist when one includes income information in the model, which means that it cannot (only) be a question of a higher likelihood of receiving public grants and family help, but that other characteristics originating from these specific class positions are relevant.

Figure 5.4 Net Effects of Social Origin on the Likelihood of Social Independence (Students, France 1992/Spain 1991)

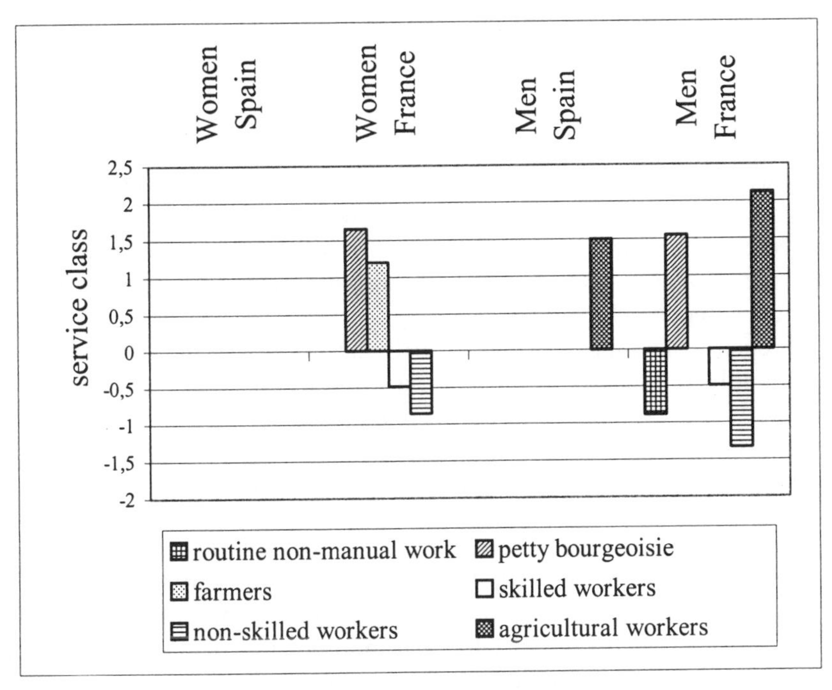

Source: author's elaboration with figures of four models, cf.Appendix, Table 1 and 2.

French men behave similarly to French women with three differences. The age effect is non-existent, while instead all educational levels exert a statistically significant effect. This means that the lower the educational level is, the less one is likely to be living outside of the parental home. With respect to social origin effects, the effect of coming from a farming background is, statistically insignificant, in contrast to women, probably because men remain more often bound to the farm than women. This is supported by the fact that small municipalities show more negative effects on males living independently than in the case of women. Male students in rural areas under 20,000 inhabitants are less likely to be living independently. Like female students, male students from a petty bourgeoisie background are more likely to live independently than their colleagues from the service class, the routine non-manual class, and the working class. Only men of agricultural working class origin also have a high probability of living independently, even higher than those from the petty bourgeoisie. As in the female case, these social class effects remain very similar once income is included in the logistic regression models. Thus, social origin differences might be related to a different accessibility to public benefits for students according to social class, since students receive grants either because their parents' income is very low (agricultural workers) or because it officially appears to be low (petty bourgeoisie), but this interpretation is not sufficient. The argument that these families have more resources than other families is not valid either, since they are more likely to have independent children than the service class, which is supposed to have higher resources. The most convincing interpretation is that these young people's families live more frequently in rural areas than service class families and that they have to leave home in order to study. However, this does not exclude their receiving public benefits and family help more frequently.

French male students' chances of living outside of the parental home are strongly influenced by their social origin and not at all by age, in contrast to what happens in Spain. French female students also display a smaller age-effect and relatively large social origin effects. It might be argued that French young people who are enrolled in education are not considered as children who have to be maintained by their parents, which would make fewer age-differences and more social class differences appear. In Spain, by contrast, large age-differences and the absence of social class effects reflect more generalised social norms about students' social dependence. It can be stated that the French male students' patterns falsify the **age-cleavage hypothesis**, while the Spanish patterns confirm it, as is shown next.

Spanish female students show few differences in their chances of living independently. Apart from the effect of a part-time job, only two other effects were found:

1. older women are more likely to be outside of the parental home than younger ones;
2. those with an already completed tertiary education are more likely than those with a maturity certificate.

Like their female counterparts, Spanish male students show few differences among themselves. Only older students, those from an agricultural worker's background and those with many siblings are more likely to be living independently than younger students of service class origin and with no siblings. Either their standard of life is very low in the parental home and thus pushes them out of the nest or they have more chances of receiving a sufficiently high scholarship to live outside of the parental home. Yet it is strange that these effects were not found for their female counterparts.

Nest-leaving of Spanish female students seems to be strongly socially regulated, since it is the attainment of a given age and the end of tertiary education which seem to guide these women's strategies. Male students are affected by a similar age effect, but also by the fact of being from a family background with a low standard of living. Unlike the patterns of their French counterparts, Spanish students' patterns confirm the **age-cleavage hypothesis**.

Economically Active Youth and Social Independence in Spain and France

If one takes the sample of young people out of formal education, it appears that first-job seekers always have less probabilities of living independently than people with long-term employment, as revealed by Figure 5.5. This type of unemployment affects Spanish men's likelihood to be socially independent the most and Spanish women's likelihood the least. First employment seeking affects more Spanish than French men.[8] Only in France did young people searching for a first employment at the end of the 1980s have access to means-tested unemployment benefits, while Spanish people were entitled to attend vocational training courses specially set up for unemployed people, but had no entitlement to unemployment benefits. In addition, French young people in need could apply for housing allowances, whereas these did not exist in Spain (cf. Chapter 9). We must also remember that many French young people leave home during their enrolment in education. Afterwards some of them return home but others remain socially independent and try to overcome brief periods without market income without returning home. These differences in social rights might explain that unemployment previous to first job in France affects the male likelihood of social independence less than in Spain. This argument is not valid for women, since in Spain the estimated coefficient of first-job seeker is not significantly different from the French one. Yet, again, this might be related to the fact that in Spain more women rely on their partners' resources than in France.

Young men who had a job and lost it are also less likely to live independently than their counterparts with a long-term job. At first sight, in Spain this type of unemployment seems to affect the likelihood of social independence more than in France, but the difference is not statistically significant. This contradicts the idea that social rights differences of unemployed people might partly explain country variations, since French unemployment insurance coverage is more extensive and more generous in terms of time than the Spanish unemployment difference (cf. Chapter 8).

In both countries, to be a fixed-term male employee decreases the likelihood of living independently compared to long-term employed men in a similar way.[9] Since Spanish employment policy is more strongly directed towards flexibilisation at the margin than in France, these policy differences might be related to the average cross-national variation. In other words, individual strategies of fixed-term employed men are similar in both countries, but Spanish employment policy is more favourable than the French short-term contracts for youth and there are more fixed-term employed young men. These context differences partly explain the higher rate of two-generation households in Spain.

Coming back to the **stability hypothesis** presented previously, it can be stated that for Spanish men, employment is more important for social independence than for French men, since unemployment previous to first job affects Spaniards' social independence more than it affects French. These findings contradict the hypothesis as it was formulated in Chapter 3, because fixed-term jobs and unemployment after a job have similar effects in both countries, but it confirms the great problem of first-unemployment in Spain.

Figure 5.5 Net Effects of Activity Situation on the Likelihood of Social Independence (Non-Students, France 1992/Spain 1991)

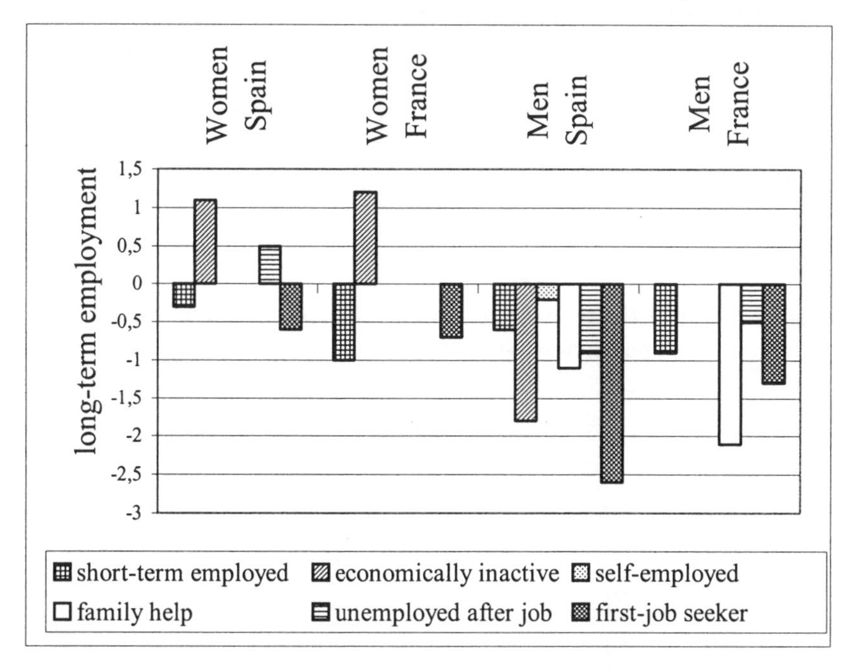

Source: author's elaboration with figures of four models, cf.Appendix, Tables 3 and 4.

In France and Spain, women who are economically inactive are more likely to be living outside of the parental home than women with long-term employment. This is not surprising, for self-definition as economically inactive is something that seldom occurs if women live in the parental home. Therefore nearly all economically inactive women are per definition living independently from their parents.

Interestingly, Spanish women who lost their jobs are more likely to be found living independently than women with long-term employment. These are surely women who had a job when leaving home and who, having lost it, maintain themselves thanks to unemployment benefits and/or their partner's income. Yet, why do we not find this pattern in France? Very likely this is connected to the fact that long-term employees, the reference category, behave differently in both countries. Above, it was shown that Spanish "privileged" women, i.e. those with long-term employment and other high resources, are less likely to be living independently than the less "privileged". The reason for this is that young women in Spain follow, more frequently than their French contemporaries, a dependent household formation strategy as shown in Chapter 4. Spanish women show less pronounced net effects of their own resources on their chance of being outside of the parental home than do their French contemporaries. This supports the **stability hypothesis** for Spain.

With respect to education the theoretical model for young people in the labour market assumed that educational level is an indicator of expectations of living standard, and of the time young people are already in the labour market. This is probably the reason why Spanish and French differences in the effect of educational level are so pronounced, as summarised by Figure 5.6.

Figure 5.6 Net Effects of Education on the Likelihood of Social Independence (Non-Students, France 1992/Spain 1991)

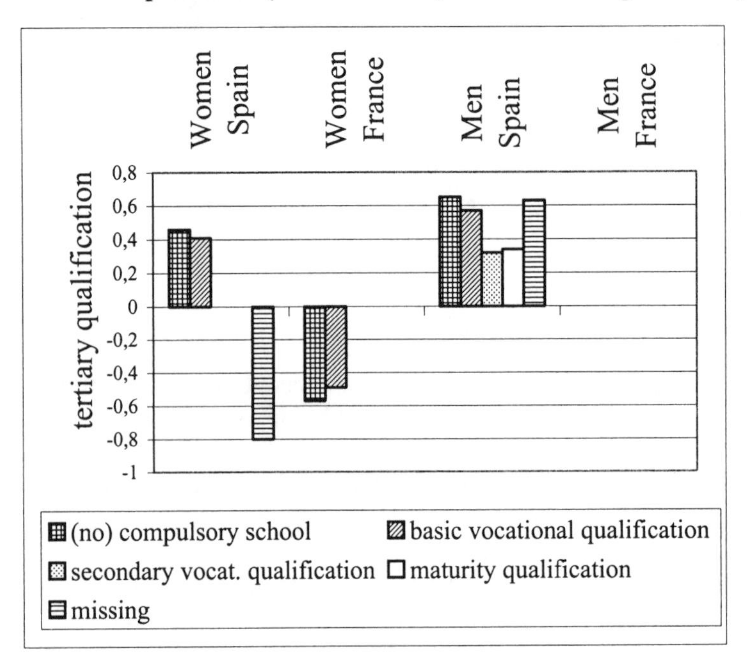

Source: author's elaboration with figures of four models, cf.Appendix, Tables 3 and 4.

Spanish women with low educational levels are more likely to be living independently than women with tertiary qualifications. This is related to the fact that women with low education credentials are found more frequently among those living in a male-breadwinner family. A logistic regression with the sample of Spanish women who live outside of the parental home, which estimated the likelihood of being an economically inactive woman against all other activity situations, shows that education has a strong net effect. Women with educational levels below tertiary qualifications are all more likely to be in a male-breadwinner family, and this is most likely for women whose highest qualification is the completion of compulsory education.[10] This explains why in the group of young women aged 20 to 29 those with the highest likelihood of living outside of the parental home are the women with the lowest educational level. However, young women with a tertiary certificate are less likely to be living independently during this life cycle phase, because they seldom follow a dependent household formation strategy. This corresponds with the predictions of the **stability hypothesis**, which foresaw that marriage with an employed husband is a very diffused strategy for female home-leaving in Spain. Apart from these relationships there are also good arguments for confirming the **low-expectation and early school-to-work transition hypothesis**, which affirms that young people with relatively low educational levels entered the labour market early and have relatively low expectations with regard to the economic standard of life outside of the parental home.

In France, we find exactly the opposite pattern. Women with a low educational level have more difficulty in living outside of the parental home than those with a tertiary qualification. This is partly due to the fact that many women with a tertiary qualification had already left home for the time they were enrolled in education. This specific French pattern is so strong that it outweighs the effect of French women with a low educational level tending to be more frequently in male-breadwinner families, like in Spain. The same logistic regression as for Spanish women was run, where the likelihood of socially independent women being economically inactive was estimated. Unlike in the Spanish case, not all educational levels below the tertiary qualification increase the chances of being in a male-breadwinner family, but the lowest educational level does. On the one hand, these findings confirm the **pluralisation hypothesis**, since they show that many French women leave home in order to enter a male-breadwinner family but that many also leave home for study or to form a one-person household, while in Spain few women leave home for study or to live alone and many more in order to live in a male-breadwinner family. On the other hand, the **low-expectation and early school-to-work transition hypothesis** has to be rejected for French women.

Spanish men with low educational levels are also more likely to be living independently as compared to men with tertiary certificates. Unlike women, this is not necessarily related to the male-breadwinner model, but is a timing effect. Men who were already out of education for some time had more employment experiences, had an income and could save some money. Garrido and Requena (1996) included years of employment experience in a logistic regression estimating the likelihood of living outside of the parental home. This variable has a quasi-linear positive effect on the probability of social independence, which is the following: the larger one's employment experience, the higher the probability of being socially independent. This effect is the net of the current activity situation, which means that accumulation of resources in the labour market has an effect independent of the current labour market situation. Thus, both the labour market career and the labour market situation are important net of all other effects, such as age and social origin. This is also a result of the fact that those who enter the labour market late have lost some years of income, but have a better chance to find a job. Young people with low educational levels enter their first employment earlier than those with higher educational levels, but at the same time, if one controls for age at leaving school, it appears that Spanish young people with higher educational qualifications are less likely to be unemployed (Garrido/Requena 1996). Thus people with low educational levels have many difficulties in the labour market but they have had nonetheless more time to accumulate savings than those with a higher educational level, in particular if we only observe young people aged 20 to 29. In addition, if we interpret educational levels as proxies for expectations then it can be argued that people with lower educational levels also have lower expectations with regard to the economic standard of life they wish to attain out of the parental home. Thus the results here and other research findings confirm, as for women, the **low-expectation and early school-to-work transition hypothesis** for Spanish men in the labour market.

French men, on the other hand, do not show different patterns according to educational level. It is as if the current labour market situation was able to indicate all differences, those related to the labour market career and those referred to the current situation. Probably, early entrance into the French labour really market means that it brings persisting disadvantages for the future labour market position, which outweigh the advantages related to early entrance. In addition, French men display many social class effects, which seem to be so important that they directly affect these people's chances without being mediated by educational level differences.

Figure 5.7 illustrates that for French men social origin plays an important role for their chances of social independence, net of many other effects. These results are in line with what was found for students. This contradicts common sense expectations about the redistributory effects of well-established Welfare States and their consequent mitigation of social class differences. Yet as is shown below, in spite of the fact that public benefits increase all young French men's chances of social independence, social class effects persist. Thus, public benefits have effects on young people's life chances, but they are not so strong as to eliminate social class effects. As in the students' case, a petty bourgeoisie background favours social independence, probably because many of those people left home when they were students. Again, as for students, a working class origin diminishes the chances of social independence, including those from an agricultural worker background. The latter had a positive effect on students' likelihood of living out of the parental home. Thus, for French men on the labour market the **low-quality-of-life hypothesis** and the **low-expectation and early school-to-work transition hypothesis** have to be falsified, as for women. Young people from lower class origin do not tend to be more frequently socially independent.

The **low-quality-of-life hypothesis** does not work either for Spanish men. Spanish men from farmers' and non-skilled workers' backgrounds are less likely to be living independently than their counterparts from the service class. The positive effect of an agricultural worker origin, which was found for students, no longer appears for non-students; it is negative, but not statistically significant.

Figure 5.7 Net Coefficients of Social Origin on the Likelihood of Social Independence (Non-Students, France 1992/Spain 1991)

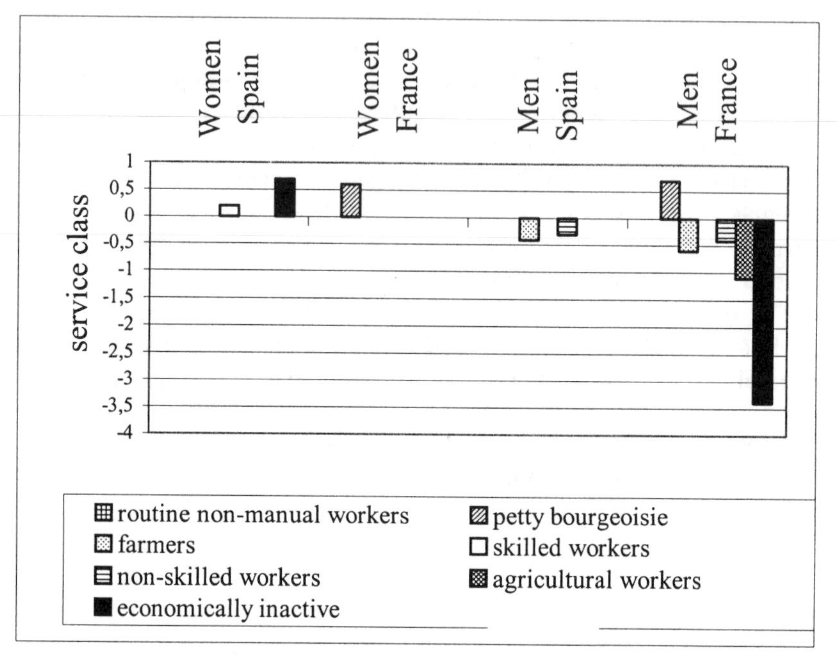

Source: author's elaboration with figures of four models, cf.Appendix, Tables 3 and 4.

Women in both countries display few social origin influences. Again, a petty bourgeoisie origin is a positive factor for French women, while a skilled workers' origin increases the probability of living outside of the parental home. It is not possible to confirm the **low-quality-of-living hypothesis** for women, either.

A curious finding is revealed by Figure 5.8: parental resources seem to be important in Spain, not as indicated by social origin but by number of siblings. Instead, in France the number of siblings has no effect on living arrangement. The costs parents face due to a larger or smaller number of children influences living arrangements in Spain. A linear relationship between the number of siblings and the likelihood of leaving home exists: the more siblings a young person has, the higher the tendency to live independently. It is as if the advantages of living in the parental home diminish when the parental resources have to be shared among many children and this applies to all social classes. The lack of this effect in France might be due to the relatively generous French family policy, which is able to equalise to some extent child costs among families with different numbers of children. These results suggest once more a falsification of the **low-quality-of life hypothesis** for French men and women, while they partially confirm it for Spaniards of both gender.

Figure 5.8 Net Coefficients of Siblings on the Likelihood of Social Independence (Non-Students, Spain 1991)

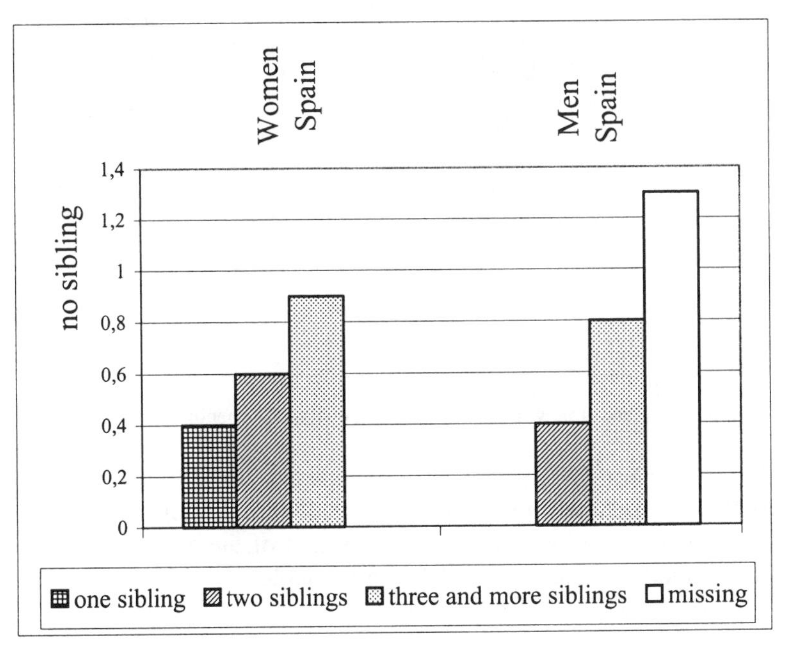

Source: author's elaboration with figures of four models, cf.Appendix, Tables 3 and 4.

Age plays a much greater role in Spain than in France, since young people aged 20 to 24 years are much more likely to stay at home than their 25 to 29 year-old counterparts. In France, differences are significantly smaller, which indicates that moving into adulthood can be achieved early in a comparative perspective. However, contrary to what happens to French students, age-differences persist in the case of French youth on the labour market. Thus for youth out of the education system, we find in both countries that the **age-cleavage hypothesis** is confirmed. The comparatively longer dependence of young Spanish people, students and non-students, on their parents is strongly institutionalised in Spanish society and is also reflected in Spanish social security and taxation law (cf. Chapter 7).

Figure 5.9 Net Coefficients of Age on the Likelihood of Social Independence (Non-Students, France 1992/Spain 1991)

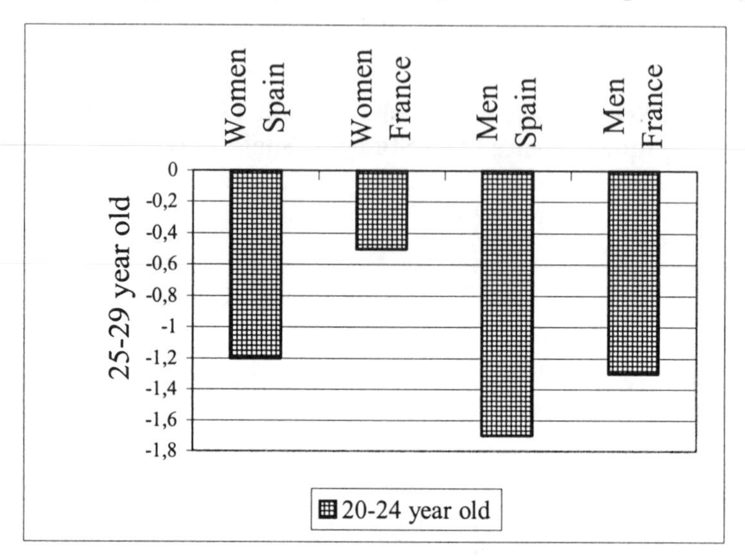

Source: author's elaboration with figures of four models, cf.Appendix, Tables 3 and 4.

Before general conclusions are drawn, we will show how much better it would be to include information on income into the logistic regressions. The French survey allows for the amelioration of the empirical test of the theoretical model, since income data are available.

Is Activity a Good Proxy for Income Level and Stability? The French Case

In Chapter 3, the theoretical model included income level and income stability as explaining variables instead of activity situation. It was necessary to take activity as a proxy for both level and stability of income, since the Spanish survey does not include information on income. On the other hand the French survey provides this information, and for France a model was computed, in which income was combined with activity. In this way we can see if the model with income level and stability explains more than the model using activity as proxy for both, as has been assumed in the cross-national empirical models. An amount slightly over the minimum wage was decided on as the cutting point for the construction of a new variable (ACTIVINC), which takes the place of the comparative variable ACTIVEST. Instead of a distinction between long-term and fixed-term employment, unemployment, etc. ACTIVINC distinguishes between long-term employment with a monthly income at or below 5,000 FF, long-term employment over 5,000 FF, short-term employment at or below 5,000 FF, short-term employment over 5,000 FF, etc.

All four French models with the variable income (ACTIVINC) instead of activity show lower –2 Log-Likelihood values, which indicates that they predict living independently better than the former French models.[11] Compared to long-term employed people with an income over 5,000 FF, an income at or below 5,000 FF has, in general, a negative effect on the probability of leaving home independently of the stability of the employment.[12] Also, male students who have an income at or below 5,000 FF are less likely to be living independently than students with a part-time job paid over 5,000 FF. First-job seeking and unemployment is negatively related to social independence, if the male or female unemployed people receive 5,000 FF income or less, but if they have access to a higher income then their chance of living independently does not differ from those having long-term employment paid over 5,000 FF. Women who are economically inactive are not more likely to be living independently than long-term employed women with a high income. Thus, income level is a significant dimension for explaining young people's living arrangements in France. It especially helps to distinguish different groups of long-term employees, which in the model without income are treated as a homogeneous group. This problem does not exist for the group of short-term employees since, compared to a long-term job paid over 5,000 FF, short-term employment always decreases men's and women's likelihood of living outside of the parental home, even if the pay is over 5,000 FF. This means that income stability is very important.

The strongest negative net effects are found for young people with a short-term job or searching for a first job and having an income of 5,000 FF or less. Full-time students with no income or with a low income also have the lowest probability of social independence compared to part-time students with an income over 5,000 FF. Yet in the case of students the net effect of some educational levels and of some social origin categories exerts similar strong effects. As before, these findings cannot confirm the **market-income hypothesis** for French young people the labour market, since having a low paid short-term employment supports social independence less than being unemployed, in particular if receiving more than 5,000 FF. For students too, market income is not the most determinant feature with respect to the strength of the influence of other variables, as for instance having a low educational level or being of petty bourgeoisie origin.

How far do these new models with ACTIVINC change the effects of all other variables? Compared to the female model without information on income, social origin, and education, effects disappear completely in the model of female non-students with income, which means that income (from market and/or spouse), income stability, and age are the only significant variables at the individual level. The inclusion of income in the male non-student model hardly alters the effects of the other variables, with two exceptions. A negative effect of being from a farming background appears and the effect of having a non-skilled father becomes statistically insignificant. Thus, for men, access to long-term employment, an income over 5,000 FF, and being from the service class or petty bourgeoisie origin are the best conditions for social independence.

Female students show very similar effects in the model with and without income, while male students show fewer social origin effects once information of income is included in the model. The positive agricultural workers' origin and the negative skilled workers' origin disappears. All in all, various social origin effects remain for both genders of students; in particular the positive petty bourgeoisie effects persist.

Thus, it can be stated that activity is quite a good proxy for income level and income stability, at least in the French case. Nonetheless, data on income provide a greater predictive power and help to discover heterogeneity within the group of long-term employees.

Conclusion: Labour Market Difficulties Affect More Spaniards than French

The socio-economic model has proven to have some explanative power, for it explains 12 to 29% of the observed variation. It performs equally well for Spain and France, but it always explains men's behaviour better than women's behaviour. Contrary to the theoretical assumption in Chapter 3, it explains students' chances of social independence better than non-students' behaviour. This does not change when income information of the young person is introduced into the model, as was done for France. This variation between students and non-students might mean two things: First, if one assumes that the relevant socio-economic variables are all included in the model, then it might mean that preferences play a larger role in non-students' decision to leave home than in students' decisions. Second, it might mean that the theoretical model of non-students has not been operationalised adequately. The non-students' leaving home process follows an individual strategy less frequently than the students' leaving home process, since non-students follow a "couple" strategy more often.

This fact is taken into account in the theoretical model but, due to technical problems, not in its empirical application. This means that, for the study of young people out of education, data which permit a better operationalisation of the theoretical model are needed. Ideally we would need as much information on the partner of the individual, in stable and non-stable partnerships, as on the individual herself. For future development it would also be better to include not only income stability and income level in the theoretical equation but also time spent in employment. This fact seems especially important in Spain because saving for a dwelling while staying in the parental home is a widely diffused strategy.

The comparative logistic regression models lead to three general conclusions and some more specific results.

1. It was shown that people with many personal resources and from a privileged social class background do not behave similarly in both countries, which means that composition effects cannot help to explain away cross-national differences. The likelihood of Spanish "privileged" people being socially independent is always low compared to their French counterparts. This points to the limits of the socio-economic model as operationalised in this analysis.
2. The findings support the **pluralisation hypothesis** for France and falsify it for Spain, i.e. young people in France show a more diversified pattern of setting up an independent household and social independence is less related to men's position on the labour market.
3. Having a stable market income is an important characteristic for increasing Spanish young men's chances of living independently, but the **market-income hypothesis** is falsified for young French men and for women in both countries.

French male students' probability of living independently is the highest for those having a job, having higher educational levels, and for those of agricultural worker, petty bourgeoisie, and service class origin. French female students show similar patterns; yet in contrast to men, being between 25 and 29 years old increases their probability of being outside of the parental home net of all other effects. French students' chances of social independence very much depend on their own resources and on the resources of their parents. These chances might also be closely related to the need of migration to university towns. Spanish students seldom leave the parental home and leaving is only favoured in the case of having personal resources and of having reached at least age 25. The redistribution of public and private resources towards students depends a lot on age in

Spain and not much on social class, while the contrary is true for French students. This means that in France we find a stronger **social class cleavage**, while in Spain the **age cleavage** is more pronounced. The fact that Spanish students' nest-leaving does not depend on their parents' resources suggests that there are social norms connecting enrolment in education with social dependence.

Spanish men not enrolled in education are the most likely to live independently if they have a stable market income, are at least age 25, have many siblings, a low educational level, and do not come from a farmer or non-skilled worker background. Complementary to this male pattern, a Spanish female non-student is most likely to live outside of the parental home if she is economically inactive or unemployed, aged 25 or more, has a low educational level, has many siblings, and her father was economically inactive when she was 16. Thus, for Spaniards out of the formal education system the **stability hypothesis**, the **low-quality-of-life hypothesis,**[13] the **low-expectation and early school-to-work transition hypothesis** and the **age-cleavage hypothesis** could be confirmed.

Patterns of their French counterparts falsify the **low-quality-of-life** and the **low-expectation and early school-to-work transition hypothesis**. The highest male probability of living independently corresponds to men with long-term employment, aged over 24, and from petty bourgeoisie or service class background. French women are the most likely to be living outside of the parental home if they are economically inactive or have long-term employment, are aged 25 to 29, have tertiary qualifications, and come from the petty bourgeoisie or from the service class.

Cross-national French-Spanish differences in the rate of young people living out of the parental home can be related to four differences:

1. French university students leave home much more frequently than Spanish students and some facts indicate that this is related to higher geographical mobility in France and to lower access of Spanish university students to economic resources.
2. Spanish men out of education find many more barriers for leaving home than their French counterparts, because of the various difficulties they encounter to find employment and in particular a long-term job in the Spanish labour market and their higher dependence on a market income.
3. French women depend less on a spouse's income in order to live independently and this is surely related to their higher chances of finding long-term employment earlier than Spanish women.
4. Spanish people leave home mostly to form a new family and only after having stabilised at least one income, whereas French young people

also leave home for studying and cohabitation and they depend less on a stable market income.

It is not possible to show here that Spanish young people having access to public benefits are more likely to live independently than those who only depend on the market or on the family. Partly because the survey provides no information on transfer income, but partly also because a whole range of public benefits do not exist for Spanish young people or are of a very limited significance, such as housing allowances, access to social housing, access to publicly subsidised residence halls and means-tested unemployment benefits. Instead, it is possible to test the importance of income diversification for young people's living arrangements in France.

Public Benefits And Market Income Help Young People Leaving Home in France

In this section the dependence-diversification hypothesis will be formulated and tested at the individual level. To confirm the dependence-diversification hypothesis at the individual level one would expect that people who have two income sources are more likely to leave home than those who have only one income source and that those who have three income sources are even more likely to live independently than those with one source. Within these differences market income will be superior to public income and the latter superior to family transfers, so that it is, for instance, more useful to receive market and public income than family transfers and public benefits. Thus, the best conditions for leaving home would be to combine market income, with public benefits and family help, the next best combination market income and public benefits, then market income and family help, followed by public benefits and family help and at last to rely only on market income. To have only family support or only public benefits should be worse for predicting social independence than to rely only on market income.

Many young French people go to a residence hall when they first leave home. Without the offer of residence halls they probably would not have left the parental home, or if they had then they would have needed parental financial help through money transfer or supply of accommodation. In Chapter 7 the importance of grants and public housing benefits for French students is discussed. Are these public benefits relevant for French students leaving home or are market income and family help more important?

Testing of the **dependence-diversification hypothesis** for non-students is more complicated than for students, because of the wide range of public benefits they can be entitled to - unemployment benefits, regulated employment measures or housing benefits - and because the effect of some of these measures on leaving home is not easy to establish, for instance, the effect of employment measures. In Chapter 8 the impact of employment measures on young people's financial autonomy and in consequence on their choice to leave home is discussed. Employment measures rarely guarantee financial autonomy but they seem to increase the pace of young people's attainment of a stable job, i.e. they open the door to financial autonomy after the measure. Besides this substantive difficulty, the retrospective part of the French survey does not provide detailed information about the types of employment measures a person had benefited from, but mixes short-term unregulated jobs with short-term regulated jobs.[14] The influence of unemployment and housing benefits for the unemployed can be studied more easily and, as shown in Chapter 8 and 9, both types of benefit, together, frequently amount to a subsistence level income, in particular for the unemployed people who had previously had a job. In addition, the comparative logistic regressions have shown important cross-national differences in unemployed people's probability of living independently. Thus, the test for non-students will concentrate on the effects of receiving versus not receiving public unemployment or housing benefits and will ignore the role of regulated employment.

The French survey permits a test of the dependency-diversification hypothesis at the individual level. The theoretical individual-level model presented above has to be changed to permit the test. The model above was:

$$(3)\ ST_{indep} = \underbrace{(I_{own} + I_{partner} - EXP_{indep} + NQUAL_{indep})}_{\text{economic factors/constraints}} + \underbrace{(SN_1 + SN_2 + SN_3)}_{\text{cultural preferences}}$$

The new model is summarised by:

$$(8)\ ST_{indep} = \underbrace{(I_{market} + I_{allowances} + I_{partner} + I_{par} - EXP_{indep} + BEN_{kind} + NQUAL_{indep})}_{\text{economic factors/constraints}} + \underbrace{(SN_1 ..)}_{\text{cultural pref.}}$$

where income is split into income from work on the market (I_{market}) and into income coming from social security or the state, such as housing allowances, unemployment allowances, grants, and minimum income transfers ($I_{allowances}$). Public benefits in kind (BEN_{kind}), such as residence halls or social housing, have to be subtracted from the expenditures of living independently. Benefits coming from parents have been added as well (I_{par}).

Translated in logistic regression language the equation becomes:

(9) $Prob_{leaving}=I_{market}+I_{allowances}+I_{partner}+I_{par}+BEN_{kind}+EDU+CLASS+PART$

Information on the expenditure of living independently and on the existence of a partner have to be omitted in the regression model, since these variables exist only for those who have left. We do not know either the expectations about expenditure in an independent dwelling of those living with their parents or the existence of a partner. As in previous models, information on education and social origin have been introduced into the statistical model.

Allowances in the case of non-students can be unemployment allowance, "indemnité de licenciement", minimum income (*RMI*), family, and/or housing allowances. The benefits in kind are "to have left home in order to go to live in a residence hall for young workers" at the time of first leaving or "to live in a social dwelling" in 1992. There is also information on income coming from a partner and from father and/or mother. Instead of activity situation the existence or non-existence of market income will be used. Grants, minimum income, family/housing allowances, and market income are relevant in the case of students, as well as the partner's and parents' contributions. As for benefits in kind, it is possible to know if the young person left home in order to live in a residence hall for students or if the individual lives in a social dwelling.

The survey does not provide information on the amount of each income type, but only on the total amount of income. Since, in this section the interest lies in the diversification of income and not in the amount of each benefit, this is not a problem. The information refers to the income of the month previous to the interview. Information on the use of residence halls refers to the moment of first leaving home in order to avoid the problem of the under-representation of people in residence halls and to avoid an over-determination of living arrangement because of the fact that all young people in residence hall are by definition outside of the parental home. The variable was created taking 7 possible situations into account (DIVERS):

1. only market income in 1992 and never lived in state-subsidised dwelling;
2. no market income or family help, but only public benefits or lives in a social dwelling in 1992 or lived in a residence hall when left home the first time;
3. only family transfers or living in a dwelling paid by the parents in 1992 and never lived in a residence hall;
4. market income and public allowances, or market income and lives in a social dwelling in 1992 or had left for a residence hall in the past;

5. market and family transfers of any type (also payment of dwelling), the latter including support from parents and partner in 1992,
6. family help in1992, and public transfers in 1992 or residence hall when left home,
7. market income, public allowances or benefits in kind and family transfers in 1992 or when left home.

Figure 5.10 reveals the diversification of young people's income sources. Most students receive some income from the family and from the state and the next most common situation is to receive income from the market and the family. All other combinations oscillate somewhere under 9 per cent. There are very small differences between the two genders. Young people in the labour market show a more diversified distribution of income sources. The most common income combination is to receive income from the market and the family, followed by the combination of market, state, and family, and by the combination of market and family and market alone. In this case we find significant gender differences, since women more frequently than men receive only family help or state and family transfers and they are less likely to combine market and family income or to receive only market income.

Figure 5.10 Diversification of Income Sources, Youth (aged 20-29), France 1992

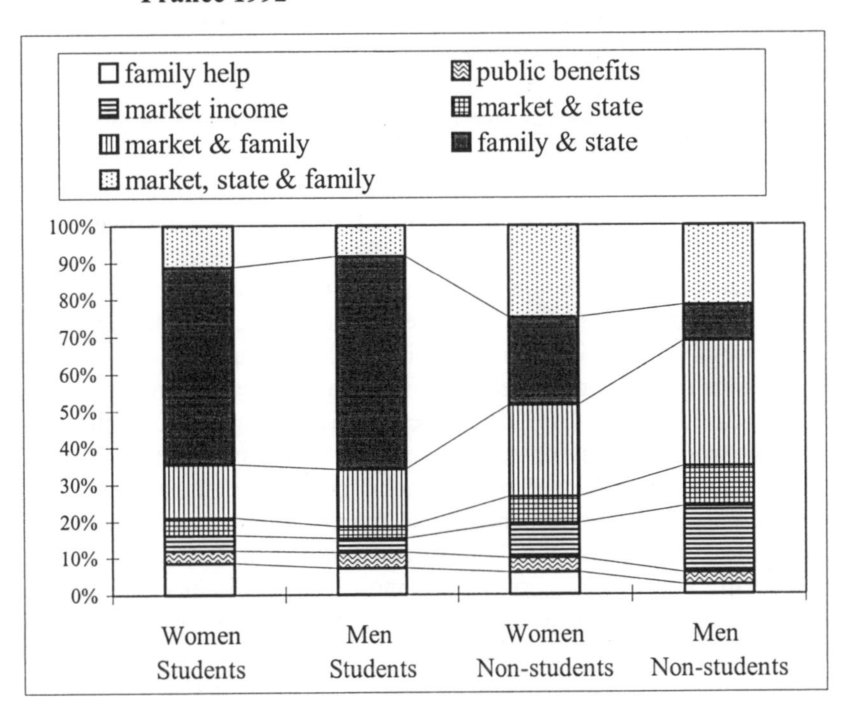

Source: author's elaboration with Franceall and with DIVERS.

In Chapter 8 we will show that financial independence through market income is reached on the average between the ages 25 and 29 in France. An analysis of the *Enquête Jeunes 1992* in order to comprehend the process of financial independence shows very clearly the important role of transfer payments in comparison to market income and to family help in the process of becoming financially independent (Caussat 1995). At age 18 only 7 per cent of the young people receive a market income, while 10 per cent receive a grant and insignificantly few receive payments from their parents. At age 23 around 15 per cent of the young people receive financial help from their parents and the same percentage receives a family or housing allowance, half of these young people obtain a market income, nearly 4 per cent receive financial help from other relatives, and 7 per cent receive an unemployment allowance. Then, at age 29 around 65 per cent obtain an income from their occupation, almost nobody receives help from their parents and only 3 per cent are helped by other relatives. Instead, 30 per cent obtain family or housing allowances, 8 per cent receive an unemployment allowance, and 2 per cent receive a RMI allowance. Market and transfer payments play a dominant role in order to allow many young adults to be financially autonomous. According to an income survey of 1990, six out of ten households, where the household head is under 30, receive more than half of their income from the state (Caussat 1995).

The presentation of the results of these new models will focus on the role of the diversification variable (DIVERS), since the effects of the other variables are mainly the same as in the models with the variable activity presented previously, as can be seen from the results of Tables 5 to 8 in the Appendix. The reference category for all models is to receive mainly market income.

Women out of education display behavioural patterns nearest to the theoretical assumptions, but they are not totally concordant with the dependence-diversification hypothesis. All situations of income combinations that are not "receives mainly market income" increase young women's likelihood to live independently. The highest probabilities are shown by women receiving family help, followed by those with market income, public benefits and family help, next come those with public benefits, those with public benefits and market income, and finally those with public benefits and family help and those with market income and family help. This model shows once more the importance of resources coming from the spouse/partner or the parents for women's social independence. In addition, it shows that a high diversification of income sources increases the likelihood of living outside of the parental home more than any other combination. Market income as the sole income source does not favour women's social independence; rather public benefits as exclusive income source do favour it. This confirms the **dependence-diversification hypothesis** partially in its dimension of diversification but not in the assumption that market income would be the most important income source. If a variable measuring the existence of a spouse/partner is introduced into the logistic regression model in order to control for the fact that many women follow a dependent household formation, different results are obtained.[15] In this case the combination of market and state income is the only value exerting a positive effect, while combinations of market and family, state and family, and market, family, and state become negatively linked to the likelihood of social independence. This shows that the only combination that favours all women's living outside of the parental home independently of their household formation strategy is the combination of market and public transfers.

In the case of male non-students, three combinations of income out of seven have a significant effect on the probability of living independently. The best situation is to receive transfers from the market and from the state, followed by the combination of market income, public benefits, and family support. The worst case is to rely only on the family and the state. To receive public benefits exclusively, family help exclusively, or to combine market income and family help do not statistically differ from living mainly from market income. The first two situations are rarely found among French men. Interestingly, the combination of public benefits and family help decreases the chances of social independence. Thus, men need a market income in order to have a high probability of living independently and if, in addition, they receive public benefits then they increase their chance of social independence considerably. Nearly all deductions from the **dependence-diversification hypothesis** are confirmed in the case of men on the labour market.

Female students show very simple patterns, since only one combination of income increases their probability of living independently compared to the situation of receiving mainly market income. As in the case of men, the best situation is to receive market and public transfers, while the worst is to rely on the family and the state only. To perform some activity on the market and to have access to state benefits or to depend mainly on market income were basic conditions to be fulfilled by female students who wanted to leave home between 1986 and 1992. Diversification of income alone is not sufficient; it is only positive if it happens to people with some market income.

Male students' likelihood to be living independently is favoured by market income, but the combination of market income with other transfers does not increase their chance of living outside of the parental home. In line with the prediction are the findings which show that receiving only public benefits or family help decreases men's chances of social independence compared to those who mainly depend on market income. As in the two previous cases, combining state and family transfers is negatively related to living independently. These findings do not mean that to receive some additional help from the state while working does not help to leave home; it only means that compared to having a market income it does not increase the chances of living independently. It is as helpful for social independence to combine market and public transfers as to live mainly from market income. Thus, the **dependence-diversification hypothesis** can only be confirmed in its negative predictions and the market income dimension, but not in its predictions about a positive link between general income diversification and social independence.

To conclude the test of the dependence-diversification hypothesis, we can state that the predictions of a negative link between receiving only public benefits or only family help and the likelihood of social independence is only confirmed for men in the labour market. The deductions about the positive influence of combining market income with public benefits or market income with family benefits or all three things together are confirmed for women in the labour market and partly for men in the labour market and women enrolled in education. The finding that a combination of family and public transfers decreases the chances of living independently in all cases except women in the labour market contradicts the previsions. The idea that the best condition for social independence is to combine market, state transfers, and family transfers is only confirmed for young people on the labour market.

Public benefits in combination with market income increase the chances of social independence of all young people except male students. In the latter case this combination appears to be as favourable as complete reliance on market income. Thus, the crucial role of public policies for living independently in France has been confirmed for all young people except male students. A corrected version of the dependence-diversification hypothesis at the individual level would be: The combination of market income and public benefits facilitates social independence more or at least as much as relying mainly on a market income. On the other hand, family help alone or in combination with market income never increases the young person's chance of social independence. This last finding is very important, since it shows that only the relatively strong division of labour between the French state and the parents with respect to the tasks of helping young people on their way to adulthood increase all young people's chances of social independence.

Test of High Property-Low Affordability Hypothesis

The price level of rents, housing ownership and mortgages is a major element in explaining different degrees of housing affordability for varying social groups and geographical areas. This idea, which forms the second part of the high property-low affordability hypothesis will be tested with a multi-level model including regional contexts in chapter 6. In this section only the first part of the hypothesis, the high property-delayed leaving statement and its individual level implications will be analysed, since it is more closely related to housing policy. The micro-level hypothesis states that young people who acquire a dwelling are more likely to have accumulated savings and to have a family formation project than those who rent a dwelling. The latter tend to have less defined personal projects, they only need to pay a monthly rent, and thus they are less tied by long-term decisions. Consequently, young single or cohabiting people will be more likely to rent a dwelling than married people, and the youngest young people will be found in owned dwellings less frequently.

These relationships are tested with a logistic regression which predicts the likelihood of a young person living independently in 1992 to have an owned dwelling in contrast to a rented or given accommodation. The samples are formed by all young people who in 1985/86 were living in the parental home and in 1991/92 were socially independent. The same logistic regression model was performed for France and Spain, where the logit of living in a rented dwelling in 1991/92 against living in dwelling that is owned property was estimated. As in the previous models, the young person's own resources, those of the parents, age, and regional and rural-urban context are assumed to influence the individual's choice of the type of dwelling. In addition, the type of living arrangement of those living independently is assumed to be related to the choice of housing tenure.

(10) logit (DWELL91/92)=α+β_1(ACTIVEST)+β_2(FACLASS)-β_3(SIBL)+ β_4(EDUC)+β_5(AGE)+β_6(LIVARR)+ β_7(RURURBAN)+β_8(REGION)

The results are in line with the **high property hypothesis**, because it was found that cohabiting couples and individuals in one-person households are more likely to rent than to own a dwelling and younger people live more frequently in rented dwellings than their older counterparts.[16] The age-effect is very similar in both countries, but the effect of cohabiting is somewhat larger in Spain than in France. In France individuals in one-person households are the most likely to rent a dwelling compared to married people, more than cohabiting and flat sharing people. By contrast, in Spain there is a decreasing linear relationship between living arrangement and type of dwelling. The highest probability of renting is found for cohabiting young people, next come those in one-person households and last those sharing a flat with peers. In any case, renting a dwelling is more strongly related to leaving home for destinations of informal family formation and for nonfamily formation living arrangements in both countries. This confirms the idea that renting a dwelling is less cost-intensive and more adequate for uncertain and transitory life cycle moments such as youth. The fact that in Spain short-term employees tend also to rent more frequently than those with a long-term job do, gives further support to this idea. In France most young people who live independently live in a rented dwelling, that is, in a more youth-adequate dwelling, whereas young people in Spain live more often in an owned dwelling, which is more adequate for the status of adulthood.

Some country-specific effects were found. In Spain there are many social class effects, since most social classes are less likely to rent a dwelling than those young people coming from the service class. Young people from the classes of the petty bourgeoisie, of farmers, of skilled workers, and of non-skilled workers rent a dwelling less frequently than those of the service class. There are also great regional differences, which will be presented later on. In France differences according to the size of the municipality where the young people lived in 1992 emerge. Compared to living in a town over 100,000 inhabitants, those living in municipalities from 20,000 to 100,000 inhabitants are more likely to rent, while those living in municipalities smaller than 5,000 inhabitants are less likely to rent a dwelling.

To conclude, the high rate of young people living in a rented dwelling in France favours early nest-leaving in this country. Since housing policy regulates prices, vacancy rates, and tenure structure of housing markets to a more or less extensive degree, an analysis of the mechanisms through which this regulation is attained will help to understand the cross-national differences in young people's living arrangements. This is the aim of Chapter 9.

Notes

[1] This presentation refers to the figures of the detailed result Tables 1 to 4 in the Appendix.

[2] A reference category is characterised by the fact that it has the value 0, which means that the logit(IND91/92) = $\alpha + \beta_1(0) + \beta_2(0) + \beta_3(0) + .. + \beta_7(0)$. Thus, the transformation of the logit into a probability for a person with the characteristics of the 7 omitted categories is: Prob(IND91/92)=$(e^{\alpha})/(1+e^{\alpha})$ (Menard 1995).

[3] Independence rates and the difference between these and the probability of the reference category are taken from Tables 1 to 4 in theAppendix.

[4] This is due to the fact that having a spouse/partner means two things at once: the fact of being socially independent and the fact of potentially having access to the partner's resources.

[5] In some cases it was necessary to check if the cross-national differences between the coefficients are significant. This has been done by merging the Spanish and French samples into one, by introducing a new variable indicating the person's country and by introducing interaction terms. In this case, an interaction between activty and country was included in the merged sample, in addition to the list of variables of the county model and to the country dummy. If the coefficients of the interaction term are significant, it means that the cross-national differences between the coefficients, as shown by the illustrative figures, are statistically significant. The detailed results are not further presented.

[6] The interpretation of this section is mainly based on Tables 1 and 2 inthe Appendix, since it was not worth illustrating all results with figures.

[7] It has to be noticed that part-time students are those people who in both questionnaires first answered that they were employed and then said that they combined their jobs with studies. Thus, these are people who perceive themselves first of all as employed and then as students. They might display other characteristics than people who consider themselves first of all as students and only sporadically combine this main activity with some jobs.

[8] Differences are statistically significant.

[9] The difference between the Spanish and French coefficients as revealed in Figure 5.4 is not statistically significant.

[10] The models control for age, social origin, number of siblings, size of municipality and region. The detailed results are not presented.

[11] Detailed results can be found in appendix, table 5 to 8.

[12] There are some exceptions, namely economically inactive men, self-employed women, and female and male family helps, but the first three categories were not significant in either comparative model.

[13] Only if one takes SIBL as indicator of parents' resources.

[14] Furthermore, there is regional variation in the number of people enroled in some employment measures, but there is very little regional variation in the likelihood of social independence in the logistic regression for French young non-student men. In the female model some more variation is found, but only four regions out of 22 show a significant effect on young female non-students' likelihood to leave home (cf. Chapter 6).

[15] The inclusion of a variable measuring the existence of a partnership overdetermines the model, because of the strong correlation between social independence and partnership formation. Yet, if one is not interested in the overall fit but only in the interaction between partnership and income diversification, then it reveals that the effects of the variable DIVERS change when partnership is controlled for. The detailed results are not presented.

[16] Detailed results are shown in Table 9 in the Appendix.

6 Bringing Regional Contexts In

At this stage it is important to have a closer look at possible contextual effects on leaving home. Ideally, these context effects would have also been studied through a cross-national comparison with many countries. This would have allowed for a test of the role of social policies in explaining the differences between Spain and France. This cannot be the scope of this work and, therefore, the role of social policies, of housing markets, and of social norms that operate at national level can only be considered in a descriptive way. A regional analysis was chosen for two reasons. First, because in Spain we find many regional variations in leaving home patterns (Jurado Guerrero 1997). Second, given the small-n problem of a two-country study, a regional comparison was chosen to study the role of context effects such as social norms and housing conditions on social independence, since they cannot be studied at the individual level with the given data.

Not only the regional context is taken into account but also the rural-urban context differences. A variable that measures the size of the place of residence in 1991/92 of each individual controls for the latter context differences. This variable will help to control for differences in living arrangement patterns in rural and urban contexts. The effect of the size of the young person's place of residence can go in two divergent directions (cf. chapter 3). First, it can be imagined that in regions with a high degree of middle-sized towns, rates of two-generation households will be low, because of more favourable housing markets. Second, areas with a high presence of rural municipalities will show a high occurrence of two-generation households due to more traditional social norms.

Regional differences in staying home rates can be due to composition effects, for instance, if in a region a social class whose children tend to leave home early is over-represented. Composition effects concerning social class of origin, activity situation, educational participation and age distribution will be analysed in the regional models, since the logistic regression with regions also includes these other variables measured at the individual level. If after the control of social origin, activity situation, educational level, and the other individual-level variables, regional differences in leaving home persist, it can mean two things. First, that regional effects are due to composition effects of individual characteristics not included in the model; for example, income. Second, it might mean that there are context effects on the probability of leaving home which are not due to composition effects of individual-level factors. These context effects have to be interpreted as specific dominant social norms, which prescribe socially non-deviant behaviour, or as a particular framework of socio-economic constraints which influence the individual's preferences, or in other words, the actor's view about which aims are worth following because they are likely to be attained. An example of the first case would be regional norms on patrilocal or neolocal family formation. The second case would be regions with very difficult youth labour markets, where young people are aware of the limited possibilities they have to find a long-term job and thus adapt their expectations to the circumstances.

In the regional quantitative models those context effects which show important regional variation will be analysed: housing markets, labour markets, and family norms. In some cases it would be better to take local instead of regional contexts as the units of analysis, but this would require very detailed and mostly unavailable data. It is possible to find provincial census data on most labour market indicators and on some family patterns, but provincial data on prices of dwellings are not reliable, since existing survey data is not representative at the provincial level. Thus, it was decided to take regions as units of analysis, but we have to be aware of the fact that within a region, within a province, and even within a town, if it is a large one, context differences may exist. In addition, to assess the extent of within-region differences in the likelihood of living independently, provincial differences are described.

The first models interpreted here are the same as those whose individual level results were presented in Chapter 5:

$$(7)\ \text{logit}\ (\text{IND91/92}) = \alpha + \beta_1(\text{ACTIVEST}) + \beta_2(\text{FACLASS}) - \beta_3(\text{SIBL}) + \beta_4(\text{EDUC}) + \beta_5(\text{AGE}) + \beta_6(\text{RURURBAN}) + \beta_7(\text{REGION})$$

Stepwise introduction of the context variables allows the observation of their effects with and without control of individual level variables, and thus permits the observation of composition effects. The next sections are organised as follows. First, bivariate relations between living arrangement and region of residence are presented in the form of cross-tabulations in order to present regional maps of living arrangements. Second, the results of the logistic regression analyses with respect to the effect of living in a given region for the probability of living independently are presented. Third, the Spanish regional differences are analysed more deeply in order to compare the role of housing, labour markets, and family norms. New multi-level models are used for this scope.

Regional Variations in Leaving Home in Spain and France

First, some remarks on data problems have to be made. In the Spanish sample, information on the region of residence is introduced as an external variable; this means it is not information provided by the individual, but it refers to the person's official registration in the 1991 census. If in the time between the census survey and the sociodemographic survey somebody changed her residence due to a regional migration, this individual appears to be living in the old place. In addition, young people registered as living with their parents, despite their real residence outside of the parental home, appear to live in the parents' region. In the French sample regional information is provided in two ways: first, it is part of the labour force survey and then it is also provided by the retrospective part of the *Enquête Jeune*. For comparative reasons it was decided to use the information from the labour force survey, thus using information for the moment of the interview.

The Spanish data problems affect students more than non-students, since the former live more frequently in residence halls or in non-registered informal living arrangements. The regional context has a very limited net effect on living outside of the parental home in the models of Spanish students, probably also due to these technical problems. These problems and the non significance of region for student's likelihood to live independently prompted the decision not to pursue a very detailed regional analysis of students' living arrangements by regions, but instead to merely present the regional differences as they appear using our limited survey data.

In this section the first step of the analysis is carried out, while the results of the multivariate analyses are discussed separately for France and Spain in the subsequent parts. Regional staying home rates for young people in Spain and France are presented in subsamples according to gender and activity situation.[1] The standard deviation is the measure chosen to compare the importance of regional differences in both countries.

French male students show regional rates of living in their parents' home (*staying home rates*) which range from 22 to 86 per cent and which display a standard deviation of 18. If one takes 5 per cent over and under the average of 58.4 per cent as cutting points, ten regions appear under this cutting point and six above of it. Champagne-Ardennes, Haute-Normandie, Bourgogne, Alsace, Franche-Comté, Bretagne, Aquitaine, Midi-Pyrénées, Limousin, and Languedoc-Roussillon all have low rates of young people living at home, while Ile-de France, Basse-Normandie, Picardie, Lorraine, Poitou-Charente, and Provence-Côte d'Azur display relatively high staying home rates for students. Later it is shown that most of these regional effects are the same if one performs a multivariate logistic regression with the individual data of the *France86* sample.

Figure 6.1 Students' Staying Home Rates in France by Region, 1992

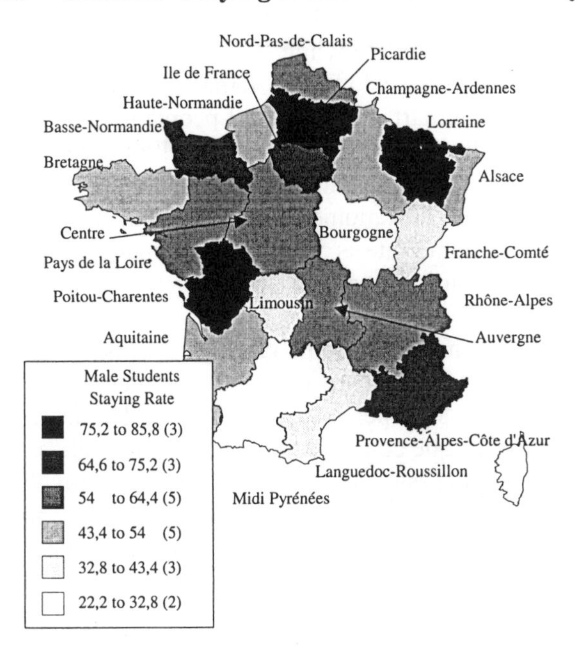

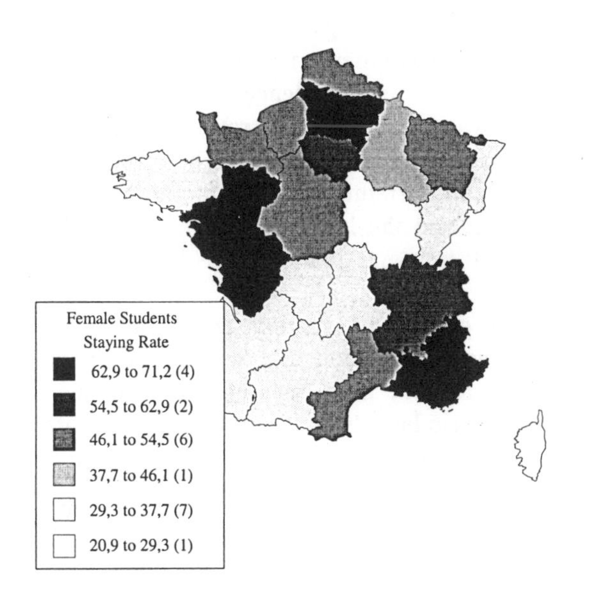

Source: own elaboration with *Franceall* and IND92.

Female students show similar regional patterns with some differences. Contrary to the male case, Haute-Normandie and Languedoc-Roussillon do not show low staying home rates, while Auvergne does. The remaining male low-staying regions also show low female rates. Female students have, like their male counterparts, high rates of people in the parental home in Ile-de France, Picardie, Poitou-Charente, and Provence-Côte d'Azur, and, unlike men, they show high rates in Pays-de la Loire and Rhône-Alpes, as well. The standard deviation of 14 is smaller than in the male case and the average staying home rate is 51.4 per cent, that is, lower than the male rate. In the multivariate analysis similar regional effects can be observed.

Regional differences in staying home rates for Spanish people enrolled in education are very low, 4 standard deviation for men and women and average rates of 90.9 and 89.5 per cent respectively. In the case of men only those living in the Basque country show a relatively high, as compared to the average, staying home rate and those in Aragon a relatively low rate. The latter occurs also in the case of women. The same results are obtained in the multivariate analyses for men and women enrolled in education.

For people in the labour market, regional differences in staying and independence rates are similar in Spain and France in terms of standard deviation. In Spain women and men show a standard deviation of 5.8 and 5 respectively and in France for women and men it is 6.1 and 6.2 respectively. The average female staying home rate in Spain is 56.2 per cent and 21.4 for their French counterparts. For men the Spanish rate amounts to 71.8 and the French independence rate 37.8 per cent. The Spanish region with the lowest staying home rate, the Balearic Islands, displays a rate, which is still higher than the highest regional rates in France, Nord-Pas de Calais and Lorraine, since the former female and male rates are 45 and 64 per cent and the latter are 36 and 49 per cent. This means 9 and 15 per cent of cross-national distance for men and women respectively.

The Spanish regional picture of staying home rates also shows differences by gender (Figure 6.2). Men and women in Cantabria, the Basque Country, and Navarre have high rates compared to the average, while those living in the Balearic Islands, and Catalonia have relatively low rates. Yet men also show relatively low rates in Andalusia and Valencia, and high rates in Asturias and Castile-Leon. In the multivariate models men and women show more regional effects than in this bivariate description.

Figure 6.2 Non-Students' Staying Home Rates in Spain, 1991

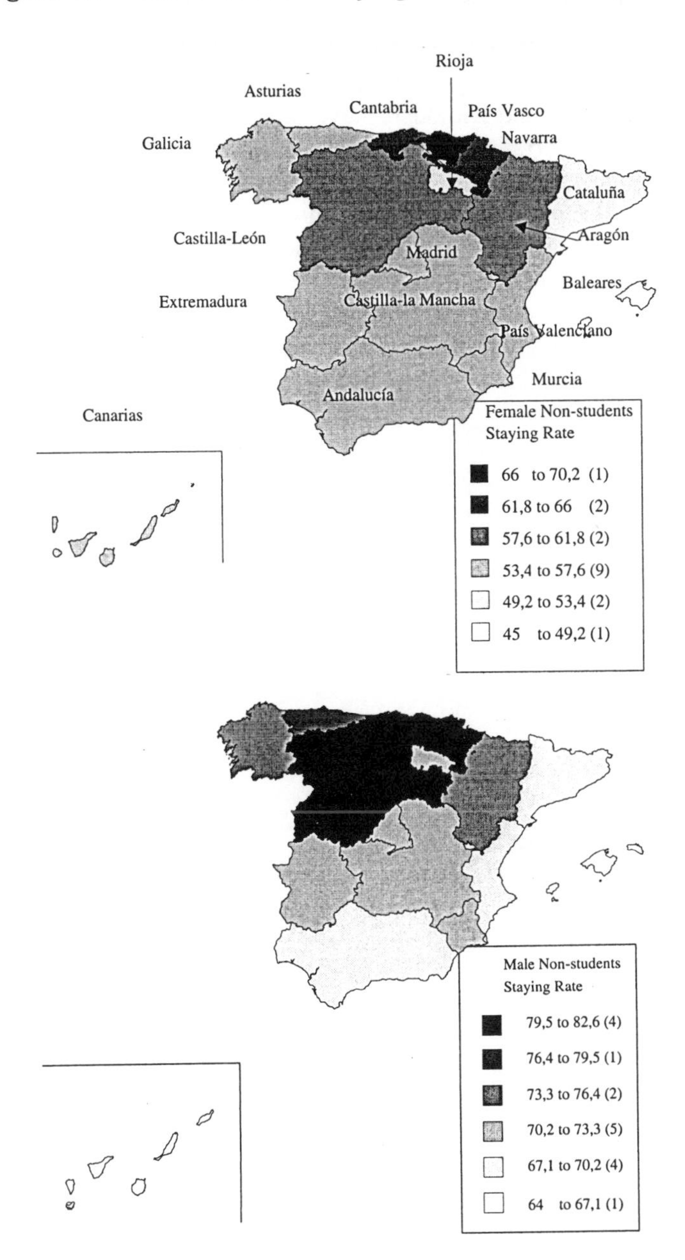

Source: own elaboration with *Spainall* and IND91.

The French picture is more complicated, since more regions differ from the average and more gender differences exist, as shown in Figure 6.3. Men and women in Bourgogne and Bretagne display relatively low staying home rates, while nearly all high rates differ by gender. Men in Centre, Pays de la Loire and Limousin have relatively low staying home rates and high ones in Lorraine, Champagne-Ardennes, Picardie, Nord-Pas de Calais, Aquitaine and Franche-Comté. Women in Haute-Normandie, Basse-Normandie, Bretagne, Pays de la Loire, Bourgogne, Alsace, and Franche-Comté have low rates, while they show high rates in Lorraine, Aquitaine and Languedoc-Rousillon. Later we will show how nearly all male regional differences disappear in the logistic regression analysis and differences for women diminish, which means that many regional differences are not statistically significant or are composition effects of individual variables.

Figure 6.3 Non-Students' Staying Home Rates in France, 1992

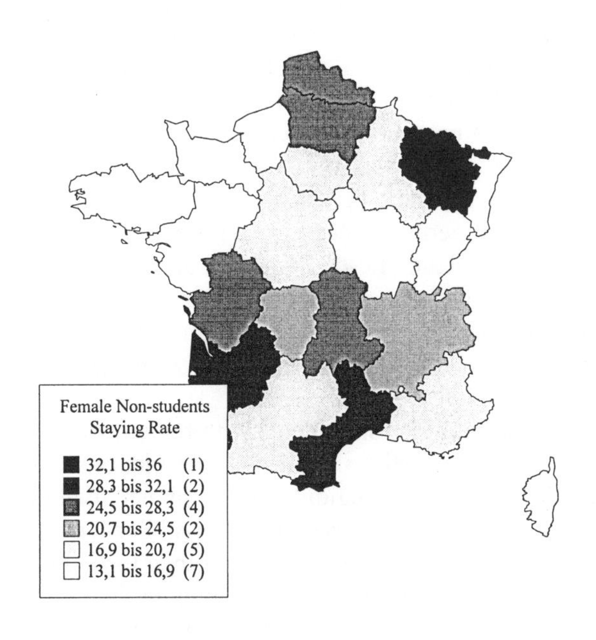

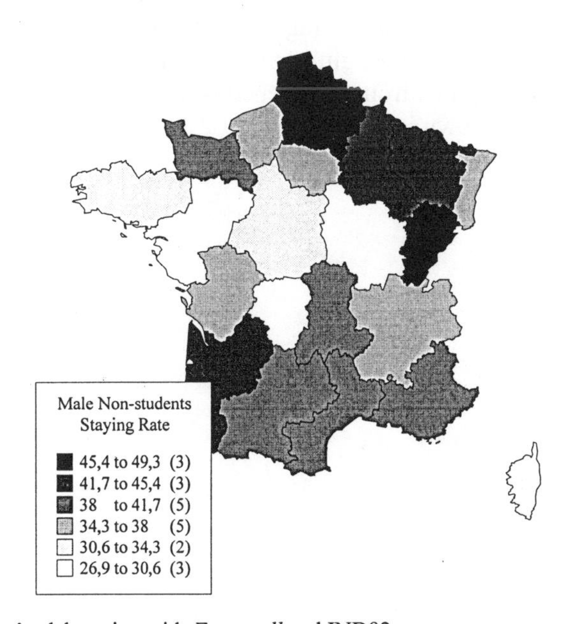

Source: author's elaboration with *Franceall* and IND92.

Regional Differences in France

Does the region of residence still have an influence on the living arrangement of young people if it is controlled for size of municipality and for other independent variables? Ile-de France, the region which includes the agglomeration of Paris, was taken as the regional reference category. This choice is justified because in the case of young people on the labour market this region displays rates of independence similar to the average rate, its characteristics are more accessible to the reader than those of other regions, and because it permits a comparison with the region of Madrid in Spain. In the case of students, Ile-de France displays relatively low rates of independence, which permits a clear analysis of those regions which facilitate living outside of the parental home. In addition it clearly highlights the importance of French centralisation in the university system (cf. chapter 4).

The multivariate analysis for students with region, size of municipality and all individual characteristics included in the model shows that young male students in 10 out of 21 regions have a higher likelihood of living independently than students in the region of Paris.[2] For female students one can observe 9 regions with a higher likelihood than those in Ile-de France. These effects are similar for men and women in five regions, namely Bourgogne, Languedoc-Roussillon, Alsace, Bretagne, Aquitaine and Midi-Pyrénées, while the remaining regional effects differ for men and women. A possible explanation for these regional effects could lie in students' migration out of the region of origin in order to enrol in a university outside the parents' region. Figures from the French Ministry of Education seem to support this idea, as shown in Table 6.1.

Table 6.1 Ranking of Export Rates of *Bacheliers* (1990) and Estimated Coefficients, 1992

rate of export		estimated coefficients men		women	
Picardie	25.9	**Bourgogne**	2.1619**	**Bourgogne**	3.1179**
Limousin	15.0	*Champagne-Ardennes*	1.7423**	Midi-Pyrénées	2.7611**
Franche-Comté	14.6	Basse-Normandie	1.6873**	**Languedoc-Roussillon**	2.7447**
Champagne-Ardennes	14.2	**Bretagne**	1.5994**	*Franche-Comté*	2.2215**
Poitou-Charente	13.1	*Auvergne*	1.5877**	*Limousin*	2.0741**
Bourgogne	12.4	**Alsace**	1.537**	**Bretagne**	1.7194**
Auvergne	11.9	*Centre*	1.2937**	**Alsace**	1.6382*
Centre	11.7	**Aquitaine**	1.1946**	Haute-Normandie	1.5137**
Languedoc-Roussillon	10.8	Midi-Pyrénées	1.0899*	**Aquitaine**	1.4732**
Provence-Côte d'Azur	10.4	Nord-Pas de Calais	1.0226**	Rhône-Alpes	0.8549**
Basse-Normandie	10.0	Lorraine	1.0179*	*Auvergne*	1.477
Rhône-Alpes	10.0	**Languedoc-Roussillon**	0.9408*	*Centre*	1.0144
Haute-Normandie	9.0	*Franche-Comté*	1.6267	*Champagne-Ardennes*	0.9087
Lorraine	8.3	*Limousin*	1.4387	Poitou-Charente	0.5682
Midi-Pyrénées	8.0	Haute-Normandie	0.4434	Nord-Pas de Calais	0.5083
Pays de la Loire	7.8	Rhône-Alpes	0.3827	Basse-Normandie	0.5079
Aquitaine	7.0	Poitou-Charente	0.1647	Pays de la Loire	0.4057
Bretagne	3.9	Picardie	-0.0454	Lorraine	-0.0079
Alsace	3.3	Provence-Côte d'Azur	-0.1102	Provence-Côte d'Azur	-0.0989
Nord-Pas de Calais	2.3	Pays de la Loire	-0.1862	Picardie	-0.1962
Ile-de-France	2.0	Ile-de-France	0	Ile-de-France	0
Metropole	8.0				

Notes: Bacheliers = people who obtained maturity certificate.
Sources: Ministère de l'Education Nationale 1994 and author's elaboration with *France86*.

The export rate is computed with the number of *bacheliers* of a given region who enrolled in a university of a different region divided by the total number of *bacheliers* of the region of origin.[3] It can be seen that most regions with high rates of export also show significant regional coefficients, be it in the male or in the female model. The exception of Picardie could be explained by the fact that this region is a neighbour region of Ile-de France and young people can probably live in the parental home despite of the fact that they go to a university in Paris. Female and male students in Alsace and Bretagne are more likely to live independently than in Paris, though they had low export rates of bacheliers in 1990. This cannot be due to rurality since the model controls for size of municipality and because people in small municipalities are less likely to live independently. As shown below, Bretagne and Alsace have a pushing-out-of-home effect also for young people on the labour market, in particular for women. There is some cultural or non-controlled socio-economic context factor in these regions which make young people, students and non-students, leave home at an early stage. The detailed explanation of students' patterns would require further analysis, which cannot be provided here.

The models for young people on the labour market have been run stepwise to allow for an analysis of composition effects. In fact composition effects and also contextual effects were found. The detailed results are shown in Table 10 in the Appendix.

1. In the first model for men the size of residence was the only independent variable and it emerges that young men out of education who live in rural areas compared to towns over 100,000 inhabitants are less likely to be living independently (Model 1).
2. By contrast, the region of residence –as sole independent variable- shows one negative regional effect on the likelihood to live outside of the parental home for Nord-Pas de Calais (Model 2).
3. If these two context variables are included in a complete model (4) with individual-level variables, it can be observed that regional effects change. The regions Pays de la Loire and Bretagne become positively linked to living independently compared to the region Ile-de-France, and the effect of Nord-Pas de Calais disappears. How can this change of regional effects be explained?

The effect of Nord-Pas de Calais is due to a composition effect of activity situation and size of municipality as shown in Model 3. It is probably due to the difficult labour market situation in this region and its relatively high urbanisation.[4] It can be observed that in Model 3 three new positive effects appear, namely those of Auvergne, Bretagne and Pays de la

Loire. The last two correspond to the findings of Model 4, the complete model. The appearance of their effects has to be explained in terms of counteracting effects.[5] The simultaneous control of size of municipality and activity situation makes them become significant, because just these individual-level effects were cancelling each other out in Model 2. The disappearance of the effect of Auvergne in the full model is due to a composition effect caused by a combination of the effects of activity, size of municipality, region and age, most probably caused by the over-representation of young people of age 25 to 29 in Auvergne.[6] To sum up, only two positive net regional effects can be observed for French men on the labour market, while there is also a strong negative effect of rural areas on the probability of living outside of the parental home.

The situation for women in the labour market is similar. The detailed results are shown in Table 11 in the Appendix.

1. Unlike men, women are not affected by the size of the municipality, in which they live (Model 1).
2. Women living in Lorraine, Aquitaine, and Languedoc-Roussilon are less likely to live outside of the parental home than those in Ile-de-France if one looks only at the bivariate relationship (Model 2).
3. These bivariate results change importantly once one introduces region and size of municipality into a model with individual level characteristics in order to control for composition effects (Model 4). All negative effects disappear and we find, instead, four positive effects: Haute-Normandie, Alsace, Pays de la Loire, and Bretagne. Besides, a negative effect of the place of residence for young women in municipalities under 5,000 inhabitants emerges, too.

The explanation of this change is similar to the male case. The disappearance of the effects of Aquitaine and Languedoc-Roussilon are due to the combined composition effects of activity and size of municipality. Both effects also make the positive effect of Bretagne appear (cf. Model 3). Then in a model where one adds the variable education to Model 3, the effect of Lorraine becomes nearly statistically non significant and the effect of Pays de la Loire appears.[7] Nonetheless, it is only the complete combination of the variables of Model 4 which explains the final four positive regional effects of Haute-Normandie, Bretagne, Pays de la Loire, and Alsace. Women enrolled in education and living in Bretagne and Alsace are also more likely to live independently, as mentioned previously. Interestingly, the same logistic regression model for women out of education with the variable income diversification instead of activity makes all regional variables disappear (cf. Table 6 in the appendix). It might be argued that in the case of women the regional effects are, indeed, composition effects due to differences in income diversification of women in different regions. Thus, as in the male case, the female model displays small regional effects, which in addition are due to composition effects. For both genders the most important context effect is that of size of municipality.

All in all, it can be stated that regional effects are rather insignificant if one wants to explain living patterns of young people in the labour market in France, while they are more important for students. It was argued that the effects of region on students are to a great extent due to their emigration to universities outside their region of origin: many students leave for Paris to enrol in a university there. The relatively small regional effects, compared to Spain, of young French people in the labour market will not be further explored in theframework of this investigation. Instead, it seems interesting to discuss the general negative effect of rurality, which was found for all four groups of young people.

All French young people in very small municipalities are less likely to live independently than those in towns with over 100,000 inhabitants. These results suggest that young people in rural areas follow other social norms than those in larger municipalities, since the study controlled for many socio-economic differences. In addition, differences in housing markets seem to be relevant, as shown below.

In a very encompassing study of rural youth in France, conducted at the end of the 1980s (Galland/Lambert 1993), it was found that independently of social class young people in rural areas were more likely to have at most a secondary school certificate and less likely to have a tertiary educational certificate. In the same study they found that these young people had more difficulties in entering employment and hence had higher unemployment rates than urban young people, young women in particular were affected by high unemployment rates. Nevertheless, at the age of 25 most young people had attained their professional integration. Young people in rural areas and in this educational and employment context live in the parental home more frequently than their urban counterparts, but this is mainly due to the behaviour of the young men, since half of them still live with their parents at the age of 25 while only one third of their urban counterparts do so. In contrast to this, young women at age 25 mostly live with their husbands (65%), whereas in urban areas not even half of all women live with husbands (44%). These differences in living arrangements are not simply a composition effect of social class, since the authors found similar rural-urban differences for all social classes. Galland proposes three possible explanations for the specific rural way of life. First, he points to the role of more traditional cultural norms which might influence all social classes. Second, there is the specific rural housing market with its low offer of small dwellings and the predominance of large parental houses, which makes intergenerational co-residence easier. Third, it might be that young people who like to live independently emigrate to larger towns. With respect to the first hypothesis, a comparison of the preferences of young rural people with those of young *lycéens* (students of upper secondary school) of a small town in *Seine-Maritime* shows that young rural people prefer marriage over cohabitation, especially to a model of cohabitation as way of life and not only as trial-period before marrying.

The model used in Chapter 5, where the likelihood of renting a dwelling was estimated for those French young people living independently in 1992, also provides some interesting information. Young people in rural areas are less likely to rent a dwelling compared to those living in large towns, net of the effects of the type of living arrangement they have (cf. Table 9 in the Appendix). This supports Galland's and Lambert's idea about the existence of specific rural housing markets. It also means that higher housing costs in large towns do not prevent young people from living more frequently outside of the parental home compared to their counterparts in rural areas.

Regional And Provincial Differences in Spain

In the Spanish case I proceed as with the French data, but different results emerge. The regional reference category is Madrid, which in every subgroup display average independence rates. As in France the reference category for size of municipality is towns of over 100,000 inhabitants.

First of all, Spanish students show little regional and rural-urban variation in their likelihood to live independently. Only male students from the Basque Country show a lower probability of living independently than those in Madrid. Female patterns are not influenced by any of the two context variables.[8] We must remember that according to our census-based surveys very few students of the sample live independently in Spain, namely 11 per cent of the men and 12 per cent of the women, while in France the respective rates are 35 per cent and 42 per cent.

Unlike in the case of the students, leaving home patterns of young men on the labour market display many regional variations (cf. Table 12 in the Appendix).

1. If one looks first at the bivariate relationships of the context variables, it emerges that the size of the municipality has no influence on leaving home (Model 1).
2. While 8 regions out of 16 have an impact (Model 2). Young men from Galicia, Cantabria, Asturias, the Basque Country, Navarre, and Castile-And-Leon tend to live with their parents more frequently compared to those in Madrid, while the contrary is the case for those in Catalonia and Andalusia.
3. In the full model with context and individual level variables the regional effects persist or even increase their coefficients (Model 4). The negative effect of Galicia disappears due to various composition effects in Model 4.[9] The interpretation of these regional effects is the objective of the next section.

The homogeneity of regional living arrangements was tested by looking at provincial differences. Model 4, as before, was run with provinces instead of regions.[10] All provinces with a positive effect are part of regions which also have a significant positive effect on men's independence, but not all provinces from a significant region are themselves significant. In the Basque Country, the provinces of Guipuzcoa and Biscay show significant negative effects, in Galicia it is the province of Pontevedra and in Castile -And-Leon the provinces of Segovia and Valladolid also show significant negative effects. The uni-provincial regions of Asturias, Cantabria, and Navarre also show significant effects. The provincial analysis shows, with respect to the regions with a positive effect, that the significant positive effect in Catalonia is due to the significant effect of Barcelona, while in Andalusia all provinces except Seville and Huelva show significant effects. In addition, within the region of Valencia the province of Valencia shows a positive effect, but it is not strong enough to push the whole region of Valencia into a significant effect. Thus, there is some interregional heterogeneity but it is not as large as to combine provinces with significant positive and significant negative effects into one region. In addition, in all significant regions all provinces have the same sign, some being significant and others not (exceptions are Huelva in Andalusia and Lerida in Catalonia). Thus, it can be concluded that regions are relatively uniform geographical units with respect to young men's living arrangements, i.e. with respect to the dependent variable.

The models for women out of education show the following results (Table 13 in the Appendix):

1. As in the male case no rural-urban effects appear (Model 1).

2. Positive relationships are more significant compared with men: seven regions are significant in shaping leaving patterns. Women who live in Galicia, the Basque Country, and Castile- And-Leon are less likely to live in an independent dwelling, while women in Catalonia, the Balearic Islands, Castile-La Mancha, and Valencia are more frequently independent (Model 2).
3. In the full model some changes occur, since the group of regions with a negative effect is joined by the Canary Islands, while the group of positive effects loses Castile-La Mancha, for it is not more positively linked to living independently. Very interestingly, women from villages of under 5,000 inhabitants are now more likely to live independently than women in towns of over 100,000 inhabitants (Model 3).

A provincial analysis shows that, as in the case of men, not all provinces of the regions which display a significant effect are themselves significant. In the region of Galicia only the province of Orense is significant, in the Basque Country the provinces of Guipuzcoa and Biscay, in the region of Castile-And-Leon only the provinces of Avila and Segovia, and in the Canary Islands only the province of Las Palmas. The situation is similar for young women in regions that affect leaving home positively. In Catalonia the provinces of Barcelona and Tarragona show a significant effect and in the Valencia only the province of Valencia does. In addition, the uni-provincial region of the Balearic Islands shows a positive effect. The important fact is that within a region significant provincial effects go in the same direction as the regional effect and no province shows an effect that goes against the regional trend, if the latter is statistically significant.

To sum up, men and women from the Basque Country and Castile-And-Leon are less likely to live independently than their counterparts in Madrid, while men and women in Catalonia live outside of the parental home more frequently. There are regional effects which vary by gender, so men in Asturias, Cantabria, and Navarre are less likely to live independently than men in Madrid, while this is not the case for women. In addition, men in Andalusia have a higher probability of living outside of the parental home, whereas this is not true for women. Men show more negative than positive regional effects compared to women. As a consequence women in the Balearic Islands and in Valencia display a significant positive probability of living independently, while men from these contexts do not. These gender differences could be related to the fact that in Madrid, the reference category, the most "privileged" men have a higher estimated probability of living independently than their female counterparts. So there are few other men who have a significantly higher probability of independence as those in Catalonia and Andalusia. Since the female reference category has a relatively low probability of independence compared to her male counterpart, more positive regional effects appear for women, whereas they show few negative regional effects.

For What Do Regional Differences Stand?

It should be possible to explain a part of the Spanish regional differences in living arrangements of non-students with the regional particularities of housing markets and social norms. If one goes back to the original hypotheses of this work (cf. Chapter 3), their validity for explaining regional differences should be posed. Not all these hypotheses are useful to apply to a regional analysis. A regional analysis with different regional context variables has to be used cautiously also due to the rapidly emerging problem of collinearity, if one introduces many context variables. The choice of the most relevant variables is to be discussed next.

Explaining Variables

The **dependence-diversification hypothesis** (cf. chapter 3) is not very useful for a regional analysis, since the greatest variations are cross-national. It could be studied through the inclusion of regional data on grants, on residence halls for students and young workers, and with figures on public benefits for young people. Since for France we are informed if individuals receive a grant or a housing allowance or if they live in a publicly subsidised dwelling, a specific individual-level model for France was performed, in which the dependence-diversification was tested and partly confirmed (cf. Chapter 5).

For Spain such an individual-level test is not possible due to lack of data. Besides, the Spanish sample excludes all those living in residence halls and thus is inappropriate for the study of regional differences in grants for students and in residence halls. The collection of regional data on other public benefits is a rather hard task[11] and without a comprehensive collection of all possible public measures the test is useless. Thus, the regional model will not include a test of the dependence-diversification hypothesis, due to the problems of lack of data in the survey itself and in official statistical publications.

The testable **precariousness hypothesis** affirms that a high occurrence of short-term employment and of unemployment among men results in a high probability of these staying at home. The female likelihood of living at home in areas with high fixed-term employment and unemployment will also be high due to their difficulties in becoming financially independent from parents and partner, and due to the relatively low number of financially autonomous male partners.[12]

This hypothesis has been tested at the individual level and it was shown that short-term employed young people are always less likely to live independently than long-term employed. This relationship is strongest for French women and men, less strong for Spanish men and the least strong for Spanish women. With respect to unemployment, it emerged that from all activity categories, first-employment seekers have the greatest disadvantages compared to long-term employed young people. This negative relationship is the strongest for Spanish men, followed by French men, French women, and Spanish women. Unemployed people who already had a job before are also less likely to have left the parental home, but the effect is less strong and, interestingly, Spanish women who are unemployed after having had a job are more likely to have left home.

Although these relationships have already been tested and confirmed at the individual level, it is important to know if contexts with very precarious labour markets reinforce individuals' likelihood of staying at home or, on the contrary, change their behavioural patterns through a decrease in their expectations. Also, it is important to compare the effects of labour markets with those of housing markets. The context question that emerges at this point is: do young people who live in contexts that are strongly marked by short-term employment and unemployment stay longer with their parents than those in more favoured areas, independently of their individual activity situation? That is, is there a specific labour market context effect, which goes beyond a mere composition effect? It is assumed that the situation of the labour market is highlighted well by taking only male rates of first employment seekers in 1991 (UNEMP) and in this way it indicates also constraints for married couples with only one-earner.

The **high property-low affordability hypothesis** is a hypothesis which can only be tested on a context level, even if an approximation on the individual level was tried in Chapter 5. On housing markets with high prices, low vacancy rates, and a low offer of rented housing, two-generation households will be more frequent and the diversity of one-generation households will be low (cf. Chapter 3). The original hypothesis can be reduced to a more manageable hypothesis for the empirical test. It can be assumed that the rate of rented dwellings in 1991 (TENRENT) is in close relation with the level of rents and thus for the multivariate analysis, the former indicator was chosen, as it is more easy to access reliable regional data in its regard. Buying a dwelling is related to leaving home, in particular, through the fact that it is a more long-term decision than that of renting a dwelling. This element together with the fact that normally people have to have some savings or obtain some money from their parents to be able to take a mortgage, leads one to presume that buying a dwelling is more related to delayed leaving than to early leaving. In Chapter 5 it is shown for France and Spain that, in fact, younger people are more likely to live in a rented dwelling than their older counterparts, and cohabiting couples are more likely to do so than married couples. Since in Spain buying a dwelling is so widespread among young people too, the regional model also tests the role of regional price differentials for the acquisition of dwellings (ACCES).

The problem with data about the housing market is that the theoretically ideal unit of analysis would be the local community, since within a region, prices of dwellings will be quite different depending on the size of the town and the spatial organisation of production. A small rural town near to an important industrial town might display high dwelling prices, since many people working in the industrial town live in the smaller rural municipality. Given the limited resources of this research we have to do with the regional average.

The estimation of the affordability of owned dwellings poses some methodological problems. For example, many estimations are based on expected prices, which can differ from real prices at the trade moment (Cortés Alcalá 1995). The most detailed information is provided by the Banco Hipotecario Español (Spanish Mortgage Bank), which processes the information of the dwellings for which they offered a mortgage. In general, their survey comprises 40,000 dwellings every year and it is more accurate for national figures than for regional or provincial ones and more for periods longer than a trimester. For the years of 1986 to 1987, 80 per cent of the sample consisted of publicly subsidised dwellings and in 1988/89, 60 per cent was made up of dwellings on the free market. The regional price structure for used dwellings, which were financed by the BHE, has not changed throughout the period 1986 to 1993. The regions where, traditionally, acquisition of housing is less expensive are Estremadura, Andalusia, and Castile-La Mancha (Sanchez Villar 1993). Based on these prices and on the annual disposable family income, Gómez Churruca and Levenfeld (1993) calculated the accessibility of dwellings by regions in 1992, first without tax deductions and then after taxes. The latter estimation is used for the regional regression model (ACCES).

Contrary to the original idea of controlling for different theoretically significant intervening variables in the logistic regression models, it was decided to construct a simple model. Indicators for regional labour markets and housing markets will be part of the model, and from the intervening variables only family norms will be included in the model due to their theoretical importance. This procedure is necessary because of the technical problems which appear when one introduces independent variables which are themselves correlated. To have, however, an idea about the role of some of the intervening variables, their regional variation will be described briefly in the next section.

Control Variables: Wealth, Consumption Standards, Mobility, and Family Norms

There are five independent control variables of the theoretical model in Chapter 3: urbanisation, education structure, geographical mobility, family norms, and wealth. Effects of urbanisation and education have been controlled for at the individual level.

Differences in wealth could not be analysed at the individual level for Spain, but only for France, since we lack information in the former case. In its place, wealth as indicated by regional GDP per head or regional average household expenditure is a measure available for Spain. The indicator chosen is average household expenditures, for it avoids problems of sub-estimation of income statistics and it permits us at the same time to take a closer look at the use of expenditure for different aims. The idea is that not only the level of wealth is important but also to see if people with lower income levels have similar or different consumption standards.

It is difficult to find regional data on young people's expenditures, since statistics of household surveys only analyse the expenditures of young people living independently but not of those living with parents. However, to give an idea of regional differences some figures from the Household Expenditure Survey (Encuesta de Presupuestos Familiares) of 1991 and of GPD per head are presented.

Figure 6.4 Average Household Expenditure Per Consumption Unit (household head aged 0-29) and GDP Per Capita (national averages=100), Spain 1991

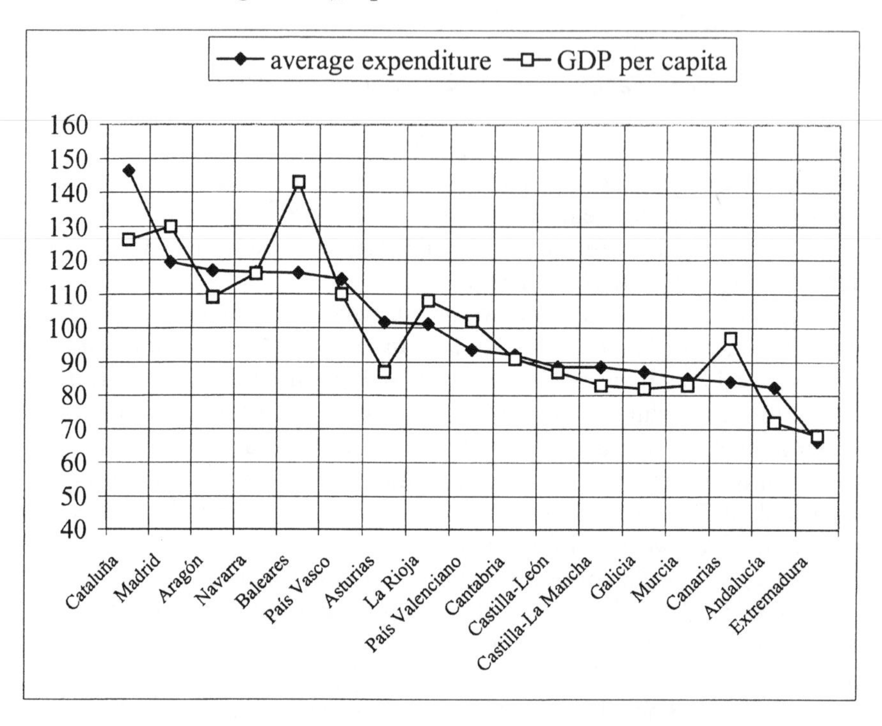

Source: author's elaboration with INE 1995 and Martín Rodríguez 1996.

The average monthly expenditure per consumption unit of those households where the head is younger than 30 amounted to 87,998 Ptas in 1991 (750 PPS). Annually, the national average is 1,055,974 Ptas, whereas the lowest average was shown by people living in Estremadura (701,267 Ptas) and the highest in Catalonia (1,545,931 Ptas). Figure 6.4 provides details of the regional distribution of the average expenditure of households with young family heads and of the GDP per capita. First, it can be observed that, in general, the households headed by a young person that spent over the national average (100) are found in those regions where the GDP per capita is also higher than the national GDP per head and vice versa. It means that the general wealth of regions is also reflected in the consumption capacity of young people living independently. Young people who left home do not seem to have risked a decrease in their consumption capacity compared to the regional standard. This is in line with the theoretical idea that young people leave home if they are able to attain a standard of living similar to that of their parents or to that of their regional context.

Interestingly, regions with low average expenditure levels and GDP per capita, for instance Andalusia, are found among the regions with low staying home rates, in particular with respect to men, and at the same time regions with high levels are also found among the early leavers (Catalonia,Balearic Islands). The same unsystematic grouping is found among regions belonging to the group of late leavers: there are "poor" regions such as Galicia and Castile-And-Leon and there are "rich" ones, such as the Basque Country and Navarre. Is the relation between wealth and leaving home mediated through differences in consumption preferences?

The theoretical model in Chapter 3 includes a hypothesis about young people's consumption preferences. It states that if young people live in a context of low average income levels, but they spend similar amounts for transport, communication and leisure as young people in contexts with higher average income levels, then in the first context the prevalence of two-generation households will be high. On the other hand, early leaving home could be a result of lower consumption levels in some important areas such as housing and leisure. It is assumed that living in the parental home is a strategy to prevent a low consumption capacity. Thus, people in regions with low income and expenditure levels, who nonetheless leave home early, might spend less on leisure, because they have lower consumption standards. Instead, regions with high income levels and high staying home rates, should display rather high amounts of expenditure for leisure, since there are high consumption standards and thus young people will only have left home after they were sure to be able to reach the regional standard.

Expenditure for leisure is indicated as a percentage of the total national average annual expenditure per consumption unit in 1991. The average national proportion spent on leisure goods was 6.4 per cent of total expenditure, which in Figure 6.5 has been transformed to 100. The smallest proportion with respect to total regional expenditure was 4.6 per cent and the highest rate 9.4 per cent. Young people who live independently in Andalusia, a "poor" region, spend less for leisure than the national average, and young people who live in the Basque Country and Navarre, "rich" regions, spend more than the average on leisure. Yet, the correlation between regional staying home rates and average consumption on leisure of those living independently seems weak. Independent youth in Madrid, Balearic Islands and the Basque Country show similar levels of expenditure on leisure, whereas their regional staying home rates are very different. Catalans spent the most of all young people in Spain in total, the most for leisure, and in addition they leave home the earliest. A possible reason for this is that they spend relatively little on accommodation. This point was discussed before and will be analysed in more detail below; however, figures related only to socially independent youth are presented here in Figure 6.5.

Figure 6.5 Part of Expenditure on Leisure/Housing of Average Household Expenditure Per Consumption Unit (household head aged 0-29, national averages=100), Spain 1991

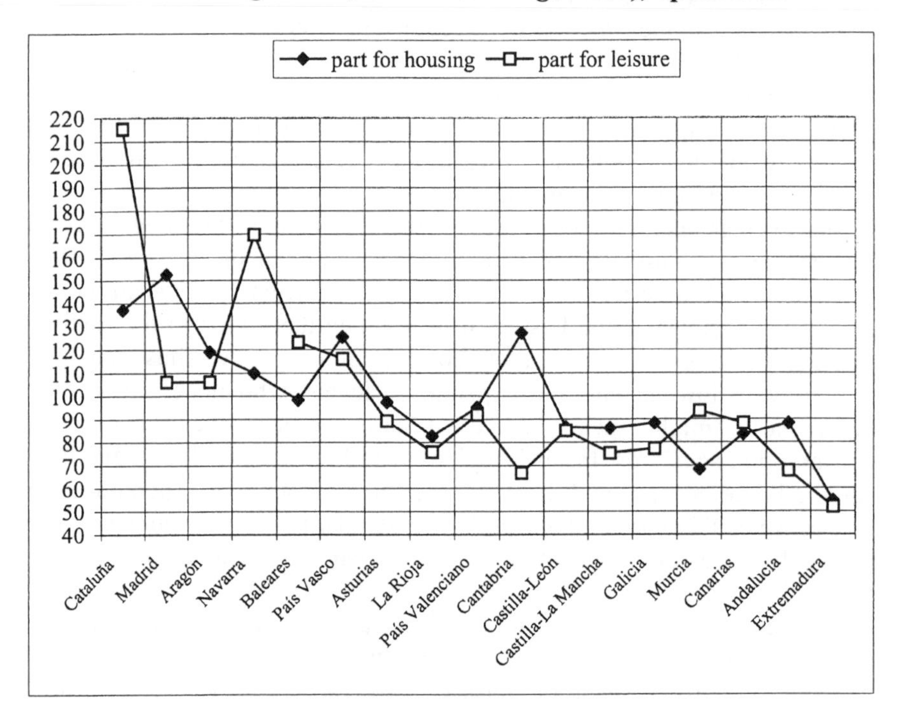

Source: author's elaboration with INE 1995.

In 1991, young people who were living independently spent on the average 16,492 Ptas per month on accommodation, heating, and electricity, which represents 18.7 per cent of their total expenditure. The annual average rates per consumption unit in relation to the respective regional total ranged from 25.9 in Cantabria to 15 per cent in Murcia. If the regional expenditure is compared to the national average, then it appears that independent young people in Madrid spent most for housing. The correlation of expenditure for accommodation with regional staying home rates is not clear, since young people in Catalonia and in the Balearic Islands pay a rather high proportion for housing despite the fact that they leave earlier, and youth in Castile-And-Leon and Cantabria spend relatively little on housing while they stay in the parental home for a long time. Yet we must take into account the fact that the part of expenditure on housing considers only those young people who have already left home, which means that it does not consider the general price levels of housing. These figures here partly reflect other regional factors favouring or hindering social independence.

Another variable that we proposed to control for in the theoretical model was *geographical mobility*. The argument there was, that areas with immigration of young people for reasons of study or work will present lower rates of two-generation households and more one-generation households, especially in the form of peer and single-person-households. To test this idea, a variable at the individual level can be introduced in order to measure the importance of having changed town, province, or region for the likelihood of living independently. Yet there are some problems. First, there is the already mentioned problem of under-registration of informal living arrangements in the sociodemographic survey, but which most probably affects the dependent and independent variable in the same way. Second, there is the problem that all those who migrated from one municipality, province or region to another have left the parental home by definition. Technically this means that it does not make any sense to include geographical mobility into any of the multivariate models, since the variable migration is part of the dependent variable. Only those who live independently have the possibility of taking a positive value on the variable migration. Of all the young people aged 20 to 29 in 1991, 6.4 per cent migrated when they left home, and there are some small regional variations. In 1991, eight per cent of those living in Madrid, in Rioja, and in the Balearic Islands had migrated when they left home, while in the Basque Country it was only 4 per cent, in Andalusia 5 per cent, and in Murcia 5.6 per cent. Thus, the relationship to the regional differences in staying home rates seems to be rather weak.

Family norms and family culture is supposed to play an important role in leaving home. In this research the perspective chosen explicitly ignores these factors most of the time. It is not because they are thought to be irrelevant, but because the aim is to explore how far one can go with a socio-economic explanation. Clearly, economy and culture are not independent from each other, as has already been mentioned. Economic and social behaviour is embedded in cultural frames and thus it is difficult to assert if a given variable indicates a cultural or an economic phenomenon. So, the decision of women to search for paid work is simultaneously linked to cultural contexts and to economic and production characteristics of those contexts. The hypothesis of the theoretical part states that areas where consensual unions are more wide-spread will present lower rates of two-generation households, since informal living arrangements favour young people's early nest-leaving. In addition, territorial units where neolocal and early marriage was important in the past will show lower rates of two-generation households, while areas, where in the past, stem-families and late and patrilocal marriage predominated, will display high rates of two-generation households. These historical patterns are only relevant in the present if the agricultural production mode in the respective region remain important.

From the 19th century until 1960/70 great regional differences in marriage patterns existed in Spain and they were relatively stable over time until well into the 20th century. In the northern coastal areas and the Canary Islands, male and female marriage was restricted as in northwestern Europe, while in the centre, in the eastern coastal regions and in the south it was intense. Reher has shown in a historical provincial analysis that the provinces of high nuptiality were "areas of high mortality, partible inheritance practices, balanced marriage markets, moderate out-migration by both sexes, low population density, and professions which facilitated marriage" (Reher 1991). If one looks at the types of families, nuclear versus pluri-nuclear, the Spanish census of 1970 shows very large regional differences in the rural areas. The pluri-nuclear family dominates in the rural areas of Galicia, the Basque Country, Asturias, and Catalonia, which are areas of small-sized and family-based agricultural production. Large nuclear families are more common in rural areas with large estates and high rates of agricultural dayworkers, such as Andalusia, the Canary Islands, and Estremadura (Pablo Masa 1976). Age at marriage among agricultural dayworkers and large estate owners was traditionally lower than among other social classes in western Andalusia (Contreras 1991). Spanish long-lasting regional differences in marriage patterns, inheritance practices, and diffusion of stem-families have been and are still the subject of controversy as to if two or more regional family models existed (Reher 1997). The interesting fact for this research is the persistence of different family models until current times.

Early family formation patterns in large estate areas are still found in present-day Spain. Following two qualitative analyses, the process of family formation of young people from agricultural dayworker origin would seem to differ from that of young people with other social origins, especially from that of young people coming from farming families. These two studies refer to the town of Lebrija, in the province of Seville, at the beginning of the 1990s, and to eight towns in western Andalusia in 1989/90 (Talego Vázquez 1995, Gavira Alvarez 1993). According to Talego, young agricultural dayworkers form, for the most part, neolocal families, i.e. outside the parental home, and, in addition, to do so earlier than other social groups. The average marital age of men is 24.9 years and of women 21.8 years, while in the small and middle agricultural owner group of the same town men marry at 28.7 and the women at 25.6 years of age, figures which are similar to the Spanish averages. The family formation process of agricultural dayworker families follows the inverse logic of most other Spanish families. The prevailing logic is not to wait in the parental home until the conditions for a particular living standard for the new couple are met, since it is only by becoming independent under precarious conditions that the new family can begin to improve its conditions. Talego explains that this phenomenon is related to the work organisation of the dayworkers' families and to the agrarian labour market.

The specific gender and age division of labour within the family, characteristic of the so-called modern nuclear family, does not apply to these families. All adult members are considered from their 16th birthday onwards or even earlier as labour power and participate in different jobs outside the house. The precarious employment and income situation of the household head, normally the father, and the particular labour market are the reasons for this massive use of the labour power of all the family members. The consequence of this is that most children go to school only for a few years and have high dropout rates (Gavira Alvarez 1993). The children begin to contribute to the family income early and, clearly, the income and services offered by the children is in the interest of the parents and other family members. To become independent means that one no longer needs to contribute to the income of the family of origin, and, in addition, men seem to find a job more easily if they are family heads.

This early home leaving, despite the very precarious economic conditions of young couples, is possible because of the very specific housing market. In Lebrija, for example, a large amount of rented accommodation ("casas de vecinos") exists, and in particular, it is possible for dayworkers with a low income to rent only a room at a very low price instead of a whole apartment (Talego Vázquez 1995). If this early neolocality of Andalusian day-workers in western Andalusia is also found in other parts of Andalusia, it makes it easy to understand why the Andalusian staying home rate is average and not high, in spite of the difficult labour market situation. Thus, the rate of agricultural dayworkers in relation to all paid workers in 1991 (DAYWORK) will be taken as an indicator of different family models and of the regional importance of agriculture.

In addition, in the southwestern coastal regions fewer people are practising Catholics and these regions had important traditions of anarchism and liberalism, whereas northern regions are more strongly determined by Catholicism. Since it was shown that in Spain young people in consensual unions are more likely to be non-practising Catholics or non-Catholics (Valero 1992), it is not surprising to see that the regional index of the number of young people who have not declared themselves to be practising Catholics relates positively to the regional index of consensual unions in relation to all partnerships (Figure 6.6 and Table 6.2). The rate of consensual unions in 1991 was chosen for the multi-level logistic regression because it reflects religious differences relatively well and because it is also an important cross-national difference between France and Spain (COHABIT). Thus, consensual unions are taken as an indicator of social norms, even if this phenomenon is also linked to socio-economic variables as shown by the correlation with the rate of rented dwellings (cf. Figure 6.6) and as theorised by some analysts.

Figure 6.6 Non-Practising Catholics (aged 15-29), Consensual Unions (all ages), and Rented Dwellings (all ages) (national averages=100), Spain 1991/92

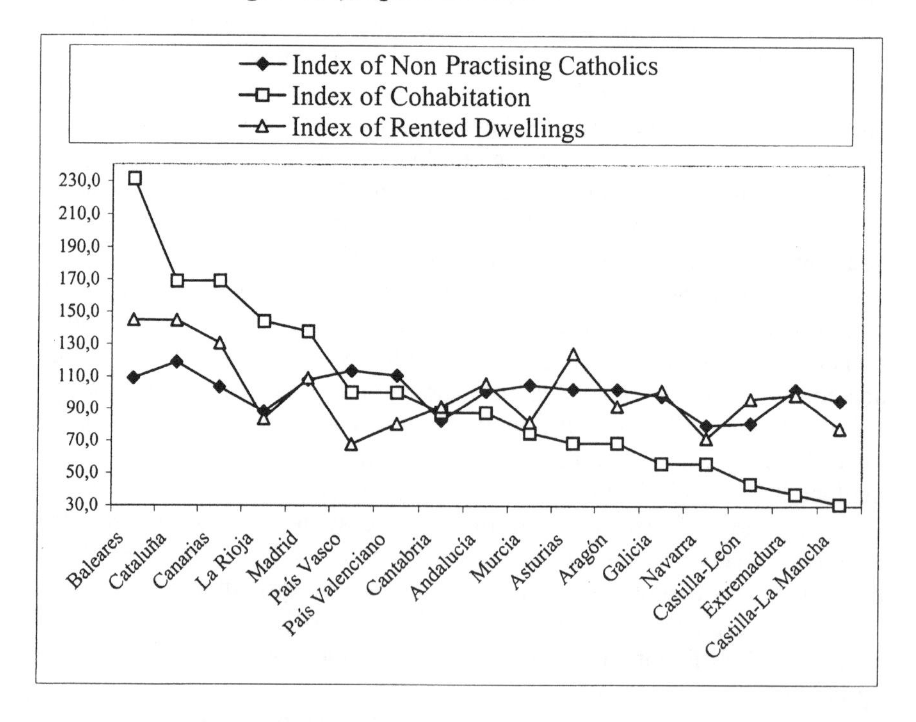

Sources: author's elaboration with INE 1994, 1995 and Navarro López/Mateo Rivas 1992.

From a modernisation perspective, some authors have seen the increase in consensual unions more as the result of general socio-economic changes than as the result of religious differences. Chafetz (1992 in: Prinz 1995) describes family change in general as a process with five phases. In the first phase, the social structure of a country changes due to technological change and economic growth. In a second phase, women's labour force participation and their enrolment in education increases. In a third phase, female employment rises among all women, including married women and mothers. In a fourth phase, family changes, such as delays in marrying, fertility decline and increase in divorce and cohabitation, can be observed, while the women's movement emerges and grows. In the last phase, public opinion regarding gender and family patterns changes and contributes to the acceleration of family change. This perspective has some problems if one wants to apply it to Southern Europe, since the fourth phase in Spain and Italy had specific features. A delay in marriage and a fertility decline can be observed, but the increase in divorce and cohabitation is very slow, as is the emergence of a women's movement. The latter is in decline instead of on the increase (Jurado/Naldini 1996, Morales 1999). However, this does not prevent a regional analysis testing for a correlation between more "modernised" regions with more cohabitation and earlier home-leaving. The question of causality nonetheless remains open, since there are arguments in favour of linking cohabitation to religious differences and in favour of relating it to socio-economic changes.

Theoretical Model for Spanish Regional Analysis and Results

Finally, it was decided to use two indicators for different regional family cultures, two indicators for the housing market and one indicator for the labour market.[13] The regional labour market will be described by the rate of young men who are searching for their first employment in relation to all young people of the age-group (UNEMP). It was decided to not include an indicator of short-term employment, because it strongly correlates with the family culture indicator DAYWORK. The housing market will be described with two indicators, one is the rate of rented dwellings (TENRENT) and the other is the price of acquisition of a used dwelling financed by the Spanish mortgage bank in relation to disposable income (ACCES). The rate of consensual unions is chosen as an indicator of tradition in terms of degree of secularisation and of prevalence of marriage as main household formation practice (COHABIT). The rate of agricultural dayworkers of all paid workers is taken as a twofold indicator, namely to represent the weight of agricultural dayworkers as an indicator of early, nuclear and neolocal family formation patterns and of the weight of agriculture (DAYWORK). The regional rates are treated as quantitative variables.

The model for Spanish young people on the labour market is as follows:

$$(11)\ \text{logit}(\text{IND91/92}) = \alpha + \beta_1(\text{ACTIVEST}) + \beta_2(\text{CLASSFA}) - \beta_3(\text{SIBL}) + \beta_4(\text{EDUC}) + \beta_5(\text{AGE}) + \beta_6(\text{RURURBAN}) + \beta_7(\text{UNEMP}) + \beta_8(\text{TENRENT}) + \beta_9(\text{ACCES}) + \beta_{10}(\text{DAYWORK}) + \beta_{11}(\text{COHABIT})$$

The inclusion of all variables into one model is problematic due to problems of collinearity. If one includes all regional indicators in one model, the predictive power of the model increases, but this is a statistical artifice, since one is including indicators measuring similar things. Thus, the decision was made to run two different models containing each time only one indicator for the housing market, labour market, and family norms. Those combinations of indicators which show less correlation were chosen.

Table 6.2 Bivariate Correlations of Regional Rates

	ACCES	TENRENT	COHABIT	DAYWORK	UNEMPM	CATHOLIC
ACCES	1.0000	0.3026	0.4401	-0.7702	-0.3189	-0.2882
TENRENT	0.3026	1.0000	0.7003	-0.1112	-0.3085	-0.4151
COHABIT	0.4401	0.7003	1.0000	-0.3223	-0.4099	-0.6535
DAYWORK	-0.7702	-0.1112	-0.3223	1.0000	0.4531	0.1441
UNEMPM	-0.3189	-0.3085	-0.4099	0.4531	1.0000	0.2978
CATHOLIC	-0.2882	-0.4151	-0.6535	0.1441	0.2978	1.0000

Note: Correlation coefficients with 2-tailed significance of p=0.000. 17,860 cases (women and men together).

There is a strong negative correlation between *daywork* and *access*, which means that in regions with high percentages of agricultural dayworkers dwellings are less expensive. A similarly strong correlation but of a positive sign exists between *cohabit* and *tenrent*, which is in line with the expectation that more people are in consensual unions in regions where higher rates of rented dwellings are found. This confirms at regional level the relation between being in a consensual union and the higher likelihood of living in a rented dwelling. As expected, there is also a strong negative relationship between the rate of practising young Catholics and cohabitation. To prevent strong correlations within one model, the following two models were computed:

(12) logit $(IND91/92)=\alpha+\beta_1(ACTIVEST)+\beta_2(CLASSFA)-\beta_3(SIBL)+\beta_4(EDUC)+\beta_5(AGE)+\beta_6(RURURBAN)+\beta_7(UNEMP)+\beta_8(TENRENT)+\beta_9(DAYWORK)$

(13) logit $(IND91/92)=\alpha+\beta_1(ACTIVEST)+\beta_2(CLASSFA)-\beta_3(SIBL)+\beta_4(EDUC)+\beta_5(AGE)+\beta_6(RURURBAN)+\beta_7(UNEMP)+\beta_8(ACCES)+\beta_9(COHABIT)$

First, each context variable was included separately into the complete model and then two multivariate models were computed. Next, the results of the separate inclusion of regional variables are presented.[14]

The regional price of dwellings in relation to disposable income is significantly and negatively linked to the probability of young active men of living independently (-0.0132**), while the rate of rented dwellings has a positive effect (0.0228**). The rate of male agricultural dayworkers as a percentage of all men employed in agriculture shows a positive effect on the likelihood of living outside of the parental home (0.0280**). The number of consensual unions in relation to all unions shows a stronger positive effect than the previous variables (0.1106**). Last, the rate of young people searching for their first employment influences living independently in a negative way (-0.0266*). All regional variables are significantly related to the dependent variable, each of them separately.

The results of both multivariate models (Models 12 and 13) are very similar.[15] In both models all three variables are significant, but the relative importance of each of them changes. In the first model the indicator of the labour market has the strongest effect, followed by the indicator of family patterns, and the indicator of housing market. In the second model the most important variable is *cohabit*, followed at some distance by *unempm* and *access*. The predictive power of the first model is somewhat higher than that of the second one (-2LL: 9321.824 and –2LL: 9366.667 respectively) and therefore Model 12 is taken in order to develop an explanation.[16]

For women, the procedure has been followed in the same way, that is to firstly introduce every context variable separately. If the effort of acquiring a dwelling (access) is introduced as unique context variable, it can be observed that this variable has no significant effect, contrary to what the male model has shown. The rate of rented dwellings, instead, has a significant positive effect on women's likelihood to live independently (0.0296**). With respect to the cultural variables, the two respective models show first a non-significant effect of *daywork* and a significant positive effect of *cohabit* (0.1695**). The male rate of first-employment seeker exerts a negative influence on women's probability of living outside of the parental home (-0.0907**). The multivariate Models 12 and 13 have more predictive power than the previous uni-variate context models.[17] The model with *unemp, tenrent* and *daywork* shows a –2 log-likelihood of 10505.475, while the model with *unemp, access* and *cohabit* provides a somewhat higher –2LL (10511.423). In both cases all three coefficients show statistically significant effects. In the first case the strongest effect comes from unemp (-0.1057**), followed equally by tenrent and daywork (0.018**). In the second model, being in a region with a high rate of consensual unions increases the likelihood of social independence more (0.1315**) than being in a region with a low first-employment seeker rate (-0.0891**). To be in a region with high dwelling acquisition prices has the smallest effect on the chances of living independently (-0.0130**). Again, as in the case of men, the more predictive model, that is Model 12, is selected for further interpretation. Martínez Granado and Ruiz-Castillo (1998) also have found that higher regional costs of renting or buying a dwelling have significant negative effects on living independently for men and women.[18]

In the male and female models the respective significance of the cultural variables changes depending on the form of the triad of independent variables. However the housing market indicators are always the less determining variables, while the labour market and the family pattern variables battle it out for first place. The models with less predictive power, which include the rate of consensual unions, the rate of effort to acquire a dwelling, and the male rate of first-employment seeker, show a larger influence of family norms than of socio-economic variables. Again, women are more strongly influenced by the labour market indicator than men. These results make the importance of the choice of indicators on social norms and culture evident, as well as the extent to which there is always some arbitrariness. This is in relation to the fact that culture is only relatively autonomous from socio-economic variables, and that cultural indicators thus always carry a socio-economic part within them.

Compared to the models with the regional dummies (Model 4), the models which give a meaning to regional differences through the combination of two economic and one cultural variable (Model 12) reach a very high predictive power.[19] The fit of the more interpretative models is as good as the model with the 16 dummy variables. For men, the differences between the –2 Log Likelihood of the model with region dummies (Model

4) and the –2LL of the best predicting model with regional rates (Model 12) number 15. The number of degrees of freedom difference is 13, because Model 4 has 16 regions and Model 12 has 3 regional variables. A χ^2 test with 13 degrees of freedom and a probability of error of 0.01 shows that the –2 LL difference of 15 is not statistically significant. This means that Model 12 predicts as well as Model 4 and thus is able to explain away the regional differences thanks to variables indicating regional differences in labour markets, housing markets and family norms. For women the –2 Log Likelihood difference is higher (26), but a χ^2 test with 13 degrees of freedom shows that the – 2 LL difference of 26 is not significantly different with an error probability of 0.01. However, our model explains men's behaviour better than women's, since Model 12 for men explains 17 per cent of the variance, while Model 12 for women explains only 14 per cent of the variance. This is what happens with all the models used in this thesis, since they are employment-oriented and take only individual strategies into account.

Table 6.3 shows that, for men, the two regions that are significantly positive are also among the first three regions according to the context indicator[20] (Andalusia and Catalonia), while of the five regions that have significantly negative coefficients four of them are among the last five regions as measured with the context indicator. For women the correlation is weaker.

To sum up, men and women in the labour market face different probabilities of living independently according to the region in which they live, and independently of their individual chances. If they live in regions with low rates of male first-employment seeker, a high offer of rented dwellings and high proportions of men working as agricultural dayworkers, they have a better chance to live outside of the parental home, than those in regions with high unemployment rates, a low offer of rented dwellings, and few men working in agriculture as dayworkers. Let us now describe the concrete situation of each region which was found to have a significant effect on the probability of living independently in comparison to Madrid.

Table 6.3 Indicator of Context Favouring Independence and Regional Differences

Indicator (tenrent +daywork-unemp)		Coefficients Men (Model 4)		Coefficients Women (Model 4)	
Andalusia	28.7	Andalusia	0.4043**	Catalonia	0.441**
Balearic Islands	24.9	Catalonia	0.2447*	Balearic Islands	0.4398**
Catalonia	23.8	Balearic Islands	0.2587	Valencia	0.2702**
Estremadura	23.0	Valencia	0.1927	La Rioja	0.1709
Canary Islands	18.1	Murcia	0.1921	Aragon	0.1038
Murcia	15.5	Estremadura	0.1812	Castile-La Mancha	0.0613
Madrid	15.5	Castile-La Mancha	0.0506	Murcia	0.0256
Valencia	15.3	La Rioja	0.0388	Estremadura	0.0032
Castile-La Mancha	15.2	Madrid	0.0000	Madrid	0.0000
Aragon	14.7	Canary Islands	-0.0405	Andalusia	-0.0319
Asturias	13.5	Aragon	-0.0621	Asturias	-0.1077
Galicia	13.3	Galicia	-0.2395	Cantabria	-0.3277
La Rioja	12.8	Castile-And-Leon	-0.3657**	Navarre	-0.294
Castile-And-Leon	11.9	Asturias	-0.3892*	Galicia	-0.2914*
Navarre	10.1	Cantabria	-0.4088*	Canary Islands	-0.3057**
Cantabria	8.0	Basque Country	-0.515**	Castile-And-Leon	-0.3406**
Basque Country	2.8	Navarre	-0.5454**	Basque Country	-0.5423**

Source: author's elaboration with census and logistic regression results of Tables 14 and 15, Appendix.

The positive regional effects of Andalusia and Catalonia on young men's probability of living independently is due to their combination of specific labour and housing market and family norms features. Andalusia has a high rate of first-employment seeking men aged 20 to 29 (9%), but it has a high rate of rented dwellings (20%) and a high rate of agricultural dayworkers (18%), which means that it has a difficult labour market for young people becoming independent, but this is compensated by a favourable housing market and a significant presence of people with family norms which favour early emancipation. Catalonia presents very good economic conditions with a low first-employment seeker rate (4%), and a high offer of rented dwellings (27%). Family norms are not shaped by a high proportion of agricultural dayworkers (0.5%), but Catalonia has the second highest rate of consensual unions (2.7 % of all unions), many Catalans are of Andalusian origin and liberal and secularised values have a long-lasting tradition.

The group of late-leaving regions has to be divided into two subgroups. First there is Navarre, which displays a low unemployment rate (5%), but also a low offer of rented dwellings (13%) and a low significance of agricultural dayworkers (1.2%). Its low rate of independence is an outcome of negative housing market conditions and a low weight of early family formation traditions. The remaining four regions, the Basque Country, Cantabria, Asturias, and Castile-And-Leon also have traditions of small-sized and family-based agricultural production (dayworker rates all under 1.5%), high rates of first-employment seekers (7-10%), and low to medium rates of rented dwellings (13-17%). Asturias is an exception with respect to housing market conditions, for it has a high rate of rented dwellings (23%), and acquisition of dwellings require an average effort, but its unemployment rate is the second highest of all regions. Difficult housing markets and a tradition of long-lasting cohabitation of children with their parents, due to the important weight of family-based small agricultural production, explain the negative influence of these contexts on young men's social independence. The position of Galicia with respect to the regional indicator leads to the expectation of finding it among the group of late leavers, and in fact, men in Galicia leave late, but this low probability of social independence is the outcome of a composition effect of activity, age, education, class, and urbanisation structures as was shown above.

The situation of women is very similar, but with two exceptions which present some major problems, if they have to be explained within the terms of the theoretical model. The regional indicators of unemployment, housing market and family norms point to a positive effect of Andalusia and the Canary Islands for women's probability of living independently, but the result of the logistic regression shows a non-significant regional effect for Andalusia and a negative effect for the Canary Islands. The lack of these effects cannot be explained as an outcome of composition effects due to activity, age, education, class, or urbanisation structures, since these regions did not appear to be significant in the bivariate models discussed above. These two exceptions show the limits of the model, which in the future will have to be revised to be able to explain these exceptions.

Conclusion: Cultural Mediation of Socio-economic Situations

The question at the beginning of this chapter was to asses how far regional differences in young people's living arrangements are due to socio-economic composition effects or to regional "culture" effects. Some composition effects were found in France and Spain, but on the other hand contextual effects also emerged after control of individual-level variables. Thus, many regional effects, in particular in Spain, are not the result of composition effects due to activity, age, education, class, or urbanisation structures.

For France few regional effects were found with the exception of students whose differential regional chances to be living away are related to migratory processes linked to decisions about where to study. French non-students, instead, show different probabilities of social independence according to their rural-urban context and very few in relation to their regional context. It was argued and partly shown that a rural context means more traditional values with respect to household formation through marriage in contrast to cohabitation, a selective emigration of young people, and a housing market dominated by owner-occupied housing. Thus varying family formation patterns and housing market structures are identified as explaining variables and the Spanish findings point to the same factors.

The Spanish regional analyses with regional indicators of family norms, labour and housing markets have shown that in the model with the highest predictive power the labour market situation exerts the strongest effect on the social independence of young Spanish people who have finished their education. A high rate of men searching for their first employment has a negative effect for men's and women's chances to be socially independent, the effect being stronger for women than for men. Family norms, as measured by the rate of agricultural dayworkers, and housing markets have a smaller influence on young people's living arrangements, but a larger influence on men's probability of social independence than on women's. In spite of these differences the **precariousness**, the **high property-low affordability** and the hypothesis about the importance of specific **family norms** have all been confirmed to some extent. Three configurations of this triad were found for Spain:

1. **Precarious-Agricultural-Daywork Regions** with precarious youth labour markets, but more favourable housing markets and family norms favouring early family formation: Andalusia.
2. **Stable-Non-Agricultural-Daywork Regions** with less precarious youth labour markets, housing markets with high rates of rented

dwellings and relatively high rates of consensual unions: Catalonia, the Balearic Islands, and Valencia.

3. **Precarious-Non-Agricultural-Daywork Regions** with precarious youth labour markets, housing markets with low to average rates of rented dwellings and no early family formation norms: Basque Country, Navarre, Cantabria, Castile-Leon, Galicia, Asturias. Asturias has a relatively favourable housing market, but because labour market features are more important than housing market characteristics it forms part of the late-leaver group.[21]

Can we draw some conclusions from this regional analysis for the cross-national comparison of France and Spain? A simple transposition of these regional results to the cross-national level is not possible, but we can suggest that if regional contexts have an influence on young people's living arrangements in Spain and to some extent in France and in the latter the rural-urban context also has an influence, then it is very probable that at the cross-national level context variations are also relevant. In fact, the cross-national models show that many Spanish-French differences persist after controlling for important socio-economic variables at the individual level. If we further assume that contexts exert similar effects be they cross-regional, cross-rural-urban or cross-national, then we can predict that cross-national differences are primarily a result of differences in the labour market and in the second place a result of differences in housing markets and family norms. If this hypothesis were to be verified in a larger cross-national study, then a final conclusion could be drawn: social policies aiming to ameliorate young people's chances of finding employment and an accessible dwelling would have a positive influence on young people's chances to reach social independence and they would diminish French-Spanish cross-national differences. Since different family cultures mediate socio-economic situations and culture is supposedly relatively autonomous from the economy, cross-national differences are not likely to disappear completely, even if socio-economic convergence were attained. However, it has to be remembered that family cultures are only relatively autonomous, since they depend to some extent on socio-economic characteristics, as was shown by the discussion of the relations between early family formation and the agricultural production mode and between consensual unions and housing market characteristics.

Notes

[1] The samples used in this descriptive part are the entire samples *Franceall* and *Spainall.* The Spanish sample was weighted (cf. Appendix).

[2] The detailed results are presented in Tables 1 and 2 in the Appendix. Only the regional coefficients are shown in Table 14 in the text. The regional coefficients are always net effects after control of all variables as presented in equation (7).

[3] *Bacheliers* are people who have obtained the highest available secondary education certificate.

[4] It is not a simple composition effect either of activity or of size of municipality, but of the combination of both. Results of these first two models are not presented.

[5] In a model with only activity and region, these two effects do not appear. The results are not presented.

[6] The results of this model are not presented.

[7] Detailed results are not shown.

[8] Detailed results are presented in Table 1 and Table 2 of the Appendix.

[9] The most plausible bivariate and trivariate combinations of variables such as activity, social class, education, etc. were analysed to see if they explained the disappearanceof the Galician effect, but they did not. Thus it is a complex composition effect of many variables together.

[10] Detailed results are not reported.

[11] The INEM (Institute for Employment), for instance, publishes data on beneficiaries of unemployment benefit by regions, but without differentiation by age (AEL 1991).

[12] The latter affirmation depends on the age-difference of spouses. If men now find more difficulties in becoming financially autonomous and if the age difference between genders does not increase, it means that women will marry later.

[13] For more details on the variables see Appendix 3.

[14] The detailed results of the models with only one independent regional variable are not reported.

[15] Detailed results for Model 13 are not reported, but for Model 12 they are shown in Table 14 inthe Appendix.

[16] To prevent the doubt that the rate of practicising Catholics (CATHOLIC) could have been a better indicator of cultural variations and that it would have been more predictive, two other male models were computed. A first one with only CATHOLIC shows a significant net coefficient of –0.0157 and another with CATHOLIC, ACCES and UNEMP shows three significant effects, whereby UNEMP displays the strongest net effect, followed by a smaller effect of ACCES and an even smaller effect of CATHOLIC. The –2LL of 9361,028 shows that the model is less predictive than Model 12. The detailed results are not presented.

[17] Detailed results of Model 12 are shown in table 15 in the Appendix.

[18] They use the Spanish Family Household Budget Survey 1991 and they perform a different model. A revised version of their working paper will be published in the "Journal of Population Economics".

[19] For detailed results see the Appendix, Tables 14 and 15.

[20] The context indicator takes one value for each region; this value is the sum of the three context variables, TENRENT, DAYWORK and UNEMP of Model12.

[21] These three household formation models are more encompassing than those developed in a previous work based on five regions and they are able to explain regional differences with fewer variables (Jurado Guerrero 1997).

7 Social Rights Careers into Adulthood

Young people move through different phases of financial dependence according to the institutions they depend upon. Before they attain legal maturity they primarily depend on their parents and, only partially, receive indirect support from the state in the form of child allowances, for instance, or they receive a marginal market income due to holiday jobs, etc. Young people move from a state of primary dependence on the parents (childhood) to a state of mixed dependencies on family, market, and Welfare State (youth) to a state of dependence on the market and the state (and less on the family), which is the normal status of an adult person in a Welfare State. This movement through different states of social status and sources of financial dependence will be labelled the social rights career, which parallels educational, employment, and housing careers. The institutionalisation of the social rights career can be considered as a crucial process for understanding young people's levels of financial and social dependence on their parents.

The dependence-diversification hypothesis affirms that social rights are crucial for understanding the differences in young people's home leaving, since they reduce dependence on parents in a life phase where young people lack financial autonomy and where uncertainty about the future is comparatively high. From this perspective, cross-national differences in young people's living arrangements emerge not only due to 1. variance in the timing of the phases of the social rights career, but also due to 2. variations in the configuration of the market-family-state triad at the starting and ending point of the career.

The aim of Chapters 7 to 9 is to describe the mechanisms through which the specific institutionalisation of social rights affects differences in the financial and social dependence of young people on their parents.

1. In a first step, the division of labour between the Welfare State and the family at the starting phase of the social rights career of young people is analysed through a description of the division of the tasks of caring for and educating children (Chapter 7).

2. Then the public definitions of age-limits of childhood and social citizenship of adults are treated through a comparison of entitlement conditions to child benefits, health services, and social assistance. This description of the timing of the social rights career finds its final development in the conclusion of Chapter 9.
3. In between, the study of entitlement conditions, of generosity and of coverage of social benefits for students, young workers, and young people on the housing market aims to provide a comprehensive picture of the extension and the timing of social rights for different groups of young people (Chapters 7 to 9).
4. Finally, the two institutional forms of social rights careers and dependency diversification degrees in Spain and France are summarised (Chapter 9).

With regard to the starting phase, it can be affirmed that some Welfare State regimes display a weak division of labour between the family and the state in the fulfilment of family tasks, while others show a rather strong division of labour. At the end of the social rights career, differences in the universality and the generosity of the Welfare State affect the financial dependence of adults on the state and the market, and to a lesser or greater extent also on the family (cf. Chapter 9). Financial transfers from the family or the state towards young people can operate in two forms, as allowances and as benefits in kind/services. Both types of benefits have to be studied in order to assess the degree of dependence-diversification young people reach in a given Welfare State. This chapter concentrates on the period of 1985 to 1992, because these are the years during which the young people analysed in this work were likely to leave home. Because in France and Spain there have been no structural reforms which have changed national configurations of social rights for young people since those years, it can be assumed that the analysis is also relevant for the current moment.

Degrees of State Intervention in Family Tasks

In most societies children's upbringing is a task families have to fulfil, but the way this is organised is subject to state regulation and is facilitated through state intervention. Family law is the favoured instrument for public regulation of family affairs, but the state also helps families through a wide range of measures, namely through the provision of public institutions for general and vocational education, through family benefits, and through helping parents in the combination of paid and unpaid work. For the purpose of studying young people's living arrangements, an analysis of public provision of education and of family benefits has to be undertaken. Family law can be important insofar as it regulates parents' and young people's reciprocal obligations in cases of need, but it is considered to be less relevant for people's decisions to leave or to stay in the parental home than welfare regulations about child maintenance and education.

The French state provides public education at all levels of general education and, in addition, it offers a wide range of publicly financed vocational training institutions. In all educational areas private institutions complete this educational offer. At some levels up to 20 per cent of the enrolled pupils go to private institutions (cf. Table 7.1), yet over 90 per cent of the students enrolled in private institutions are part of schools, whose teaching staff is paid by the French state (DEP 1995).

Education in France is divided into three main levels:

1. primary education from ages six to eleven;
2. secondary education, which lasts until age 15 in the lower level (*collège*) and until age 17, 18, or 19 in the upper level depending on the path taken;
3. tertiary education until approximately ages 20 to 28 depending on the levels, which go from short-cycle technological courses lasting two years to certain medical specialisations and doctorates which last approximately ten years. A specificity of the French system is the dual system of universities formed by public and private elite institutions named *Grandes Écoles* (OECD 1996).

In France, compulsory schooling lasts until age 16 and until this age parents do not need to pay for education. Even private schools, which are publicly recognised, do not require a major financial effort from parents, since they are publicly subsidised (Dienel 1993). Tertiary education foresees the payment of academic fees, which are low at universities, higher at the *Grandes Écoles* and very high at the private *Grandes Écoles* (Eurydice 1993). The dominance of the state as the provider of education is also reflected in the relatively small number of apprenticeships, even if great efforts have been undertaken in order to increase the dual system elements of French vocational education. It can be stated that the French state helps parents considerably in matters of education through the provision of a wide net of public and publicly subsidised institutions.

Table 7.1 Public and Private Education by Level in France and Spain, 1991/1994

	Students in France 1994-95 (in thousands)*				Students in Spain 1991-92 (in thousands)			
	Public	Private	Total	Private as % of Total	Public	Private	Total	% of Private
Primary Education	5643	900	6.543	13.8	3.016	1.634	465	35.1
Secondary Education:	4.828	1.146	5.974	19.2	1.799	708	2.507	28.3
General	3.793	992	4.785	20.7	1.185	447	1.631	27.4
Vocational	1.035	153	1.189	12.9	619	262	881	29.8
Tertiary Education	1.975	133	2.108	6.3	1.154	40	1.194	3.3

Notes: General education of secondary level in France includes "1er cycle secondaire" and "2e cycle général et technologique". * university enrolment for 1993-94.
Sources: DEP 1995, Consejo de Universidades 1992, MEC 1994.

Like the French state, the Spanish Welfare State provides its citizens with public schools at all levels of compulsory education. This situation is rather new, since for a long time the Catholic Church was the main provider of education. During the transition to democracy (1978-1982) and in particular during the period the socialists were in power, the public educational offer was enlarged, its quality increased, and private schools were subjected to rather detailed regulation. Unlike in France, the Spanish education system has experienced several structural reforms: the *LODE* in 1986 (regulation of right to education) and the *LOGSE* in 1990 (new educational system). Many private schools persist, in particular in primary and secondary education, but since 1985 they are strongly regulated by the Spanish state, in particular at the compulsory level. As in France, the state offers subsidies to private schools according to some conditions, such as cost-free admission of students according to the norms of the public schools. There are two types of subsidies to private schools: 1. subsidies which cover all the costs (*concierto general*) and which secure cost-free education for all pupils, and 2. subsidies which cover only some part of the costs of private schools (*concierto singular*), so that these are allowed to take tuition fees within given limits. In 1985-86, over 90 per cent of private schools of primary level received some state support, most of them the most encompassing type. Private secondary level institutions receive only the second type of subsidy, since free education at these levels is not guaranteed by the Spanish state (MEC 1988). Thus, despite increasing subsidies for private schools throughout the last decade, in 1993, the rate of non-state subsidised private schools of primary and secondary level in Spain was higher than in France (OECD 1995, Fernández Mellizo-Soto 2000).

The young people of this analysis went to school in the system as it was designed by the *LGE* (General Law on Education) in 1970, since the step-wise implementation of the new education system began only after 1990. As in France, education can be divided into three levels:

1. Primary school (*Enseñanza General Básica, EGB*), which ends at age 14, and which was the age-limit for compulsory education until the reform of 1990.
2. Secondary school with its general path (*Bachillerato Unificado y Polivalente, BUP* and *Curso de Orientación Universitaria, COU*) and with its first and second level professional education paths (*Formación Profesional, FP*). The complete general path, which gives access to university, lasts until age 18 and the first degree professional path finishes normally at age 16 and the second degree at age 18.
3. Tertiary education goes until age 21 if somebody follows a short course and until age 23/24 if a five-year path is the aim. Clearly, it frequently lasts longer than the theoretically foreseen time, as is also the case if somebody undertakes doctoral studies. Unlike in France, there is no system of elite universities, even if private universities are increasing in number in recent years.

Like in France and even more than there, in Spain formal vocational education is dominated by the school system and dual-system vocational training is mostly non existent. Education at primary level is free in the public system, whereas fees have to be paid in private schools at secondary level. Enrolment in tertiary education is not free, and relatively high tuition fees have to be paid. For children from low-income families and from large families exemption from fee payment is granted. The Spanish Welfare State helps families considerably in their education tasks. This has been one of main developments in the Spanish Welfare State in the last decades. Yet, in secondary and tertiary education Spanish families have to pay, on average, more than French families (see below).

Another well-known indicator of public help for families is the rate of very young children in childcare. France belongs, together with the Scandinavian countries, to those societies which have the highest rate of children aged 3 to 5 covered by public child care services (Duncan 1996). In France in 1993-94, 35 per cent of children aged 2 were enrolled in public child care and 99 per cent of those aged 3 were enrolled (DEP 1995). This French environment of early public care of children in combination with a high rate of employed mothers might have long-term consequences on young people's values about independence from parents and on their degree of individualism, and thus indirectly influence young people's decisions of leaving home.

One important Welfare State shortcoming in Spain is the lack of child-care services for very young children (0-3 years of age) and the inadequacy of most child care services in terms of quality and time schedules, so that it is difficult for women to combine family and work. In 1992/1993 only around 8 per cent of children aged 2 were enrolled in a pre-school, while the enrolment rate of older children was higher and attained a maximum of around 100 per cent at the age of 5 (Eurydice 1996). The number of children under age 2 cared for in public centres was in 1991-1992 one of the lowest among EU countries: 0.1 per cent for those under 1 year; 0.5 per cent for 1-year-olds and 1.4 for 2-year-olds (MEC 1994, Valiente 1995). Thus, compared to France the Spanish Welfare State cares for very young children less, and for employed mothers help from family members is very important.

To sum up, children in France are not only a private affair, since the state recognises their financial support and well-being as a priority of public social policies, in particular through pre-school education and education in general. State intervention in education and in family policy, as described below, socialises the tasks of bringing up children to a much greater extent than in countries with poor family policy. Let us illustrate this further by describing the role of child benefits in France and Spain.

Family benefits are social rights of parents, who receive allowances due to the assumption that children depend on their parents and that the state aims to redistribute child costs horizontally. Child-related social rights will be described for two reasons: first, to clarify which are the categories of young people, for whom parents are entitled to benefits; and second, to look for the public definition of dependent childhood.

Family policy in France is a very developed and differentiated strand of the Welfare State with a long history and high levels of generosity from a comparative perspective (Lenoir 1991, Commaille/Singly 1996). Around twenty different family and child allowances exist in France nowadays, which can be divided into four different types: 1. income-maintenance allowances; 2. birth and young-child allowances; 3. one-parent allowances; 4. housing allowances.[1]

1. Universal child allowances from the second child onwards (*allocations familiales*); means-tested child allowances for families with three or more children (*complément familial*); means-tested allowances for children in school (*allocation de rentrée scolaire*).
2. Allowances for very young children, which are universal until the child is three months old and means-tested until age three (*allocation pour jeune enfant*); universal allowances for mothers with three children, who have left the labour force (*allocation parentale d'éducation*); universal allowances for employed parents who employ someone to take care of their children aged under three (*allocation de garde d'enfant à domicile*); universal allowances for paying a publicly recognised mother's help (*aide à la famille pour l'emploi d'une assistante maternelle agréée*).
3. Means-tested allowances for single mothers or fathers with children under age three (*allocation de parent isolé*); allowances for single parents (*allocation de soutien familial*).
4. Universal housing allowances for families receiving child allowances, for young married couples, and for families with a dependent elderly relative (*allocation de logement familiale*); means-tested housing allowances (*allocation de logement sociale*).

In addition, the French state concedes tax exemptions for families with children (*quotient familial*). Income tax is based on a progressive rate and on the household unit, and it takes family obligations into account through a mechanism whereby the taxable income is divided by a factor representing the number of dependent family members. A single, divorced, or widowed person without a child is assigned factor one, a married person factor two, a married or widowed person with one dependent child scores factor two and a half, with two dependent children factor three, and so on. For the calculation of the taxable income of a couple with two children, for instance, it means that first the total household income is divided by factor three in order to calculate the tax due to one part taking advantage of the lower tax rate for lower amounts, and then this amount of income tax is multiplied by three to obtain the total tax amount. This very specific form of income tax, which was introduced in 1946 and only slightly changed since then, has some drawbacks in terms of vertical redistribution, since it offers families with high income and children relatively better tax conditions than families with low income and children (Trotabas/Cotteret 1990, Glaude 1991, Villac 1993).

Universal benefits for all families are lacking in the Spanish social security system, as are benefits for specific family problems such as one-parent families, and advance maintenance payments for separated mothers and their children. Since the creation of child benefits in 1938, the goals of Spanish family policy have undergone major changes. Initially, pronatalism and horizontal redistribution following family criteria through wage supplements and social security predominated, whereas since 1985 an anti-poverty policy with special focus on poor families has been enforced. From 1971–85 social security family benefits were nearly non-existent in quantitative terms, partly due to the ideological connection of family policy to the dictatorship. Non-recurrent benefits and benefits for dependent spouses, which had lost most of their real monetary value during the 1970s, were discontinued in 1985. At the same time a monthly supplement of 1050 Ptas for every dependent child was created for retired employees and for those receiving unemployment benefits (Coll Cuota and Martín Jadraque, 1993). This supplement meant that in 1990, an unemployed family head with two children received child benefits worth 5% of the minimum wage. But for other recipients the value of the child benefit for two children decreased to 1% of minimum wage in 1990.

With the introduction of non-contributory social transfers in 1991, family benefits changed completely: benefits for dependent children (*prestación familiar por hijo a cargo*) were introduced, and all legal residents of Spain with dependent children under 18 are eligible, whether or not they are enrolled in social security.[2] But this benefit is subject to a means test that takes the number of children into account. In 1991 income ceilings for recipients of child benefits were fixed at 1 million Ptas per year for one child (1,123,084 Ptas in 1996) and increased by 15% for every additional child (INSS 1996). Children under 18 received 36,000 Pta. per year (1996). For a family with two children this represents benefits equivalent to 10% of the minimum wage. Benefits for disabled children are not subject to a means test and vary with the degree of handicap. After the age of 18 child benefits are restricted to children with a handicap over 65% or more. In 1995 a new law on large families was passed to include families with three children into the category of large families. As of October 1995, the main benefit for large families was a 50 per cent reduction in children's university registration fees (*El País*, 2 October 1995). As in France, the Spanish state concedes tax exemptions for children. In 1991 parents could deduce 18,100 Ptas for each child, which represents less than 3 per cent of the annual minimum wage. In comparative European studies on family policies, Spain ranks among the lowest positions in generosity in child benefits for a couple with children (Bradshaw et. al 1993, Flaquer 2000). Again, the conclusion is that in Spain families have to cope with more tasks than in France. Last, the definition of childhood by the state is to be analysed, to see how the two states define the timing of the social rights career.

In France, we find three age-limits for children's entitlement to any family allowance. General entitlement to child benefits lasts until age 16, if the child is effectively enrolled in education. Children can continue to be entitled until age 18 if they are out of the labour force or their market income does not exceed 55 per cent of the national minimum wage (*SMIC*). Allowances can be received until age 20, if the child accomplishes an apprenticeship, a vocational training stage, is enrolled in education or if he/she is unable to enter the labour force for reasons of illness or handicap (Julliot 1991). Tax exemptions for a dependent child display a very similar regulation of age-limits. Children up to age 18 are taken into account; children up to age 21 can be considered as if they are single, studying or fulfilling their military service; and for children in education the age-limit goes up to 25 (Trotabas/Cotteret 1990).[3] To sum up, the French social security system offers parents entitlement to child benefits during the children's period of transition into social independence, since by age 20 around 50 per cent of young people had already left home once. The French Welfare State does not consider children aged 25 to be dependent on their parents, but to be citizens with entitlement to means-tested social benefits (cf. below).

In Spain, means-tested child benefits can be obtained while the child is under 18 years old, while tax exemptions for children go until age 30 (25, in 1988), if the child does not have his or her own family (since 1989, or if this new family has an annual income under 618,000 Ptas.) and if the child's income does not exceed 123,000 Ptas (1991). Older handicapped children with an income under 123,600 Ptas (1991), who are part of family unit can benefit from tax exemption without age-limit (Delgado Diaz et al. 1989). In contrast to France the age-limit for entitlement to child benefits is lower in Spain, but it is higher for tax exemptions instead. On one hand, the Welfare State does not consider young people over 18 as dependent on their parents, but on the other hand it is as if tax exemptions for children had been designed taking into consideration that leaving home in Spain is a long process which lasts frequently until age 30, and which entitles the family to a tax reduction if the child's income is low. Further on it will be shown that the Spanish Welfare State defines childhood in most cases as a situation which lasts longer than in France (cf. conclusion of Chapter 9).

Another important field where the definition of childhood can be studied is entitlement to health services. What are the conditions that have to be met in order to be entitled to health services as a dependent child or as a citizen? In general in France, young people are entitled to health care services until age 20 in the frame of their parents' insurance. Indirect entitlement to health services is not linked to the fact of sharing the household with the parents, but it depends on age-limits and enrolment in education. The following differences in entitlement can be listed:

1. Young unemployed people receiving an unemployment allowance continue their previous affiliation to social security automatically and are directly entitled to health benefits. First-employment seekers, who have not contributed to social security, are directly entitled to health services in case of illness and maternity. Unemployed people who have finished their unemployment benefit period are also directly entitled to health services for an unlimited time period as long as they continue seeking employment. Thus, the fact of entering the labour market, be it as an employee or as an unemployed person turns young people into citizens.
2. Students under 20 are entitled to health services indirectly through their parents, while young apprentices are entitled directly, since they have a labour contract giving them rights to social security affiliation. Students from 20 to 26 enrolled in a university or a preparatory class for a *Grande École* have access to a special social security scheme for students and are thus directly entitled to health services.
3. Economically inactive young people over 20 can sign up to a special health insurance scheme which is open to all people living in France who have no right to another type of health insurance (*assurance personnelle*). If they are not able to pay the contributions themselves, then the social assistance assumes the costs (Dupeyroux 1988). In July 1992 a new law on cost-free health services for needy people has increased the conditions for access to health services (Delhoume 1995).

Unlike in France, in Spain in 1990 there was no age limit which restricted children's indirect access to health services. The conditions were to live with the insured father or mother, to be maintained by them, and not to receive an income higher than twice the minimum wage. Also, no other entitlement to health insurance should exist. Young people enrolled in education or unemployed people with unemployment protection are also entitled to health services.

1. Young people enrolled in secondary or tertiary formal education institutions and who are younger than 28 are automatically insured by a special school insurance (*seguro escolar*), which entitles them to health services.
2. First-employment seekers have no direct entitlement to health services, but unemployed people receiving unemployment benefits continue to

be covered by health insurance. Unemployed people who have finished their unemployment protection can benefit from health services if they pass a means-test, continue searching for employment and are not entitled to health services by other means (MTSS 1991).

3. Since 1989, every citizen resident in Spain whose annual income is the same or below the minimum wage is entitled to health services under the same conditions as those insured through social security (MTSS 1991).

In contrast to France young people who live with their parents and who depend on them can be insured with them in their health insurance as long as necessary. As is the case for tax law, long-lasting cohabitation of young people with their parents is recognised by the Welfare State. Dependent childhood depends less on age and more on the current financial situation and living arrangement.

Finally the question of social assistance for young people will now be dealt with. Besides family and housing benefits, which to some extent serve as social assistance measures, a specific social assistance exists in France. The minimum allowance for integration (*revenu minimum d'insertion or RMI*) was created by a December 1988 law. To be eligible the individual has to be aged 25 or under with family obligations, and he has to live alone or with a partner as a couple. It is a means-tested measure for people with very low resources. The aim of this benefit is to guarantee an income of 2,000 FF for one person and 600 FF for a child (1988), i.e. around 50 per cent of the minimum wage. An individual entitled to RMI is also automatically entitled to health services and to APL housing allowance (cf. Chapter 9). People who receive RMI can profit from specific subsidised employment measures and special loans for housing (cf. Chapter 8 and Chapter 9). The profile of beneficiaries goes from marginalised young people, some unemployed young people, and many old people. At the beginning of the 1990s a third of the beneficiaries were under 30 years old (Raymond 1995, Delhoume 1995). There are also other social assistance benefits under regional and municipal responsibility, but directed towards old-aged people and handicapped people (Delhoume 1995).

Unlike in France, there is no national social assistance scheme, but by 1996 all regions (*Comunidades Autónomas*) had enacted laws guaranteeing a minimum income for families (*rentas mínimas de inserción* or *salarios sociales*), and by 1990 the regions of The Basque Country, Navarre, Andalusia, Cantabria, Catalonia, and Madrid had introduced this new 'social assistance', financed by the regions (Estivill 1993, Sanzo 1993). Despite the differences between the various regional social assistance programs, some common characteristics can be pointed out. As in France, these allowances are for very poor people and all these programs relate the allowances to activities of re-integration into society, mainly through work requirements. In addition, and most importantly for this research, nearly all regions have two age conditions, age 25 as minimum age-limit or to be under 25 with family obligations.[4] As in France, beneficiaries have to live alone or in a new family unit. The basic allowance for one person in 1993 amounted on average to 34,337 Ptas. per month, representing, as in France, 50 per cent of the minimum wage. At the beginning of the 1990s and based on a sample of five regions, the rate of households headed by a young person aged 16 to 24 who received some benefit, in relation to the total number of households benefiting from an allowance, ranged from 5 to 19 per cent (Aguilar et al. 1995). Thus, in France and in Spain young people aged 25 can benefit from social assistance, but only if they live independently.

To conclude, the French Welfare State does not relate indirect and direct social rights for young people to the condition of living in the parental home, but to age-limits and handicap only.[5] Child benefits last until age 20/25 and direct social rights to social assistance are acquired by age 20/25. A possible gap without rights exist between 20 to 25 years for young people without family obligations, who live independently, have not yet entered a job with social security and who do not seek employment. These people have no right to income maintenance. In consequence, young people do not receive incentives to live with their parents, since living away does not reduce their parents' transfer income nor does it reduce the range of social rights available to youth. Instead, having their own dwelling allows young people to claim housing benefits (cf. Chapter 9).

In Spain child benefits are so low that, even if health services and tax exemptions for children are related to living and being maintained by parents, they do not represent any incentive to staying at home. Indirect rights to health services through co-residence with parents could be a more important incentive, but health services are universal in Spain, so that everybody on a low income has access to them, independently of their living arrangement.

Let us now move to the acquisition of direct social rights according to the category a young person belongs to. Social rights for students, young employees, and young unemployed people have to be studied separately.

Multiple Social Benefits for Students

Students in France receive state support in the form of services (residence halls, health insurance, refectories, reduced costs for public transport, and some cultural activities) and in the form of allowances (grants and housing allowances). For female students the dependence-diversification hypothesis has been confirmed by the empirical analysis, in the sense that the combination of market income and public benefits is the most determinant combination of resources to explain the likelihood of students living independently (cf. Chapter 5). It was also shown that many more French than Spanish people left home in order to live in residence halls, that full-time students in France are more likely to live independently than their Spanish counterparts and that a great number of French young people living in one-person households are students. In this section public benefits for students will be described for the period from 1986 to 1992 by looking at entitlement conditions, coverage rates, and their generosity.

In March 1991, a reform of public benefits for students was undertaken in France, which resulted in an increase in the number and in the amount of student grants and in the institution of a system of loans, which are guaranteed by the state. In 1992, 16.6 per cent of the tertiary education system students received a grant, which represented five times more students than in 1960 (Massit-Folléa/Epinette 1992).

In Spain in 1991 the law in force, which regulated university grants, dated from 1983. In 1991, 17 per cent of the students received some form of grant, but many of them were a very low amount. In 1989/90 a new type of grant was created for those students whose parental home is so far away from the university town that they cannot commute every day, but have to live away from home. In November 1998, a new benefit for students was created. The Ministry of Education and Culture offers students in the last year of their studies the possibility of asking for a loan with a very low interest rate (approximately 1.3 %). The loan can reach the maximum annual amount of 630,000 Ptas and will be paid monthly for a period of nine months. It means a maximum monthly amount of 70,000 Ptas, i.e. around 419 ECU.[6] The only condition to be fulfilled is to have passed all the previous academic courses successfully. These loans are intended to facilitate the finishing off of one's studies and the search for a first employment (Mercado de Trabajo, 27.11.98).

Public-funded Housing for Students in France

An important help for French students is the public residence halls. In France, two institutions are responsible for the social and economic well being of students. The *Centre National des Oeuvres Universitaires et Scolaires* (CNOUS) at the national level and the *Centres Regionaux des Oeuvres Universitaires et Scolaries* (CROUS) at the regional level. These institutions have a tradition that goes back to 1920, a time when young people from lower social class origin began to enrol in university, and different university towns therefore created some help for them. By law the CNOUS and the CROUS exist since 1955. The CROUS provide three different types of student accommodation:

1. residence halls of old and new construction,
2. subsidised social flats, and
3. information about private accommodation.

Students' entitlement to housing benefits depends on the student's income, on the income of her or his parents, on the distance of the university from the parents' residence and on academic performance. Places are primarily reserved for students with limited financial means. Students pay only for the running costs (heat, electricity, water and staff) and, thus, they have to pay rather low rents. The contracts for rooms in the residence halls are, in general, concluded for a period of 9 months, since it is assumed that students will stay at their parents' homes during holidays. Alternatively, apartments in residence halls can be rented for a period of 12 months.

At the beginning of the 1990s, around 240 residence halls were administered by the CROUS and some additional places were available in subsidised social flats (Schäferbarthold 1993). In 1996 the places offered were: 96,000 rooms in halls, 45,500 apartments, 6,750 dwellings in public social housing (*Habitation a loyer modéré, HLM*), and 1,450 beds in associated halls (CNOUS 1998). In 1988, the sum of places in residence halls, *HLM* dwellings and associated halls was 116,833 places, which, divided by the number of students in the academic year 1988/89 (1,477,077) yields a coverage rate of 8 per cent (OECD 1989).

In 1992 and in 1997, the average rent for a room (9 m^2) in a hall built in the 1960s was 700 FF per month, which represents 12% of the national minimum wage in 1992 and 100 PPS.[7] Since 1991 students living in a hall can apply for a housing allowance (*allocation de logement a caractère social, ALS*), which in 1997 amounted to 285 FF per month and by this means the final rent for a room was 415 FF per month.[8] In 1997, an apartment (18m^2) in one of the new halls had to be paid at 1,700 FF per month, but this rent could be reduced to around 700 FF per month after subtracting the housing allowance. Students under some conditions can receive an APL-housing allowance (*aide personnalisée au logement*), which according to the zone of habitat amounted from 1,102 to 1,227 FF per month in 1997.[9]

Social flats, *named habitations à loyer modéré*, are owned by semi-public institutions, but furniture is provided by the CROUS. In 1992, the monthly rent for a social flat amounted to approximately 1,200 FF, i.e. 27% of the minimum wage and 173 PPS.[10] These flats are aimed at young couples and these can ask for an APL-housing benefit.

In addition, the CROUS informs students about private accommodations in town and they advertise in the press to find additional rooms for students. In 1992, the rent of a private room amounted to around 1,200 to 2,000 FF (27-44% of the minimum wage) depending on the town (Schaeferbarthold 1992, CNOUS 1998).

With respect to the coverage rate, two representative surveys and one quasi-representative survey on students at the beginning of the 1990s offer figures on the use of public housing by students. In 1992, the CREDOC (*Centre de Recherche pour l'Étude et l'Observations des Conditions de Vie*) conducted a survey directed towards French students in universities and technological university institutes (*Institut Universitaire Technologique or IUT*). This survey reports that 36 per cent of the students were living in the parental home, 13 per cent in a residence hall and 51 per cent in a private dwelling. Two other surveys, conducted by the Sociological Observatory of Change in 1992 and by the Observatory of Students' Life in 1994, show very similar results. The percentage of students living with their parents is much higher in Paris (63%) than out of the area of the capital (33%). This difference is related to the high rents in Paris, which are around two and a half times higher than in other parts of the country. Universities in regional capitals, on the other hand, receive students coming from municipalities that are rather far away from the university town, forcing these students to find a dwelling outside the parental home. One third of the students who come from provincial towns of middle to large size have their parents more than 100 km away from the location of their university. Consequently, students of provincial origin live in residence halls more often. Students who live in halls are also more frequently from lower social class origin and they are more likely to receive a public grant (Galland/Oberti 1996). Following my own elaboration with the *Enquête Jeunes 1992*, 9 per cent of the full-time students who lived independently were living in a rented and furnished dwelling or residence hall, 9 per cent had rented an HLM dwelling, 10 per cent were in a dwelling given by relatives, friends, etc., 28 per cent were living in a self-owned dwelling (by them or their parents), and 44 per cent had rented a dwelling on the private market. Irrespective of the type of dwelling, as many as 80 per cent of the students who lived independently were receiving financial help from their parents, since the parents were paying the rent or the mortgage or were allowing their children to stay in a dwelling owned by the family.[11]

Residence Halls in Spain

In Spain, there is no equivalent to the CNOUS nor is there another type of central institution responsible for students' social affairs. All facilities and services except state grants are provided by the universities themselves. This results in scarce statistical information on the socio-economic situation of students. However, some general information and figures can be provided. In most university towns two different types of residence halls for students can be found: 1. *Colegios Mayores* and 2. *Residencias*. The first have a long tradition, they are maintained by universities, by public or by private organisations and they offer students half or full board. In 1998 there were 163 Colegios Mayores. 15 per cent were public, 25 per cent depended on non-religious institutions, and 60 per cent on religious organisations. Most of the halls are uni-sex, since only 38 halls accept female and male students together. There are long waiting lists for acceptance into the *Colegios Mayores* and there can be up to 300 applications for 30 available places. Applicants are chosen according to their qualifications. Students have to re-apply every year and they can live in the residence halls during the nine months of the academic year, like in France. In 1992, the monthly rent oscillated between 32,000 and 60,000 Ptas, which means 273 to 512 PPS. These amounts are much higher than the 100 PPS a French student had to pay for a room in a residence hall. In Spain, some special scholarships (approximately 15% of the places) are awarded for students from the Colegios Mayores, where academic performance is the main selection criterion. The other type of residence halls, the *Residencias* are most of them private commercial enterprises. Rents in these places vary greatly. In 1998 they ranged from 60,000 to 90,000 Ptas (Schäferbarthold 1992, El País 13.10.1998).

Table 7.2 shows the number of places in residence halls in France and Spain and the respective coverage rates. In Spain, the most dominant residence hall is the Colegio Mayor. The coverage rate in Spain is less than half that of France, though the Spanish figures are from 1991, while the French ones are from 1988.

Table 7.2 Residence Halls in Spain 1991/France 1988

Spain			France	
Type of Residence	Number	Places	Places	Type of Residence
Colegios Mayores	155	21,060	102,760	Cité Universitaire
Residencias	50	5,555	10,778	H.L.M
			3,295	Foyers Agréés
Total	205	26,615	116,833	Total
Students	1,137,228		1,471,900	Students
Places/students * 100	2.3%		7.9%	Places/students * 100

Source: Consejo de Universidades, 1991, 1992; INSEE 1993, OECD 1989.

We have already mentioned that the Spanish sociodemograpic survey used for this research does not offer accurate information on students living outside of the parental home during their study period. Valenzuela Rubio (1994) offers some data on the situation of students who left home in order to study in another town. According to these figures in 1991/92 the proportion of students living away from home out of all students in their respective universities reaches a maximum of 62 per cent in the university of Castile-La Mancha, 48 per cent in Valladolid, and only 9 per cent in Seville and 11 per cent in the "Universidad Autónoma" in Madrid. The proportion of these students living outside of the parental home in relation to places offered in residence halls goes from 3 per cent in the University of the Basque Country to 26 per cent in the "Universidad Complutense" in Madrid. The expansion of enrolment in higher education in Spain has been characterised by the creation of universities in many regions, so that universities have got closer to young people's homes, instead of sparking off geographical mobility in order to study at a university (Garrido/Requena 1996).

At the beginning of the 1990s some public efforts were made to augment the number of residence halls for students, but their number is limited and their nature is rather erratic. A first example is the central plan of the Ministry of Social Affairs of 1990. The Ministry devised a programme for the construction of housing for students who left the parental home to go to a university town. The Ministry signed conventions with regions, municipalities, and universities, which foresaw the construction of housing to be used by students during the academic year and by other people during the summer. Entitlement to places in these residence halls would follow criteria of income, distance to parental home, and academic achievement. This plan foresaw the construction of residence halls in nine university towns and the creation of 1200 places per year, around 3000 places in total (MAS 1994). Another example is the construction of a residence hall in the *Universidad Autonoma* of Barcelona. In 1992 the municipality of Barcelona organised the Olympic Games, and it decided to construct accommodation for the participants of the Games at some distance from the city in a place easily protected by the police. After the Games, it was decided that this building should be transformed into a residence hall for students, professors, and employees of the above-mentioned university.

To conclude, public housing is especially important for those students whose parents have low resources and who live in rather rural areas. In Spain public provision of residence halls is more or less non-existent, but private institutions are not very diffused either. Thus, French students can afford to study in a town far away from their parents' home more easily, since they receive public help for accommodation and for maintenance.

Grants for Students

The French Welfare State offers two types of grants for students:

1. grants according to social criteria (*bourses sur critères sociaux*) and
2. grants following academic criteria (*bourses à caractère spécial*).

The first group of grants is thought to be a complement to the family help a student receives in order to be able to maintain herself during the period of studies. Entitlement to the first type of grant depends on resources and expenditure of the student and of her/his parents, on age, school certificate, type of tertiary studies to be followed and performance during study time. The potential beneficiary has to be under 26 years old when asking for the grant the first time and every year he/she has to show some progress according to established criteria. Grants cover the study phase of nine months a year and they are granted for the first and second phases of studies, i.e. until the level of Licence. Beneficiaries are exempted from tuition fees and from contribution to students' social security system. Normally, they have priority for obtaining a place in of residence hall and also for obtaining a job as school assistant in secondary schools (*surveillant scolaire*).

The second type of grant is assigned according to academic performance and by the president of the university's proposal. These grants are mainly used by students of the third phase of studies (*DEA* and *DESS*) and to some extent also by students who prepare a competition to enter the public administration, such as the competitions for *l'agrégation* (examination to become a teacher in a public secondary school), for l'ENA (*Ecole Nationale de l'Administration*), etc. (cf. Table 7.3). These latter grants are named grants for public service (*bourses de service public*). Students who continue their studies after the completion of the third phase can apply for a research grant (*allocation de recherche*).

In addition, students, who do not receive a grant, can apply for special loans (*prêts d'honneur*), which are interest-free. Their amount is similar to the amount of a grant, but their number is rather small (OECD 1989). In 1993, in addition to the grant system, academic assistance funds for specific urgent cases (*aides individualisées exceptionnelles, AIE*) were offered for especially needy students like students who are bringing up children (EURYDICE 1993, Schäferbarthold 1992). Since 1991 the state guarantees additional loans given to students by banks. Due to the rather unattractive interest conditions, the total number of loans in 1991/92, 36,000, was rather low (Massit-Folléa/Epinette 1992).

In 1992 in France, the level of a grant ranged from 4,680 and 16,236 FF a year and between 6,210 and 17,442 for students who had committed themselves to work in the public sector for ten years, i.e. 670-2323 PPS and 888-2495 PPS respectively. The highest possible monthly amount for normal scholarships was thus of 335 PPS. Following the CREDOC survey the average monthly amount of a grant was 1,460 FF in 1992, i.e. 210 PPS (Richter 1992, EURYDICE 1993, Galland/Oberti 1996). The exact distribution according to type and amount of grant and the main beneficiaries are illustrated in Table 7.3 for the academic year 1993/94. In this year many beneficiaries of means-tested grants (around 43%) are found among those who receive the highest grant amount, which is nearly the same distribution as in 1987/88 (OECD 1989).

Table 7.3 Amounts and Distribution of Grants in France, 1993-94

	Means-tested grants			Special grants	
	Annual amount (FF)	% beneficiaries		Annual amount (FF)	% beneficiaries
1er échelon	6,588	12.6	Licence	17,442	0.1
2e échelon	9,882	13.7	Service public	17,766	4.5
3e échelon	12,744	15.8	DEA	19,440	52.4
4e échelon	15,498	14.7	DESS	19,440	28.1
5e échelon	17,766	43.2	Agrégation	21,006	14.9
total		100	total		100
number		374,380	number		12,693

Source: DEP, 1995.

In Spain in 1991, grants for students were regulated by a royal decree of 1983 and annually a government decree specifies the details of the grants. Two types of national grants can be distinguished:

1. Grants based on a means test and on academic performance (*ayuda compensatoria*) and
2. scholarships for an assistantship with a professor or lecturer or for co-operation in research projects during the final two years of the longer *licenciatura* studies and for the final year of the shorter *diplomatura* studies (*proyecto fin de carrera* or *becas de colaboración*).

In addition to national grants, regional authorities award various scholarships to students from their respective regions. Both types of national grants are conditioned by academic achievement and family income (Schäferbarthold 1992). Like in France, beneficiaries of grants are exempted from tuition fees. In addition, there are also students, who do not get a scholarship, but who are exempted from paying tuition fees (EURYDICE 1993).

In Spain in 1990/91, students applying for an *ayuda compensatoria* were entitled to 214,000 Ptas for the academic year, that is 1,824 PPS. This grant could be complemented with a travel grant depending on the distance (cf. Table). If the distance of the student's home residence from the university town required living away from the parents' home, an accommodation benefit could be awarded (208,000 Ptas). Also, students received an annual amount of 20,000 Ptas for study materials and of 50,000 Ptas for a project at the end of their studies. Students entitled to a grant are exempted from payment of study fees, which in Spain are relatively high (around 44,000 to 62,000 Ptas in 1990). Students who received a *beca de colaboración* were entitled to annual grants of 300,000 Ptas (1992), if they were studying in their home town, and 500,000 Ptas for other, i.e. 2,558 and 4,263 PPS respectively (Schäferbarthold 1993, Consejo de Universidades 1992). Thus, a student who received a grant with accommodation and study material supplements, received in 1990/91 an annual amount of 436,200 Ptas which is equivalent to 3,717 PPS and to 310 PPS per month. Table 7.4 shows that out of all the beneficiaries, only 21 per cent received a maintenance grant and 38 per cent a residence grant. However, all beneficiaries received a grant for material. In 1990-91, the average annual amount of a grant awarded to the beneficiaries was 181,398 Ptas, i.e. 129 PPS per month (Consejo de Universidades 1992).[12]

Table 7.4 Amount and Distribution of Means-tested Grants, Spain 1989/91

		Annual amount (Ptas)		
		1989/90	1990/91	% beneficiaries of total, 1990/91
Ayuda compensatoria		200,000	214,000	20.47
Transport	5-10 km	13,000	14,000	4.72
	10-30 km	30,000	32,000	15.22
	30-50 km	63,000	67,000	7.09
	> 50 km	75,000	80,000	2.80
	urban	12,000	12,000	12.67
Residence		195,000	208,000	37.50
Material		20,000	20,000	100.00
End of studies project			50,000	0.50
Total beneficiaries				161,446

Source: MEC 1992, Consejo de Universidades 1992.
Note: scholarships for material are for all beneficiaries and they can be added to other types of scholarships.

It has become clear, that French grants and Spanish grants are organised in different ways. This makes it necessary to compare average amounts or highest amounts. The average monthly amounts in France and

Spain, as published by the CREDOC in 1992 and by the Consejo de Universidades in 1991 are 210 PPS and 129 PPS respectively. This means the French average amount is nearly twice as high as the Spanish one. Nevertheless, the difference between the highest possible amounts in Spain (1991) and in France (1992) is very small. The highest monthly amount in Spain is 310 PPS and 335 PPS in France. This means that the French means-test allows more students to receive a rather generous grant, while this is not the case in Spain. Finally, the question of how many students receive a grant will be looked at.

Due to the differences in the organisation of the grants system in both countries, the calculation of comparable coverage rates presents several problems. First, one has to distinguish which types of scholarships are considered in the total amount. The Spanish Ministry of Education calculates the rate including all types of grants, it means exemptions of tuition fees, benefits for the acquisition of books, support for transport, grants for living outside the parental home, and allowances for maintenance. This rate reached approximately 20 per cent in 1992 and it is very frequently compared with the rates calculated in other countries (Eurydice 1993, Schäferbarthold 1992). But the French grants system is different and the calculation of the coverage rate, is too. In France different types of grant exist, but these are all aimed at helping the student to cover maintenance costs, there are no specific transport or book benefits. Thus, if one wants to compare Spain with France, only allowances for maintenance have to be considered in the Spanish case. A second problem lies in the definition of student, which is taken as the denominator. In both countries the respective ministries take the current number of enrolled students, but in the above-mentioned publications the base for France is only those students who depend on the Ministry of Education. Students who depend on other ministries or who are in private institutions are excluded. This yields a coverage rate of 18 per cent in 1992/93 (EURYDICE 1993). In Spain public and private university students are all included in calculations instead. To solve these problems I had to do my own calculations, differentiating according to the type of grant and taking students in all types of tertiary institutions as the base.

Table 7.5 Grants and Coverage Rates of Grants in Spain, 1988/89-1990/91

	Number of grants by type				Exemp-tions	Total	Students	Coverage		
Year	Compen-sation	Transport	Resid-ence	Other*	Tuition fees	Beneficiaries		Compen-sation	Resid-ence	All
1988-89	37,781	102,925	-	159,335	1,032	191,395	1,027,018	3.7	-	18.6
1989-90	38,388	81,531	59,960	169,311	34,976	201,836	1,067,874	3.6	5.6	18.9
1990-91	32,886	79,301	60,233	163,894	36,231	197,677	1,140,572	2.9	5.3	17.3

Note: Students in Spain means enrolled students in all types of public and private tertiary education excluding doctoral students. In Spain, students who receive a grant are also exempted from tuition fees, but some students are exempted from fees, while they do not receive a grant. In addition, students can accumulate different types of grants. * In 1988-89, "other" includes benefits for material and plane. In 1989-90, "other" includes material, plane and general allowances. In 1990-91, it includes those of the previous year and benefits for end of studies project. Sources: Consejo de Universidades 1990, 1991, 1992.

Table 7.5 shows for Spain that the coverage rate of students who receive the most generous grants, compensation and residence grants, oscillates around 3 to 5 per cent (1990/91), which is a much smaller percentage than the usually published coverage rate of 18-20 per cent.

Table 7.6 Number of Grants and Coverage Rates of Grants in France, 1987/88-1993/94

	Grants				Students	Coverage		
	Special[a]	Means-tested	Other[b]	Total		Special in %	Means-tested in %	all grants in %
1987-88	8,643	188,177	3,640	200,460	1,417,487	0.6	13.3	14.1
1988-89				224,344	1,477,077			15.2
1989-90				248,228	1,585,300			15.7
1990-91				272,996	1,698,716			16.1
1991-92				303,071	1,840,307			16.5
1992-93				337,792	1,951,994			17.3
1993-94	12,693	347,380	33,381	393,454	2,074,591	0.6	16.7	19.0

Note: Students in France refers to all enrolled students in all types of public and private tertiary education without overseas regions.[a] Special grants include "allocataires d'études, boursiers d'agrégation, boursiers de service public", which are all grants depending on academic performance.[b] other includes "prêts d'honneur" (loans), grants for "Intsituts Universitaires de Formation des Maîtres". Sources: OECD 1989, DEP, 1995; INSEE 1993.

If the coverage rate is calculated with all students, then in 1991/92 and 1992/93 the French coverage rate is 17 per cent (Table 7.6). This coverage rate is near to the 18% reported above, which takes only students in institutions administered by the Ministry of Education into account. Coverage rates differ by type of tertiary institution. According to administrative sources, in 1988/89, 15 per cent of the university students, 32 percent of IUT students and 16 per cent of *classes préparatoires* students received a grant (Richter 1992). The previously mentioned representative survey conducted by CREDOC in 1992 found 23 per cent of the students who reported that they were receiving a scholarship, which is about the same rate as that reported by administrative sources, since the survey did not include students of the *classes préparatoires* (Galland/Oberti 1996).

To conclude, it can be said that the French grants system is more generous and that it covers more students than the Spanish system. In 1990/91, French maintenance grants covered around 16 per cent of all students, while Spanish maintenance grants covered around 4 per cent of all students. In France, on the average, students can pay 30 to 50 per cent of their expenses with the amount of the grant, since they live frequently in subsidised residence halls.[13] There is no official estimation of the living cost of students in Spain, but for 1991 an amount of between 55,000 and 75,000 Ptas, excluding fees, can be assumed (Schäferbarthold 1992). This means that on average students could finance 20 to 28 per cent of their maintenance costs. Besides public help most parents of students have to help their children financially and they do so in both countries, but in Spain financial support of parents is more necessary than in France.

Public housing for students in combination with grants facilitates leaving home for French students in order to study, whereas Spanish public help is very limited, so that Spanish parents have necessarily to finance most of the costs. Mobility of students in Spain is a very costly affair, and it is a burden mainly financed by the family. Thus, public social policies for students in France are more extensive and more generous. Let us next describe the situation of young people who left school or university and entered the labour force.

Notes

[1] This description of social security benefitsrefers to the general regime of the French social security, which protects around 80 per cent of the inhabitants of France. For the situation in other regimes, cf. Julliot 1991.

[2] Law about child allowances (Ley 26/90, 20 de diciembre sobre Prestaciones no contributivas). All citizens living in Spain and disposing of small incomes are entitled to these allowances. In 1991 a Royal Decree specified the Law (Real Decreto 356/1991, 15 de marzo).

[3] For children over 18 years of age the factor for tax exemption moves from one to half. Married children until 21 or 25, if studying, can also be considered for tax exemptions in the household of one of the parents.

[4] Two regions have different rules: 1. Andalusia has no age-limit for young people if these do not live alone, but if they live alone they have to be over 35, and Aragon applies the same rules as the majority but with a minimum age-limit of 18.

[5] One exception is young workers' entitlement to ALS housing allowance, which is incompatible with his/her parents entitlement to child benefits (cf. Chapter 9).

[6] The current exchange rate of 1 ECU is 167 Ptas.

[7] PPS=Purchasing Power Standard. In 1992, 1 PPS was worth 6.94 FF.

[8] The ALS-housing allowance exists since 1971, but students were not entitled to apply for it until 1991/93 (cf. Chapter 9).

[9] The student has to live in an apartment or a room in a residence hall regulated by the state. The dwelling has to be the official residence and has to fulfil certain norms concerning the size of the dwelling (cf. Chapter 9).

[10] The monthly SMIC was calculated by taking the SMIC per hour before social contributions and multiplying it by 169, which are the working hours in a month (39 hours week) (INSEE 1993).

[11] These calculations are based on the *France86* sample, which means that the base of calculation are those young people who in 1986 were living in the parental home and who faced the opportunity of leaving during a six-year time period until 1992.

[12] The average amount includes the amount for tuition fees.

[13] For 1992, the average monthly living costs for French students were estimated to be on average 4,200 FF for students benefiting from CROUS services living in Paris and 3,800 for those living in other parts. Students without access to CROUS services had higher expenses, 4,800 and 4,400 FF respectively (Schäferbarthold 1992).

8 Public Regulation of Youth Labour Markets

Labour market careers of young people are regulated by the State through an active employment policy. The interesting aspects of this regulation for the leaving home process are twofold. First, there is the question of whether active employment policies affect young people's income level and income stability and thus facilitate their financial autonomy; and secondly, whether these policies increase the velocity of young people's entrance into a long-term employment and in consequence provide them with a stable income at an early age. The second point has to be postponed until the end of this section.

The answer to the first question is that young people have access to income through employment measures, but that their income level is not always sufficiently high to enable financial and social independence. Caussat (1995) performed a logistic regression analysis with survey data on French young people aged 15 to 29 receiving a market income in order to estimate the likelihood of living in the parental home.[1] After having controlled for sex, age, educational level, professional category of the father, type of parental family, region of residence, duration of employment, occurrence of unemployment, and short-term employment spells, he found that young people with an apprenticeship contract, a subsidised contract, a short-term contract, or a job as family help were more likely to live in the parents' home than young people with another type of job in the market sector. This supports our findings that people with short-term jobs tend to stay in the parental home more than those with long-term contracts (cf. Chapter 5). It will be shown for France and Spain that subsidised jobs are paid very little in comparison to non-regulated jobs, especially compared to long-term employment. Since market-income is not the only resource on which young people rely, it is important to see access to employment in combination with access to transfer income as described in below. The question of the stability of market income is dealt with when discussing the role of unemployment benefits and some data have already been presented in the section on labour market characteristics.

The scope of this part is to present the range of public measures available from 1985 to 1992 in Spain and France focusing on their quantitative importance, their generosity, their relation to social rights, and the evaluation of their effects on young people's way and pace of integration into stable employment relations.

In France during the period of 1986 to 1992, the state created three different types of employment measures for young people. First, subsidies for employment in the market sector in the form of contracts of alternation between work and training; second, subsidies for jobs in the non-market sector; and third, since 1989 the comprehensive programme for individual training (*crédit formation individualisé or CFI*), which includes various kinds of employment measures. Besides these programmes targeted at youth there are general employment measures to which young people can also have access, and which are described further on (Charraud Ses 1993).

In Spain for the period under study, 1985 to 1991, four main types of employment measures for young people can be distinguished. These have been in place in part since 1981, were revised in 1984 at the time of a general labour market reform in Spain, and were partly created in 1985. Of these four types, two were specific types of labour contracts in the market sector for young people from 16 to 28 years of age (*contratos en prácticas* and *contratos de formación*); one type consisted of grants and specific contracts for training in public institutions (*Escuelas-taller* and *casas de oficios*); and the third type consisted of subsidies for the conversion of temporary contracts into long-term contracts (*contratos indefinidos para trabajadores jóvenes*). In addition to these specifically youth-oriented contracts, the labour market reform of 1984 eased the use of short-term and part-time contracts, which had a significant effect on young people (Flórez Saborido 1994). In 1992 exemptions from social security contributions for the first two types of contracts (*contratos en prácticas y formación*) were ended and in 1993-94 a new labour market reform changed these forms of contracts (Cachón Rodríguez 1997). In October 1991 the competent authorities dealing with occupational training were decentralised: first to Catalonia, in 1992 to Valencia, in 1993 to Galicia and Andalusia, and in 1994 to the Canary Islands.

It is not the aim of this work to analyse the behaviour of the political actors and their aims, but it is worth mentioning that in 1988 the Spanish government tried to implement a plan for youth employment, which it had to shelve due to a general strike organised by the Spanish trade unions in 1988. The result of this strike was the increase of expenditure for unemployment protection and the withdrawal of the plan for youth employment (Márquez 1992, Garrido/Requena 1996).

Special Employment Contracts for Youth

In France, the most important group of employment measures for young people are those that aim to provide young people aged 16 to 25 with a vocational qualification through an employment contract alternating work in an enterprise with theoretical training in public or private education courses. Four types of contracts can be distinguished:

1. Practical training for initiation into professional life (*stage d'initiation à la vie professionelle, SVIP,* following a collective agreement in 1984 and in place until 1991), orientation contract (*contrat d'orientation* following a law of December 1991) and long-term contract for low qualified young people ("exo-jeunes" since October 1991);
2. Qualification contract (*contrat de qualification* following a law of February 1984);
3. Adaptation contract (*contrat d'adaptation* following a law of February 1984);
4. Apprenticeship contract (*contrat d'apprentissage* as reformed in 1987).

With respect to the length of the contract, the apprenticeship contract is the most generous, since it can be signed for one to three years and, in general, it lasts two years. Next comes the qualification contract, which lasts six months to two years and which aims to provide a professional qualification for young people with little formal education. The "adaptation" contract exists in two forms, one offering a contract for a period of six to twelve months and the other offering long-term employment. People applying for an "adaptation" contract have to already have a professional qualification and have to be able to integrate themselves into a job very quickly. The shortest contract time, six months, is provided by the orientation contract, whose aim is to provide a first experience of professional life for young people aged 16 to 22 without a professional qualification and with a relatively low general education. Its predecessor, the practical training for initiation into professional life (SVIP), had the same scope, it lasted between 3 to 6 months but was not an employment contract and had no training aims. (Juès1996, Bouder/Mansuy/Werquin 1995, Charraud Ses 1993). In October 1991, a new contract called "exo-jeunes" was introduced as a provisional project with the aim of filling the gap that appeared after the elimination of the SVIP. Young people with low qualifications aged 18 to 25 can benefit from this subsidised long-term contract (Tuchszirer/Gélot/Zilberman 1993).

All these first five measures entitled their beneficiaries to social security benefits and in all cases, except for the "adaptation" contract, the state paid the enterprise's social security contribution. In the case of "exo-jeunes" the state pays all social security contributions during the first year and a half of the contributions for the following six months within the limit of 120 per cent of the minimum wage.

The non-market measures for young people under 26 have only a marginal interest in providing some kind of qualification. In 1984, the state created collective utility jobs (*travaux d'utilité collective or TUC*). Young people had the legal status of a *stagaire* (person in practical training) of vocational training and were employed in part-time jobs in associations or in the public administration for a period of 3 to 12 months (later increased to a maximum of two years). In 1989 the TUC were replaced by employment-solidarity contracts (*contrats emploi-solidaritè or CES*). Unlike the TUC, this new measure is a real employment contract and the beneficiaries' pay is subjected to greater regulation. These contracts have a length of 3 months to one year - for some groups even three years - and are part-time. The state pays the entrepreneur's social security contribution with the exception of unemployment insurance (Nicole-Drancourt/Roulleau-Berger 1995, Meron/Minni 1995, Abbrosimov 1995).

The individualised training loan programme (CFI) is targeted at young people with few qualifications and it attempts to create a new training trajectory including practical training in enterprises, alternation contracts, and CES contracts (Charraud Ses 1993).

Table 8.1 Contract Duration and Monthly Earnings of People Aged 16 to 25 by Type of Youth-Specific Contract, France 1986-1992

Earnings and Duration	range of monthly earnings or average earning	average duration
Apprenticeships 1971-	25-78 [a]	2 years
Adaptation 1984-	80 [b] and at least SMIC	long-term
Qualification 1984-	30-75 [a] or [b]	> 1 year
SVIP 1984-1991	17-27 [a] plus 535-1580 FF	3-6 months
Orientation [c] 1992-	30-65 [a]	six months
TUC [c] 1984-1989	1,250 FF (+ max. 500 FF) in 1986	3-12 months (part-time)
CES 1990-	100 [a]	six months (part-time)
Exo-jeunes 1991-	71%, less than 6,000 FF in 1992	long-term

Note: [a] % of SMIC. [b] % of minimum fixed by collective agreement. [c] youth aged 16-21.
Sources: Juès 1996, Clémençon/Coutrot 1995, Abrossimov/Gelot/Roguet 1993, Catala 1989, Tuchszirer 1993, Villalard 1986.

Table 8.1 provides a summary of the wage amounts and the duration of the employment measures for young people for the period of interest for this study. France has a statutory national minimum wage (*salaire minimum de croissance or SMIC*), which can be improved by collective agreements. In 1986 the system was modified to enable young workers with integration contracts to be paid 45 to 90% of the national minimum wage (OECD 1994). As can be seen from Table 8.1 young people's wages differ from one contract type to the other and also in relation to age and duration of the contract. Nearly all young people with an alternation contract attain three quarters of the national minimum wage by the end of their contract, i.e. on average after two years, in particular those with an apprenticeship, an adaptation and a qualification contract. The TUC contract offered a low income, for it offered only part-time employment and this was paid below the minimum wage level. The CES contract increased the wage level to the SMIC norm, but since it offers only part-time employment, it provides half of the minimum wage. The statistical information on "exo-jeunes" measures shows that these young people earned on average less than 6.000 FF, which is an amount somewhat over the SMIC.[2]

Forgeot (1997) analysed the income levels of first jobs of young people interviewed in the *Enquête Jeunes 1992* and his analysis confirms the previous institutional information. In general, 72 per cent of those interviewed received a salary equal or inferior to the SMIC in their first job. The overwhelming majority of young people with an apprenticeship contract earned less than the SMIC and the majority of those with another type of subsidised contract also earned less than the SMIC. On the other hand, most young people who did not have these contracts or a part-time contract received a wage at SMIC level, many had a salary over this level and a minority earned less than the minimum wage. In other words, more than 60 per cent of first jobs that are paid below the minimum wage level correspond to an apprenticeship or a subsidised contract. Youth-specific employment is important in order to get into contact with the professional world - around half of the first jobs of young people in 1992 were youth-specific jobs (Forgeot 1997) - but it cannot insure a subsistence income by itself.

In Spain, there are four specific types of publicly regulated measures for the integration of young people into employment. The majority as modified by the labour market reform of October 1984:

1. contract for practical training (*contrato en prácticas*, Royal Decree 1992 of 1984) for young people aged 16 to 28,
2. contract for qualification (*contrato para la formación*, Royal Decree 1992 of 1984) for young people aged 16 to 19,
3. grants and contracts for workshop-schools and training houses (*programas de Escuelas-Taller y Casas de Oficio*, since 1985/88),
4. long-term contracts for young people under 26 years of age and young people with short-term contracts (*contratos por tiempo indefinido de trabajadores jóvenes y de otros colectivos*, from 1985 until 1988, from 1992 onwards).

Table 8.2 Contract Duration and Earnings of Contracts for Youth, Spain 1985-1991

Earnings and Duration	range of earnings or average earnings	legal duration	Ø duration 1987
Practical training Contract < 29, 1981-	fixed by collective agreement, but not lower than minimum base [a]	3 months – 3 years	16.8 months
Qualification Contract < 20, 1981-	80% of SMI in first year [b] 100% of SMI in second year	3 months – 3 years	14.5 months
Workshop/Profession schools 1985-88	1. phase: 550 PTA/day of course 2. phase: practical training or qualification contract	1.phase: 3–6 months 2.phase:6–30months	no information
Long-term contracts<26, 1985-88	normal wage corresponding to enterprise and work	long-term	no information

Note: [a] minimum base of the corresponding social security contribution group of the enterprise. In 1991, for workers aged 17 or less it was of 1,367 Ptas per day and for others it ranged from 62,130 to 92,820 Ptas per month according to professional situation. [b] Only the hours of work are paid, not those of qualification. SMI= minimum wage, which in 1991 amounted to 53,250 Ptas a month for those aged 18 or over and 35,160 Ptas per month for those aged under 18. Sources: Cachón Rodríguez 1997, Segura et al. 1991, MTSS 1991, RD 1992/1984 de 31 de octubre.

Getting a practical training contract is subjected to other conditions besides age. First, one has to be officialy registered as unemployed and one has to have obtained a formal education certificate (secondary or tertiary level) in the four years preceding the beginning of the employment. The programs of workshop-schools and training houses allowed the financing of projects of public employment or jobs in non-profit organisations with the granting of some qualification. In a first phase the beneficiary received some theory lessons and in the second phase she or he signed a practical training or qualification contract with a public or non-profit employer. The state subsidised the qualification part of the employment, the grants and salaries of the beneficiaries and teachers, and if necessary, costs for accommodation and transport. The European Social Fund co-financed these two types of employment-qualification programs. At the end of a period of practical training, of a qualification contract, or of another short-term contract, young people's long-term employment was subsidised by the state for some years. From 1985 to 1988, if employers hired young unemployed people under 26 or young people having passed through an employment measure, the state subsidised these new contracts. In 1992 a similar measure was reintroduced for young people under 30 (MTSS 1988, 1991, Flórez Saborido 1994).

Qualification and practical training contracts give rights to social security protection, but they are not subjected to contributions for old-age pensions. Also, practical training contracts of under 6 months of duration do not entitle the worker to unemployment insurance (Segura et al. 1991). Practical training and qualification contracts exempt the employer from paying all or a part of the social security contributions. In the case of practical training, the employer is entitled to an exemption of 75% of the contribution,[3] and in the case of qualification contracts to a 100% exemption for small enterprises and to a 90% one for large enterprises. In addition, according to the National Plan for Qualification and Professional Integration (*Plan FIP*) in 1988, employers could receive subsidies if the employed young person in practical training had been unemployed for at least two years, as well as subsidies for the theory courses in the programme of qualification contracts. The enterprise was entitled to 90 Ptas per worker and hour/day of theory course (Royal Decree of 1990), if a qualification project was presented to the INEM (Spanish Institute of Employment). Long-term contracts for young people under 26 enabled employers to pay a social security contribution of 12 per cent instead of one of 24 per cent for the whole period of the contract (MTSS 1988).

In 1993 the practical training and qualification contracts were changed. The use of the first was limited and the wage to be paid was lowered to the minimum wage. The second contract form was replaced by an apprenticeship contract (Flórez Saborido 1994, Cachón Rodríguez 1997).

Also, young Spanish people could and can participate in a variety of programs of vocational training, which were created and co-ordinated by the National Plan of Qualification and Professional Integration (*Plan FIP*) of 1985 and prolonged afterwards. Some of these qualification measures allowed young people to receive a grant for the time of the course. Table 8.3 shows the courses targeted at young unemployed people or at young people in rural areas. Young people over 25 or with family responsibilities received, in general, a grant for the time of the course of 75 per cent of the SMI without supplements and, if necessary, they were also entitled to some supplementary amount for transport, maintenance and accommodation. Furthermore, courses or practical training for other groups were offered: young people under 16 who had not completed formal education, young people in formal vocational training (*FP II*) or in the last two years of university, young men in military service, self-employed people, women with family responsibilities and in a difficult economic situation, etc. In general in 1991, courses lasted at least 200 hours and grants were paid at the end of the course (MTSS 1991). Thus, if one estimates a five-day week with 5 hours of course per day, it means that courses would last on average two months and so too the grant. This is clearly a very temporary possibility of receiving some income and it gives no right to affiliation to social security.

Table 8.3 Vocational Training Courses with Grants for Unemployed/Rural Youth, Spain 1991

Grants and Duration	Conditions	Amount of grant
Youth < 25	unemployment, low qualification	12,620 Ptas/month 75% of SMI [b] + 19,390 Ptas/month for transport and maintenance [a]
Youth >=25 and <=30	never worked more than 3 months	75% of SMI without supplementary payments + 19,390 Ptas/month for transport and maintenance [a]
Long-term Unemployed (> 1 year)	income <= SMI without supplementary payments	12,620 Ptas/month if age <25 75% SMI if family responsibilities or >25 [c] + 19,390 Ptas/month for transport and maintenance [a]
Youth under 25	practical training after completion of course	12,620 Ptas/month 75% of SMI [b] + 19,390 Ptas/month for transport and maintenance [a]
Youth in rural areas	workers in rural areas	12,620 Ptas/month 75% of SMI [b] [d] + 19,390 Ptas/month for transport and maintenance [a]

Notes: a If the young person has to live outside of the current residence in order to take part in the course she/he can receive a help of 5,203 Ptas a day instead of the 19,390 Ptas a month. b Amount conceded to young first employment-seeker with family responsibilities. c SMI without supplementary benefits for holidays, Christmas and so on. [d] If aged over 25.

Source: MTSS 1991.

It is difficult to know exactly the wage young people were earning in the above-mentioned regulated employment contracts. They earned more or less the minimum wage (more in the practical training contract and less in the first year of a qualification contract), which in 1991 was 1,775 Ptas a day or 53,250 Ptas a month for those aged 18 or over and 1,172 Ptas a day or 35,160 Ptas a month for those aged under 18. The amount could be increased if the employer paid supplements for long appartenance to the enterprise, for holidays, Christmas, and so on. All in all including supplements the annual minimum wage could not fall under 745,500 Ptas for those aged 18 or over and 492,240 for the younger ones. Assuming a young person aged over 18, working full-time and earning the minimum wage, the monthly wage was around 62,125 Ptas including supplements, it means 484 ECU and 530 PPS.[4] Compared with 75 per cent of the French minimum wage, which is the amount young people attained in the third year of an apprenticeship contract, on average young people in regulated contracts for integration in France earned 482 ECU and 488 PPS in 1991.[5] Thus, in absolute terms and within the limit of an institutional – not statistical – analysis, it can be stated that French and Spanish young people were entitled to similar wages in their entrance jobs, but in relative terms the Spanish amounts were more generous than the French ones.

The remaining question is how long these situations in regulated short-term contracts and in temporary employment in general persist in both countries. That is if on average in both countries young people need the same amount of time to acquire a long-term contract. The comparison of the activity structures in Chapter 4 suggests that young people in Spain stay in unstable employment conditions for longer than in France. This question is treated further on.

Other Employment Measures Affecting Youth

In addition to measures for young people the French state encouraged other employment contracts by subsidising employers or private households who employed people. Households who employed individuals for domestic work, for instance, could profit from a tax reduction. The state also subsidises enterprises (*entreprises d'insertion*, since 1982) and associations (*associations intermédiaires,* since 1987) who offer service or public utility jobs in the form of short-term contracts to unemployed people (Abbrosimov 1995). The stock of young people in *entreprises d'insertion* was of 5,000 people in December 1992 and it is, thus, a measure of minor numerical significance (Abrossimov/Gelot/Rouget 1993).

Another measure not directly targeted at young people is the total exemption of the employer's contribution to social security for two years if a first employee is hired. This subsidy was introduced in January 1989 in order to provide an incentive to self-employed people who offer a long-term contract to a first employee. In December 1991, the possibility of exemption from social security contributions for one year in case of employment of a second or third employee was added to the first measure. Around 72,000 people were hired taking advantage of these subsidies in 1991, and 31 per cent were young people under 25 years and 22 per cent were aged 25 to 29 years. This yields a rather small absolute number of young people (22,176), but is still higher than the SIVP practical training measure (cf. Figure 8.1) (Gaye 1995).

As already mentioned, nearly all youth-specific employment contracts are short-term contracts (exceptions are adaptation and *exo-jeunes* contracts). In addition to the whole range of these specific contracts, in 1986, the legislative restrictions on general fixed-term contracts were reduced. Short-term contracts did not need to follow specific reasons anymore, but a maximum duration of 24 months was fixed. In 1990, the law again regulated the use of fixed-term contracts, restricting them to cases of seasonal work, of replacement of another employee, or of temporary increase in workload. In addition, the general duration was reduced to 18 months (only under certain circumstances to 24 months) (OECD 1994).

In December 1989, a contract for re-entrance into employment (*contrat de retour à l'emploi or CRE*) was created for the RMI beneficiaries and for long-term unemployed people. Its duration could be from 6 to 18 months and the wage was fixed by collective agreement. The state liberates the employer from social security contributions and it offers a premium for each CRE employee (Clémençon Coutrot 1995, Raymond 1995). In December 1992, 10,300 young people under 25 benefited from a CRE contract, which is a smaller number than that of the beneficiaries of exemption for a first employee (Abrossimov/Gélot 1994).

Unlike in France, subsidised employment measures not directly targeted at young people were and are of great quantitative relevance for young people's employment in Spain (cf. Figure). The labour market reform of 1984 enlarged the conditions under which fixed-term contracts are allowed. Short-term contracts were more clearly defined than before, the maximum duration of given fixed-term contracts was shortened and a new short-term contract for the creation of new activities was introduced. The most important innovation was the possibility of hiring unemployed people through a short-term contract independently of the type of employment. In this way, in practice short-term contracts can be concluded with all types of workers. Unlike in Spain, fixed-term contracts in France (1990) are restricted to extraordinary conditions of the enterprise and limited to two years. In Spain in 1991, one could find nine different types of short-term contracts, a first group restricted to special circumstances of the enterprise (ordinary short-term), a second group targeted at unemployed people (promotion short-term), and a third group (specific short-term).

Ordinary short-term contracts:

1. service contract (*obra y servicio*);

2. temporary for production circumstances (*eventual por circunstancias de producción*);
3. interim contract (*interinidad*);
4. for new activity (*nueva actividad*).

Promotion short-term contracts:

5. temporary for augmentation of employment (*temporal de fomento de empleo*);

Specific short-term contracts:

6. job sharing (*relevo*);
7. practical training (*de prácticas*);
8. qualification (*de formación*);
9. substitution for retirement at 64 years (*sustitución por jubilación a los 64 años*).

In both countries short-term contracts convert themselves into long-term contracts, if the employee continues working for the enterprise after the time-period foreseen in the fixed-term contract (Segura et al. 1991).

In Spain, short-term contracts increased substantially after the labour market reform at 1984. In the second trimester of 1987, 1,225,800 employees had temporary contracts and they reached the number of 3,927,400 in 1991. In this same year they represented 32 per cent of all employees (Segura et al 1991, AEL 1992). The administration which registers fixed-term contracts does not distinguish them by age, but only by type, which does not permit us to understand the number of young people in ordinary and promotion short-term contracts. The expert committee of the report on temporary employment in Spain (Segura et al. 1991) had access to information which permitted them to estimate the number of young people in ordinary and specific fixed-term contracts. For 1989 they estimated that in the under 20 age-group 18 per cent of those who had a short-term contract had a general contract not specifically directed to young people, while 82 per cent had a contract for training or for qualification. In the group of young people aged 20 to 24, 72 per cent had a general temporary contract and in the group of those aged 25 to 29 as many as 83 per cent had a general fixed-term contract, while 16 per cent had a contract for practical training. Thus, unlike in France, Spanish young people from age 16 to 24 profited mostly from short-term contracts not targeted at young people and, consequently, without a qualification content (cf. Figure

8.2 and Figure 8.3). The average duration of short-term contracts was 15 months during the 1987-1995 period (García Polavieja 1998), which means that they were rather unstable, but also that most people were entitled to unemployment allowance.

Beneficiaries of Active Employment Policy for Youth in France and Spain

The comparison of the respective national effort on active employment policies for young people can be undertaken through an estimation of expenditures or through an estimation of beneficiaries. In this work the second option was chosen, since these figures allow for a better representation of the significance of these measures for young people's lives. However, the quantitative comparison of different employment policies has to overcome problems of definition and data availability. This section is a first attempt at this comparative task.

The quantitative significance of special contracts for youth in France and their development in time can be seen from Figure 8.1, where the annual stocks of contracts were measured. In 1987, special employment measures for young people under 26 years reached a peak and afterwards they dropped until 1991, but at the same time they reached absolute levels similar to the number of unemployed young people (aged 15 to 24). At the beginning of the period the two most important contract types were apprenticeships and TUC contracts, while at the end a third contract form, the qualification contract, became similarly significant.

Figure 8.1 Special Employment Contracts for Young People Aged 16 to 25, France 1986-1992 (average annual stock)

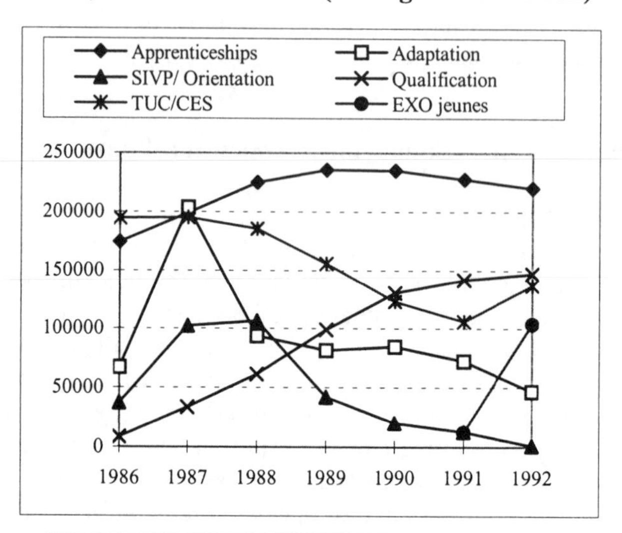

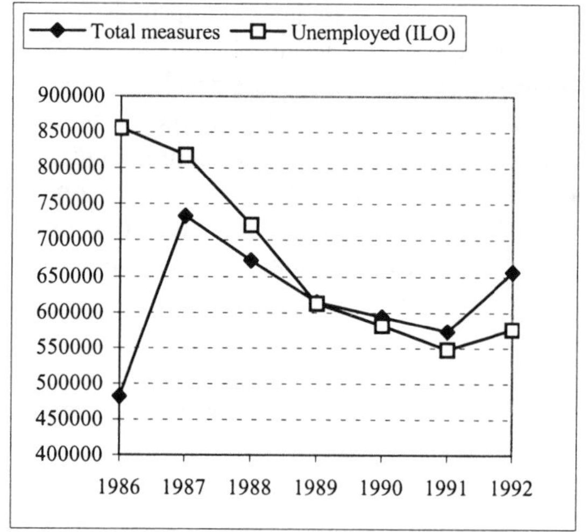

Note: unemployed as measured by labour force surveys (aged 15 to 24).
Sources: For employment measures 1986-1991: Ministère du Travail, de l'Emploi et de la Formation professionnelle in: Meron/Minni1995; for 1992: estimation of stock in December 1992 in: Abrossimov/Gelot/Rouget 1993; figures on unemployment: INSEE 1994.

The quantitative importance of the Spanish employment measures can be observed in Figure 8.2. The figure provides complete data on the number of registered youth-specific and general promotion short-term contracts until 1989. Published figures for later years were not available. Unlike the French stock data, Spanish figures refer to registered contracts, which in general are significantly higher than stock figures. This means that Spanish figures cannot be compared with the French figures, but are to be compared only with each other. In Spain, the most extended contract types are promotion fixed-term contracts for young people under age 25 and qualification contracts, which are for people aged 16 to 19. Of less quantitative importance are promotion short-term contracts registered by people aged 25 to 29 and practical training contracts, which can be used by young people until age 29. Thus, state subsidised contracts are more important for the younger age group (16 to 24) than for those aged 25 to 29. Unlike in France, young people have found more regulated jobs in non-youth-specific promotion measures than in youth-specific programmes.

Figure 8.2 Employment Contracts for Young People (aged 16 to 29), Spain 1985-1991 (annual registered contracts)

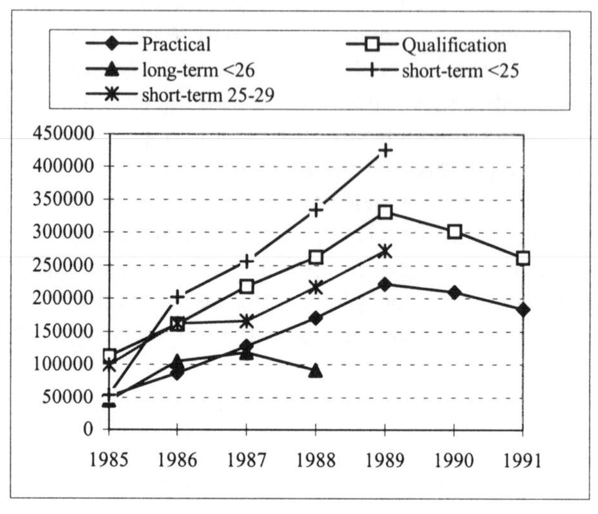

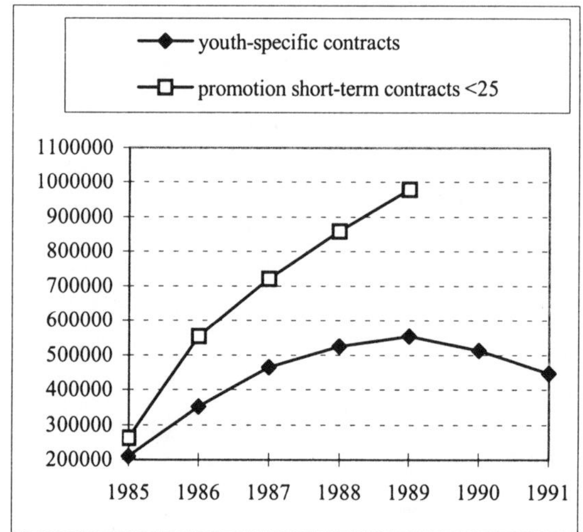

Note: Young people in subsidised short-term contracts are estimations made by Segura et al (1991) for the years of 1985 to 1989; they therefore lack data for 1990 and 1991. Unemployed as measured by labour force surveys (aged 16 to 24).

Sources: For employment measures: Cachón Rodríguez 1997; Segura et al. 1991; MTSS 1991. For unemployed: BEL 1994.

In order to estimate the public involvement in employment measures for young people and to make it comparable with French figures, existing stock statistics of the Spanish Labour Force Survey have been compared to the number of unemployed young people (Figure 8.3). The comparison is to be interpreted taking into account that the very important group of young people in general promotion fixed-term contracts is lacking and that the unemployed people taken into account include only young people aged 16 to 24, though youth-specific contracts are available for people aged 16 to 29. All these differences are not very important, since the emerging relationships are very clear. The stock of youth-specific contracts oscillated around 60,000 people during 1986 to 1991. If we multiply this figure by three[6] to obtain, more or less, an estimate of the total number of young people in subsidised contracts, the result is still a very small number (18%) in comparison to the average one million unemployed people aged 16 to 24. Thus, Spanish public effort to supply subsidised employment contracts for young people is much smaller than the French. This result corresponds with comparative estimates about expenditure on active employment measures made in a study for the European Parliament. This study estimated that in 1992/93 France invested one per cent of its GDP in active employment policy, while Spain invested one-half per cent of its GDP. Of these amounts France spent 35 per cent on young people, while Spain spent only 15 per cent for youth-specific measures (Parlamento Europeo 1995).

Figure 8.3 Stock of Youth-Specific Contracts (aged 16-29) and Unemployed (aged 16-24), Spain 1986-1989

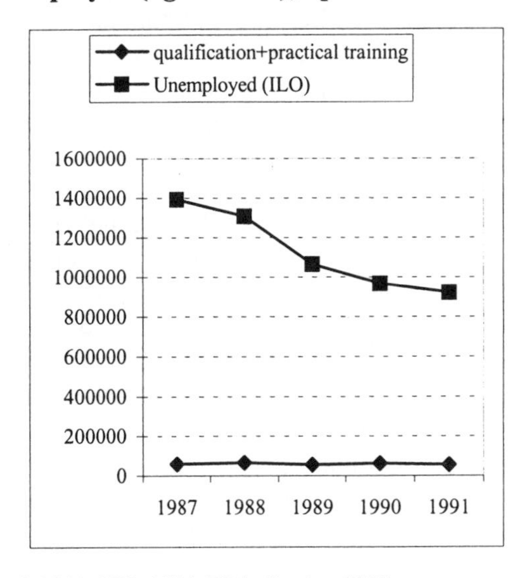

Sources: Segura et al. 1991, BEL 1994, EPA, II. trim. 1991.

To conclude, in the period from 1985/86 to 1988 the number of young people benefiting from a regulated short-term contract in comparison to the number of unemployed people aged 14/16 to 24 was higher in France than in Spain; that is, the effort of the French state in active employment policy for youth was greater. The next paragraph explores the average time young people need to wait until they earn on average a subsistence-level income.

Short French Queues: Financial Autonomy at Age 25

What role do all these public employment measures play in the integration of young people into employment? The evaluation of employment and training measures for young people is a very controversial field. Some French analysts have found that vocational training measures such as SIVP and TUC have no statistically significant effect on the transition into a long-term employment; in particular, they are not able to help women and young people whose fathers have a low educational level to find a stable job (Magnac 1997). Other studies have found that certain types of employment measures do help young people to enter stable employment or to avoid unemployment, while other types of measures do not change their probabilities of doing so (Clémençon/Coutrot 1995).

For the comparative question of why French young people leave home earlier than Spaniards it is important to know if young people in France receive a subsistence income earlier than in Spain and if they have a better chance of receiving it over a long period. The condition of benefiting from a subsistence income and from financial autonomy through market income is considered fulfilled when an individual receives at least the minimum wage. This occurs mainly when a young person moves into a non-regulated job. Three French studies provide information on the timing of moving into employment providing at least the minimum wage. First, there are the results of a study on the labour market career of young people leaving school at the end of the academic year 1988-89 (Werquin 1997).[7] This analysis is limited to young people who left school without a maturity certificate, but with professional qualifications and it reports on their activity situation in December in the years 1990, 1991, 1992, and 1993, and in January-February 1995. By the time of their entrance into the labour market in December 1989, around 20 per cent of the young women were unemployed, 30 per cent had employment, 8 per cent were economically inactive, and around 40 per cent had a subsidised employment contract, most of them CES contracts. Two years later, in December 1991, more young women had employment (around 50%), less were in a public measure (25%), and similar proportions were unemployed or economically inactive. At the same time, in December 1991, men were very frequently doing their military service and they profited less from public measures: around 15 per cent of the men were unemployed, 55 per cent had a job, 15 per cent were economically inactive, and 15 per cent were in an employment measure. Hence, women profited more from public employment contracts and they found unregulated jobs less quickly than men. A comparison with a previous study of the same author shows that for a previous cohort, those who left school in December 1986, employment measures were even more important for the transition into employment, since the unemployment situation was worse. Thus, French public employment measures seem to have helped young people with secondary educational level to receive some income during their first period in search of a first employment, and to make contact with the professional world, and they were especially important for women's access to an income. With respect to the timing question it can be stated that half of these young people had a unregulated job two years after their entrance into the labour market, that is, when they were 18 to 20 years old. Did these jobs provide people with a subsistence income?

In 1993, the CEREQ again asked a sample of people who entered the labour market in 1989 about their trajectories during these four years.[8] This sample includes youth who had no general maturity certificate, who had left school before finishing lower secondary education, those who had attained a certificate of vocational competence (CAP), who had attended a preparatory apprenticeship class (CPPN) or had a diploma of vocational studies (BEP) or an equivalent certificate, people with a vocational maturity certificate (BAC pro) or with a technician's diploma (BT), and young people who had already completed an apprenticeship. These people were on average between 16 and 18 year old when they entered the labour market and four years later they were between 20 and 24 years old. By this age, 75 per cent of all the young people and 60 per cent the of young women had reached financial independence, for they earned at least the minimum wage (SMIC) for full-time employment (4,500 FF). To begin the labour market career with an alternation contract seems to have positive effects on improving the employment situation, since 77 per cent of these young people reached financial autonomy after four years, even if on average they earned less than those who began with a normal fixed or long-term contract. Instead, beginning their career in a CES or TUC employment measure allowed only 52 per cent to reach financial autonomy after four years. There is almost no difference in the attainment of financial autonomy if one has gone through long-term or fixed-term contracts. Frequently, young people interrupt long-term contracts, while short-term contracts seem to be used by large enterprises, which after some time offer long-term contracts and relatively high salaries (Bordigoni/Mansuy 1997). To conclude, by age 20 to 24 three out of four French young people without a general maturity certificate and without university qualifications had reached financial autonomy and some of them had already reached it before. Does this picture change when young people with higher educational levels are included?

By including young people with a higher educational level the age limits to obtain financial independence through market income move upwards. Based on the *Enquête Jeunes 1992*, Moncel et Rose (1995) found that there is a cutting line at age 25 with respect to the position youth occupy on the labour market. Nearly half of the young people under age 24 are unemployed, are in an employment measure, or have a short-term contract, while from age 26 to 29 young people are less likely to be in these positions. Correspondingly, 50 per cent of the people aged 18 to 25 earned less than 5000 FF per month, i.e. the minimum wage or less (714 ECU and 720 PPS), while those aged 26 to 29 received on average 6500 FF (929 ECU and 937 PPS).[9] The access to a job, in particular to a stable job with at least a minimum wage, can be perceived in terms of a queue, in which young people have to wait for a given time until they access such a job. Some of them, moreover, do not arrive at the end of the queue and remain in a chronic situation of precariousness. In 1992 in France, it would appear that on average the queue lasted until age 25 (Moncel/Rose 1995).

In Spain there are nearly no evaluation studies about the effects of employment policies for young people, and there is only a very small number of studies on income and wages of young people. A review of the statistics and reports published by the National Employment Office (INEM) reveals that there are no analytical studies on the integration into the labour market of young people who benefited from some employment measure. The INEM offers only some cross-sectional analyses of people who followed a vocational training course and the percentages of those who then entered a regulated job or another type of job. The INEM describes the situation of those pupils 11 months after they had finished the courses. In 1991, from 206,449 unemployed people who had finished a course successfully, 37 per cent had employment, 50 per cent were searching for employment, and 14 per cent were no longer registered in the INEM (INEM 1992).

For the region of Catalonia there are some retrospective and panel studies, which follow young people in their trajectories from school to work, but they do not analyse as a specific group those who had benefited from a regulated job. One study analyses the integration into employment of young people who have finished university. Catalan university leavers were asked retrospectively in 1989/90, 1991/92 and 1993/94 about their careers after their graduation in 1986, 1987 and 1988/89 respectively. Of interest here are the results concerning the economic independence of these young people, whose age at the moment of the interview ranged from 25.9 years to 30.7 years and from 21.9 to 26.7 when they finished university. The percentage of those still economically dependent on their parents at the moment of the interview ranges from 0.8 for Engineers to 27.5 for agricultural technical engineers. If we take a group in between, for instance those who finished with a law qualification, it can be observed that 10.5 of them were still economically dependent on their parents three years after having obtained their degree and of those who were already independent, the average age of becoming economically independent had been 23.7 years (Masjuan et al. 1996). Catalan young people with university degrees seem to stay in a similarly long queue for economic independence as French young people in general, but a real comparison is rather difficult to make.

In Spain, studies on earnings of young people are scarce, mainly because of a lack of data, since in the regular surveys on wages the units of analysis are enterprises and not individuals, which prevents an analysis by age. There are few other surveys, which have been used for a more detailed study. In 1985 a large survey on informal employment and other related matters was conducted and this is the source of many studies (Segura et al. 1991). In one article based on this survey, Toharia and Muro (1988) analysed the wage distribution of people with long-term contracts according to age. In 1985, young people aged 20 to 24 in long-term jobs earned, on the average, 50,000 Ptas per month and the group aged 25 to 29 earned 60,000 Ptas, while the age-group with the highest average wage were people of 35 to 39 years, who earned around 70,000 Ptas. This study is of very limited value, since it excludes many young people, namely those in fixed-term jobs. Another study based on the same survey estimated a wage equation taking age, sex, educational level, civil status, seniority, type of contract, economic sector, and region into account. They found that there was a wage differential of 8 per cent in favour of long-term employment, but this was a study of the situation in 1985 when short-term contracts were not yet very diffused (Segura et al. 1991). Finally, Jimeno and Toharia (1992) had access to an experimental labour force survey of the Spanish National Statistical Office (INE) conducted in 1991, where questions on income were asked. They found that, if one controls for age, sex, occupation, educational level, years passed in the enterprise, sector and activity of the enterprise, and region of residence, workers with short-term contracts earn approximately 11 per cent per hour less than long-term workers (cited and reproduced in García de Polavieja 1998).

Apart from these general studies on wages, there are two other ways of studying young people's earnings. First, some youth surveys have asked about income and earnings and second, family budget surveys provide some information on age. Comparative data on wage levels of young people in Spain and France can be obtained by comparing the Spanish Youth Survey of 1992 with the French Youth Survey of 1992.[10] More than 15 per cent of the young people aged 20 to 29 earn less than the Spanish minimum wage (Table 8.4). In France, more than 17% of this age group earn less than the French minimum wage. Yet, if one takes the wage category of 403 to 604 PPS as the subsistence level for both countries, then it can be observed that 15 per cent of Spanish young people with a market income receive a wage below the subsistence level, while only 10 per cent of the French do so. Sixty-one per cent of Spaniards earn 805 PPS or less, while only 43 per cent of the French fall into this wage category. In addition, 48 per cent of the Spanish young people aged 20 to 29 said they were employed and received an income, while 55 per cent of the French said the same. These figures correspond more or less to the respective employment rates of 48.6 and 52 per cent in the *Spainall* and *Franceall* samples. To conclude, young Spanish people are not only less present in the paid labour force, but, those who receive a market income also receive less than their French counterparts. The Spanish waiting queue for obtaining a subsistence wage is longer than the French one.[11]

Table 8.4 Monthly Earnings as Reported in Spanish and French Youth Surveys, 1992

Wage in PPS[12]	Spain % of aged 20-29	France % of aged 20-29	Spain, cum % of aged 20-29	France, cum % of aged 20-29
< 403	15.1	10.0	15.1	10.0
403-604	18.7	7.1	33.8	17.1
604-805	27.0	25.4	60.8	42.5
806-1,006	17.4	24.7	78.2	67.3
1,007-1,207	9.9	16.2	88.1	83.5
>1,208	11.9	16.5	100.0	100.0
	100.0	100.0		
Total with earnings	1,509	4,233		
Total sample	3,131	7,703		
% with earnings	48.2	55.0		
minimum wage in PPS	529	673		

Sources: author's elaboration according to Navarro López/Mateo Rivas 1993 and *Franceall*.

Conclusion

In France and Spain important efforts have been undertaken in the period from 1985 to 1992 to integrate young people into the labour market. Yet, the relative effort compared to the number of unemployed young people was much greater in France than in Spain. The generosity of youth-specific employment measures, as indicated by the average wage amount regulated by law, was greater in Spain than in France. However, the relative weight of these youth-specific jobs compared to all fixed-term jobs was much lower in Spain than in France. Average wages of young people aged 20 to 29 measured in PPS are lower in Spain than in France. Given the importance of income stability for leaving home, are there adequate insurance schemes for going through periods of unemployment? Does public unemployment protection mitigate the problem of job rotation?

Unemployed Youth and State Support, 1986-1992

It is nothing new to state that job security is becoming a scarce commodity, which does not necessarily constitute a problem in terms of financial autonomy, provided that the unemployed young person receives a subsistence level benefit until she or he finds a new job. Young unemployed people are not a homogeneous group, either in terms of their socio-economic condition or with respect to social rights. To understand their position in the Welfare State they have to be divided into four groups:

1. first-employment seekers;
2. unemployed people who had a job, which did not entitle them to benefits;
3. unemployed people who had a job with social security affiliation;
4. long-term unemployed people who had a job with social security affiliation.

There are two guiding questions: 1. which of these four groups of unemployed people are entitled to which unemployment benefits within the respective Welfare States? 2. are the levels of unemployment benefits and their duration adequate to guarantee financial autonomy between jobs?

First-Employment Seekers And Very Short-Term Workers

In France, first-employment seekers and young people who were dependent workers for a rather short period, from 3 to 6 months, or who had a job without unemployment insurance, e.g. CES-contract or an informal job, had the right to a means-tested unemployment allowance called integration allowance (*allocation d'insertion or AI*), if they fulfilled some conditions. Young people had to be aged 16 to 25 and they had to fulfil one of the following three conditions:

1. they had to have finished a practical training programme (*stage de formation professionnelle*), they had to have obtained a professional training qualification or they had to have finished a complete cycle in secondary or tertiary education in the 12 months preceding their enrolment as job seekers;
2. not more than six months should have passed since the end of their military service;
3. they had to help their family financially and the family had to have a monthly family income lower than 200 times the daily SMIC amount (i.e. lower than 6,460 FF or 923 ECU in 1991).[13]

The monthly income of the person should not exceed 90 times the daily amount of the AI, i.e. an income limit of 3,726 FF or 532 ECU per month, and if the person has a partner, their income should not exceed 180 times this amount.[14] Young people had to complete a given waiting time until they received the allowance: young men who had finished their military service had to wait for one month, those having gone through a practical training course lasting 3 to 6 months had to wait for 3 months and those entitled to AI due to their educational qualifications had to wait for 6 months. Once they had reached the entitlement moment they received a fixed daily allowance of 41.4 FF for the duration of one year (Dupeyroux 1988). This amount was not increased after 1985 and in January 1992 the AI for young people was abolished (Bolot-Gittler 1992, Amira 1996). In 1991 the monthly AI amount of 1,159 FF represented 26 per cent of the minimum wage, 166 ECU and 163 PPS. From the point of view of financial autonomy the problem with this allowance was the waiting period, during which the person had to live from savings, from an informal job income or from family help, and from the low allowance amount.

The extension of this allowance can be roughly estimated using published statistics. Figures on the beneficiaries of the AI allocation include not only young people but also other entitled categories, for instance single mothers, refugees and ex-prisoners. Since in 1992 single mothers and young people were no longer entitled to AI, the number of the other beneficiaries can be approximately calculated and deduced from the whole number for the previous years in order to obtain an idea on the volume of young beneficiaries. In 1986, there were around 165,000 young people and single mothers who benefited from AI and this number decreased over the period until it reached approximately 80,000 in 1991 (Amira 1996). This means that around 12 to 17 per cent of young unemployed people (15-24) were covered by an AI allowance during the period under observation.

Following the previously mentioned study of Werquin (1997), around 25 per cent of the unemployment periods of young women, who left secondary school without a maturity certificate in 1989, were immediately after they left school, while this was the case for circa 15 per cent of the men. The unemployment previous to first job spell lasted on average seven months for this cohort of young people, which means that most of them would in theory be covered during a part of their unemployment by the AI allowance (after a waiting period).

In Spain, no public unemployment benefit is foreseen for first-employment seekers. They can only be entitled to an occupational training course for a limited time period (cf. above).

In addition, the second group of unemployed people, namely young people in informal jobs or in jobs that in total did not exceed six months of contribution to unemployment insurance during the four years preceding unemployment, have no rights to unemployment benefits, with the exception of those with family responsibilities (MTSS 1991). This is unlike in France, where young people without family duties who contributed for three months to unemployment insurance, could receive an unemployment allowance (*allocation de base minorée or ABE*), provided these three months of contribution were concentrated in the last year preceding unemployment (cf. following). If one takes the worst case, i.e. somebody in an employment contract of only three months, she would have been entitled to unemployment benefits in France after the end of her employment, but not in Spain. There she would have to find another contract of at least three months duration in the following four years in order to be able to benefit from protection. In Spain in 1987 the average duration of regulated short-term contracts was around 15 to 17 months, which means that on the average, short-term employed people had access to unemployment benefits after the end of the contract (Segura et al. 1991, Polavieja 1998).

Unemployed People with Entitlement to Contributory Unemployment Allowance

The third group of unemployed young people, those who had had an employment contract and who had contributed to unemployment insurance for at least three months are entitled to unemployment benefits within the insurance scheme in France. They have to fulfil the general conditions of having lost their job involuntarily and of being in search of employment through the local agency for employment (ANPE).[15] Entitlement duration and the amount of the allowance depends on the contribution time and on age (cf. Table 8.5): people over age 50 received more generous benefits than those under this age. There is no waiting period for the allowances originating from the insurance scheme.

Table 8.5 Duration and Amount of Allowances by Type of Unemployment Benefit for Beneficiaries under Age 50, France 1992

Contribution time during last 12 months		3 months	6 months	12 months	24 months during last 36 months
Basic allocation (AB)	duration	3 months (allocation de base minorée, ABE)	8 + (2 months prolongation)	14 + (5 months prolongation)	21 + (12 months prolongation)
	amount[a]	30% of SR[b] + 32.9 FF a day (30.3%/37.1 FF)[c]	40% of SR + 43.87 per day[b] (40.4%/49.5)[c] allocation during prolongation is degressive: 0.85 every six months		
	Min./Maximum	Min: 79 FF p. day Max: 56.25% SR[b] Min: 89.7 FF p.d.[c]	Min: 105.5 FF per day Max: 75% SR[b] Min: 119.8 FF p.d.[c]		
Allocation of end of right (AFD)	duration	0	6 + (1 month prolongation)	12 + (4 months prolongation)	15 +(9 months prolongation
	amount[a]	0	64 FF per day[b], 76.6 FF[c]		
Max. duration	all allowances	3 months	15 months	30 months	45 months

Note: [a] the rate and fixed amounts refer to 1986. They have been increased until 1992 (cf. Bolot-Gittler 1992) [b]Amounts in 1986. SR = reference salary. [c]Amounts in 1990.

Sources: Bolot-Gittler 1992, Commission of the EU 1991.

Again, according to Werquin (1997) the second and third unemployment spell of young people who have left the education system without a maturity certificate lasted longer than seven months on the average, but not more than nine months. Those young people who had had a regulated employment contract, which lasted at least three months, would normally have contributed to unemployment insurance for three months and are thus very likely to be entitled to the reduced basic unemployment allowance (*allocation de base minorée or ABE*). These unemployed people will be protected for a duration of three months, which on the average seems to be too short a time to bridge the period of unemployment. In addition, they will receive a very low amount in terms of a subsistence income. Those unemployed people who have contributed for 6 or more months to the insurance scheme were better off in terms of duration and of income substitution, but here again, if the young person was earning only a minimum wage or less, the substitution income will be too low to be considered to be at the subsistence level. According to the previously mentioned study of Forgeot (1997) very young employees and workers are very likely to earn the minimum wage or less and, hence, if they become unemployed they will receive the minimum amount of the unemployment allowance, 3,594 FF per month in 1990, and will thus have less than the minimum wage. In addition, a high percentage of unemployed young people have no coverage of this sort, either because they are first-employment seekers or because they cannot fulfil the conditions of the insurance allowance or because they do not ask for benefits. In 1990, around 35 per cent of the unemployed under age 30 were covered by the unemployment insurance scheme (EC 1992).[16]

The duration of the allowances is quite long for people having contributed at least 6 months during the last year. If they have contributed more than six months a commission of employees' and employers' representatives decides on the possible prolongation of the allowance, which cannot, however, surpass a maximum duration (cf. Table 8.5). If no prolongation is conceded and the basic allocation is exhausted, then the unemployed person is entitled to "end of rights" allocation (AFD), which consists of a flat-rate for a given duration which depends on previous contributions, as can be seen from Table 8.5.

In Spain, laws and decrees about unemployment insurance and benefits have changed continuously since 1978 and so I have decided to describe the situation only for 1991 (for a detailed description cf. Jurado Guerrero 1995). In this year, young people could have access to the contributory unemployment allowance, if they had contributed for at least six months to the insurance.[17] Compared to France this is less favourable, in particular for the people employed for a short-term who worked for less than six months. According to their contribution time they could receive the allowance for up to 24 months. Afterwards, they could get a prolongation in the form of a non-contributory allowance up to 18 months if they had exhausted a duration period of the contributory allowance of at least 3 months. If they had been entitled to a contributory allowance for at least 6 months the prolongation could last up to 24 months. However, the non-contributory unemployment allowance is restricted to the unemployed with family responsibilities and it is means-tested. This allowance is not an individual right, but is a sort of family allowance for low-income one-earner couples, where the family head is unemployed.

As in France, the unemployed have to fulfil the general conditions of having lost their job involuntarily and of being in the process of searching for an employment through the public agency for employment (INEM). Entitlement duration and the amount of the allowance depends on the contribution time and on age (cf. Table 8.6): people age 45 or over receive more generous benefits than those under this age. There is, in general, no waiting period for the allowances originating from the insurance scheme (MTSS 1991).

Table 8.6 Duration and Amount of Allowances by Type of Unemployment Benefit for Beneficiaries under Age 45, Spain 1991

Contribution time during the last four years	Contributory Allowance (Prestación de nivel contributivo)			Non-contributive Allowance (subsidio por desempleo) for Unemployed With Family Responsibilities[c]	
	duration	amount[a]	Minimum/ Maximum	duration or prolongation	amount
3 months				3 months	
4 months	no rights			4 months	
4 months				5 months	
6-12 months	3 months			6–18 months	
12-18 months	6 months	80 % of BR[a]			
18-24 months	9 months				75 % of SMI
24-30 months	12 months		SMI+1/6 SMI/ 170% SMI + 1/6 SMI[b]		
30-36 months	15 months	70 % of BR[a]		6-24 months	
36-42 months	18 months				
42-48 months	21 months	60 % of BR[a]			
48 months	24 months				

Note: [a] BR= base reguladora (regulatory base), which is the average of the contribution base for the unemployment insurance during the last 180 days preceding the legal situation of unemployment or at the moment of ceasing to contribute. [b] if the unemployed person has dependent children the maximum amount is increased to 195% for one child, to 220% for two or more. [c] family responsibility means being responsible for the maintenance of the spouse or another relative up to the second degree of kin relationship inclusively, who lives with the unemployed person and if the total family income divided by the number of dependent members does not exceed the SMI.

Sources: MTSS 1991.

In Andalusia and Estremadura, a specific means-tested unemployment allowance for agricultural dayworkers was created in 1983. These people have to have contributed at least for 60 real working days to the specific agricultural social security scheme during the previous 12 months before unemployment. In these cases they can receive an unemployment allowance for a maximum of 20 days a month or 180 days a year and of 75% of the corresponding minimum wage. The duration of the allowance depends on age and family responsibilities. Within the group of young workers, the worst protection is given to those under 20 years without family responsibilities and the best to those aged over 25 independently of their family duties. The means-test is not individual, but it depends on the components of the household. A single person should not have an annual income over the annual SMI and if this person lives with another person over 16 years of age the limit is fixed at twice the SMI. If he or she lives with two other people then it is 2.75 times the SMI, and so on. As a consequence, young agricultural dayworkers over age 16 living with their parents and perhaps siblings, have worse unemployment protection than those living alone or with a partner, and in addition they reduce the amount of the allowance the father will receive, if he required it. The amount of the allowance is as high as the amount of the non-contributory unemployment allowance, but it is limited to 180 days a year (MTSS 1991). The type of work organisation, the particular form of family formation, and the institutionalisation of the unemployment allowance for dayworkers pushes young dayworkers towards leaving home early. These particularities are reflected in the regional variance of leaving home (cf. Chapter 6).

At this point it is time to compare the generosity of the contributory unemployment allowance of France and Spain. Considering that the average duration of qualification and practical training contracts in Spain is about 15 months (cf. Table 8.), it means that on the average young people who became unemployed after such a contract were entitled to six months of contributory unemployment allowance. Assuming further that the young unemployed person had had a special employment contract, was 18 or over, and that on the average she will have contributed according to a regulatory base similar to the minimum wage if not less, it means that she will be entitled to the minimum amount, which is the minimum wage plus supplements (the latter are 1/6 of SMI). In 1990, the SMI was 50,010 Ptas a month and with supplements it reached 58,345 Ptas. In France a young person with the same contribution time was entitled to a minimum allowance of 119.8 FF per day in 1990, which is equivalent to 3,594 FF per month.[18] Thus, for 1990 in purchasing power parity units, the Spanish allowance reached 496 PPS and the French one 505 PPS, which means that they were of similar generosity.[19]

With respect to coverage in 1991, approximately 16 per cent of young Spanish unemployed people under 25 were covered by the contributory unemployment insurance scheme, 16 per cent by the non-contributory allowance and 33 per cent were covered by one of the two allowances (AEL 1992).[20] In 1995 the corresponding Spanish rates were: 7 per cent, 8 per cent, and 15 per cent, much lower than in 1991 (BEL 1996).[21] Labour force survey figures show for 1990 a rate of young unemployed people under 30 covered by an unemployment allowance of 18 per cent. In any case, the comparison of coverage rates for 1990 shows that the French coverage of 35 per cent of the unemployed people under 30 receiving some allowance is higher than the Spanish rate (EC 1992).

Again, this ideal-typical young person who had contributed 15 months to the unemployment insurance (average of youth-specific contracts and of short-term contracts), would have the right to a 14-month allowance with a possible prolongation of 5 months in France, whereas in Spain the same person would receive the allowance only for a period of 6 months without the possibility of a prolongation. In terms of length, the French system is more generous than the Spanish system, and this applies also to long-term unemployed people outside the contributory scheme, as shown below.

However, published data show that in 1992 the average length of the contributory allowance in Spain was 11 months for those aged 20 to 24 and 14 months for those aged 25 to 29. This means that the younger age group might have contributed between 18 to 30 months on the average and the older group between 30 to 36 months (AEL 1991). It seems, thus, that on the average most young people with an entitlement to contributory benefits have worked before for a period of around two years. This does not change the fact that under the same conditions their French counterparts will be entitled to longer periods of unemployment insurance.

Long-term Unemployed Youth

The forth group, long-term unemployed people, who have lost entitlement to unemployment allowance due to its expiration, might be eligible for a means-tested unemployment assistance (*allocation de solidarité spécifique or ASS*) in France. The beneficiaries must prove they have worked as a dependent worker for five years during the last ten years preceding their entrance into entitlement to unemployment allowance and they have to pass a means-test. The unemployed person's income has to be lower than 90 times the daily amount of the ASS, and if living with a partner, it has to be lower than 180 time the ASS. The assistance is paid for six months and can then be prolonged without limit every six months (Dupeyroux 1988). This allowance is rather insignificant for young people given its contribution conditions: in 1996, only 15 per cent of its beneficiaries were under age 35 (Amira/Favre 1996).

In Spain, young people who have exhausted their entitlement to contributory unemployment allowance can benefit from a non-contributory allowance according to the months they originally contributed to unemployment insurance under two conditions: 1. they must pass a means-test and 2. have family responsibilities. Only in these cases can young long-term unemployed people profit from a prolongation of the unemployment allowance (cf. Table 8.6).

Unemployed People's Social Security

The last question to be treated is whether unemployed people receiving some kind of benefit have other social rights as well. In France, an unemployed person who receives an allowance is normally obliged to pay a contribution for health and old-age insurance. All unemployed people receiving benefits are at least entitled to health services. After the expiration of unemployment benefits the right to health services is prolonged for one year, after which they do not lose entitlement if they can prove that they are still searching for employment; otherwise they have to rely on a personal insurance and social assistance. Also, those unemployed people who were not affiliated to an insurance scheme before and are not entitled to unemployment benefits have to rely on cost-free medical help. Besides general unemployment benefits, other measures have been created to help unemployed people to find a job: allowance for training-reclassification, allowances for taking up part-time employment, local allowances for long-term unemployed people, etc. (Dupeyroux 1988).

In Spain, the National Institute for Employment pays the contributions of the employer and the dependent worker to the main social security insurances (old-age, family, transitory illness, health, and so on), so that the beneficiary of the contributory unemployment allowance remains insured. The beneficiaries of the non-contributory unemployment insurance are automatically insured against health risks and for family reasons, but lose other insurances. In addition, those unemployed who have lost the right to any unemployment allowance and whose income does not surpass the minimum wage continue to be entitled to health services and to child allowance (MTSS 1991). Apart from these general entitlements, there is the right for unemployed people with entitlement to contributory allowances to receive the total amount of the unemployment allowance and a part of the compulsory social security contribution, if she wants to become self-employed, a member of a co-operative, or a member of an employment enterprise (*sociedad laboral*).

Conclusion on Unemployment Protection

Unemployment benefits in France and Spain in their institutional form of 1991 provided a stable income to a minority of young people. The amount of the allowance young people could receive was structurally low, since many young people either had not worked before or had paid a low contribution to the unemployment insurance scheme. The same is true for the duration of the unemployment allowance. A comparison of the French and the Spanish situations yields the following results:

1. First-employment seekers were entitled to a means-tested allowance in France, while in Spain there was no such allowance. The French allowance amounted to 26 per cent of the minimum wage in 1991, i.e. 166 ECU or 163 PPS per month, and it covered around 12 to 17 per cent of the unemployed people aged 15 to 24 in the period from 1986 to 1992.
2. Young people with a job and a contribution time of under six months during the previous year were entitled to a reduced basic allowance in France, but in Spain they had no entitlement to unemployment allowance if they had no family duties. But if the Spanish young person had accumulated six months of contributions within the last four years, then she was entitled to unemployment benefits.
3. Young people with entitlement to contributory unemployment allowance and who had earned low wages received similarly generous minimum unemployment allowances in Spain and in France. In 1990 it stood at 496 PPS per month in Spain and 505 PPS in France. However, contributory unemployment allowances last twice as long in France as in Spain in the case of 15 months of contribution payment to the insurance.
4. Non-contributory and means-tested allowances in Spain are restricted to young unemployed people with family responsibilities, while in France young people without family obligations can benefit from them.
5. In 1990 and according to labour force survey data, unemployment allowances covered around 35 per cent of the unemployed people under 30 in France, while in Spain they covered around 18 per cent of the same age group of unemployed people.

To conclude with respect to the significance of these policies for income stability and for leaving home, it can be stated that French unemployment insurance might have favoured early home-leaving by providing the first-employment seeker with a low unemployment subsidy of one-year's duration. For young people who had contributed for at least three months to the insurance scheme, the system guaranteed an income stability of three months at a low level, but for those who had contributed for at least 6 months a maintenance income at a quasi-subsistence level was guaranteed for at least 14 months. In France more young people are covered by the contributory unemployment insurance than in Spain.

In Spain, only those who had had a job and who had contributed for at least six months were granted a transfer income at a quasi-subsistence level for six months. After this period young people without family duties, no longer had public help. The main problem with the Spanish system for income maintenance is, thus, the short duration of the unemployment allowance for young single people, the lack of help for first-employment seekers, and the lower coverage of unemployed youth.

Notes

[1] He used the *Enquête Jeunes 1992*.

[2] The SMIC in 1991 was of 32,30 FF gross per working hour, which corresponds to 4500 FF net per month (INSEE 1993).

[3] Only if it is a full-time employment.

[4] To compute the ECU amount the annual average exchange rate was used, which in 1991 was 128.47 Ptas for one ECU and 7 FF for one ECU. The PPS are also annual averages, whose rates were 6.92 FF and 117.3 Ptas (EUROSTAT 1995).

[5] The same was done for the conversion of the Franc to the ECU, in 1991 6.9 Francs for one ECU (INSEE 1996).

[6] This estimation is based on the relative distribution of youth-specific contracts registered in the INEM in 1991 (cf. Figure 8.3).

[7] The study is based on three phone panels undertaken by the CEREQ (*Centre d'études et de recherches sur les qualifications*). These surveys suffer from a relatively high panel mortality of around 20 per cent at each wave. To solve the bias problem a weighting procedure was applied and a supplementary sample was taken (Werquin 1997).

[8] This survey is of a retrospective nature and it had the form of personal interviews undertaken by interviewers of the INSEE (Bordigoni/Mansuy 1997).

[9] Survey informations on earnings always have to be taken with caution.

[10] The Spanish figures have been taken from the publication, Table 2.17 and they have been re-elaborated to obtain the wages only for those aged 20 to 29 (Navarro López/Mateo Rivas 1993). Then the wage levels of the publication have been transformed into the Purchasing Power Standard. The resulting wage groups have been reproduced with the *Franceall* sample in order to make both surveys comparable.

[11] This is also supported by the comparative findings on financial independence published by Barailler (1997).

[12] In Ptas the wage groups are as follows: <50,000; 50-75,000; 75-100,000; 100-125,000; 125-150,000; >150,000. In FF they are: <2,795; 2,795- 4,193; 4,193- 5,591; 5,591- 6,989; 6,989- 8,386; >8,386.

[13] Daily gross SMIC in 1991 was 32.3 FF.

[14] Daily AI amounted to 41.4 FF in 1991.

[15] For a good reason voluntary loss of employment can also not block entitlement to allowance (MISSOC 1992).

[16] This figure comes from the labour force survey and not from administrative information, which makes it less reliable but also more easily comparable with Spanish figures.

[17] In 1992 it was changed to one year (MTSS 1992).

[18] Assuming the payment for 30 days per month. French unemployment insurance covers all seven days of the week.

[19] The exchange rate in 1990 was of 117.7 Ptas for 1 PPS and of 7.12 FF for 1 PPS (Eurostat 1995).

[20] These figures are provided by the National Employment Agency (INEM) in different way. The INEM publishes the total number of beneficiaries by type of allowance in annual averages, but the table on beneficiaries by age and type of allowances contains only percentages and refers to beneficiaries in December. I have estimated the coverages rates with these figures and with the number of unemployed people as published by the Labour Force Survey. The number of beneficiaries of the non-contributory allowance includes the beneficiaries of the agricultural dayworker allowance.

[21] Since October 1996 the INEM publishes the total annual average number of beneficiaries by age and type of allowance for 1994 onwards, which permits us to know the rates of coverage for young people more accurately. The number of beneficiaries of the non-contributory allowance includes the beneficiaries of the agricultural dayworker allowance.

9 Youth and Housing Policies

Young people's decisions to leave the parental home are supposed to be influenced by the supply of dwellings. One exception is young people who decide to undertake studies, mostly university studies, which are not offered at their parents' place of residence, and which require leaving the parental home. These students have to adapt to the supply of housing in the university town. For all other young people, the evaluation of the affordability of a dwelling is a major element in their decision to leave the parental home as opposed to staying. The **high property-low affordability hypothesis** presented in Chapter 3 states that on housing markets with high prices, low vacancy rates, and low supply of rented housing, two-generation households will be more frequent and the diversity of one-generation households will be low. In Chapter 5, a simpler version of this hypothesis was tested with two logistic regression models for Spain and France. These models estimate the probability that those young people who live independently will live in a rented dwelling compared to the likelihood that they will live in an owned dwelling. It was found that cohabiting couples and individuals in one-person households are more likely to rent than to own a dwelling compared to young married people, and younger people live more frequently in rented dwellings than their older counterparts.

Thus, housing policy favouring young people's early home-leaving is mainly housing policy favouring an adequate supply of rented accommodation through the private or the public sector and financial help for people who are not able to afford the rent without a subsidy. Next, a comparative framework for the comparison of Spanish and French housing policies is elaborated.

Increasing Income and Rented Accommodation

The degree to which the state helps students on the housing market is one element for understanding cross-national differences in home-leaving patterns (cf. Chapter 7). The state also helps young economically active people on the housing market. The forms of public housing policy are manifold and not all have the same relevance in helping young people.

Studies of housing policy normally distinguish between governmental action in regulating the supply of housing by home constructors and regulating the demand of households by increasing the affordability of housing for needy social groups. In France supply side intervention receives the name of *aide à la pierre* (bricks and mortar aid), while demand side housing benefits are referred as *aide à la personne* (personal aid)(Blanc/Bertrand 1995). In Spain this difference is often referred to in the same way or through the distinction of *ayudas de carácter personal* (help for people) and *ayudas a la oferta de vivienda* (help for the housing supply) (Rodríguez 1993). Lundqvist (1990 in: Boelhouwer/Van der Heijden 1992) proposes an interesting framework for comparative research on housing policies, which helps to determine which regulations governments opt for and which they do not. He conceptualises the demand for housing through the household's purchasing power, which in its turn is influenced by general income policies, by income transfers, and in particular by housing allowances. On the supply side, Lundqvist depicts the dwelling price, which depends on the costs of dwelling production, as the most important element. The state might intervene in home production through capital cost subsidies, through rent, access and sales price regulations, and through the financing of management, repair and maintenance costs. Both, household purchasing power and dwelling price are, in addition, influenced by possession regulations, and income, property, and sales taxation. For the scope of the present study a more simplified model is thought to be adequate (Figure 9.1).

Figure 9.1 Housing Policy Favouring Very Young People Leaving Home

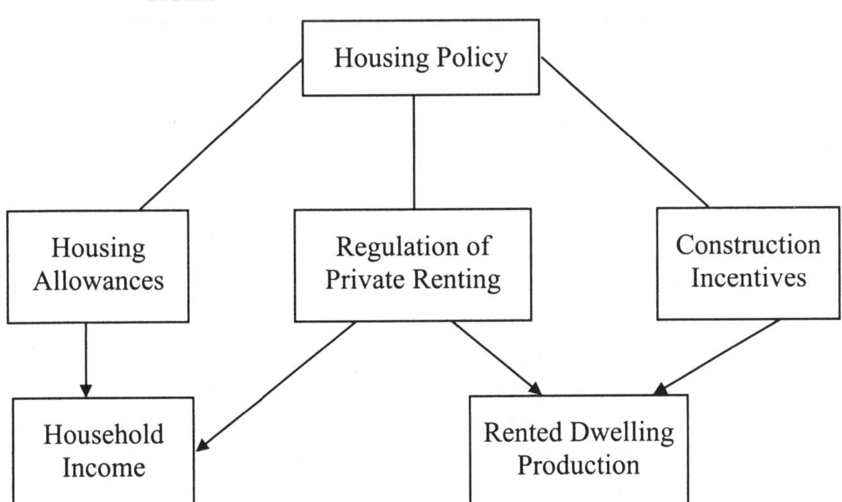

The previous discussion and results have shown that renting is the housing arrangement that most facilitates leaving the family of origin early and setting up informal living arrangements. Formal family formation through marriage, by contrast, is more strongly related to acquiring a dwelling and thus depends more on the investment capacity of young people. Consequently, the central housing policy benefits to be studied are housing allowances for tenants of rented housing, regulation of rents, and public incentives for the construction of dwellings to be rented. Thus, tax exemptions that seek to help buy a dwelling and public subsidies directed towards building houses to be sold to owner-occupiers are of minor relevance, even though these might help people who leave home in order to marry and, indirectly, help single young people to leave home by giving their parents incentives to acquire a dwelling for their child. Since this research focuses on the French particularities in contrast to Spain, it is important to analyse those mechanisms that help very young single people to leave home and which differ from one country to the other.

Overview of French and Spanish Housing Policies in 1985-1992

Boelhouwer and Van der Heijden (1992,1993), in their comparative housing policy study, characterised French housing policy from 1985 to

1990 as a policy of great emphasis on housing quality, on problems of housing distribution, and on targeting specific groups. In 1986, measures for the deregulation of the housing market had been implemented with the election of a Liberal government: firstly, through relaxing rent controls; secondly, through easing the sale of social rented housing; and finally, by reforming the system of housing finance. In spite of this liberalisation of housing policy, the state increased its involvement due to the reappearance of quantitative and qualitative housing shortages. Housing construction in the private rented and owner-occupied sectors was favoured through state benefits. Financial conditions affecting the private rented sector were eased and tax exemptions were granted to those who bought a dwelling and rented it out for more than six years.

Grants for social housing construction were increased in 1990 by 17 per cent and rent subsidies (APL) by 7.6 per cent. In 1990, the Ministry of Equipment and Housing had a budget which was second in size after the budget of the Ministry of Education and it represented the most important public investment programme. It is in this housing policy context that the young people studied with the *Enquête Jeunes 1992* left their parental homes. With regard to rent controls, a new Rent Act was passed in 1986, by which more freedom was conceded to landlords. They were obliged to offer tenants a contract for three years, instead of the average six years in 1982, and after the expiration of the contract they were allowed to give notice without giving reasons for it. As a consequence, enormous rent increases going from 51 to 180 per cent were witnessed, particularly in large cities. In 1989, the Rent Act was amended to limit rent increases for sitting tenants, and since then, rent regulation has passed under the control of the regions. In May 1990, a bill relating to housing vacancies was approved in order to enable HLM institutions (non-profit organisations who offer social rented housing) to purchase private housing and to rent it out at low rent levels. In addition, low-income households and those receiving social security benefits became entitled to a housing allowance enabling them to pay their rent.

In Spain housing policy was for a long time strongly dominated by the goal of favouring economic growth through public intervention into housing construction. This situation changed in 1987 when a construction boom took place. Public intervention into housing construction was reduced and, instead, goals of redistribution and equality were given more weight. Spanish housing policy of this period has been centred firmly on the availability of and access to home-ownership (Ghékiere 1991, Coll Cuota/Martin Jadraque 1989, Alberdí/Levenfeld 1996).

Since 1983/84 housing policy began to be decentralised in Spain, while in France regions did have few competencies. The Spanish constitution of 1978 defined housing policy as a matter of regional competence, but the transfer of the highly centralised housing directorate was slow and accompanied by many conflicts. The current state of decentralisation of Spanish housing policy can be described as a situation, in which the central state fixes the norms of public help for housing, determines the framework of their implementation by the regions, and exerts financial control. Every year the central state and the regions sign a convention on housing policy. But, housing policy of a fiscal and monetary character is not decentralised, since regions do not have any competencies in these areas. Despite the importance of central housing policy design, regions do carry out self-financed housing policies specific to their territories, in particular public housing, and they administer public housing benefits. Municipalities constitute the third administrative level of housing policies. Their role is to design plans of urbanisation and to assure the land necessary for new housing construction. The institutional change from a centralised housing policy to a partially decentralised one had negative consequences on the overall efficiency of Spanish housing policies (Leal 1992, Trilla et al. 1998).

In Spain, there are three important pieces of legislation for the period 1985 to 1991: a new rent act in 1985, a housing plan in 1984, and single measures in 1987.

1. First, like in France rent controls were changed in 1985 after many decades of very strict public regulations on rent contracts. Since the end of the Civil War and until 1964 a freeze on rents was decreed. In 1964 a new law on leasing was enacted, which only affected contracts signed after the law. New leases allowed for annual revision of rents according to inflation, but the rent contract period was not fixed. In practice this meant that dwellings once rented remained normally in the hands of the tenant, even for one or two generations. In 1985 a royal decree liberalised the rent sector to a very great extent, since price and duration were to be decided totally freely.
2. Second, in December 1983 the government decided a four-year plan for housing (1984-1987), whose results were an increase of the economic activity of the housing sector, a rather insignificant construction of publicly developed dwellings, and a deviation of public subsidies to second residence acquisition contrary to the theoretical aims of the plan.
3. Last, a Royal Decree of December 1987 changed housing policy in order to establish a clearer differentiation of public policy by type of beneficiary instead of by type of constructor as had been the case before, and by the amount of household resources. Yet in fact these

measures meant the disappearance of a housing plan until 1991 and the quasi-ceasing of subsidised housing construction (cf. Chapter 4).

Basic changes were also introduced after 1991, but this does not affect the young people studied in this research. Out of the new measures of the 1992-95 housing plan two are of relevance for young people: the creation of a specific benefit for the acquisition of a first dwelling, the application of tax exemptions for the payment of a rented dwelling, and new subsidies for rented housing with regulated rent. But in November 1998 tax exemption for rented housing was abolished after just nine years of existence (Valenzuela Rubio 1994, El País 13.11.1998). There are other important legal reforms that affect the housing market in this period, but which are not looked at here. The application of a new house census (catastro) (1984-89) and a new law on housing transactions in order to bring informal activities and camouflage of real housing values into public light. Other laws were enacted in the fields of urban and ground administration and on investment funds for housing (1992). An important step on the rented housing market was a new reform of the Rent Act in 1994 (cf. Valenzuela Rubio 1994, Cortés Alcalá 1995).

In the second half of the 1980s, the financing of Spanish housing policies had a stable distribution according to the sources. Around 40 per cent of the costs were financed via the budget of the central state and the regions and directed towards direct housing benefits, 50 per cent originated from tax exemptions and 10 per cent were financial costs supported by financial institutes. Together they amounted to 1.1 per cent of the GDP in 1987, while in France housing policy expenditures accounted for 2 per cent of the GDP in the same year. Also, the structure of housing policy expenditure in France was less biased in favour of tax exemptions, since in 1987 these stood at only 27 per cent of the public housing expenditure, while brick and mortar subsidies and personal benefits accounted for up to 73 per cent of the total expenditure. In contrast to Spain, where no personal benefits exist, France invests around 26 per cent of its housing budget for the three different housing allowances (Leal 1992, Levenfeld 1990, Alberdi 1993).

Converting Spanish Youth into Proprietors and Helping Tenants in France

It is not the aim of this work to undertake a comprehensive analysis of housing policies in France and Spain, but to draw a rough picture of the main similarities and differences between the two policy models. As has already been argued, public benefits for young people in rented accommodations represent the main public incentive for leaving home and therefore these benefits will be described for the French case. Since in Spain there are no direct housing allowances for tenants, existing direct, financial and fiscal benefits will be discussed from young people's perspective and possible reasons for the non-existence of housing allowances for tenants will be proposed.

Housing Allowances in France

Unlike in the Spanish section on housing benefits, the description of French housing benefits excludes all bricks and mortar aids, and benefits for the acquisition or rehabilitation of dwellings, for they are of less relevance for young people. It should suffice to mention that the French housing policy comprises a wide range of these measures (Guékière 1991).

The French state provides three different types of housing allowances:

1. *allocation de logement à caractère familial* (housing allowance for families or ALF);
2. *allocation de logement à caractère social* (housing allowance for social reasons or ALS);
3. *aide personnalisée au logement* (personal housing help or APL).

The ALF housing allowance was created in 1948 and the group of eligible beneficiaries was enlarged in 1972. The aim of this allowance is to reduce the real housing expenditures of families. The following categories of beneficiaries were eligible for the ALF in 1991:

1. beneficiaries of a family allowance;
2. households and individuals with only one child and without family allowance entitlement;
3. young family heads without children for a period of five years from the beginning of the marriage onwards;
4. households with elderly dependants;
5. households with handicapped relatives.

The individual has to fulfil three other conditions, which are to occupy the dwelling as the main residence, to have a certain number of square metres and to have a minimum of general infrastructure (toilette, etc.). The amount of the allowance depends on resources, rent, and family obligations. The allowance is not intended to reach the total amount of the rent, since the beneficiary has to pay a part of the rent by him or herself (*loyer minimum*). The amount of the *loyer minimum* is fixed by decree and takes the number of children or other regularly cohabiting people into account. Consequently, ALF is paid only in those cases where the rent exceeds the *loyer minimum*. In addition, a ceiling for rent expenditures, which enters the calculation of the allowance amount, exists.

The second type of housing allowance, ALS, has existed since 1972 and was modified in 1985, 1988, 1991, 1992, and 1993 in order to include, first, long-term unemployed people as a new group of eligible beneficiaries; second, low-income people receiving the public minimum income allowance (*revenu minimum d'insertion* or RMI); third, individuals living in the region of Paris and overseas regions and not eligible for other housing benefits; fourth, individuals from municipalities of over 100,000 inhabitants; and fifth, all other individuals not eligible for other housing benefits. By 1993, the ALS had become a universal means-tested allowance, since all individuals living in France are eligible for this benefit. The winners of this progressive extension of eligibility criteria have been students, who before had to have family obligations to be entitled to ALF or had to live in a public regulated dwelling to be entitled to APL. Unlike the ALF, this allowance does not derive from family obligations, but from a situation of need. In 1986, at the beginning of the period under analysis, there were seven categories of social groups eligible for the ALS:

1. people over 65 years old (in some cases over 60);
2. handicapped individuals not able to work;
3. young dependent workers under 25 with a regular contract giving right to social security affiliation and living outside of the parental home;
4. long-term unemployed people, who had lost entitlement to the basic unemployment allowance;
5. beneficiaries of an integration allowance (*allocation d'insertion, AI*) (cf. Chapter 8);
6. long-term sick people living in health institutions;
7. individuals having their dwelling in the *départements* of Paris, Hauts-de-Seine, Seine-Saint-Denis, Val-de-Marne, Seine-et-Marne, Yvelines, Essonne, Val-d'Oise, and in the over-seas *départements*.

Entitlement conditions are very similar to those of the ALF with three specific characteristics. Firstly, ALS can be received if the dwelling is a hall of residence (*logement-foyer*); secondly, people renting a dwelling from a relative are not eligible for ALS; and thirdly, old people being kept in a household for payment according to the conditions of the social security law are entitled to ALS. A young person cannot receive the ALS allocation if his/her parents receive child allowances for him/her. In these cases the parents have to renounce the child allowance in order to allow their child to benefit from ALS. The amount of the allowance is calculated in a similar way as the ALF (Rassat 1995, Julliot 1991).

At the end of the 1970s, the French government redirected housing policy from a supply side policy towards more demand-side oriented benefits. The cornerstone of this reform was the creation of a new personal housing benefit (*aide personnalisée au logement or APL*) in 1977. It is the aim of the APL to progressively replace the other two housing allowances. The APL aims to facilitate the acquisition of a dwelling, to facilitate the improvement of the quality of existing housing, and to help tenants to pay their rent.

The basic condition for entitlement to APL is that an agreement between the state and the constructor/owner exists. Only in these cases can people become beneficiaries of the APL under certain conditions. All individuals are eligible for APL independently of age, family situation, or nationality. One of the following housing conditions has to be fulfilled by tenants of rented housing in order to receive APL:

1. The dwelling has to be the main residence, which means that it has to be occupied for at least 8 months a year. This condition might affect some students, but in general they will stay at least 8 months in a residence hall.
2. The dwelling has to be owned or administered by an HLM organisation or other organisations having an agreement with the state.
3. The accommodation has to have been built, acquired, or improved after 1977 with public subsidies or under conditions determined by the state.
4. The individual lives in a residence hall for young workers (*foyers de jeunes travailleurs*) or in similar housing following public norms.
5. Individuals who have a rent-acquisition contract according to the 1984 bill.
6. The amount of the housing allowance is calculated according to a complex formula, which takes three elements into account: 1. resources of the beneficiary, her/his spouse/partner, and all other persons living regularly in the dwelling; 2. monthly rent; 3. individuals maintained by the beneficiary (children, elderly parents, handicapped relatives).

The rent is considered only within the limits of a ceiling fixed by decree according to family obligations and the geographic location of the dwelling. In addition, as for ALF and ALS a minimum rent is determined, which represents the rent amount the tenant has to pay him/herself after resources and family obligations have been taken into consideration (Julliot 1991).

As summarised by Table 9.1, in 1992 all young people were eligible for APL if they fulfilled two main conditions: living in a publicly regulated dwelling and having limited resources. In addition, nearly all young people were entitled to ALS if they passed a means test. Young people with dependent children and those married recently formed the group of individuals with the greatest support through housing allowances. This clearly shows how two important features of the French Welfare State work together, assistance for the needy and assistance for those with family obligations. Housing policy is rather unconnected with the social security mechanism of the French Welfare State, since regular employment is not a criterion to receive housing benefits and hence it helps to alleviate the typical support gaps inherent in social security provisions.

Table 9.1 Entitlement to Housing Allowances by Year of Institution and Type of Allowance for Young People Living in an Independent Dwelling, 1986-1993

Year	Students	Dependent workers	Long-term unemployed	With dependent child	Married recently	Entitled to RMI
1986			APL			APL
1987		APL		APL	APL	
1988	APL	ALS[a]		ALF	ALF	
1989						
1990						
1991	APL ALS[b]	APL ALS[a,b]	APL ALS	APL ALS[b] ALF	APL ALS[b] ALF	APL ALS
1992	APL ALS[c]	APL ALS[a,c]		APL ALS[c] ALF	APL ALS[c] ALF	
1993	APL ALS	APL ALS		APL ALS ALF	APL ALS ALF	

Notes: [a] Condition: under 25 years. [b] Condition: live in certain départements. [c] Condition: live in certain municipalities. An individual has to choose one housing allowance in those cases she or he is entitled to different housing allowances.

Source: author's elaboration.

With regard to the coverage of the three housing allowances it is possible to find general statistics, while figures related to young people are seldom published with. At the beginning of the 1990s, one in four households were receiving a housing allowance (APL, ALS, or ALF). The highest rate of beneficiaries was found among people living in HLM and other social-rented housing. At the end of 1988, forty four per cent of HLM tenants received an allowance, most of them an APL benefit, while 32 per cent of the tenants of a private-rented dwelling without furniture received a housing allowance (Curci/Taffin 1991, Blanc / Bertrand 1996). In 1992, the beneficiaries of ALS amounted to 1,309,620, of which 21 per cent were students. Out of all the students receiving housing benefits, 78 per cent received ALS, 20 per cent APL, and 2 per cent ALF (Rassat 1995). At the end of the 1980s the *foyers de jeunes travailleurs* (residence halls of young workers) in France were estimated to be 450, which meant around 50,000 places. Most of the young people taking advantage of this living arrangement were students of vocational training and of tertiary education, while one third had an unstable employment, and around one tenth, respectively, were unemployed or in an apprenticeship (Guide 1990). In the *Enquête Jeunes 1992* young people were asked in one question if they received family allowances or housing allowances, which means that it is difficult to know how many were receiving only housing allowances. If young people with children are not taken into account, it can be stated that all others answering positively to this question were receiving a housing allowance.[1] Out of all the young people without children and living independently in 1992, 9 per cent were receiving a housing allowance and out of all the young people living on their own 30 per cent were receiving a family and/or housing allowance.[2]

The quantitative importance of housing allowances within general housing policy can be deduced from figures on public expenditure. In 1986, the amount spent for housing allowances amounted to only 37 per cent of the total expenditure and APL represented 45 per cent of the expenditures for housing allowances. Later, in 1992, 46 per cent of the total public expenditure for housing was for housing allowances, and more than half of it was directed towards APL.[3] The increase of the relative importance of the expenditure for housing allowances has meant a parallel decrease of the State's expenditure for supply side benefits (Geindre 1994).

Different surveys conducted by the national statistical office (INSEE) in 1984 and 1988 permit some calculations on the relative amount of housing allowances in relation to the disposable income of beneficiaries. Tenants without allowances paid an average of 17 per cent of their income for rent and related housing costs, while tenants receiving a housing allowance paid an average of 14 per cent. Tenants of private-rented housing received the highest amount of housing allowance in relation to income (18%), while tenants of HLM dwellings received the least (15%). Tenants can pay, depending on the type of allowance, one third to one half of their housing costs with public help (Curci/Taffin 1991).

Housing Benefits in Spain

Spanish housing policy almost exclusively subsidises owner-occupied accommodation through direct and fiscal benefits. Subsidies for rented accommodation are very scarce and were subject to frequent changes. If one distinguishes public regulation of the housing market following the type of tenure for which benefits are designed and according to the beneficiaries, then we obtain a fourfold distinction:

1. Benefits for owner-occupied accomodations for individuals and families;
2. Benefits for owner-occupied accomodations for construction enterprises;
3. Benefits for rented dwellings for individuals and families;
4. Benefits for rented dwellings for construction enterprises.

Table 9.2 Types of Housing Policy Measures in Spain 1985-1991

Beneficiaries: families/individuals	Beneficiaries: enterprises
Benefits for owner-owned accommodation	
1984-87	1984-87
Financial and direct benefits: ▪ benefits for **acquisition** of **new** constructions (for family incomes under 2.5 SMI, between 2.5 and 3.5 SMI, and over 3.5 SMI): loan subsidies, regulated interest rates ▪ benefits for **rehabilitation** of owned dwellings: loan subsidies, regulated interest rates Tax benefits: ▪ reduced VAT for new dwellings ▪ tax deduction of loan interests from tax bill for **acquisition** of dwelling (up to 800,000 Ptas annually, since 1986) ▪ tax deduction from tax quota for repayment of loans (15% for main residence, 10% for other residence with a limit of <= 30% of tax sum, in 1988)	▪ subsidies in form of regulated loans for constructors of **new** dwellings for ownership
new in 1989-1991	new in 1989-1991
▪ benefits for **acquisition** of **used** dwellings ▪ families with income over 2.5 SMI are excluded from direct benefits and with income over 5 SMI from any benefits ▪ no tax deduction for **secondary** residence (since 1991) and **house-saving accounts** are considered like loans	▪ subsidies in form of regulated loans for enterprises that rehabilitate **used** dwellings
Benefits for rented dwellings	
1984-87	1984-87
▪ benefits for tenants of **newly** constructed **public housing**: allowances ▪ benefits for **rehabilitation** of rented dwellings: loan subsidies, regulated interest rates	▪ subsidies for constructors of **new** dwellings for rent: regulated loans
new in 1989-1991	new in 1989-1991
▪ no benefits for tenants of public housing ▪ tax deduction of 15% for payment of rent with a maximum of 75,000 Ptas per year and an annual income limit of 2,000 Mia Ptas (Law, June 1991, applicable in May 1992)	▪ subsidies for enterprises that rehabilitate **used** dwellings for rent

Sources: MOPU 1987; BOE 224/1998, 3.3.1989; Alberdí/Levenfeld 1996; Delgado Diaz, José et al. 1989; Levenfeld 1993; Ley 18/1991, 6.6.1991.

In Spain most housing policy measures are directed towards home-ownership, be it as benefits to families that purchase a dwelling or as benefits for construction enterprises (Table 9.2). The measures directed towards families and individuals are threefold: 1. financial measures in the form of state-regulated mortgage interest rates below market rates; 2. loan subsidies in order to reduce interest-rates or down-payments; 3. fiscal benefits in the form of tax reliefs for the acquisition of housing. Spanish housing policy from 1985 to 1987 was very strongly biased towards the construction of new dwellings, since mainly the constructors of these and the families in these new dwellings were entitled to some type of housing benefit. Also, families who wanted to restore their rented or owned dwelling could benefit from some public help.

From 1989 until 1991, public support for restoring dwellings was increased, people with an income equal to or over five times the minimum wage were excluded from entitlement to public subsidies, and for the first time subsidies were given for the acquisition of used dwellings. Finally in 1990, tax exemptions for a second dwelling were lifted and in 1991 house-saving accounts were considered as mortgages and entitled to tax deductions. For the first time expenditure for rent gave the right to tax deductions if certain conditions were met.

It becomes clear, as mentioned before, that the logic of the housing policy of this period was to subsidise the economic activity of the housing sector. Housing policy during the 1980s did not primarily follow a social policy logic of helping families who could not afford a dwelling on the free market, but was mostly an economic policy for the benefit of the construction industry and for employment in this sector (Valenzuela Rubio 1994). A further indicator of this conception is the fact that the Ministry of Housing did not publish any statistics on the number of families benefiting from housing benefits, but offers only figures on subsidised dwellings (cf. Ministerio de Fomento 1996, 1992). Moreover, tax deductions for the acquisition or restoration of owner-occupied dwellings have a regressive character and subsidise higher incomes more than lower ones.[4] This had an effect on the distribution of the total amount of tax exemptions for housing according to income groups. In 1989, 70 per cent of the total tax sum which the state lost due to exemptions for housing was accumulated by the three highest income decimal points (Levenfeld 1993, Cortés Alcalá 1995). Housing policy changed its economic policy character with the housing plan of 1992-1995 and became more oriented towards social redistribution aims (Rodríguez 1993).

What did this policy mean for young people who wanted to leave home in the period 1985 to 1991? First of all, only young people with a sufficiently high income to be able to benefit from tax deductions were entitled to public benefits, while young people without income or with an income under the taxable income level did not have any access to housing benefits. Second, young people who rented a dwelling could not apply for any public help until 1992, when for the first time rents gave rights to tax exemptions. Third, since young people earn, on the average, less than older people and tax exemptions have a regressive character, young people tend to receive fewer subsidies than older people. Spanish housing policy is designed for adults and for people who want to acquire a private dwelling, but it ignores the needs of young people with low and unstable incomes, who cannot afford to buy a dwelling.

Social Housing, Construction Incentives, and Regulation of Private Renting

In France in the 1960s, social housing construction was very important in solving the housing problems of migrants and it took almost exclusively the form of large housing estates. From 1984 to 1993 the proportion of social dwellings in the French housing infra-structure had stabilised at around 17 per cent (Blanc/Bertrand 1995). In 1977, a new system of grants and subsidised loans for rent purposes (*prêts locatifs aidés* or PLA) was set up. These subsidies are mainly given to HLM institutions in order to construct or renew social dwellings. Tenants of these dwellings are entitled to the APL housing benefit. In addition, the state offers subsidised loans for the construction of accommodation for very low-income households (*prêts locatifs aidés 'très sociaux'* or PLATS). Since the mid-1980s, grants for the restoration of the existing HLM housing stock were created (*prime à l'amélioration des logements à usage locatif e à occupation sociale* or PALULOS). In addition, HLM institutions can profit from tax exemptions: for instance, they pay lower VAT, lower duties on the sales of dwellings, and lower land taxes. Also, they do not need to pay corporate taxation (*impôt sur les sociétés*). Constructors of housing for private renting are freed from land tax for two years and private landlords can deduct a part of their expenses for their rented housing from their income tax. In 1991 a law was passed by which towns of over 200,000 inhabitants were required to organise social housing construction through building new social dwellings or through paying a special tax for the increase of the whole social-rented stock in the town (Blanc/Bertrand 1996).

In contrast, social housing plays a very insignificant role in Spanish housing policy, because many of them have been sold to their tenants and because few new public dwellings were constructed, so that Spain has a very small sector of social housing for rent. Cause and effect of this situation is the small number of organisations and enterprises dedicated to the construction and administration of social housing. Around 50 such institutions at the local, regional, and central levels act in this field in Spain, whereas in France there are around 300 H.L.M. institutions. These few institutions have large problems of administration of their social accommodation units, they work without profits, their target population is exclusively composed of very low-income groups and they normally have to bear higher construction costs than private constructors (Leal 1992, Prats 1992).

Rent regulation in France can be divided into three periods from 1948. The rent act of 1948 offered tenants of rented housing security of tenure and tightly controlled rents. In 1988 14 per cent of all private rented dwellings built after 1948 were still subject to this rent act. In 1982, a new rent act was passed, which stipulated the obligation of a written rent agreement and which regulated the duration of the tenancy, the increase of the rent, the possibilities of giving notice, the right of renewing the contract and of buying the dwelling if the landlord wanted to sell it. A private landlord was allowed to choose between a contract of at least six years (with the possibility of giving notice to the tenant) and one of three years (without the possibility of giving notice within this period). After the expiration of the tenancy period the contract had to be renewed, if the landlord was not able to put forward one of the following three reasons. Firstly, that he intended to live in the dwelling; secondly, that the tenant had failed to comply with the terms of the tenancy agreement; or thirdly, that he intended to sell the dwelling. Rent levels were determined by a national commission composed by tenants, landlords and municipalities. In 1986, the third rent act was passed with the aim of deregulating the private rent housing sector and it was slightly modified in 1989. Rent levels can be freely decided by landlords at the beginning and at the end of the tenure agreement, and in addition the duration of rent contracts was reduced to three years and the conditions to serve notice were abolished. If the rent contract ends, the tenant has six months to search for an alternative dwelling. Landlords having signed the contract in 1986 or later were allowed to revise rents after the three-year lease period had expired (Boelhouwer/Heijden 1992, Curci/Taffin 1991). In 1994 the INSEE estimated that 80 per cent of all rent contracts were written contacts as stipulated by a 1982 law (Cases 1995).

A new rent act was passed in Spain three years later than in France. The innovations of this 1985 decree were the abolition of the automatic prolongation of the contract, the free choice of the length and rent increases of the tenancy, the possibility of adapting the dwelling to economic activities, and the extension of fiscal exemptions to the second and third dwellings. The consequences for the supply of rented accommodation were insignificant, since in 1991 this decree affected only 18 per cent of the dwellings. These dwellings display high rents and short contract periods (on average one year) (Valenzuela Rubio 1994). This decree and the new Rent Act of 1994 did not solve a problem that prevented and still prevents many property-owners from renting out their dwellings. In Spain it is difficult to get redress through the courts in cases of non-paying tenants. With the new law on civil processes (January 2001), it is expected that effective court decisions in cases of non-paying tenants will be more rapid. The current tenancies can be divided into three groups: those previous to 1964 with very low rents, the contracts signed after July 1964 with free prices but with long-term contracts, and those described above from May 1985 onwards. In 1989, 26 per cent of the rented accommodations were long-term contracts without price revision, 52 per cent were long-term contracts with price changes, and 22 per cent were leases with the price and the length of the contract freely agreed upon by both parts (Alberdí/Levenfeld 1996).

In Spain, in the last years a few isolated and innovative projects have been started aiming to ease young people's access to rented dwellings. In Madrid and Barcelona special services have been created, where young people get information and help in order to find a dwelling to rent. In Barcelona this service was created in May 1996 and it expanded in June 1997 (*Servei d'Habitatge i Allotjament per als Joves i Grups Juvenils*). It is financially supported by the regional government of Catalonia and around 18,000 persons had passed through it from 1996 to 1998. Young people aged 18 to 35 can search a database of rented dwellings in order to find an accommodation to live alone, or if they are under 31 they have access to a specific offer of flats to share with others. The service checks the dwellings before they are included in the database and it offers the landlord a free insurance against the risk of non-payment for the first ten months and a liability insurance during the first year. In 1998 young people could find rooms this way for around 25,000 Ptas per month. On the average young people taking advantage of this service are around 27 years old, are highly qualified, and have temporary contracts. More women than men asked for a one-person dwelling. In addition, the service also helps in searching for places in residence halls for students and for lodgings.[5]

The municipality of Barcelona has another specific project, which consists of building of 431 dwellings for young people on ground expropriated by the municipality for the construction of a road. This project forms part of the municipal action program (PAM) of 1996-1999. Young people under 31, with income not exceeding 2.5 times the minimum wage, whose income comes mainly from employment, and who normally live in

Barcelona will be able to apply for these dwellings. Young people were expected to be able to rent those dwellings for 24,000 to 41,000 Ptas - depending on the number of rooms- at the beginning of 1999 (CJB 1998, El País, Catalonia, 9.11.1998).

To sum up, young people in France receive help in the form of housing allowances and indirectly through the offer of social housing. In particular those young people who do not reach the subsistence income level because they are students or young workers with short-term contracts can profit from housing allowances. This, undoubtedly, helps young people leave home despite a low market or transfer income. Unlike in France, Spanish young people cannot receive any direct housing allowances for rented accommodation and nor do they have access to social housing, since it is almost non existent.

The negative effects of Spanish housing policy on young people's ability to find a dwelling have been noted and commented on by many Spanish experts and even by a former Minister of Housing (cf. Borrell 1992). Nonetheless little had been done until 1992, and no structural change took place afterwards, either. To conclude, I would like to reflect on the possible reasons for the existence and permanence of this specific Spanish housing policy.

First, housing policy has been conceived of as a sort of economic and fiscal policy, but within the social security system no benefits similar to the French ALS or ALF were created. The historical importance and the separate administrative institutionalisation of an encompassing family policy is surely one factor, which facilitated the creation of these housing benefits in France. In addition, in 1977 the French housing administration created a new housing allowance for the acquisition and renting of accommodations. Unlike France, Spain did not pursue any explicit and significant family policy from 1978 on, and thus has no specific administration in this field. Moreover, the Spanish Welfare State had to be constructed and extended in the 1980s, which means that the most basic social needs were given priority: universalisation of old-age pensions and of health and education services, and the extension of unemployment benefits.

In 1992 the committee for the reform of Spanish housing policy pointed to the necessity of structural changes but also to the difficulties of eliminating existing tax advantages. One problem lies in the necessity of creating a costly administration able to administrate and control new direct benefits, while the fiscal administration could continue administering new types of fiscal benefits without additional costs. Another problem was considered to be the heavy social costs and possible conflict a structural change of the fiscal housing policy could create, since the acceptance of the existing income taxation system by higher income earners was and is partly based on tax exemptions for housing. In 1989 over 24 per cent of taxpayers benefited from tax deductions for investment in housing (Leal 1992, Cortés Alcalá 1995).

A third reason can be sought in the belief that Spanish citizens have a cultural preference for home-ownership and against renting, which induces politicians to design housing policy accordingly. This might be true, but there are other arguments which help to understand these supposed cultural preferences. First, there is the significance of the informal economy in Spain which might be favouring saving for old-age through house acquisition instead of through social security contributions. Second, alternative investment opportunities were scarce for a long time in the Spanish financial market, which nowadays has changed, but at the same time the liberalisation of the bank sector created a very dynamic mortgage market (cf. Ferrera/Castles 1996, Gomez 1989). Last, under the old rent acts before 1985 and 1994, proprietors had low incentives to rent dwellings out, while the Spanish state had a very limited supply of public housing.

Social Policies for Youth: Differences in Diversification, Not in Timing

The aim of Chapters 7 to 9 on the social rights careers of young people in France and Spain was to describe the mechanisms through which social policies might be contributing to early home-leaving in France. Cross-national differences in the timing of the social rights career were shown to be less important than differences in the range of social benefits. Social benefits help young people to take the decision to leave home because they reduce uncertainty through the promise of maintenance allowances and services under given conditions. These social rights reduce the risk of leaving home and they disconnect the standard of life to some extent from the availability of market income or family help. This dependence diversification mechanism works only if three conditions are fulfilled:

1. if social benefits cover the main needs of young people leaving home, that is stability of a minimum income and access to a dwelling (**extension condition**);
2. if coverage occurs in an adequate way, which is that maintenance allowances are relatively generous and subsidised dwellings are accessible without any requirement of previous investment (**generosity condition**);
3. if entitlement conditions are not restricted to a minority of young people (**coverage condition**).

The first question of this chapter was about the timing of the social rights career. Do French young people lose their child status and acquire adulthood earlier than Spanish young people? The French Welfare State defines children as dependent family members, who have to be supported as such, up to age 20/25, when they are supposed to reach adulthood. The French state provides some special rights for young people aged 16 to 25 and then it opens the door to full social citizenship by age 25. The process of acquiring full social rights is guided by age criteria and it ignores whether young people live with their parents or independently. At age 25 young people have social rights through their contribution to social security insurance or through a means-test. The Spanish Welfare State, on its part, cares less for children and it assumes that children depend mainly on family solidarity. The family is supposed to take care of their dependent children as long as necessary, frequently without any age-limit, but in any case longer than in France. The Spanish Welfare State conceives of its beneficiaries frequently in terms of family units and not in terms of individuals and, in consequence, age-limits mark resource-sharing realities less.

Table 9.3 illustrates this conclusion through a summary of entitlement conditions to child benefits and to social rights for young people. It shows very clearly that the definition of dependent child in different social security laws varies in France and Spain. In France a child is considered dependent on her parents if she is not employed, but studying. But this sort of dependence cannot last for a long time, since at age 20 the young person's enrolment in education loses significance and the young person is no longer considered to be dependent on her parents. French fiscal law is somewhat more generous in defining childhood, since until age 24 a young person can be considered as a child. In Spanish social security law childhood is defined in two ways: 1. a child is a child until age 18, and 2. a child is a child as long as he is financially dependent on his parents. The first definition applies only to means-tested child benefits, while the second definition applies to health services and non-contributory unemployment benefits. Fiscal law defines childhood as lasting until age 29, if the child is financially dependent on her parents. Despite the heterogeneity of the Spanish legal definitions of childhood, it clearly is a state which lasts longer than in France. In Spain, financial dependence on parents is a fact that turns young people into children, while this infantilisation is something French law conceives of as possible only until age 20/25.

Table 9.3 Parents' Rights to Child Benefits in France and Spain, 1991

Public Benefits	Students	Dependent Workers	Unemployed	Economically inactive
ALS-housing allowance	up to **age 20** (F)	up to **age 18** if income under 56% of SMIC (F)	up to **age 16** (F)	up to **age 18** (F)
APL and ALF-housing allowance	up to **age 20** (F)			
Child allowance	up to **age 20** (F) up to **age 18** (E)	up to **age 18** if income under 56% of SMIC (F) up to **age 18** (E)		up to **age 16** (F) up to **age 18** (E)
Health services	up to **age 20** (F) **dependent** child without age-limit (E)	up to **age 16** (F) **dependent**, without age-limit, but income limit (E)		up to **age 16** (F) **dependent** child without age-limit (E)
Non-contributory unemployment assistance	no dependent child supplement (F) / **dependent** child supplement, no age-limit (E)			
Tax exemptions	up to **age 25** (F) up to **29**, if low income (E)		up to **age 21** (F) / up to **age 29** if low income (E)	

Note: F = France, E = Spain. For handicapped children and young people there are special rules, which are not considered in this table.
Sources: Julliot 1991, Trotabas/Cotteret 1990, Raymond 1995, MISSOC 1992, Aguilar et al. 1995, MTSS 1991, EURYDICE 1993.

The other side of the coin is the age starting at which young people have access to the two types of existing social rights. Young people can be entitled to 1. specific rights for youth, and 2. to general social rights for adults. The latter can be of contributory, universal, or of a means-tested nature.

Specific rights for young people exist as means-tested and universal rights (cf. Table 9.4). These are social rights related to enrolment in education: a special health insurance for students and means-tested scholarships. In France these benefits are regulated according to age, while in Spain they are only regulated according to the fact of being enrolled in education. In France two other specific means-tested social benefits exist(ed), which are not available in Spain: 1. housing allowances for young workers, and 2. non-contributory unemployment allowances for first employment seekers. These are benefits for young people aged 16-25 trying to enter the labour market.

Table 9.4 Range of Social Rights of Young Single People without Children, Aged 20-29, in France and Spain 1991

	Public Benefits	Students	Dependent Workers	Unemployed	Economically inactive
Housing Benefits	ALS-allowance **means-tested**	in certain regions (F) no (E)	**Under 25 years** in certain regions (F) no (E)	if benefit period exhausted or if AI beneficiary (F) no (E)	if able to pay minimum rent (F) no (E)
	APL-allowance **means-tested**	yes (F) no (E)			if able to pay minimum rent or if receiving **RMI** (F) / no (E)
	ALF-allowance **means-tested**	no (F and E)			
	Public dwellings **means-tested**	yes (F) / very limited (E)			
	Residence halls	yes (F) / limited (E)	yes (F) / no (E)	no (F and E)	No (F and E)
Income Maintenance	**Contributory** unemployment allowance	no (F and E)		3 months contribution (F) 6 months contribution (E)	No (F and E)
	Means-tested unemployment allowance	no (F and E)		**16-25 years** old, other conditions (F) / no (E)	No (F and E)
	University grants **means-tested and achievement**	until **age 26** (first time) (F) no age-limit (E)	-	-	-
	RMI **means-tested**	in practice incompatible with integration measures (F, E)	if low resources, no entitlement to other benefits, and **over 24** (F, E)		
Health Services	**Contributory and universal** health services	from **20 years** upwards (F) from **15 years to 27** (E)	if **contribution** to social security (F, E)	if **contribution** (F, E)	**means-tested** (F, E)

Note: grey background means specific rights for young people. AI = allocation d'insertion.

Sources: Julliot 1991, Trotabas/Cotteret 1990, Raymond 1995, MISSOC 1992, Aguilar et al. 1995, MTSS 1991, EURYDICE 1993.

General contributory benefits are independent of age, since the condition is to have contributed to an insurance scheme. In these cases age plays an indirect role through young people's chances of finding employment with social security coverage. Means-tested benefits such as housing allowances and health services are, in general, not limited to any age, yet general social assistance is conditioned to a minimum age of 25 years in both countries. Thus, social rights for young people are in both countries related to employment with a contribution to social security and to a means-test. Unlike cross-national differences in the definition of childhood, nearly no cross-national differences exist in the definition of an adult citizen with social rights. In both countries adulthood is related to an employment with social security and to the attainment of age 25. All in all, differences between Spain and France in the legal timing of the social rights career are small.

The second conclusion of this chapter is not unexpected: the French Welfare State fulfils more tasks of caring for and maintaining children and young people than the Spanish Welfare State. As shown in Table 9.4, in France the extension condition is better complied with than in Spain. In Spain, young people are entitled to contributory and means-tested income maintenance programs nearly to the same extent as their French counterparts. Only a Spanish means-tested unemployment benefit for first-employment seekers is missing, but this benefit was abolished in France in 1992. Health services in Spain and France are organised according to the contributory scheme, but in fact they are universal. The great and crucial difference between the two countries is housing benefits. No housing allowances and scarce public social housing supply exist in Spain, while a wide range of housing benefits are accessible to French young people.

The Spanish Welfare State does not fulfil the extension condition adequately nor the generosity and coverage conditions either. The relative generosity of different public benefits measured in Purchasing Power Standards are reported in Table 9.5. The average Spanish wage in youth-specific contracts and the minimum amount of contributory unemployment allowance for somebody who contributed for 15 months to unemployment insurance are as generous, as, or more generous than, the equivalent French measures. The problem with the Spanish allowances is their lower generosity in terms of the length of time the allowance can be paid. Rooms in halls of residence halls are more expensive in Spain than in France and, in addition, students receive on the average lower scholarship amounts.

Table 9.5 Comparative Generosity (benefit amounts in monthly PPS), 1991/92

PPS per month	France	Spain
Average wage in youth-specific contract	488	530
Minimum amount of unemployment allowance (15 months contribution)	505	496
Minimum contribution time	3 months (last year)	6 months (last 4 years)
Benefit length (15 months of contribution)	14 months	6 months
Room in residence hall (costs)	100-246	273-512
Average grant amount	210	129

Source: author's elaboration with information of Chapters 7 to 9.

As has already been mentioned, the calculation of coverage rates is a rather difficult task due to differences in benefit systems and due to a lack of good administrative statistics. However, some estimates were possible and they are summarised in Table 9.6. In general, benefits for students and young people in the labour force cover fewer young people in Spain than in France.

Table 9.6 Indicators of Coverage in France and Spain, 1991/92

	France	Spain
% of students with grant	17 %	ca. 8 %
Places in halls per 100 students	7.9 %	2.3 %
% unemployed (under age 30) with unemployment coverage	ca. 35 %	ca. 18 %
% youth-specific contracts per 100 unemployed (16-24)	ca. 100%	ca. 18%

Source: author's elaboration with information of chapters 7 to 9.

Young Spanish people in their transition into adulthood have to rely mainly on the market and on the family, while French young people are able to diversify their income across the market, the family and the state. This lower degree of income diversification in Spain does not favour early home leaving for Spanish people. Most likely it also obstructs geographic and social mobility, as well as experiments with nonfamily living arrangements.

Notes

[1] This is based on the fact that family allowances are given for having dependent children (cf. Chapter 7).

[2] These figures were calculated with the *Franceall* sample.

[3] The 46 per cent spent in housing allowances includes allowances for rent and for acquisition of housing. Housing allowances directed exclusively to subsidise rents are estimated to represent around 26 per cent of public housing expenditure (Levenfeld 1990).

[4] In 1991, two tax deductions were possible in Spain. First, one could deduce mortgage interests from income before tax rate application. This means that people with lower income received a higher tax benefit relative to their income but a lower public subsidy in absolute terms than people with higher income, due to the progressivness of the tax rate. Second, 15 per cent of some investments for housing could be deducted from the tax sum after tax rate application with a limit of 30 per cent of the taxable income. Again, people with lower incomes benefit from lower absolute benefits than people with higher incomes (cf. Coopers & Lybrand 1993).

[5] Information was personally communicated by the director of the service in November 1998 (cf. www.habitatgejove.com).

10 Configurations Favouring and Hindering Nest-Leaving

There are many popular beliefs about why, since the 1980s, young people tend to stay at home longer in West-European countries and many people offer ad-hoc explanations for international differences. Since the family is something everybody is familiar with from their own experience, it is an area in which sociological thinking has to compete with popular beliefs. During the research, I heard many opinions of non-sociologists about why young people in Spain stay with their parents longer than in France and I would like to conclude this research by contrasting these opinions with the results of this work. Popular beliefs can be divided into four statements.

1. In Spain Catholicism is still strong, which explains the dominance of marriage and the poor development of consensual unions. Thus, in Spain people stay at home until they marry and this delays leaving home (Traditional-values statement).
2. The difficult employment situation of young people and the obstacles of the housing market are the reasons that so many young people stay at home with their parents for so long (Socio-economic statement).
3. The creation of universities all over Spain explains why students do not need to leave home for study reasons (Students-particularity statement).
4. In France students receive many public benefits and this helps them to leave their parents early (Social-policies statement).

First of all and obviously, there is no mono-causal explanation for understanding the diversity of living arrangements in Spain and France. There are specific configurations of social factors which favour high staying home rates and others which make these less likely. What a sociologist can do is to explore which factors are irrelevant and analyse relevant factors systematically, and try to falsify current explanations or put them into a broader context. In this conclusion the research strategy and the main results are summarised, and lastly possible future developments of young people's living arrangements are discussed.

In this research, an optimal research design could not be applied, since not all the necessary information was available. Some information was available at the individual level for both countries, some information exists only for France and not for Spain, and again other data could only be found at the regional or national level. This situation prevents a strict statistical multivariate test, but it does not prevent a systematic interpretation of the situation and a confrontation of hypotheses with statistical evidence. This analysis followed three strategies of hypothesis testing:

1. Parameterisation of socio-economic characteristics at the individual level through statistical multivariate analysis (French and Spanish individuals from representative samples).
2. Parameterisation of some context variables through a systematic choice of cases (France and Spain, Spanish regions, French regions).
3. Descriptive comparison of some very specific subgroups of young people (young people living independently in Spain and France).
4. Statistical test of hypotheses in only one unit of analysis (France).
5. Descriptive comparative institutional analysis of social benefits in two contexts (France, Spain).

The first strategy allowed for the confirmation of the **stability,** the **low-quality-of-life,** the **low-expectation and early school-to-work transition** and the **precariousness hypotheses** at the individual level for Spain. In addition, for Spanish men the **market-income hypothesis** was confirmed. For France the **precariousness** and the **pluralisation hypotheses** were confirmed. The second strategy holds some independent context variables in Spain and France constant and thus excluded them as possible explanative factors: Catholic denomination, strength of intergenerational solidarity, average age at first marriage, school-based vocational training system, enrolment rates in universities, perception of youth unemployment as a social problem and importance of agricultural production in the national economy. The third strategy permitted the confirmation of the **high-property hypothesis** for Spain and France. The fourth strategy partly confirmed the **dependency-diversification hypothesis** for France at the individual level and tested how the consideration of income increased the predictive power of the logistic regression models for France. Lastly, the fifth strategy discussed through which mechanisms and to what extent cross-national differences in social policies might be related to variations in intergenerational co-residence and provided in this way arguments in favour of the **dependency-diversification hypothesis** at the macro-sociological level.

This work does not test any causality relations, but it proposes a causal interpretation of correlations and an explanation in terms of configurations favouring intergenerational co-residence and those favouring early nest-leaving. If one takes the frequently used concepts in youth research of status transitions, then the results of this research can be summarised as follows. The comparatively late Spanish social transition is not an outcome of a late school-to-work transition nor of a late entry into marriage, since the former occurs, on the average, earlier than in France, and the latter at similar times. The late Spanish social transition is, instead, the result of a late financial transition and a late and incomplete social rights acquisition.

It was shown that the socio-economic theoretical model and, in particular, its statistical application, can reduce the unexplained variance in social independence patterns by 12 to 29 per cent, depending on gender and relation to studies. The statistical models explain students' patterns better that non-students' living arrangements and men's social independence better than women's. In the future the operationalisation of the socio-economic model has to be improved in three ways: First, information on income (from market, state, and family) and on expenditures has to be introduced. Second, the time spent in a job has to be added to the income level and income stability. Third, more information on the socio-economic situation of stable and informal partners has to be introduced in order to explain women's behaviour better. Probably an event history technique would also increase the explained variance.

Figure 10.1 summarises the findings of this research by relating different contexts with each other and by showing the influence of these configurations on individuals' strategies and on national living arrangements of young people.

Figure 10.1 Configurations Favouring and Hindering Early Nest-Leaving, 1985-1992

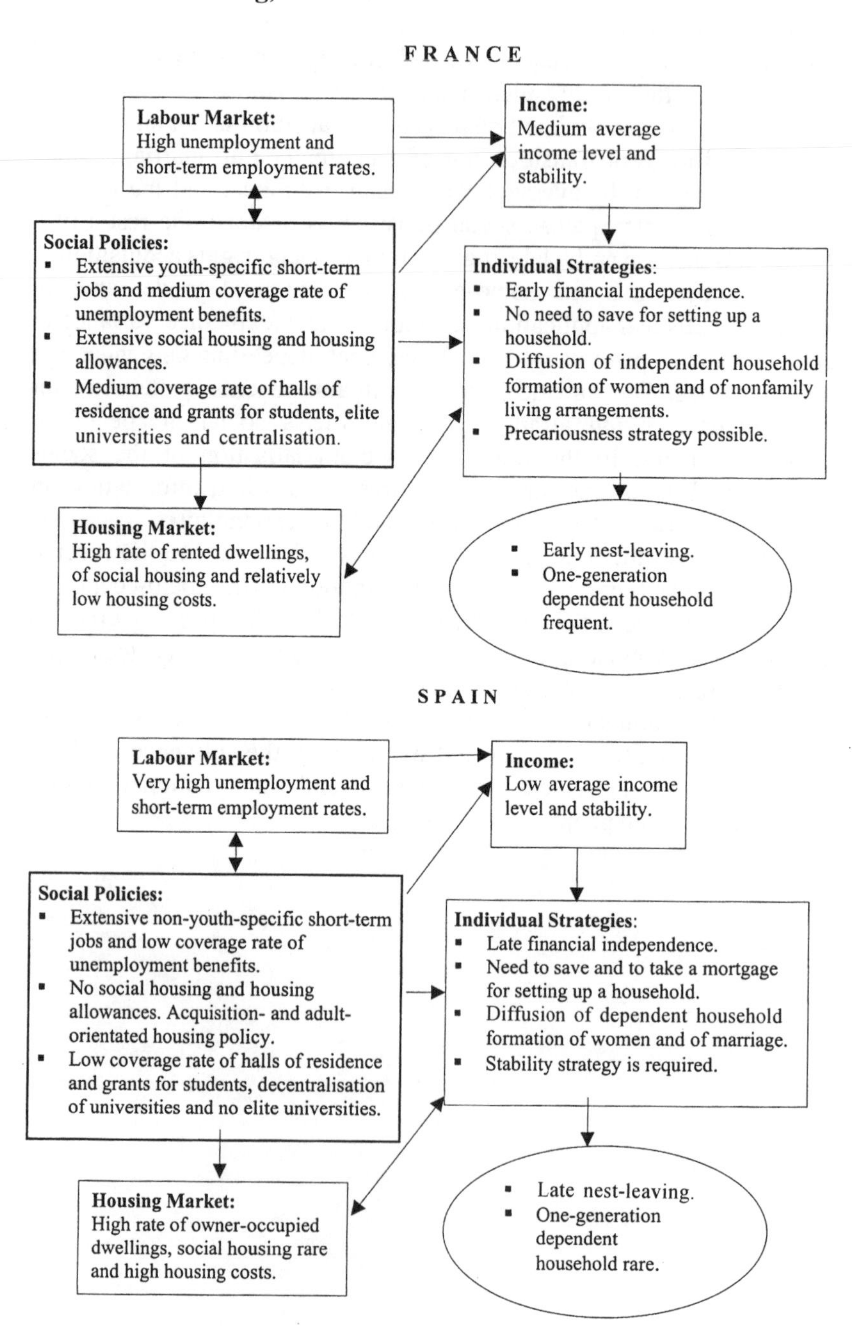
FRANCE
Labour Market:
High unemployment and short-term employment rates.
Income:
Medium average income level and stability.
Social Policies:
Extensive youth-specific short-term jobs and medium coverage rate of unemployment benefits.
Extensive social housing and housing allowances.
Medium coverage rate of halls of residence and grants for students, elite universities and centralisation.
Individual Strategies:
Early financial independence.
No need to save for setting up a household.
Diffusion of independent household formation of women and of nonfamily living arrangements.
Precariousness strategy possible.
Housing Market:
High rate of rented dwellings, of social housing and relatively low housing costs.
Early nest-leaving.
One-generation dependent household frequent.
SPAIN
Labour Market:
Very high unemployment and short-term employment rates.
Income:
Low average income level and stability.
Social Policies:
Extensive non-youth-specific short-term jobs and low coverage rate of unemployment benefits.
No social housing and housing allowances. Acquisition- and adult-orientated housing policy.
Low coverage rate of halls of residence and grants for students, decentralisation of universities and no elite universities.
Individual Strategies:
Late financial independence.
Need to save and to take a mortgage for setting up a household.
Diffusion of dependent household formation of women and of marriage.
Stability strategy is required.
Housing Market:
High rate of owner-occupied dwellings, social housing rare and high housing costs.
Late nest-leaving.
One-generation dependent household rare.

Late nest-leaving in Spain is an outcome of lower income levels of Spanish youth compared to French young people. Financial independence is reached earlier in France and this is the result of an earlier entrance into subsistence-level guaranteed jobs and of a more extended access to more generous public allowances: grants for students, unemployment benefits, and housing allowances. Income stability is a resource, which French young people also attain earlier than their Spanish counterparts, while Spanish young people show high rates of rotation from one short-term job to the next. These lower Spanish chances for attaining an early stable and adequately paid job have a deep impact on young people's likelihood to be socially independent, because Spanish youth is surrounded by a housing market and housing policy context which exasperate their difficulties on the labour market. Spanish short-term employed people are more likely to rent than to buy a dwelling, since a precarious income situation in a context of poorly developed social policies for young people makes the taking on of a mortgage a risky enterprise. Also, the Spanish housing market offers few rented dwellings and the few available ones were very expensive during the period of 1985 to 1991. Even with parental help for the down-payment of an owner-occupied dwelling, the acquisition of an accommodation was a very costly affair after Spain's entrance into the European Community. By contrast, in France young short-term employed people had access to extensive subsidised social housing and housing allowances. In this respect the Spanish Welfare State neglects Spanish youth totally: housing allowances do not exist and social dwellings for rent are nearly impossible to find. If socio-economic opportunities to leave home early are so rare for Spanish young people aged 20 to 29, does it make sense to pose the question of national differences in preferences and social norms?

For most young people in Spain social independence is an alternative with very high opportunity costs, but what about young people who one might expect to have enough resources to leave home early? First, one thinks of the children of service class origin with high resources, a high educational level and a long-term job. The logistic regression models have shown that in Spain there are nearly no class differences in the probability of living independently and that "privileged" Spanish people tend to live in the parental home much more than their French counterparts. What counts a lot in Spain are age differences, much more than in France. Let us interpret these findings for students and non-students separately.

For students, parents' resources are expected to be of some relevance for their chances to be socially independent. In fact, French students from the service class and from the petty bourgeoisie have a high chance of being socially independent compared to working class children, because they frequently emigrate for study reasons and they can combine family help with market income and sometimes even with public benefits for students (housing allowances). In Spain, students have to rely mainly on market income and family help, since public benefits for students are restricted to few students and they are less generous than in France. However, Spanish students from service class origins are not more likely to live independently than those from other social classes. There seem to be two reasonable explanations for this cross-national difference. First, the Spanish university system is less centralised and there are no elite universities, which means that migration for study reasons is less important than in France. Second, young people of service class origin do not seem to want to live away while studying, even if it is in the same town as their parents, and/or their parents do not conceive of the possibility of helping them economically in a way other than allowing them to remain at home. The findings for Spanish students point to strong social norms connecting enrolment in education with living in the parental home. Since students living away might not be adequately recorded in the Spanish survey, this lack of social class differences in the likelihood of social independence needs further confirmation. The fact that few students live away in Spain also has an influence on the diffusion of nonfamily living arrangements, since these are traditionally more frequent among students. In most countries the expansion of consensual unions in the 1960/1970s was largely due to their diffusion in the student subculture. Later cohabitation diffused into other social groups.

The situation of non-students is somewhat different, since they are supposed to depend less on parents' resources and mainly on their own resources. The Spanish "privileged" non-students have lower chances of being socially independent than their French counterparts. Different answers – cultural and socio-economic are possible. The socio-economic explanation affirms that social dependence of "privileged" young people is the result of the specific Spanish labour and housing market. Young people in Spain attain financial autonomy later than in France, mainly because their wages are lower. Wages are lower because Spanish young people enter long-term employment later than their French contemporaries and it might be that a long-term employed Spanish person earns less than her French counterpart. The latter question was not answered here, because it requires use of income data in the statistical models for both countries. Apart from this labour market question, there is clear evidence concerning housing market differences. Spanish young people with adequately paid long-term jobs have access to public incentives to buy a dwelling, but there is no public help for renting accommodations and tax exemptions are useless for people with low earnings. Besides, rented accommodations were as expensive as a mortgage during the period of observation (1985-1991).

Buying a dwelling is for most young people more rational than renting one, but this implies the need to accumulate some savings. In its turn, this requires not only a long-term job but also some time in such an employment. In fact, the cross-national logistic regression results have shown that young people with few qualifications are more likely to be socially independent, partly because they have passed more time in the labour market than their counterparts with a higher education. For young people out of education there are few opportunities to receive adequate public benefits, subsistence-guaranteeing employment is a scarce resource for which one has to queue a long time, and acquisition of a dwelling requires some savings. In this context it seems rational for Spanish "privileged" young people, who very often have passed a long time enrolled in education and who normally have to pass through a phase of short-term employment before entering a long-term job, to stay in the parental home as long as less "privileged" people. If there were more long-term jobs, more extensive and more generous public benefits for young people, and rented dwellings were more accessible, then one could expect to find more Spanish young people in a condition of social independence and more people moving out of home in order to live in consensual unions and fewer in married couples.

It has been shown that there is a larger number of young people stating that they approve of consensual unions and that they would like to move in with a partner to form a consensual union than the real number of young people doing so. Thus, there is some potential for nonfamily living arrangements, but these people are hindered from fulfilling their wishes for three reasons. First, because of the low supply of rented housing. There is a strong correlation between consensual unions and rented dwellings, whose causality might go in both directions, but a difficult housing situation clearly affects young people's decisions. Second, young Spanish people might face more social pressure against consensual unions and in favour of marriage from their parents than in France. This social pressure is strengthened by the fact that young people in Spain need their parents' economic and emotional help more than in France, since they receive fewer public benefits and they have to face more adverse and unstable employment conditions. Third, the particularly difficult labour market situation for women is strengthening the institution of marriage.

High rates of unemployment, of irregular work, and of short-term jobs have particularly negative effects on women's social independence. Assuming that as many of them would like to have a job and to choose an independent household formation as do their French counterparts, it is much more difficult for Spanish women than for French women to enter a job and, in particular, long-term employment. Hence, a higher rate of male-breadwinner families are found among Spanish than among French young people. French women rely more than French men on public benefits in order to be able to live independently. In Spain women cannot count on public benefits as French women do and thus cannot counterbalance their bad employment prospects with public help. Spanish regional labour markets with high male unemployment rates influence women's chances of social independence more than they do men's. The Spanish labour market favours dependent family formation for women through marriage and reinforces in this way the institution of marriage. Spanish young couples might face social pressure from their parents to marry, more than French young people do, but even so, a Spanish couple composed of young people with short-term jobs, in addition, has to face the problem of more difficult access to owned or rented dwellings. It means that a different housing market situation and housing policy would most probably reduce the rate of young people moving out to marry and increase the number of consensual unions and nonfamily arrangements. This does not exclude the possibility that in such a context, different social norms about consensual unions might persist between France and Spain, but they would be smaller than in the current configuration.

Young people in Spain choose a stability strategy in order to leave home, i.e. men's likelihood to live independently depends strongly on employment, in particular on long-term employment, and women's probability is strongly linked to setting up a household with an employed partner. Employment or, in other words market-income, is less relevant for French men's chances to be socially independent, since they often combine market income with public benefits and even with family help, for instance from a female partner, and this increases their chances of living independently compared to men who only rely on market income. Thus, young French people do not follow a stability strategy as frequently as Spanish men, but can more frequently afford to leave home under precarious conditions, due to the more favourable housing market and social policies context.

It is not necessary to argue in terms of different family cultures and social norms in order to explain cross-national differences in intergenerational co-residence in Spain and France, since a large part of the differences are related to very different opportunity structures.[1] So, coming back to popular explanations about long-lasting intergenerational co-residence in Spain, we can state that the traditional-values statement might explain a part of the cross-national differences, but the socio-economic statement already explains a large amount of the French-Spanish variation. The students-particularity and the social-policies statements are important explanative factors, but they have to be embedded into their respective contexts, since they can explain cross-national differences only in relation to other factors.

One can speak of the relevance of differences in social norms with respect to the institutionalisation of the division of labour between the Welfare State and the Family. An important argument throughout this work has been that social policies affect young people's life chances, in particular their chances to become socially independent. It was shown for France that public benefits influence young people's living arrangements more than parental help does. However, public benefits do not eliminate social class differences, as shown in the results for France. More research on social policies for youth has to be done, in particular with respect to Southern Europe. The mechanisms through which social policies affect young people's life chances and social class differences within youth have to be clarified.

The Spanish Welfare State is based on the assumption that children are mainly their parents' affair, and that they might depend on their parents as long as they live with them in one household. Social policies for young people focus on active employment policy through flexibility at the margin, which means a flexibility concentrating exclusively on new entrants into employment. These measures created a specific youth labour market with high job rotation and low earnings, which is not being alleviated through adequate housing benefits and only to a small degree through unemployment benefits.

Social policies can alleviate problems related to crowded labour markets, but they cannot remedy the difficult labour market integration of young people. They can help young people to maintain their income through phases of unemployment and to reduce housing costs, they can help them to come into contact with the labour market or to acquire more employment-related qualifications, and they might reduce general uncertainty about future consequences of leaving home under economically precarious conditions. It has been shown for France that public benefits affect young people's life chances mainly in combination with market income and they affect women more than men. Thus, the problem of employment shortage, especially in Spain, has to be solved in the first place by the creation of more employment, be it due to economic growth or due to the redistribution of paid work. It was shown that, if one wants to favour the social independence of young people, employment has to be of long-term nature. In France and in Spain young people in fixed-term jobs have more difficulties living independently. The main conclusion of this work is that an alleviation of employment and housing problems of young people through adequate social policies will increase the Spanish rate of socially independent young people and, hence, will accelerate young people's nest-leaving.

If social policies for young people and young families are not developed more intensively in Spain or were further restricted in France, then several problems related to long-lasting intergenerational co-residence might increase and emerge.

1. The fertility decline in Spain might still go on for some years with all its subsequent future problems for the economy and the Welfare State.
2. Patriarchal gender relations will be more difficult to change or will even be reinforced, if the Welfare State does not support families in their tasks and a large majority of women have to pass from economic dependence on the father to economic dependence on the spouse.
3. The transition from intergenerational co-residence to marriage will persist in Spain, reducing young people's experimentation with different forms of living arrangements and their capacity for social innovation.
4. Young people's frustration about their incapacity to manage an important part of their own lives and become economically, socially, and emotionally independent will persist or even increase.

With respect to social policies for young people in Spain there is still a long way to go in order to change the strong assumption about the division of labour between the Family and the Welfare State. Political decisions or the absence of these are the main factors which determine the form of this division of labour. We can argue that in some socio-economic contexts there are more limits on the redistribution of resources through the Welfare State than in others, but within these limits Welfare States are able to organise them differently and they do so. Like social policies for young people, family policies have not only vertical but also horizontal redistribution aims and there are large differences in how family policies are organised among similarly "rich" and developed Welfare States. These differences can be observed simply by comparing French and German family policies (Kaufmann et al. 1997, Neubauer 1993).

The Spanish Welfare State is a late comer, experiencing its expansion phase when Welfare State expansion was coming to an end in other countries and the crisis of the Welfare State was proclaimed. In a context of high unemployment, Spain had to develop basic public benefits which did not exist before, such as universal health care, unemployment benefits, minimum old-age pensions and a comprehensive public education system. Most public social resources are transferred via the social security and the tax system to the older dependents, while young dependents and potential children are neglected due to political, social, and economic reasons (Garrido Medina 1997). The current challenge of the Spanish Welfare State is to support families in their tasks with respect to children's maintenance and socialisation and to lower the costs of children, young and adult children. Spanish young people's access to income maintenance allowances through scholarships and unemployment benefits, and state-regulated youth-specific employment measures increasing the pace of entrance into adequately paid jobs has to be ameliorated. The most important dimension of this new social policy orientation should be to change and develop housing policy in a direction that helps more youth and young families to rent their first dwelling rather than support adults' acquisition of a second dwelling.

Note

[1] It is not clear if this statement also applies to students, since the limited evidence found in this work makes it more reasonable to see social norms as the main cause of students' social dependence.

[illegible]

[illegible] support [illegible] make [illegible] [illegible] and to [illegible] young and [illegible] children; Spanish young people [illegible] and [illegible] allow [illegible] youth, respectively [illegible] measures [illegible] the [illegible] children [illegible] adequately paid [illegible] to be [illegible]. The [illegible] direction [illegible] the new social policy [illegible] studying [illegible] and [illegible] housing policy [illegible] that helps young [illegible] and single [illegible] their [illegible] rather than [illegible] adults [illegible] dwellings.

Note

[illegible] independent.

Appendix

Description of Encuesta Sociodemográfica 1991 and Enquête Jeunes 1992

French Survey

The French survey "Enquête Jeunes 1992" was conducted in March 1992 by the French Statistical Office among 10,000 young people who were leaving the general French Labour Force Survey sample, after having been interviewed for three consecutive years. Thus the information of the specific "young people" survey can be complemented by the information these young people gave one to two weeks before in the Labour Force Survey. The survey was aimed at young people aged 18 to 29 and born between January 1963 and December 1974 inclusively. The survey asks detailed information for the professional and family situation and for retrospective information since the young person's 16th birthday (Meron 1993).

The sample of the Enquête Jeunes is a sub-sample of the Labour Force Survey and it excludes people who live in residence halls. In order to have at least some representation of this population in the survey the interviewers were instructed to interview people who live outside of a family dwelling but who can still be considered as members of the household and thus to interview them (cf. Villeneuve-Gokalp 1997). They form 4 per cent of the *Franceall* sample (cf. below). However, the retrospective part of the Enquête Jeunes allows one to know the number of young people who left home for the first time and went to a residence hall.

Since the Enquête Jeunes is a sub-sample of the Labour Force Survey, the sampling method of the latter has to be described. The French Labour Force Survey is conducted by the French Statistical Office (INSEE) in March of every year and in 1992 it had a sample of around 65,000 households and 135,000 individuals. The INSEE applies a three-stage sample (échantillon aréolaire) with stratification in the first-stage units (LASMAS 1998). The first-stage sample units are 210 zones including municipalities and urban agglomerations, which are the outcome of crossing 21 regions with 10 categories of municipalities. The second-stage units are the result of the division of the former zones in groups of areas of ca. 200 dwellings. Of these groups one group of every 60 groups is chosen with the same probability and then the latter groups are divided in 5 areas of around 40 dwellings. The third-stage units are all the dwellings of the chosen area. This method (méthode aréolaire) prevents a sub-registration of informal households.

For the chosen household information on all members is collected. Within one household one household member can answer for all the others, so that the interviewer is not forced to interview all members personnally. The informant is chosen randomly from the whole sample following the "Kish" method (LASMAS 1998). In cases of non-response the chosen household is replaced by another household with similar characteristics. For the 1990 Labour Force Series, the non-response rate varies from 2 to 3%. Weighting in order to make up for random errors is done with the help of census information and the same coefficients are used every year.

Spanish Survey

The Spanish survey is called "Encuesta Sociodemográfica 1991" (further on called ESD) and it was conducted by the Spanish Statistical Institute during October, November, and December 1991. The universe of the survey are all people having their residence in Spain, aged 10 or over and registered in the Population Census of 1991. People living in residence halls were not taken into consideration, but we have some information on them in the retrospective part of the survey.

The Statistical Office applied a three-stage sample with stratification in the first-stage units (INE 1993, 195). The first-stage sample units are the census enumeration districts of the 1991 census and the second-stage units are the main family dwellings and fixed dwellings. The third-stage units are the individuals living in fixed family dwellings and who were born before the first of January 1982. The first-stage units were stratified using a geographic and habitat size criterion following the province and the number of inhabitants of the municipality. Given the different distribution of municipality size among different provinces, a non-uniform stratification was applied, excluding for instance the category of very small municipalities in regions were they are insignificant. The sample consists of 7,969 census districts and 20 second-stage units in each district. This results in 159,154 dwellings and, because in each one individual was selected, the same number of interviewees is the result.

The distribution of the sample among the different *Comunidades Autonomas* (CCAA) was done following a compromise between an equal sample allocation and a proportionally allocated sample giving a higher weight to small CCAA composed of only one province (Asturias,

Cantabria, Murcia, Navarre, Rioja) with the aim of obtaining a representative sample. Within each CCAA the allocation by province and district followed the criterion of the proportionality of the population.

The selection of the sample followed a random procedure at the first-stage unit, a systematic procedure for the selection of dwellings and a random selection of individuals. Two reserve samples were chosen following the principles of the general sample. This permitted for the substitution of dwellings in given cases where it was not possible to conduct the interview. The census information was used to ameliorate the estimation and to establish weighting factors with the aim of correcting for possible bias due to non-responses.

Interview Process The information was collected via a personal interview of the selected person (INE 1993, 219). The dwelling and the individual to be interviewed could be substituted by a reserve dwelling or a reserve individual only in cases of an erroneous selection or when it was impossible to conduct the interview. In the following cases a substitution was admitted:

1. dwelling could not be found;
2. dwelling could not be reached (due to weather, etc.);
3. dwelling no longer existed;
4. dwelling was a collective establishment instead of a family dwelling;
5. nobody was living in the dwelling;
6. a household different from that of the individual to be interviewed was living in the dwelling;
7. if all residents of the household were absent and would continue to be absent during the whole period of the field work;
8. if at the end of the field work it had not been possible to contact a member of the household;
9. if all the members of the household refused to answer;
10. if the household did not have its main residence in the dwelling.

In all these cases a reserve dwelling was chosen. In some other cases the dwelling was not substituted but another member of the household was interviewed (selection by random).

1. if the individual to be interviewed had died after the time of the census interview;
2. if the individual was absent and would be absent during the whole time of the field work. In this case another family member was asked to give information about the absent selected individual;

3. if the individual had changed dwelling since the time of the census;
4. if the selected individual was not able to answer to questions because of a strong illness or handicap;
5. if the individual was aged under 16 years;
6. if the individual refused to answer. In case he/she did not refuse to allow another family member to answer for him/her, another member could give the information about her/him. If the refusal was total a new household was selected;
7. if no adequate substitute informant was found or another family member did not have sufficient knowledge to answer all the questions about the selected individual;
8. if the individual was not ten years old at moment of the interview.

Problems During the Field Work In 76,3% of the cases the interview was done in the originally selected dwelling and with the selected individual. In 15,8% of the cases the interview was conducted in a first substitute dwelling, in 5,2% in a second substitute and in 2,8% in a third substitute dwelling. In some autonomous communities substitution was more frequent than on the average. This was the case inthe Balearic Islands, the Canary Islands,and Madrid.

In 10,2% of the cases a substitution was necessary because of a refusal to answer and in 8,3% of the cases because of a long-lasting absence. In the autonomous communities of Madrid, Navarre, and the Basque Country, the refusal to answer was higher than in other autonomous communities (16,6%, 13,4%, and 13% respectively). If one takes the total sample as the basis (as in the French case), the non-response rate amounts to 2.4%. It is important to notice that the over-proportional refusals occurred in highly urbanised autonomous communities like Madrid and the Basque Country, which for our study could mean that young people living in informal living-arrangements tended to refuse the interview and thus could be underrepresented.

Weighting The INE offers two weighting factors, one for the estimation of the real population and one for the dwelling. They not only estimate the whole population but also correct for bias. A comparison of the weighted and non-weighted sample of young people aged 25 to 29 years show the following corrections:

Some autonomous communities increased their weight (Galicia 0.4%, Catalonia 2%, Valencia 1.4%, Andalusia1.9%, Castilla-And-Leon 0.3%, and Madrid 1.8%). If *Spainall* is weighted then we can observe that by this procedure men become up-weighted (2.8%), while women were down-weighted. Full-time students and unemployed people become up-weighted

(2.1% and 0.2% respectively) while economically inactive people become down-weighted (2%). Young people living with parents increase their percentage by 12.2%. Despite the weighting procedure the results of the ESD differ from those of the census of 1991, not only compared to the total population but also compared to the population living in family dwellings.

Estimation of the Excluded Youth Population For the study of leaving the parental home the survey presents two sorts of problems. First, the ESD did not take into account people living in residences and this is in particular a problem for analyses of the youth population due to the fact that students might live in residences. It is absolutely necessary to estimate this population to be able to make some affirmation on the overestimation of young people living with their parents in Spain. Different sources permit an estimation of this figure. The census of 1991 counted 7,826 young people aged 25-29 years living in residences of different types (hotels, students' residence halls, hospitals, prisons, etc.)(INE 1994, 385). This means that 0.3% of young people of this age group are not represented in the ESD. In the age group between 20 and 24 years of age the percentage is only 0.2% despite the fact, that it is the age group with the highest proportion of students. These figures suggest that the ESD does not really underestimate the youth population due to the low figures of young people living in residence halls. According to the 1991 census, the total number of people who live in a residence hall for students, for workers or in an educational institution amount to 2,625. This number represents 0.08% of all the young people aged 20 to 24 and 0.3% of those young people in this age group enrolled in education (INE 1994). Another possible estimation is to see how many places in residence halls there are in Spain in relation to the registered student population. Table 7.2 in the main text shows that in 1991 there were 2.3 places per hundred students.

The second problem is probably a sub-estimation of informal living arrangements in the sense that young people living with flat mates or with a partner but are officially still registered as living with their parents will not have been adequately interviewed. If such a person was chosen at random two possibilities exist.

1. They were absent from their parents' home during the whole field work period and somebody else, e.g. the mother, was asked to inform about the young person or the person was replaced by another member of the household. In the first situation the young person counts as living with the parents and in the second situation he or she is eliminated from the sample.

2. They were interviewed during the time of a visit to the parents, e.g. during the week-end, and thus they were classified as living with their parents.

To sum up, we cannot know how many young people live in informal households with a survey which bases its selection process on official registration information. Other types of surveys such as youth surveys can give some information, but even these have other types of problems, such as problems related to quota sampling. The published report of the youth survey of 1992 permits only a rough estimation of these informal living arrangements, because it contains aggregated information on young people aged 15 to 29 years. According to this survey, 2% of the young people live alone, 2% live in cohabitation, and 5% live with friends (Navarro/Rivas 1993). The respective figures of the ESD for young people aged 20 to 29 are: 5%, 4%, and 7% (cf. Figure 4.4). Since in Spain those aged 15 to 29 live mostly at home, the figures of the ESD suggest a similar recording of non-family households as the Youth Survey.

Samples of Logistic Regression

Both surveys were reduced to smaller samples following theoretical and technical reasons of the research question as described in Chapter 3.

French Samples

The sample used in this research includes only individuals aged 20 to 29, that is 7,734 young persons, of whom 3,838 are aged 20 to 24 and 3,906 are aged 25 to 29 (*Franceall*). The decision to concentrate only on those aged 20 to 29 and thus to exclude the 18- and 19-year-olds is because this way all young people in the analysis have reached legal maturity as well as the age by which the maturity certificate is obtained in most of cases.

For the logistic regression analysis, a sub-sample of *Franceall* was used by selecting only those young people who in 1986 were living with their parents. The information of the retrospective part of the survey was used (*calendrier*) and those who in 1986 were not yet 16 years old and thus had not given any information for 1986 were supposed to live with their parents and counted as such. The question of the first leaving home moment could have been used alternatively, but since in France it is rather frequent for young people who have left home to come back again, the retrospective question of the *calendrier* was preferred. In addition and for comparative reasons, young people living in residence halls like students' halls or army barracks were treated as missing values. In this way, 258 young people were lost, that is 4.8 per cent of the new sub-sample.

This new sub-sample (*France86*) misses the individuals who left their parental home before 1986 and before reaching the age of 23, and it contains 5,393 cases. By this procedure 30% of the *Franceall* sample is excluded from *France86* and the sample is not more representative for the age group 20 to 29 years, since it under-represents some young people. Compared to *Franceall, France86* over-represents the age-group of the 20- to 24-year-olds by 15%, men by 2%, those living in the parental home by 12%, young people in education by 7%, and finally young people with the maturity certificate by 3%. Individuals in employment are underrepresented by 5% and economically inactive people by 2%. Thus, many young people in France left before age 23 and most of them were in employment or economically inactive in 1992. However, *France86* is representative of young people aged 14 to 23 who in 1986 were living at home. Thus it can be used to estimate age-specific conditional probabilities of leaving home for all ages from 14 to 29.

I decided not to weight *Franceall* since the weighted results are very similar to the non-weighted results. In the non-weighted sample the variable IND92 counts 34.9% young people living with their parents, while in the weighted sample it shows 35.2% young people at home. It was decided not to weight *France86* for the logistic regression neither, since the coefficients of the regression with the weighted sample and those with the non-weighted sample were almost the same.

Spanish Samples

From the general Sociodemographic Survey only those individuals aged 20 to 29 were selected for the same reasons as in the French case (*Spainall*), which results in a sample with 25,557 cases. For the logistic regression only those young people who in 1985 were living with their parents were selected (n=21,748). This new sub-sample (*Spain85*) misses individuals who left their parental home before 1985 and before reaching the age of 23. By this procedure 16% of the *Spainall* sample is excluded from *Spain85* and as a consequence it over-represents the group of people aged 20-24 by 6%, women by 3%, those staying with their parents by 9%, those in education by 2% and those with a maturity certificate by 4%. Economically inactive people are underrepresented by 3% and those with primary education by 4%. As in the French case Spain85 is representative of young people aged 14 to 23 who in 1985 were living at home. Thus it can be used to estimate age-specific conditional probabilities of leaving home for all ages from 14 to 29.

It was decided not to weight the sub-sample for the individual-level logistic regression, since the coefficients of the regression with the weighted sample and those with the non-weighted sample were almost the same. Only in the case of men did the coefficients of social origin, educational level, and number of siblings differ somewhat; in particular the positive effect of having two siblings becomes statistically insignificant. Nevertheless, the non-weighted sample was used in the individual-level models. In the context-level models, on the other hand, the differences between the weighted and non-weighted samples were larger and thus it was decided to weight the samples. The weighted sample was used, also, for bivariate calculations and frequencies with *Spainall*, since there are rather large differences after weighting, as shown above. This is partly due to the explicit over-sampling of some regions.

Spanish Activity Figures Compared The figures on activity resulting from my own calculations with *Spainall* were compared with the Spanish labour force survey figures in order to assess divergences between both sources.

Table A Comparison of Author's Elaboration of ESD and Results of Spanish Labour Force Survey, 1991

	Labour Force Survey (EPA)			% of population in family households	
	20-24	25-29	20-29	EPA	ESD
economically inactive	1045600	577800	1623400	26.9	27.6
active	2145600	2189000	4334600	71.8	70.5
military service	69000	11800	80800	1.3	1.3
total population	**3191200**	**2766800**	**5958000**	**98.7**	**99.4**
employed	1489700	1685800	3175500	52.6	48.5
no longer employed searching employment	417500	367200	784700	13.0	14.7
first-employment seekers	238400	136000	374400	6.2	7.3
total economically active	**2145600**	**2189000**	**4334600**	**71.8**	**70.5**
students	782400	138800	921200	15.3	16.8
other economically inactive	263200	439000	702200	11.6	10.8
total economically inactive	**1045600**	**577800**	**1623400**	**26.9**	**27.6**
long-term employment	399400	762300	1161700	19.2	16.1
short-term employment	880800	640700	1521500	25.2	25.2
not possible to classify	1000	600	1600	0.0	0.6
total dependent workers	**1281200**	**1403600**	**2684800**	**44.5**	**41.9**
population in family households, EPA	3260200	2778600	6038800		
total population without Ceuta/Melilla*			6318640		
estimated population in ESD			6254861		

Note: Students in ESD include those who only study and those who work and study.
* Census 1991.

Sources: Labour Force Survey (EPA), 4. Trimester 1991 and Sociodemographic Survey (ESD), author's elaboration.

Table 1 Coefficient Estimates and Standard Errors of Logistic Regression of Living Independently in France in 1992 and in Spain in 1991. Young People Aged 20-29 in 1991/92 Who in 1985/86 Were Living at Home and in 1991/92 Were in Education

WOMEN		**France**			**Spain**		
Total Cases		979			1720		
Cases in Analysis		910			1712		
-2 Log Likelihood		1011.15			1000.51		
-2 LL initially		1238.00			1238.55		
Diff. of -2 LL		18.32%			19.22%		
Variables	Cases	Coefficients	St. Error	Cases	Coefficients	St. Error	Variables
Activity							
part-time student	180			664			part-time student
full-time student	730	-1.1041**	0.2202	1048	-1.1022**	0.1945	full-time student
Agegroup							
25-29 year old	76			427			25-29 year old
20-24 year old	834	-0.6819**	0.3035	1285	-1.3485**	0.1843	20-24 year old
Completed Education							
tertiary certificate	60			188			tertiary certificate
<=compulsory cert.	78	-1.165**	0.3840	169	0.0352	0.2961	<=compulsory cert.
basic vocational cert.	141	-0.5201	0.3381	111	-0.1098	0.3041	basic vocational cert.
secondary vocat. cert.	431	-1.0339**	0.2820	993	-0.347	0.3512	secondary vocat. cert.
maturity certificate	192	-0.2636	0.2026	10	-0.5476*	0.2273	maturity certificate
missing	8	-0.1481	0.8114	241	0.1533	0.7694	missing
Father's Social Class							
service class	317			442			service class
routine non-manual	114	-0.2092	0.2538	304	0.1305	0.2571	routine non-manual
petty bourgeoisie	53	1.6469**	0.4046	184	0.511	0.2812	petty bourgeoisie
farmers	43	1.1893**	0.4030	105	-0.2618	0.4398	farmers
skilled workers	266	-0.4824**	0.2039	267	-0.1456	0.2775	skilled workers
non-skilled workers	95	-0.8516**	0.3030	329	-0.1479	0.2632	non-skilled workers
agricultural workers	2	74782	25.6343	35	-0.5042	0.6083	agricultural workers
economic. inactive	12	-65262	10.0438	20	0.3364	0.6462	economic. inactive
missing	8	12138	0.8070	26	-61649	10.8356	missing
Siblings							
no sibling	103			100			no sibling

one sibling	292	-0.2188	0.2665	550	0.19	0.4494	one sibling
two siblings	225	-0.1218	0.2777	528	0.5767	0.4440	two siblings
three and more sibli.	242	-0.0007	0.2845	528	0.7688	0.4419	three and more sibli.
missing	48	-0.3836	0.4170	6	0.4816	1.2924	missing
Size of municipality							
> 100.000 inhabitants	588			302			> 100.000 inhabitants
>= 20.000 and < 100.000	80	-0.1705	0.2919	403	-0.2029	0.2670	>= 20.000 and < 100.000
>= 5.000 and < 20.000	75	-0.4213	0.3108	476	0.1164	0.2506	>= 5.000 and < 20.000
< 5.000 inhabitants	167	-1.1264**	0.2481	531	-0.1036	0.2745	< 5.000 inhabitants
Region							
Ile-de-France	206			312			Madrid
Champagne-Ardennes	15	1.7423**	0.5969	105	0.1628	0.3772	Galicia
Picardie	37	-0.0454	0.4754	56	-0.5223	0.5442	Asturias
Haute-Normandie	32	0.4434	0.4353	34	-0.1463	0.5914	Cantabria
Centre	36	1.2937**	0.4275	120	-0.7614	0.4514	País Vasco
Basse-Normandie	15	1.6873**	0.5987	48	-0.134	0.5758	Navarra
Bourgogne	36	2.1619**	0.4722	61	0.3632	0.4192	Aragón
Nord-Pas de Calais	87	1.0226**	0.2977	238	-0.0421	0.2835	Cataluña
Lorraine	31	1.0179*	0.4361	46	0.0726	0.4583	Baleares
Alsace	29	1.537**	0.4441	138	0.0116	0.3339	País Valenciano
Franche-Comté	7	16267	0.8921	47	-0.0867	0.5333	Murcia
Pays de la Loire	39	-0.1862	0.4616	195	-0.5422	0.3391	Andalucía
Bretagne	73	1.5994**	0.3332	35	0.3068	0.6012	Extremadura
Poitou-Charente	10	0.1647	0.7963	60	-0.0597	0.4861	Castilla-La Mancha
Aquitaine	42	1.1946**	0.3940	124	-0.7337	0.4595	Castilla-León
Midi-Pyrénées	26	1.0899*	0.4955	22	-56766	12.0852	La Rioja
Limousin	5	14387	0.9806	71	-0.1193	0.4798	Canarias
Rhône-Alpes	86	0.3827	0.3051				
Languedoc-Roussillon	26	0.9408*	0.4764				
Provence-Côte dAzur	57	-0.1102	0.3727				
Auvergne	15	1.5877**	0.6289				
Intercept		1.3275**	0.3940		-0.7225	0.5224	
probability refer. categ.		0.79			0.33		
rate of independence		0.42			0.12		
Delta in %		53			36		

* statistically significant at <= 0.05 ** statistically significant at < =0.01

Table 2 Coefficient Estimates and Standard Errors of Logistic Regression of Living Independently in France in 1992 and in Spain in 1991 Young People Aged 20-29 in 1991/92 Who in 1985/1986 Were Living in the Parental Home and in 1991/92 Were in Education

MEN		**France**			**Spain**		
Total Cases		810			1694		
Cases in Analysis		727			1688		
-2 Log Likelihood		672.47			888.802		
-2 LL initially		945.71			1187.79		
Diff. of -2 LL		28.89%			25.17%		
Variables	Cases	Coefficients	St. Error	Cases	Coefficients	St. Error	Variables
Activity							
part-time student	133			678			part-time student
full-time student	594	-1.4532**	0.2798	1010	-1.561**	0.2206	full-time student
Agegroup							
25-29 year old	82			479			25-29 year old
20-24 year old	645	-0.6914	0.3186	1209	-1.5623**	0.1939	20-24 year old
Completed Education							
tertiary certificate	55						tertiary certificate
<=compulsory cert.	73	-2.1765**	0.4958	218	-0.1971	0.3496	<=compulsory cert.
basic vocational cert.	124	-1.4018**	0.4204	156	0.4591	0.3465	basic vocational cert.
secondary vocat. cert.	292	-1.4343**	0.3374	118	0.5352	0.3830	secondary vocat. cert.
maturity certificate	163	-0.7029**	0.2541	1023	0.0974	0.2781	maturity certificate
missing	20	-2.3939**	0.8850	9	11207	0.8085	missing
Father's Social Class							
service class	269			447			service class
routine non-manual	85	-0.8934**	0.3483	304	-0.0516	0.2850	routine non-manual
petty bourgeoisie	45	1.548**	0.4393	173	0.1319	0.3432	petty bourgeoisie
farmers	23	-0.0842	0.6267	104	0.0797	0.4243	farmers
skilled workers	220	-0.4868**	0.2511	285	0.3991	0.2861	skilled workers
non-skilled workers	62	-1.3339**	0.4557	302	0.12	0.2871	non-skilled workers
agricultural workers	8	2.1281*	0.9678	36	1.5161**	0.4952	agricultural workers
economic. inactive	10	-74421	102073	10	-53469	17.4433	economic. inactive
missing	5	16815	12285	27	11375	0.6207	missing

Siblings							
no sibling	64			108			no sibling
one sibling	247	-0.1176	0.3690	551	-0.0799	0.4537	one sibling
two siblings	189	0.2483	0.3842	506	0.6022	0.4419	two siblings
three and more sibli.	188	0.2947	0.3874	519	0.8627*	0.4393	three and more sibli.
missing	39	-0.2494	0.5486	4	19572	1.2803	missing
Size of municipality							
> 100.000 inhabitants	487			277			> 100.000 inhabitants
>= 20.000 and < 100.000	79	-0.5047	0.3640	361	-0.2131	0.2779	>= 20.000 and < 100.000
>= 5.000 and < 20.000	53	-1.2724*	0.4443	525	-0.4402	0.2650	>= 5.000 and < 20.000
< 5.000 inhabitants	108	-1.6232**	0.3672	525	-0.5191	0.2935	< 5.000 inhabitants
Region							
Ile-de-France	170			317			Madrid
Champagne-Ardennes	11	0.9087	0.7910	111	-0.0903	0.3891	Galicia
Picardie	24	-0.1962	0.7950	46	-0.9963	0.6719	Asturias
Haute-Normandie	23	1.5137**	0.5837	38	-0.9238	0.8086	Cantabria
Centre	29	10144	0.5487	108	-1.6603**	0.6333	País Vasco
Basse-Normandie	16	0.5079	0.7991	43	0.4298	0.5750	Navarra
Bourgogne	15	3.1179**	0.9394	69	0.5733	0.4266	Aragón
Nord-Pas de Calais	79	0.5083	0.3614	220	-0.3498	0.3082	Cataluña
Lorraine	22	-0.0079	0.7031	42	-1269	0.6944	Baleares
Alsace	15	1.6382*	0.6852	145	-0.1895	0.3642	País Valenciano
Franche-Comté	9	2.2215**	0.8710	54	-10383	0.7713	Murcia
Pays de la Loire	20	0.4057	0.6288	209	-0.1131	0.3035	Andalucía
Bretagne	45	1.7194**	0.4405	30	0.9831	0.6065	Extremadura
Poitou-Charente	7	0.5682	11977	48	-0.8788	0.6660	Castilla-La Mancha
Aquitaine	35	1.4732**	0.4873	93	0.1636	0.4048	Castilla-León
Midi-Pyrénées	40	2.7611**	0.4722	23	-6133	11.4187	La Rioja
Limousin	10	2.0741**	0.8097	92	-0.3733	0.4200	Canarias
Rhône-Alpes	77	0.8549**	0.3550				
Languedoc-Roussillon	19	2.7447**	0.5911				
Provence-Côte dAzur	54	-0.0989	0.4152				
Auvergne	7	1477	1.0207				
Intercept		1.6218**	0.4916		-0.8171	0.5346	
probability refer. categ.		0.84			0.31		
rate of independence		0.35			0.11		
Delta in %		42			37		

* statistically significant at <= 0.05
** statistically significant at < =0.01

Table 3 Coefficient Estimates and Standard Errors of Logistic Regression of Living Independently in France in 1992 and in Spain in 1991 Young People Aged 20-29 in 1991/92 Who in 1985/1986 Were Living in the Parental Home and in 1991/92 Were on the Labour Market

WOMEN			**France**			**Spain**		
	Total Cases		1706			8908		
	Cases in Analysis		1673			8863		
	-2 Log Likelihood		1862.769			10479.962		
	-2 LL initially		2120.414			12197.808		
	Diff. of -2 LL		12.15%			14.08%		
Variables		Cases	Coefficients	St. Error	Cases	Coefficients	St. Error	Variables
Activity	long-term employment	831			1354			long-term employment
	short-term employment	225	-0.9729**	0.1678	2264	-0.2576**	0.0753	short-term employment
	economically inactive	187	1.207**	0.2513	1837	1.0985**	0.0823	economically inactive
	self-employed	21	0.3296	0.5811	298	0.253	0.1364	self-employed
	family help	14	0.4374	0.6869	150	-0.1896	0.1918	family help
	unemployed	155	-0.3379	0.1960	1860	0.4499**	0.0782	unemployed
	first-job seeker	240	-0.7404**	0.1645	1100	-0.5966**	0.0990	first-job seeker
Agegroup	25-29 year old	756			4708			25-29 year old
	20-24 year old	917	-0.5416**	0.1193	4155	-1.2298**	0.0498	20-24 year old
Completed Education								
	tertiary certificate	361			4696			tertiary certificate
	<=compulsory cert.	713	-0.5646**	0.2229	999	0.4595**	0.0803	<=compulsory cert.
	basic vocational cert.	200	-0.4922**	0.1975	636	0.4074**	0.0981	basic vocational cert.
	secondary vocat. cert.	145	-0.4361	0.2388	1270	0.1731	0.1114	secondary vocat. cert.
	maturity certificate	16	-0.4341	0.2560	1158	0.1491	0.0933	maturity certificate
	missing	238	0.1286	0.6357	104	-0.7886**	0.2384	missing
Father's Social Class								
	service class	246			863			service class
	routine non-manual	263	0.2119	0.2159	1072	0.083	0.1022	routine non-manual
	petty bourgeoisie	114	0.6067*	0.2929	794	0.0825	0.1104	petty bourgeoisie
	farmers	117	-0.1949	0.2729	840	-0.1047	0.1119	farmers
	skilled workers	570	-0.2862	0.1838	1826	0.1982*	0.0945	skilled workers
	non-skilled workers	306	-0.0196	0.2110	2747	0.0779	0.0903	non-skilled workers
	agricultural workers	35	-0.417	0.4094	431	0.1508	0.1356	agricultural workers
	economic. inactive	20	-6675	4.8226	159	0.6572**	0.1915	economic. inactive
	missing	2	-0.5187	1.4521	131	0.1713	0.2114	missing

Siblings	no sibling	126			415			no sibling
	one sibling	378	0.0185	0.2363	2293	0.4134**	0.1241	one sibling
	two siblings	396	0.1716	0.2366	2416	0.5694**	0.1238	two siblings
	three and more sibli.	714	0.1202	0.2282	3703	0.9041**	0.1216	three and more sibli.
	missing	59	0.5839	0.3799	36	0.4593	0.3924	missing
Size of municipality								
	> 100.000 inhabitants	778			1478			> 100.000 inhabitants
	>= 20.000 and < 100.000	255	0.1306	0.1864	2027	0.0011	0.0777	>= 20.000 and < 100.000
	>= 5.000 and < 20.000	182	0.0503	0.2059	2633	0.0509	0.0729	>= 5.000 and < 20.000
	< 5.000 inhabitants	458	-0.3063*	0.1565	2725	0.1594*	0.0804	< 5.000 inhabitants
Region	Ile-de-France	334			967			Madrid
	Champagne-Ardennes	36	0.1633	0.4096	490	-0.2914*	0.1285	Galicia
	Picardie	64	-0.0264	0.3282	248	-0.1077	0.1619	Asturias
	Haute-Normandie	63	0.8828*	0.3662	204	-0.3277	0.1771	Cantabria
	Centre	66	0.0642	0.3123	564	-0.5423**	0.1294	País Vasco
	Basse-Normandie	42	0.4819	0.4078	211	-0.294	0.1748	Navarra
	Bourgogne	36	0.8975	0.4970	285	0.1038	0.1495	Aragón
	Nord-Pas de Calais	125	-0.113	0.2442	1114	0.441**	0.0984	Cataluña
	Lorraine	71	-0.5204	0.3005	193	0.4398**	0.1743	Baleares
	Alsace	57	0.7126*	0.3687	790	0.2702**	0.1069	País Valenciano
	Franche-Comté	31	0.6549	0.4722	337	0.0256	0.1417	Murcia
	Pays de la Loire	92	0.6236*	0.2892	1616	-0.0319	0.0927	Andalucía
	Bretagne	80	0.8677**	0.3282	343	0.0032	0.1423	Extremadura
	Poitou-Charente	39	-0.1345	0.3895	442	0.0613	0.1300	Castilla-La Mancha
	Aquitaine	93	-0.1504	0.2797	512	-0.3406**	0.1257	Castilla-León
	Midi-Pyrénées	73	0.3942	0.3239	111	0.1709	0.2251	La Rioja
	Limousin	19	0.0992	0.5394	436	-0.3057**	0.1305	Canarias
	Rhône-Alpes	158	0.059	0.2328				
	Languedoc-Roussillon	66	-0.1913	0.3187				
	Provence-Côte dAzur	99	0.0073	0.2713				
	Auvergne	29	-0.3688	0.4279				
	Intercept		1.549**	0.2836		-0.9596**	0.1708	
	probability refer. categ.		0.82			0.28		
	rate of independence		0.67			0.45		
	Delta in %		81			162		

* statistically significant at <= 0.05 ** statistically significant at < =0.01

Table 4 Coefficient Estimates and Standard Errors of Logistic Regression of Living Independently in France in 1992 and in Spain in 1991 Young People Aged 20-29 in 1991/92 Who in 1985/1986 Were Living in the Parental Home and in 1991/92 Were on the Labour Market

MEN			France			Spain		
	Total Cases		1726			9045		
	Cases in Analysis		1708			8997		
	-2 Log Likelihood		1980.35			9306.583		
	-2 LL initially		2367.64			11247.944		
	Diff. of -2 LL		16.36%			17.26%		
Variables		Cases	Coefficients	St. Error	Cases	Coefficients	St. Error	Variables
Activity	long-term employment	1033			2308			long-term employment
	short-term employment	237	-0.908**	0.1689	3341	-0.5772**	0.0628	short-term employment
	economically inactive	25	-0.642	0.4559	370	-1.8335**	0.1836	economically inactive
	self-employed	77	-0.4242	0.2793	906	-0.2067*	0.0873	self-employed
	family help	17	-2.0645**	0.8142	296	-1.0603**	0.1645	family help
	unemployed	124	-0.4767*	0.2129	1316	-0.9191**	0.0863	unemployed
	first-job seeker	195	-1.3156**	0.1919	460	-2.5907**	0.2638	first-job seeker
Agegroup	25-29 year old	908			5010			25-29 year old
	20-24 year old	800	-1.2534**	0.1142	3987	-1.6606**	0.0581	20-24 year old
Completed Education								
	tertiary certificate	405			5481			tertiary certificate
	<=compulsory cert.	908	-0.2876	0.2271	1060	0.654**	0.1068	<=compulsory cert.
	basic vocational cert.	142	-0.1652	0.2047	701	0.5728**	0.1247	basic vocational cert.
	secondary vocat. cert.	75	-0.1279	0.2639	1032	0.3177*	0.1363	secondary vocat. cert.
	maturity certificate	171	0.0573	0.3181	641	0.3415**	0.1265	maturity certificate
	missing	7	-0.1071	0.9586	82	0.6227*	0.3050	missing
Father's Social Class								
	service class	239			752			service class
	routine non-manual	209	-0.2583	0.2231	1046	-0.1132	0.1173	routine non-manual
	petty bourgeoisie	125	0.6689**	0.2690	829	0.0722	0.1231	petty bourgeoisie
	farmers	146	-0.5927*	0.2693	957	-0.398**	0.1233	farmers
	skilled workers	556	-0.3502	0.1875	1906	-0.1554	0.1074	skilled workers
	non-skilled workers	382	-0.4073*	0.2055	2786	-0.2455*	0.1041	non-skilled workers
	agricultural workers	31	-1.0886*	0.4532	477	-0.225	0.1432	agricultural workers
	economic. inactive	19	-3.3738**	1.0605	113	-0.2088	0.2451	economic. inactive
	missing	1	-57043	13.5037	131	-0.0419	0.2352	missing

Siblings	no sibling	135			416			no sibling
	one sibling	362	-0.1148	0.2288	2326	0.1291	0.1379	one sibling
	two siblings	376	-0.0828	0.2272	2511	0.3659**	0.1365	two siblings
	three and more sibli.	740	0.3201	0.2144	3696	0.7893**	0.1339	three and more sibli.
	missing	95	-0.0748	0.3055	48	1.2913**	0.3489	missing
Size of municipality								
	> 100.000 inhabitants	750			1479			> 100.000 inhabitants
	>= 20.000 and < 100.000	229	0.2983	0.1872	2135	0.0268	0.0824	>= 20.000 and < 100.000
	>= 5.000 and < 20.000	171	-0.1567	0.2003	2698	0.0291	0.0781	>= 5.000 and < 20.000
	< 5.000 inhabitants	558	-0.7322**	0.1523	2685	0.0648	0.0863	< 5.000 inhabitants
Region	Ile-de-France	316			944			Madrid
	Champagne-Ardennes	50	-0.059	0.3504	501	-0.2395	0.1404	Galicia
	Picardie	89	0.358	0.2939	242	-0.3892*	0.1842	Asturias
	Haute-Normandie	67	0.5472	0.3106	196	-0.4088*	0.2002	Cantabria
	Centre	61	-0.003	0.3233	560	-0.515**	0.1475	País Vasco
	Basse-Normandie	54	0.339	0.3570	213	-0.5454**	0.2003	Navarra
	Bourgogne	38	0.6762	0.4272	306	-0.0621	0.1595	Aragón
	Nord-Pas de Calais	137	-0.3153	0.2358	1131	0.2447*	0.1053	Cataluña
	Lorraine	62	-0.2892	0.3226	249	0.2587	0.1668	Baleares
	Alsace	64	0.5613	0.3189	800	0.1927	0.1154	País Valenciano
	Franche-Comté	36	-0.0557	0.4079	353	0.1921	0.1496	Murcia
	Pays de la Loire	92	0.9108**	0.2860	1608	0.4043**	0.1002	Andalucía
	Bretagne	91	0.6931*	0.2843	359	0.1812	0.1484	Extremadura
	Poitou-Charente	44	0.5881	0.3727	466	0.0506	0.1359	Castilla-La Mancha
	Aquitaine	86	0.215	0.2894	575	-0.3657**	0.1338	Castilla-León
	Midi-Pyrénées	56	0.0148	0.3529	115	0.0388	0.2309	La Rioja
	Limousin	16	0.2455	0.5819	379	-0.0405	0.1480	Canarias
	Rhône-Alpes	149	0.2894	0.2283				
	Languedoc-Roussillon	45	0.5317	0.3675				
	Provence-Côte dAzur	115	0.2945	0.2499				
	Auvergne	40	0.7144	0.4019				
	Intercept		1.2906**	0.2875		-0.5923**	0.1933	
	probability refer. Categ.		0.78			0.36		
	rate of independence		0.50			0.32		
	Delta in %		64			89		

* statistically significant at <= 0.05 ** statistically significant at < =0.01

Table 5 Coefficient Estimates and Standard Errors of Logistic Regression of Living Independently in France in 1992
Young People Aged 20-29 in 1992 Who in 1986 Were Living in the Parental Home and in 1992 Were on the Labour Market

MEN		Model without Income			Model with Income			Model with Income Diversification		
	Total Cases		1726			1726			1726	
	Cases in Analysis		1708			1646			1681	
	-2 Log Likelihood		1980.35			1737407,00			1895.44	
	Variable	Cases	Coefficient	St. Error	Variable	Coefficient	St. Error	Variable	Coefficient	St. Error
Activity	long-term employ.	1033			long-term >5000			market income		
					long-term <=5000	-0.9421**	0.1812	public benefits	0.5314	0.3039
	short-term employ.	237	-0.908**	0.1689	short-term <=5000	-1.7001**	0.2656	family help	-0.726	0.4006
					short-term >5000	-0.7522**	0.2295	market and state	1,5872**	0.2353
	economically inactive	25	-0.642	0.4559	enco. inactive <=5000	-0.9957	0.5352	market and family	0.2054	0.1580
					econ. inactive >5000	-0.1899	12.539	state and family	-0.9463**	0.2285
	unemployed	124	-0.4767*	0.2129	unemployed <=5000	-0.8581**	0.2568	market. state. family	0.7318**	0.1844
					unemployed >5000	-0.62	0.4752			
	first-job seeker	195	-1.3156**	0.1919	first-job seeker <=5000	-1.5208**	0.2122			
					first-job seeker >5000	0.7981	0.8932			
	self-employed	77	-0.4242	0.2793	self-employed <=5000	-1.146**	0.4632			
					self-employed >5000	0.2998	0.4586			
	family help	17	-2.0645**	0.8142	family-help <=5000	-63821	54.851			
					family-help >5000	n	n			
Agegroup	25-29 year old	908			25-29 year old			25-29 year old		
	20-24 year old	800	-1.2534**	0.1142	20-24 year old	-1.2602**	0.1226	20-24 year old	-1.4029**	0.1168
Compl. Education	tertiary certificate	405			tertiary certificate			tertiary certificate		
	<=compulsory cert.	908	-0.2876	0.2271	<=compulsory cert.	-0.0102	0.2486	<=compulsory cert.	-0.3792	0.2318
	basic vocational cert.	142	-0.1652	0.2047	basic vocational cert.	-0.0346	0.2239	basic vocational cer.	-0.1237	0.2088
	secondary vocat. cert.	75	-0.1279	0.2639	secondary vocat. cert.	-0.0408	0.288	second. vocat. cert.	-0.0375	0.2677
	maturity certificate	171	0.0573	0.3181	maturity certificate	0.033	0.3513	maturity certificate	0.0385	0.3314
	missing	7	-0.1071	0.9586	missing	0.3433	11.941	missing	-0.0977	0.9012
Father's Class	service class	239			service class			service class		
	routine non-manual	209	-0.2583	0.2231	routine non-manual	-0.2924	0.2383	routine non-manual	-0.1237	0.2278
	petty bourgeoisie	125	0.6689**	0.269	petty bourgeoisie	0.6414*	0.2943	petty bourgeoisie	0.7304**	0.2752
	farmers	146	-0.5927*	0.2693	farmers	-0.6166*	0.2946	farmers	-0.6858**	0.2631
	skilled workers	556	-0.3502	0.1875	skilled workers	-0.4474*	0.2021	skilled workers	-0.3065	0.1928
	non-skilled workers	382	-0.4073*	0.2055	non-skilled workers	-0.4192*	0.2209	non-skilled workers	-0.3665	0.2104
	agricultural workers	31	-1.0886*	0.4532	agricultural workers	-1.0492*	0.4836	agricultural workers	-1.1013*	0.4718
	economic. inactive	19	-3.3738**	10.605	economic. inactive	-3.2373**	10.797	economic. inactive	-3.631**	10.911
	missing	1	-57043	135.037	missing	-65624	22.243	missing	-53845	135.042

Siblings	no sibling	135			no sibling			no sibling		
	one sibling	362	-0.1148	0.2288	one sibling	-0.0952	0.2417	one sibling	-0.2494	0.2364
	two siblings	376	-0.0828	0.2272	two siblings	-0.0541	0.2409	two siblings	-0.1228	0.2354
	three and more sibli.	740	0.3201	0.2144	three and more sibli.	0.3068	0.2274	three & more sibli.	0.1818	0.2223
	missing	95	-0.0748	0.3055	missing			missing	-0.1014	0.3169
Size mun.	> 100.000 inhabitants	750			> 100.000 inhabitants			> 100.000 inhabitants		
	>= 20.000 and < 100.000	229	0.2983	0.1872	>= 20.000 & < 100.000	0.351	0.2013	>=20.000&<100.000	0.2393	0.1915
	>= 5.000 and < 20.000	171	-0.1567	0.2003	>= 5.000 & < 20.000	-0.0408	0.2164	>= 5.000 & < 20.000	-0.1421	0.2056
	< 5.000 inhabitants	558	**-0.7322****	0.1523	< 5.000 inhabitants	**-0.7013****	0.1633	< 5.000 inhabitants	**-0.6191****	0.1567
Region	Ile-de-France	316			Ile-de-France			Ile-de-France		
	Champagne-Ardennes	50	-0.059	0.3504	Champagne-Ardennes	-0.1924	0.3859	Champagne-Ardenne	0.0729	0.3606
	Picardie	89	0.358	0.2939	Picardie	**0.5991***	0.3328	Picardie	0.3438	0.3022
	Haute-Normandie	67	0.5472	0.3106	Haute-Normandie	**0.6975***	0.3322	Haute-Normandie	0.4742	0.3187
	Centre	61	-0.003	0.3233	Centre	0.031	0.3382	Centre	-0.0332	0.3334
	Basse-Normandie	54	0.339	0.357	Basse-Normandie	0.4031	0.3791	Basse-Normandie	0.2272	0.3691
	Bourgogne	38	0.6762	0.4272	Bourgogne	0.7967	0.46	Bourgogne	0.5004	0.4286
	Nord-Pas de Calais	137	-0.3153	0.2358	Nord-Pas de Calais	-0.3437	0.2503	Nord-Pas de Calais	**-0.524***	0.2420
	Lorraine	62	-0.2892	0.3226	Lorraine	-0.2139	0.3389	Lorraine	-0.1285	0.3325
	Alsace	64	0.5613	0.3189	Alsace	0.6052*	0.3649	Alsace	**0.7296***	0.328
	Franche-Comté	36	-0.0557	0.4079	Franche-Comté	-0.2415	0.4215	Franche-Comté	-0.362	0.4489
	Pays de la Loire	92	**0.9108****	0.286	Pays de la Loire	**0.8543***	0.2972	Pays de la Loire	**0.7651****	0.2859
	Bretagne	91	**0.6931***	0.2843	Bretagne	**0.8058***	0.3064	Bretagne	**0.6319***	0.2869
	Poitou-Charente	44	0.5881	0.3727	Poitou-Charente	**1.0289***	0.4293	Poitou-Charente	0.6733	0.3861
	Aquitaine	86	0.215	0.2894	Aquitaine	0.2177	0.3054	Aquitaine	0.1692	0.3025
	Midi-Pyrénées	56	0.0148	0.3529	Midi-Pyrénées	0.056	0.4018	Midi-Pyrénées	0.1399	0.3568
	Limousin	16	0.2455	0.5819	Limousin	0.4237	0.6091	Limousin	0.1029	0.5755
	Rhône-Alpes	149	0.2894	0.2283	Rhône-Alpes	0.3284	0.2409	Rhône-Alpes	0.2114	0.2334
	Languedoc-Rouss.	45	0.5317	0.3675	Languedoc-Roussillon	0.5229	0.3947	Languedoc-Roussillo	0.5001	0.3757
	Provence-Côte dAzur	115	0.2945	0.2499	Provence-Côte dAzur	0.1424	0.2688	Provence-Côte dAzur	0.0632	0.2617
	Auvergne	40	0.7144	0.4019	Auvergne	0.6591	0.4542	Auvergne	0.6208	0.4050
	Intercept		**1.2906****	0.2875	Intercept	**1.359****	0.3086	Intercept	**0.7857****	0.3075
	prob. of refer. categ.		0.78			0.80			0.68	
	rate of independence		0.50			0.51			0.50	
	Delta in %		64			64			73	

* statistically significant at <= 0.05 ** statistically significant at < =0.01

Table 6 Coefficient Estimates and Standard Errors of Logistic Regression of Living Independently in France in 1992
Young People Aged 20-29 in 1992 Who in 1986 Were Living in the Parental Home and in 1992 Were on the Labour Market

WOMEN		Model without Income			Model with Income			Model with Income Diversification		
	Total Cases		1706			1706			1706	
	Cases in Analysis		1673			1597			1647	
	-2 Log Likelihood		1862.8			1754.56			1895.02	
	Variable	Cases	Coefficient	St. Error	Variable	Coefficient	St. Error	Variable	Coefficient	St. Error
Activity	long-term employ.	831			long-term >5000		0.1820	market income		
					long-term <=5000	-0.5063**	0.2247	public benefits	0.7395*	0.3317
	short-term employ.	225	-0.9729**	0.1678	short-term <=5000	-1.3904**	0.2963	family help	1.5178**	0.3347
					short-term >5000	-1.1138**	0.2919	market and state	0.7208**	0.2676
	economically inactive	187	1.207**	0.2513	econ. inactive <=5000	0.8489	1.0598	market and family	0.4285*	0.1887
					econ. inactive >5000	16605	0.2362	state and family	0.5202**	0.1996
	unemployed	155	-0.3379	0.1960	unemployed <=5000	-0.6417**	0.5739	market. state. family	1.0969**	0.2050
					unemployed >5000	-0.626	0.2010			
	first-job seeker	240	-0.7404**	0.1645	first-job seeker <=5000	-1.1836**	0.7070			
					first-job seeker >5000	0.0153	0.8011			
	self-employed	21	0.3296	0.5811	self-employed <=5000	0.4386	1.1819			
					self-employed >5000	-0.2417	0.7161			
	family help	14	0.4374	0.6869	family-help <=5000	-0.0947				
					family-help >5000					
Agegroup	25-29 year old	756			25-29 year old			25-29 year old		
	20-24 year old	917	-0.5416**	0.1193	20-24 year old	-0.4382**	0.1255	20-24 year old	-0.6717**	0.1170
Education	tertiary certificate	361			tertiary certificate			tertiary certificate		
	<=compulsory cert.	713	-0.5646**	0.2229	<=compulsory cert.	-0.4257	0.2400	<=compulsory cert.	-0.4905**	0.2216
	basic vocational cert.	200	-0.4922**	0.1975	basic vocational cert.	-0.3698	0.2131	basic vocational cert.	-0.4879**	0.1984
	secondary vocat. cert.	145	-0.4361	0.2388	secondary vocat. cert.	-0.3342	0.2534	secondary vocat. cert.	-0.4417	0.2374
	maturity certificate	16	-0.4341	0.256	maturity certificate	-0.3914	0.2747	maturity certificate	-0.3489	0.2563
	missing	238	0.1286	0.6357	missing	0.1782	0.6617	missing	-0.0612	0.6202
Class	service class	246			service class			service class		
	routine non-manual	263	0.2119	0.2159	routine non-manual	0.2181	0.2294	routine non-manual	0.2025	0.2144
	petty bourgeoisie	114	0.6067*	0.2929	petty bourgeoisie	0.4857	0.3052	petty bourgeoisie	0.6696*	0.2901
	farmers	117	-0.1949	0.2729	farmers	-0.1119	0.2908	farmers	-0.0983	0.2685
	skilled workers	570	-0.2862	0.1838	skilled workers	-0.3407	0.1945	skilled workers	-0.3119	0.1831
	non-skilled workers	306	-0.0196	0.2110	non-skilled workers	-0.032	0.2218	non-skilled workers	-0.0272	0.2087
	agricultural workers	35	-0.417	0.4094	agricultural workers	-0.4253	0.4410	agricultural workers	-0.4372	0.4038
	economic. inactive	20	-6675	48.226	economic. inactive	-67319	5.0261	economic. inactive	-69323	4.7920
	missing	2	-0.5187	14.521	missing	-0.4825	1.4527	missing	-10533	1.4543

Siblings	no sibling	126			no sibling			no sibling		
	one sibling	378	0.0185	0.2363	one sibling	0.0821	0.2437	one sibling	0.1624	0.2350
	two siblings	396	0.1716	0.2366	two siblings	0.2549	0.2450	two siblings	0.2996	0.2349
	three and more sibli.	714	0.1202	0.2282	three and more sibli.	0.2203	0.2353	three and more sibli.	0.2879	0.2266
	missing	59	0.5839	0.3799	missing			missing	0.4711	0.3795
Size municipality	> 100.000 inhabitants	778			> 100.000 inhabitants			> 100.000 inhabitants		
	>= 20.000&< 100.000	255	0.1306	0.1864	>= 20.000 & < 100.000	0.2004	0.1977	>= 20.000 & < 100.000	0.1276	0.1835
	>= 5.000 & < 20.000	182	0.0503	0.2059	>= 5.000 & < 20.000	0.053	0.2191	>= 5.000 & < 20.000	0.1015	0.2020
	< 5.000 inhabitants	458	-0.3063*	0.1565	< 5.000 inhabitants	-0.3606*	0.1640	< 5.000 inhabitants	-0.2622	0.1550
Region	Ile-de-France	334			Ile-de-France		0.4323	Ile-de-France		
	Champagne-Ardennes	36	0.1633	0.4096	Champagne-Ardennes	0.2595	0.3742	Champagne-Ardennes	0.0481	0.4070
	Picardie	64	-0.0264	0.3282	Picardie	0.256	0.3828	Picardie	-0.3189	0.3254
	Haute-Normandie	63	0.8828*	0.3662	Haute-Normandie	0.9746**	0.3396	Haute-Normandie	0.6116	0.3571
	Centre	66	0.0642	0.3123	Centre	0.265	0.4178	Centre	0.0246	0.3092
	Basse-Normandie	42	0.4819	0.4078	Basse-Normandie	0.4843	0.5410	Basse-Normandie	0.2255	0.4091
	Bourgogne	36	0.8975	0.4970	Bourgogne	1.0686*	0.2585	Bourgogne	0.8348	0.4934
	Nord-Pas de Calais	125	-0.113	0.2442	Nord-Pas de Calais	-0.108	0.3169	Nord-Pas de Calais	-0.3126	0.2389
	Lorraine	71	-0.5204	0.3005	Lorraine	-0.526	0.3996	Lorraine	-0.5162	0.3002
	Alsace	57	0.7126*	0.3687	Alsace	0.8969*	0.5011	Alsace	0.6099	0.3712
	Franche-Comté	31	0.6549	0.4722	Franche-Comté	0.8323	0.2977	Franche-Comté	0.3856	0.4649
	Pays de la Loire	92	0.6236*	0.2892	Pays de la Loire	0.6872*	0.3451	Pays de la Loire	0.2406	0.2845
	Bretagne	80	0.8677**	0.3282	Bretagne	0.994**	0.4027	Bretagne	0.5552	0.3230
	Poitou-Charente	39	-0.1345	0.3895	Poitou-Charente	-0.0795	0.2926	Poitou-Charente	-0.2649	0.3810
	Aquitaine	93	-0.1504	0.2797	Aquitaine	-0.0248	0.3419	Aquitaine	-0.4048	0.2776
	Midi-Pyrénées	73	0.3942	0.3239	Midi-Pyrénées	0.6267	0.5462	Midi-Pyrénées	0.1211	0.3165
	Limousin	19	0.0992	0.5394	Limousin	0.2023	0.2464	Limousin	-0.1783	0.5243
	Rhône-Alpes	158	0.059	0.2328	Rhône-Alpes	0.1606	0.3487	Rhône-Alpes	-0.0345	0.2297
	Languedoc-Roussillon	66	-0.1913	0.3187	Languedoc-Roussillon	0.0273	0.2869	Languedoc-Roussillon	-0.4094	0.3126
	Provence-Côte dAzur	99	0.0073	0.2713	Provence-Côte dAzur	-0.0043	0.4543	Provence-Côte dAzur	-0.0222	0.2685
	Auvergne	29	-0.3688	0.4279	Auvergne	-0.2564		Auvergne	-0.4936	0.4237
	Intercept		1.549**	0.2836	Intercept	1.5704**	0.2973	Intercept	0.7737**	0.3066
	probab. of referc cat.		0.82			0.83			0.68	
	rate of independence		0.67			0.68			0.67	
	Delta in %		81			82			97	

* statistically significant at <= 0.05 ** statistically significant at < =0.01

Table 7 Coefficient Estimates and Standard Errors of Logistic Regression of Living Independently in France in 1992 Young People Aged 20-29 in 1992 Who in 1986 Were Living in the Parental Home and in 1992 Were in Education

WOMEN	Model without Income			Model with Income			Model with Income Diversification		
Total Cases		979			979			979	
Cases in Analysis		910			876			898	
-2 Log Likelihood		1011.15			974.685			976.786	
Variables	Cases	Coefficients	St. Error	Variables	Coefficients	St. Error	Variables	Coefficients	St. Error
				part-time>5000			market income		
part-time student	180			part-time<=5000	-0.4614	0.4000	public benefits	-0.6	0.6370
full-time student	730	-1.1041**	0.2202	full-time<=5000	-1.4006**	0.3652	family help	-0.755	0.5117
				full-time>5000	-0.1786	0.6608	market and state	1.8209*	0.7535
							market and family	-0.5773	0.4842
							state and family	-0.9234*	0.4604
							market. state. family	0.1989	0.5070
Agegroup									
25-29 year old	76			25-29 year old			25-29 year old		
20-24 year old	834	-0.6819**	0.3035	20-24 year old	-0.5366	0.3123	20-24 year old	-0.9528**	0.3067
Completed Education									
tertiary certificate	60			tertiary certificate			tertiary certificate		
<=compulsory cert.	78	-1.165**	0.3840	<=compulsory cert.	-1.058**	0.3907	<=compulsory cert.	-0.9801**	0.3879
basic vocational cert.	141	-0.5201	0.3381	basic vocational cert.	-0.3792	0.3441	basic vocational cert.	-0.3027	0.3394
secondary vocat. cert.	431	-1.0339**	0.2820	secondary vocat. cert.	-1.0238**	0.2906	secondary vocat. cert.	-0.9722**	0.2915
maturity certificate	192	-0.2636	0.2026	maturity certificate	-0.1674	0.2074	maturity certificate	-0.1728	0.2091
missing	8	-0.1481	0.8114	missing	-0.0158	0.8077	missing	-0.289	0.8678
Father's Social Class									
service class	317			service class			service class		
routine non-manual	114	-0.2092	0.2538	routine non-manual	-0.1664	0.2578	routine non-manual	-0.2894	0.2619
petty bourgeoisie	53	1.6469**	0.4046	petty bourgeoisie	1.5809**	0.4064	petty bourgeoisie	1.6934**	0.4129
farmers	43	1.1893**	0.4030	farmers	1.438**	0.4400	farmers	0.9883*	0.4105
skilled workers	266	-0.4824**	0.2039	skilled workers	-0.433*	0.2083	skilled workers	-0.4779*	0.2091
non-skilled workers	95	-0.8516**	0.3030	non-skilled workers	-0.8427**	0.3042	non-skilled workers	-0.9396**	0.3166
agricultural workers	2	74782	25.6343	agricultural workers	76784	25.6603	agricultural workers	75847	25.655
economic. inactive	12	-65262	10.0438	economic. inactive	-65132	10.4662	economic. inactive	-64342	9.9751
missing	8	12138	0.8070	missing	13065	0.9410	missing	11984	0.8381

Siblings	no sibling	103			no sibling			no sibling		
	one sibling	292	-0.2188	0.2665	one sibling	-0.1952	0.2701	one sibling	-0.2117	0.2713
	two siblings	225	-0.1218	0.2777	two siblings	-0.1629	0.2834	two siblings	-0.1614	0.2840
	three and more sibli.	242	-0.0007	0.2845	three and more sibli.	-0.0099	0.2875	three and more sibli.	-0.06	0.2920
	missing	48	-0.3836	0.4170	missing	-0.4394	0.4300	missing	-0.2974	0.4206
Size of municipality										
	> 100.000 inhabitants	588			> 100.000 inhabitants			> 100.000 inhabitants		
	>= 20.000 and < 100.000	80	-0.1705	0.2919	>= 20.000 and < 100.000	-0.1741	0.2999	>= 20.000 and < 100.000	-0.1825	0.3008
	>= 5.000 and < 20.000	75	-0.4213	0.3108	>= 5.000 and < 20.000	-0.4258	0.3137	>= 5.000 and < 20.000	-0.5215	0.3211
	< 5.000 inhabitants	167	-1.1264**	0.2481	< 5.000 inhabitants	-1.0936**	0.2544	< 5.000 inhabitants	-0.9692**	0.2496
Region	Ile-de-France	206			Ile-de-France			Ile-de-France		
	Champagne-Ardennes	15	1.7423**	0.5969	Champagne-Ardennes	1.6263**	0.5976	Champagne-Ardennes	1.7048**	0.6207
	Picardie	37	-0.0454	0.4754	Picardie	0.0531	0.4842	Picardie	0.1329	0.4821
	Haute-Normandie	32	0.4434	0.4353	Haute-Normandie	0.5045	0.4494	Haute-Normandie	0.3579	0.4555
	Centre	36	1.2937**	0.4275	Centre	1.1725**	0.4342	Centre	1.3585**	0.4275
	Basse-Normandie	15	1.6873**	0.5987	Basse-Normandie	1.4862*	0.6243	Basse-Normandie	1.6165**	0.6104
	Bourgogne	36	2.1619**	0.4722	Bourgogne	2.0994**	0.4737	Bourgogne	2.1767**	0.4768
	Nord-Pas de Calais	87	1.0226**	0.2977	Nord-Pas de Calais	1.0026**	0.3018	Nord-Pas de Calais	1.0292**	0.3059
	Lorraine	31	1.0179*	0.4361	Lorraine	0.9574*	0.4541	Lorraine	1.0448*	0.4438
	Alsace	29	1.537**	0.4441	Alsace	1.5237**	0.4448	Alsace	1.3782**	0.4611
	Franche-Comté	7	16267	0.8921	Franche-Comté	17438	0.9635	Franche-Comté	15865	0.9099
	Pays de la Loire	39	-0.1862	0.4616	Pays de la Loire	-0.1692	0.4631	Pays de la Loire	-0.3359	0.5014
	Bretagne	73	1.5994**	0.3332	Bretagne	1.7122**	0.3454	Bretagne	1.56**	0.3424
	Poitou-Charente	10	0.1647	0.7963	Poitou-Charente	0.1546	0.8002	Poitou-Charente	0.2868	0.8235
	Aquitaine	42	1.1946**	0.394	Aquitaine	1.1221**	0.3965	Aquitaine	1.0468**	0.4104
	Midi-Pyrénées	26	1.0899*	0.4955	Midi-Pyrénées	1.0056*	0.4995	Midi-Pyrénées	1.1068*	0.5015
	Limousin	5	14387	0.9806	Limousin	13804	0.9900	Limousin	14962	0.9959
	Rhône-Alpes	86	0.3827	0.3051	Rhône-Alpes	0.4225	0.3081	Rhône-Alpes	0.3726	0.3086
	Languedoc-Roussillon	26	0.9408*	0.4764	Languedoc-Roussillon	0.8962	0.4843	Languedoc-Roussillon	1.087*	0.4734
	Provence-Côte dAzur	57	-0.1102	0.3727	Provence-Côte dAzur	-0.138	0.3813	Provence-Côte dAzur	0.0248	0.3711
	Auvergne	15	1.5877**	0.6289	Auvergne	1.5721**	0.6312	Auvergne	1.5065*	0.6525
	Intercept		1.3275**	0.3940		1.4196**	0.4479		1.2342*	0.5424
	prob. of reference cat.		0.79			0.81			0.77	
	rate of independence		0.42			0.43			0.41	
	Delta in %		53			53			53	

* statistically significant at <= 0.05

** statistically significant at < =0.01

Table 8 Coefficient Estimates and Standard Errors of Logistic Regression of Living Independently in France in 1992 Young People Aged 20-29 in 1992 Who in 1986 Were Living in the Parental Home and in 1992 Were in Education

MEN		Model without Income			Model with Income			Model with Income Diversification		
	Total Cases		810			810			810	
	Cases in Analysis		727			692			716	
	-2 Log Likelihood		672.47			610.76			640.185	
		Cases	Coefficients	St. Error		Coefficients	St. Error		Coeffic.	St. Error
					part-time>5000			market income		
	part-time student	133		0.2798	part-time<=5000	-1.0162*	0.4874	public benefits	-1.6141*	0.7805
	full-time student	594	-1.4532**		full-time<=5000	-2.0782**	0.4066	family help	-2.5468**	0.7443
					full-time>5000	0.367	0.9624	market and state	0.7809	0.8841
								market and family	-11387	0.6217
								state and family	-1.627**	0.5934
								market. state. family	-0.5848	0.6549
Agegroup										
	25-29 year old	82			25-29 year old			25-29 year old		
	20-24 year old	645	-0.6914	0.3186	20-24 year old	-0.4912	0.3553	20-24 year old	-0.824**	0.3182
Completed Education										
	tertiary certificate	55			tertiary certificate			tertiary certificate		
	<=compulsory cert.	73	-2.1765**	0.4958	<=compulsory cert.	-2.1667**	0.5170	<=compulsory cert.	-2.0363**	0.5167
	basic vocational cert.	124	-1.4018**	0.4204	basic vocational cert.	-1.5222**	0.4500	basic vocational cert.	-1.1499**	0.4173
	secondary vocat. cert	292	-1.4343**	0.3374	secondary vocat. cert.	-1.361**	0.3539	secondary vocat. cert.	-1.5297**	0.3516
	maturity certificate	163	-0.7029**	0.2541	maturity certificate	-0.8319**	0.2695	maturity certificate	-0.5777*	0.2623
	missing	20	-2.3939**	0.8850	missing	-3.0989**	1.0034	missing	-1.8601*	0.8260
Father's Social Class										
	service class	269			service class			service class		
	routine non-manual	85	-0.8934**	0.3483	routine non-manual	-0.912**	0.3687	routine non-manual	-0.7534*	0.3555
	petty bourgeoisie	45	1.548**	0.4393	petty bourgeoisie	1.583**	0.4683	petty bourgeoisie	1.4865**	0.4523
	farmers	23	-0.0842	0.6267	farmers	0.05	0.6847	farmers	0.1677	0.6492
	skilled workers	220	-0.4868**	0.2511	skilled workers	-0.5403*	0.2638	skilled workers	-0.5261*	0.2615
	non-skilled workers	62	-1.3339**	0.4557	non-skilled workers	-1.3614**	0.4852	non-skilled workers	-1.5472**	0.4902
	agricultural workers	8	2.1281*	0.9678	agricultural workers	12124	1.1641	agricultural workers	18762	1.0173
	economic. inactive	10	-74421	10.2073	economic. inactive	-73201	10.5807	economic. inactive	-79752	10.0433
	missing	5	16815	1.2285	missing	15689	1.2292	missing	16932	1.2122

Siblings										
	no sibling	64			no sibling			no sibling		
	one sibling	247	-0.1176	0.3690	one sibling	-0.0052	0.3886	one sibling	-0.2465	0.3826
	two siblings	189	0.2483	0.3842	two siblings	0.4425	0.4073	two siblings	0.1785	0.4003
	three and more sibli.	188	0.2947	0.3874	three and more sibli.	0.451	0.4065	three and more sibli.	0.2439	0.4008
	missing	39	-0.2494	0.5486	missing	-0.1538	0.5994	missing	-0.4074	0.5591
Size of municipality										
	> 100.000 inhabitants	487			> 100.000 inhabitants			> 100.000 inhabitants		
	>= 20.000 & < 100.0	79	-0.5047	0.3640	>= 20.000 & < 100.00	-0.3669	0.3826	>= 20.000 &<100.000	-0.6811	0.3792
	>= 5.000 & < 20.000	53	-1.2724*	0.4443	>= 5.000 & < 20.000	-1.3553**	0.4802	>= 5.000 & < 20.000	-1.2506**	0.4531
	< 5.000 inhabitants	108	-1.6232**	0.3672	< 5.000 inhabitants	-1.6036**	0.3937	< 5.000 inhabitants	-1.7293**	0.3796
Region	Ile-de-France	170			Ile-de-France			Ile-de-France		
	Champagne-Ardenne	11	0.9087	0.7910	Champagne-Ardennes	0.9105	0.8125	Champagne-Ardennes	14681	0.8360
	Picardie	24	-0.1962	0.7950	Picardie	-0.6017	0.9884	Picardie	0.1363	0.7895
	Haute-Normandie	23	1.5137**	0.5837	Haute-Normandie	1.967**	0.6231	Haute-Normandie	1.7221**	0.5897
	Centre	29	10144	0.5487	Centre	1.1373*	0.5604	Centre	1.2185**	0.5546
	Basse-Normandie	16	0.5079	0.7991	Basse-Normandie	0.624	0.7876	Basse-Normandie	0.7244	0.7865
	Bourgogne	15	3.1179**	0.9394	Bourgogne	3.3843**	0.9973	Bourgogne	3.1417**	0.9256
	Nord-Pas de Calais	79	0.5083	0.3614	Nord-Pas de Calais	0.6494	0.3784	Nord-Pas de Calais	0.6859	0.3752
	Lorraine	22	-0.0079	0.7031	Lorraine	-1209	1.0958	Lorraine	0.0065	0.7823
	Alsace	15	1.6382*	0.6852	Alsace	1.7023*	0.7111	Alsace	1.773**	0.6971
	Franche-Comté	9	2.2215**	0.8710	Franche-Comté	2.9401**	1.0819	Franche-Comté	2.694**	0.8509
	Pays de la Loire	20	0.4057	0.6288	Pays de la Loire	0.3337	0.6841	Pays de la Loire	0.7443	0.6436
	Bretagne	45	1.7194**	0.4405	Bretagne	1.7519**	0.4607	Bretagne	1.7512**	0.4611
	Poitou-Charente	7	0.5682	11977	Poitou-Charente	0.1364	1.2542	Poitou-Charente	-44107	13.5033
	Aquitaine	35	1.4732**	0.4873	Aquitaine	1.726**	0.5108	Aquitaine	1.6113**	0.4960
	Midi-Pyrénées	40	2.7611**	0.4722	Midi-Pyrénées	2.8874**	0.4853	Midi-Pyrénées	2.8387**	0.4934
	Limousin	10	2.0741**	0.8097	Limousin	2.1913**	0.8191	Limousin	2.1273**	0.7986
	Rhône-Alpes	77	0.8549**	0.3550	Rhône-Alpes	0.8889*	0.3747	Rhône-Alpes	0.9581**	0.3708
	Languedoc-Roussillo	19	2.7447**	0.5911	Languedoc-Roussillon	2.9282**	0.5999	Languedoc-Roussillon	3.007**	0.6097
	Provence-Côte dAzur	54	-0.0989	0.4152	Provence-Côte dAzur	0.0145	0.4305	Provence-Côte dAzur	-0.0286	0.4288
	Auvergne	7	1477	1.0207	Auvergne	0.4243	1.1802	Auvergne	19458	1.0209
	Intercept		1.6218**	0.4916		1.8922**	0.571		1.8279**	0.7054
	probab. of refer. categ.		0.84			0.84			0.84	
	rate of independence		0.35			0.35			0.35	
	Delta in %		42			42			40	

* statistically significant at <= 0.05 ** statistically significant at < =0.01

Table 9 Coefficient Estimates and Standard Errors of Logistic Regression of Living in a Rented Dwelling in France in 1992 and in Spain in 1991 Young People Aged 20-29 in 1992 Who in 1985/1986 Were Living in the Parental Home and in 1991/92 Were Living Independently

			France		Spain			
	Total Cases		2635		7279			
	Cases in Analysis		2494		6953			
	-2 Log Likelihood		1578.24		8644.697			
Variables		Cases	Coefficients	St. Error	Coefficients	St. Error	Cases	Variables
Activity	long-term employment	1207					1600	long-term employment
	short-term employment	178	-0.0906	0.2639	0.2503**	0.0773	1684	short-term employment
	part-time student	174	0.1001	0.3035	-0.1044	0.1424	289	part-time student
	full-time student	376	0.5121	0.3261	-0.2596	0.2585	79	full-time student
	economically inactive	170	-0.1917	0.2421	0.127	0.0860	1221	economically inactive
	self-employed	55	-0.5322	0.3515	0.0366	0.1126	518	self-employed
	family help	11	-0.2040	0.8605	-0.194	0.2220	111	family help
	unemployed	153	-0.0023	0.2774	0.128	0.0851	1217	unemployed
	first-job seeker	170	0.6052	0.3232	-0.05	0.1531	234	first-job seeker
Agegroup	25-29 year old	1247					5133	25-29 year old
	20-24 year old	1247	0.5714**	0.1535	0.5221**	0.0603	1820	20-24 year old
Completed Education								
	tertiary certificate	417					659	tertiary certificate
	<=compulsory cert.	956	0.2943	0.2613	-0.1033	0.0992	4131	<=compulsory cert.
	basic vocational cert.	255	0.04	0.2091	-0.2009	0.1175	796	basic vocational cert.
	secondary vocat. cert.	375	0.3494	0.2759	-0.3399**	0.1367	453	secondary vocat. cert.
	maturity certificate	24	-0.327	0.2489	-0.1849	0.1134	858	maturity certificate
	missing	467	15304	1.0819	0.0721	0.3030	56	missing
Class	service class	532					649	service class
	routine non-manual	353	-0.2579	0.2315	-0.2138	0.1124	819	routine non-manual
	petty bourgeoisie	253	0.2167	0.2786	-0.3918**	0.1210	664	petty bourgeoisie
	farmers	157	0.2599	0.3110	-0.3602**	0.1244	628	farmers
	skilled workers	736	-0.1116	0.2055	-0.3136**	0.1041	1486	skilled workers
	non-skilled workers	421	0.2806	0.2476	-0.3713**	0.1009	2110	non-skilled workers
	agricultural workers	31	-0.1785	0.5733	-0.2547	0.1424	379	agricultural workers
	economic. inactive	1	57817	60.4347	-0.4042	0.2151	122	economic. inactive
	missing	10	48351	18.715	-0.1192	0.2330	96	missing
Siblings	no sibling	207					237	no sibling

	one sibling	608	-0.2578	0.2731	0.0292	0.1542	1489	one sibling
	two siblings	598	-0.0015	0.2783	0.0671	0.1524	1835	two siblings
	three and more sibli.	968	0.2675	0.2718	0.1859	0.1491	3357	three and more sibli.
	missing	113	-0.1682	0.3787	0.5768	0.3850	35	missing
Living Arrangement	married	816					5943	married
	cohabiting	838	0.7333**	0.1625	0.9687**	0.1299	281	cohabiting
	one person	578	1.3931**	0.2371	0.7336**	0.1193	336	one person
	with peers	199	-0.136	0.2829	0.3456**	0.1218	355	with peers
	other		-0.199	0.3781	0.7841**	0.3400	38	other
Size of municipality	> 100.000 inhabitants	1363					1157	> 100.000 inhabitants
	>= 20.000 and < 100.000	361	0.6176*	0.2714	0.0096	0.0836	1629	>= 20.000 and < 100.000
	>= 5.000 and < 20.000	233	-0.3353	0.2539	0.0187	0.0787	2145	>= 5.000 and < 20.000
	< 5.000 inhabitants	537	-1.0902**	0.1776	-0.1231	0.0870	2022	< 5.000 inhabitants
Region	Ile-de-France	495					752	Madrid
	Champagne-Ardennes	53	-0.2909	0.4764	0.4628**	0.1411	320	Galicia
	Picardie	83	-0.2086	0.3746	0.5205**	0.1821	160	Asturias
	Haute-Normandie	104	0.9869*	0.4775	0.1201	0.2131	118	Cantabria
	Centre	92	0.5136	0.4308	-0.6064**	0.1723	292	País Vasco
	Basse-Normandie	62	0.6786	0.4990	-0.4447*	0.2231	137	Navarra
	Bourgogne	83	0.0705	0.4249	0.2378	0.1562	247	Aragón
	Nord-Pas de Calais	187	-0.4916	0.2729	0.0386	0.1039	1043	Cataluña
	Lorraine	71	-0.6439	0.3463	0.5664**	0.1678	202	Baleares
	Alsace	105	-0.1975	0.3189	-0.5202**	0.1208	690	País Valenciano
	Franche-Comté	44	0.4629	0.5352	-0.3406*	0.1586	279	Murcia
	Pays de la Loire	131	-0.1137	0.3143	-0.0259	0.1004	1330	Andalucía
	Bretagne	168	0.152	0.3221	0.8923**	0.1467	288	Extremadura
	Poitou-Charente	51	0.0858	0.4620	0.0876	0.1392	357	Castilla-La Mancha
	Aquitaine	123	-0.2108	0.3337	0.6534**	0.1365	340	Castilla-León
	Midi-Pyrénées	101	0.0626	0.3521	0.4534*	0.2337	95	La Rioja
	Limousin	28	15211	1.0724	0.2448	0.1442	303	Canarias
	Rhône-Alpes	241	0.4588	0.3084				
	Languedoc-Roussillon	77	-0.9555**	0.3517				
	Provence-Côte dAzur	148	0.7232*	0.3587				
	Auvergne	47	59962	8.3628				
	Intercept		1.3976**	0.3281	-0.6222**	0.2021		
	probability refer. categ.		0.80		0.35			
	rate of renting dwelling		0.88		0.37			

* statistically significant at <= 0.05

** statistically significant at < =0.01

Table 10 Coefficient Estimates and Standard Errors of Logistic Regression of Living Independently in France in 1992 (Regional Analysis) Young People Aged 20-29 in 1992 Who in 1986 Were Living in the Parental Home and in 1992 Were on the Labour Market

MEN		MODEL 1		MODEL 2		MODEL 3		MODEL 4	
Total Cases		1726		1726		1726		1726	
Cases in Analysis		1711		1708		1708		1708	
-2 Log Likelihood		2331.508		2339.429		2175.971		1980.35	
Variables	Cases	Coefficients	St. Error	Coefficients	St. Error	Coefficients	St. Error	Coefficients	St. Error
Activity									
long-term employment	1033								
short-term employment	237					-1.1458**	0.1579	-0.908**	0.1689
economically inactive	25					-0.7716	0.4252	-0.642	0.4559
self-employed	77					-0.1712	0.2462	-0.4242	0.2793
family help	17					-2.3155**	0.7667	-2.0645**	0.8142
unemployed	124					-0.56**	0.1971	-0.4767*	0.2129
first-job seeker	195					-1.4677**	0.1794	-1.3156**	0.1919
Agegroup									
25-29 year old	908								
20-24 year old	800							-1.2534**	0.1142
Completed Education									
tertiary certificate	405								
<=compulsory cert.	908							-0.2876	0.2271
basic vocational cert.	142							-0.1652	0.2047
secondary vocat. cert.	75							-0.1279	0.2639
maturity certificate	171							0.0573	0.3181
missing	7							-0.1071	0.9586
Father's Social Class									
service class	239								
routine non-manual	209							-0.2583	0.2231
petty bourgeoisie	125							0.6689**	0.269
farmers	146							-0.5927*	0.2693
skilled workers	556							-0.3502	0.1875
non-skilled workers	382							-0.4073*	0.2055
agricultural workers	31							-1.0886*	0.4532
economic. inactive	19							-3.3738**	1.0605
missing	1							-5.7043	13.5037

MEN		MODEL 1		MODEL 2		MODEL 3		MODEL 4	
Siblings									
no sibling	135								
one sibling	362							-0.1148	0.2288
two siblings	376							-0.0828	0.2272
three and more sibli.	740							0.3201	0.2144
missing	95							-0.0748	0.3055
Size of municipality									
> 100.000 inhabitants	750								
>= 20.000 and < 100.000	229	0.3214*	0.1539			0.1845	0.1739	0.2983	0.1872
>= 5.000 and < 20.000	171	-0.0892	0.1697			-0.2747	0.1876	-0.1567	0.2003
< 5.000 inhabitants	558	-0.5631**	0.1132			-0.7822**	0.1396	-0.7322**	0.1523
Region									
Ile-de-France	316								
Champagne-Ardennes	50			-0.4622	0.3079	0.017	0.3272	-0.059	0.3504
Picardie	89			-0.2971	0.2407	0.2078	0.2693	0.358	0.2939
Haute-Normandie	67			0.0101	0.2697	0.5371	0.2954	0.5472	0.3106
Centre	61			-0.3038	0.2806	0.0289	0.3024	-0.003	0.3233
Basse-Normandie	54			-0.2879	0.2953	0.2057	0.3256	0.339	0.3570
Bourgogne	38			0.0718	0.3452	0.6039	0.3928	0.6762	0.4272
Nord-Pas de Calais	137			-0.5086**	0.2072	-0.2361	0.2199	-0.3153	0.2358
Lorraine	62			-0.5315	0.2824	-0.2577	0.3015	-0.2892	0.3226
Alsace	64			0.3052	0.2799	0.4875	0.2965	0.5613	0.3189
Franche-Comté	36			-0.5914	0.3600	-0.0575	0.3846	-0.0557	0.4079
Pays de la Loire	92			0.1673	0.2392	0.6783**	0.2640	0.9108**	0.2860
Bretagne	91			0.1482	0.2400	0.6424**	0.2661	0.6931*	0.2843
Poitou-Charente	44			0.135	0.3246	0.5739	0.3501	0.5881	0.3727
Aquitaine	86			-0.3261	0.2442	0.1587	0.2651	0.215	0.2894
Midi-Pyrénées	56			-0.5005	0.2941	0.004	0.3214	0.0148	0.3529
Limousin	16			-0.3908	0.5164	0.233	0.5415	0.2455	0.5819
Rhône-Alpes	149			0.117	0.2000	0.2497	0.2144	0.2894	0.2283
Languedoc-Roussillon	45			-0.1839	0.3188	0.4966	0.3497	0.5317	0.3675
Provence-Côte dAzur	115			-0.1221	0.2180	0.2606	0.2347	0.2945	0.2499
Auvergne	40			0.266	0.3419	0.8091**	0.3797	0.7144	0.4019
Intercept		0.1711	0.0733	0.1395	0.1128	0.4644**	0.1214	1.2906**	0.2875
probability refer. categ.						0.61		0.78	

* statistically significant at <= 0.05 ** statistically significant at < =0.01

Table 11 Coefficient Estimates and Standard Errors of Logistic Regression of Living Independently in France in 1992 (Regional Analysis) Young People Aged 20-29 in 1992 Who in 1986 Were Living in the Parental Home and in 1992 Were on the Labour Market

WOMEN		MODEL 1		MODEL 2		MODEL 3		MODEL 4	
Total Cases		1706		1706		1706		1706	
Cases in Analysis		1885		1673		1673		1673	
-2 Log Likelihood		2131.243		2082.955		1957.924		1862.769	
Variables	Cases	Coefficients	St. Error	Coefficients	St. Error	Coefficients	St. Error	Coefficients	St. Error
Activity									
long-term employment	831								
short-term employment	225					-1.0584**	0.1599	-0.9729**	0.1678
economically inactive	187					1.0684**	0.2395	1.207**	0.2513
self-employed	21					0.4997	0.5687	0.3296	0.5811
family help	14					0.4557	0.6712	0.4374	0.6869
unemployed	155					-0.4613**	0.1877	-0.3379	0.1960
first-job seeker	240					-0.9288**	0.1568	-0.7404**	0.1645
Agegroup									
25-29 year old	756								
20-24 year old	917							-0.5416**	0.1193
Completed Education									
tertiary certificate	361								
<=compulsory cert.	713							-0.5646**	0.2229
basic vocational cert.	200							-0.4922**	0.1975
secondary vocat. cert.	145							-0.4361	0.2388
maturity certificate	16							-0.4341	0.2560
missing	238							0.1286	0.6357
Father's Social Class									
service class	246								
routine non-manual	263							0.2119	0.2159
petty bourgeoisie	114							0.6067*	0.2929
farmers	117							-0.1949	0.2729
skilled workers	570							-0.2862	0.1838
non-skilled workers	306							-0.0196	0.2110
agricultural workers	35							-0.417	0.4094
economic. inactive	20							-6.675	4.8226
missing	2							-0.5187	1.4521

WOMEN		MODEL 1		MODEL 2		MODEL 3		MODEL 4	
Siblings									
no sibling	126								
one sibling	378							0.0185	0.2363
two siblings	396							0.1716	0.2366
three and more sibli.	714							0.1202	0.2282
missing	59							0.5839	0.3799
Size of municipality									
> 100.000 inhabitants	778								
>= 20.000 and < 100.000	255	0.092	0.1549			0.1386	0.1790	0.1306	0.1864
>= 5.000 and < 20.000	182	0.0223	0.1763			0.0189	0.1981	0.0503	0.2059
< 5.000 inhabitants	458	-0.2101	0.1235			-0.3108*	0.1485	-0.3063*	0.1565
Region									
Ile-de-France	334								
Champagne-Ardennes	36			-0.157	0.3732	-0.0053	0.3991	0.1633	0.4096
Picardie	64			-0.4055	0.2827	-0.1653	0.3112	-0.0264	0.3282
Haute-Normandie	63			0.4026	0.3257	0.6635	0.3470	0.8828*	0.3662
Centre	66			-0.2244	0.2846	-0.08	0.3037	0.0642	0.3123
Basse-Normandie	42			0.0661	0.3619	0.3142	0.3916	0.4819	0.4078
Bourgogne	36			0.7591	0.4629	0.7928	0.4886	0.8975	0.4970
Nord-Pas de Calais	125			-0.3775	0.2193	-0.2289	0.2320	-0.113	0.2442
Lorraine	71			-0.7091**	0.2663	-0.6478*	0.2859	-0.5204	0.3005
Alsace	57			0.3691	0.3375	0.539	0.3563	0.7126*	0.3687
Franche-Comté	31			0.2059	0.4275	0.5405	0.4519	0.6549	0.4722
Pays de la Loire	92			0.0814	0.2606	0.4639	0.2796	0.6236*	0.2892
Bretagne	80			0.3866	0.2932	0.768*	0.3164	0.8677**	0.3282
Poitou-Charente	39			-0.4872	0.3468	-0.2654	0.3772	-0.1345	0.3895
Aquitaine	93			-0.5687*	0.2411	-0.3106	0.2644	-0.1504	0.2797
Midi-Pyrénées	73			-0.0094	0.2817	0.3579	0.3079	0.3942	0.3239
Limousin	19			-0.3112	0.4904	0.0447	0.5174	0.0992	0.5394
Rhône-Alpes	158			-0.2228	0.2053	-0.0723	0.2217	0.059	0.2328
Languedoc-Roussillon	66			-0.5448*	0.2762	-0.2559	0.3045	-0.1913	0.3187
Provence-Côte dAzur	99			-0.1112	0.2459	-0.077	0.2606	0.0073	0.2713
Auvergne	29			-0.6425	0.392	-0.519	0.4203	-0.3688	0.4279
Intercept		0.7535**	0.0769	0.8502**	0.1195	0.9976**	0.1292	1.549**	0.2836
probability refer. categ.		0.68		0.70				0.82	

* statistically significant at <= 0.05   ** statistically significant at < =0.01

Table 12 Coefficient Estimates and Standard Errors of Logistic Regression of Living Independently in Spain in 1991 (Regional Analysis) Young People Aged 20-29 in 1991 Who in 1985 Were Living in the Parental Home and in 1991 Were on the Labour Market

MEN		MODEL 1		MODEL 2		MODEL 3	
Total Cases		9045		9045		9045	
Cases in Analysis		9045		8997		8997	
-2 Log Likelihood		11297.529		11120.558		9306.583	
Variables	Cases	Coefficients	St. Error	Coefficients	St. Error	Coefficients	St. Error
Activity							
long-term employment	2308						
short-term employment	3341					-0.5772**	0.0628
economically inactive	370					-1.8335**	0.1836
self-employed	906					-0.2067*	0.0873
family help	296					-1.0603**	0.1645
unemployed	1316					-0.9191**	0.0863
first-job seeker	460					-2.5907**	0.2638
Agegroup							
25-29 year old	5010						
20-24 year old	3987					-1.6606**	0.0581
Completed Education							
tertiary certificate	5481						
<=compulsory cert.	1060					0.654**	0.1068
basic vocational cert.	701					0.5728**	0.1247
secondary vocat. cert.	1032					0.3177*	0.1363
maturity certificate	641					0.3415**	0.1265
missing	82					0.6227*	0.3050
Father's Social Class							
service class	752						
routine non-manual	1046					-0.1132	0.1173
petty bourgeoisie	829					0.0722	0.1231
farmers	957					-0.398**	0.1233
skilled workers	1906					-0.1554	0.1074
non-skilled workers	2786					-0.2455*	0.1041
agricultural workers	477					-0.225	0.1432
economic. inactive	113					-0.2088	0.2451
missing	131					-0.0419	0.2352

MEN		MODEL 1		MODEL 2		MODEL 3	
Siblings							
no sibling	416						
one sibling	2326					0.1291	0.1379
two siblings	2511					0.3659**	0.1365
three and more sibli.	3696					0.7893**	0.1339
missing	48					1.2913**	0.3489
Size of municipality							
> 100.000 inhabitants	1479						
>= 20.000 and < 100.000	2135	0.0503	0.0723			0.0268	0.0824
>= 5.000 and < 20.000	2698	0.0428	0.0692			0.0291	0.0781
< 5.000 inhabitants	2685	-0.0905	0.0698			0.0648	0.0863
Region							
Madrid	944						
Galicia	501			-0.3588**	0.1251	-0.2395	0.1404
Asturias	242			-0.3906*	0.1660	-0.3892*	0.1842
Cantabria	196			-0.4181*	0.1825	-0.4088*	0.2002
País Vasco	560			-0.5783**	0.1255	-0.515**	0.1475
Navarra	213			-0.4979**	0.1794	-0.5454**	0.2003
Aragón	306			-0.0959	0.1433	-0.0621	0.1595
Cataluña	1131			0.2185*	0.0932	0.2447*	0.1053
Baleares	249			0.2467	0.1485	0.2587	0.1668
País Valenciano	800			0.1284	0.1020	0.1927	0.1154
Murcia	353			0.0237	0.1336	0.1921	0.1496
Andalucía	1608			0.2451**	0.0869	0.4043**	0.1002
Extremadura	359			0.0749	0.1319	0.1812	0.1484
Castilla-La Mancha	466			0.0384	0.1210	0.0506	0.1359
Castilla-León	575			-0.3417**	0.1191	-0.3657**	0.1338
La Rioja	115			0.2485	0.2050	0.0388	0.2309
Canarias	379			-0.0054	0.1307	-0.0405	0.1480
Intercept		-0.7638**	0.0558	-0.7639**	0.0699	-0.5923**	0.1933
probability of reference categ.		0.32		0.32		0.36	

* statistically significant at <= 0.05 ** statistically significant at < =0.01

Table 13 Coefficient Estimates and Standard Errors of Logistic Regression of Living Independently in Spain in 1991 (Regional Analysis) Young People Aged 20-29 in 1991 Who in 1985 Were Living in the Parental Home and in 1992 Were on the Labour Market

WOMEN		MODEL 1		MODEL 2		MODEL 3	
Total Cases		8908		8908		8908	
Cases in Analysis		8908		8863		8863	
-2 Log Likelihood		12259.619		12071.925		10479.962	
Variables	Cases	Coefficients	St. Error	Coefficients	St. Error	Coefficients	St. Error
Activity							
long-term employment	1354						
short-term employment	2264					-0.2576**	0.0753
economically inactive	1837					1.0985**	0.0823
self-employed	298					0.253	0.1364
family help	150					-0.1896	0.1918
unemployed	1860					0.4499**	0.0782
first-job seeker	1100					-0.5966**	0.0990
Agegroup							
25-29 year old	4708						
20-24 year old	4155					-1.2298**	0.0498
Completed Education							
tertiary certificate	4696						
<=compulsory cert.	999					0.4595**	0.0803
basic vocational cert.	636					0.4074**	0.0981
secondary vocat. cert.	1270					0.1731	0.1114
maturity certificate	1158					0.1491	0.0933
missing	104					-0.7886**	0.2384
Father's Social Class							
service class	863						
routine non-manual	1072					0.083	0.1022
petty bourgeoisie	794					0.0825	0.1104
farmers	840					-0.1047	0.1119
skilled workers	1826					0.1982*	0.0945
non-skilled workers	2747					0.0779	0.0903
agricultural workers	431					0.1508	0.1356
economic. inactive	159					0.6572**	0.1915
missing	131					0.1713	0.2114

WOMEN		MODEL 1		MODEL 2		MODEL 3	
Siblings							
no sibling	415						
one sibling	2293					0.4134**	0.1241
two siblings	2416					0.5694**	0.1238
three and more sibli.	3703					0.9041**	0.1216
missing	36					0.4593	0.3924
Size of municipality							
> 100.000 inhabitants	1478						
>= 20.000 and < 100.000	2027	-0.0259	0.0687			0.0011	0.0777
>= 5.000 and < 20.000	2633	0.0642	0.0652			0.0509	0.0729
< 5.000 inhabitants	2725	-0.0076	0.0648			0.1594*	0.0804
Region							
Madrid	967						
Galicia	490			-0.2366*	0.1139	-0.2914*	0.1285
Asturias	248			-0.1531	0.1454	-0.1077	0.1619
Cantabria	204			-0.2528	0.1591	-0.3277	0.1771
País Vasco	564			-0.3797**	0.1102	-0.5423**	0.1294
Navarra	211			-0.0454	0.1540	-0.294	0.1748
Aragón	285			0.2544	0.1351	0.1038	0.1495
Cataluña	1114			0.4189**	0.0885	0.441**	0.0984
Baleares	193			0.3828*	0.1581	0.4398**	0.1743
País Valenciano	790			0.3097**	0.0964	0.2702**	0.1069
Murcia	337			0.2123	0.1269	0.0256	0.1417
Andalucía	1616			0.1133	0.0820	-0.0319	0.0927
Extremadura	343			0.1669	0.1262	0.0032	0.1423
Castilla-La Mancha	442			0.3347**	0.1152	0.0613	0.1300
Castilla-León	512			-0.2716*	0.1126	-0.3406**	0.1257
La Rioja	111			0.1993	0.2008	0.1709	0.2251
Canarias	436			-0.0344	0.1168	-0.3057**	0.1305
		-0.2086**	0.0522	-0.2895**	0.0650	-0.9596**	0.1708
Intercept		0.45		0.43		0.28	
probability refer. categ.							

* statistically significant at <= 0.05 ** statistically significant at < =0.01

Table 14 Coefficient Estimates and Standard Errors of Logistic Regression of Living Independently in Spain in 1991 (Regional Analysis with Dummies). Young People Aged 20-29 in 1991 Who in 1985 Were Living in the Parental Home and in 1991 Were on the Labour Market

MEN		**MODEL 4**		**MODEL 12**		
Total Cases		9045		9045		Difference in -2 LL
Cases in Analysis		8997		8997		(Model 12 - 4)
-2 Log Likelihood		9306.583		9321.824		15.241
-2 LL initially		11247.944		11247.944		
Diff. of -2 LL		17.26%		17.12%		
Variables	Cases	Coefficients	St. Error	Coefficients	St. Error	Variables
Activity						
long-term employment	2308					long-term employment
short-term employment	3341	-0.5772**	0.0628	-0.5867**	0.0626	short-term employment
economically inactive	370	-1.8335**	0.1836	-1.8298**	0.1834	economically inactive
self-employed	906	-0.2067*	0.0873	-0.2157**	0.0869	self-employed
family help	296	-1.0603**	0.1645	-1.0708**	0.1642	family help
unemployed	1316	-0.9191**	0.0863	-0.9221**	0.0861	unemployed
first-job seeker	460	-2.5907**	0.2638	-2.5921**	0.2636	first-job seeker
Agegroup						
25-29 year old	5010					25-29 year old
20-24 year old	3987	-1.6606**	0.0581	-1.6562**	0.0580	20-24 year old
Completed Education						
tertiary certificate	5481					tertiary certificate
<=compulsory cert.	1060	0.654**	0.1068	0.6585**	0.1064	<=compulsory cert.
basic vocational cert.	701	0.5728**	0.1247	0.5691**	0.1244	basic vocational cert.
secondary vocat. cert.	1032	0.3177*	0.1363	0.3064*	0.1360	secondary vocat. cert.
maturity certificate	641	0.3415**	0.1265	0.3455**	0.1262	maturity certificate
missing	82	0.6227*	0.3050	0.6119*	0.3042	missing
Father's Social Class						
service class	752					service class
routine non-manual	1046	-0.1132	0.1173	-0.1115	0.1170	routine non-manual
petty bourgeoisie	829	0.0722	0.1231	0.0743	0.1227	petty bourgeoisie
farmers	957	-0.398**	0.1233	-0.4285**	0.1218	farmers
skilled workers	1906	-0.1554	0.1074	-0.1564	0.1071	skilled workers
non-skilled workers	2786	-0.2455*	0.1041	-0.2473**	0.1038	non-skilled workers
agricultural workers	477	-0.225	0.1432	-0.2271	0.1419	agricultural workers
economic. inactive	113	-0.2088	0.2451	-0.2101	0.2455	economic. inactive
missing	131	-0.0419	0.2352	-0.0586	0.2347	missing

MEN		MODEL 4		MODEL 12		
Siblings						
no sibling	416					no sibling
one sibling	2326	0.1291	0.1379	0.1347	0.1375	one sibling
two siblings	2511	0.3659**	0.1365	0.3692**	0.1361	two siblings
three and more sibli.	3696	0.7893**	0.1339	0.7861**	0.1332	three and more sibli.
missing	48	1.2913**	0.3489	1.3077**	0.3484	missing
Size of municipality						
> 100.000 inhabitants	1479					> 100.000 inhabitants
>= 20.000 and < 100.000	2135	0.0268	0.0824	0.0377	0.0816	>= 20.000 and < 100.000
>= 5.000 and < 20.000	2698	0.0291	0.0781	0.0515	0.0774	>= 5.000 and < 20.000
< 5.000 inhabitants	2685	0.0648	0.0863	0.0663	0.0814	< 5.000 inhabitants
Region						
Madrid	944			-0.0734**	0.0139	UNEMP
Galicia	501	-0.2395	0.1404	0.022**	0.0065	TENRENT
Asturias	242	-0.3892*	0.1842	0.0427**	0.0047	DAYWORK
Cantabria	196	-0.4088*	0.2002			
País Vasco	560	-0.515**	0.1475			
Navarra	213	-0.5454**	0.2003			
Aragón	306	-0.0621	0.1595			
Cataluña	1131	0.2447*	0.1053			
Baleares	249	0.2587	0.1668			
País Valenciano	800	0.1927	0.1154			
Murcia	353	0.1921	0.1496			
Andalucía	1608	0.4043**	0.1002			
Extremadura	359	0.1812	0.1484			
Castilla-La Mancha	466	0.0506	0.1359			
Castilla-León	575	-0.3657**	0.1338			
La Rioja	115	0.0388	0.2309			
Canarias	379	-0.0405	0.1480			
Intercept		-0.5923**	0.1933	-0.723**	0.2541	
probability refer. categ.		00.36		0.33		

* statistically significant at <= 0.05   ** statistically significant at <= 0.01

Table 15 Coefficient Estimates and Standard Errors of Logistic Regression of Living Independently in Spain in 1991 (Regional Analysis with Dummies). Young People Aged 20-29 in 1991 Who in 1985 Were Living in the Parental Home and in 1992 Were on the Labour Market

WOMEN		**MODEL 4**		**MODEL 12**		
Total Cases		8908		8908		
Cases in Analysis		8863		8863		Diff. in -2 LL (Model 12 - 4)
-2 Log Likelihood		10479.962		10505.475		25.513
-2 LL initially		12197.808		12197.808		
Diff. Of -2 LL		14.08%		13.87%		
Variables	Cases	Coefficients	St. Error	Coefficients	St. Error	Variables
Activity						
long-term employment	1354					long-term employment
short-term employment	2264	-0.2576**	0.0753	-0.261**	0.0751	short-term employment
economically inactive	1837	1.0985**	0.0823	1.0901**	0.0818	economically inactive
self-employed	298	0.253	0.1364	0.2571	0.1360	self-employed
family help	150	-0.1896	0.1918	-0.1728	0.1913	family help
unemployed	1860	0.4499**	0.0782	0.4443**	0.0779	unemployed
first-job seeker	1100	-0.5966**	0.0990	-0.6112**	0.0985	first-job seeker
Agegroup						
25-29 year old	4708					25-29 year old
20-24 year old	4155	-1.2298**	0.0498	-1.2206**	0.0496	20-24 year old
Completed Education						
tertiary certificate	4696					tertiary certificate
<=compulsory cert.	999	0.4595**	0.0803	0.471**	0.0798	<=compulsory cert.
basic vocational cert.	636	0.4074**	0.0981	0.4233**	0.0977	basic vocational cert.
secondary vocat. cert.	1270	0.1731	0.1114	0.1836	0.1111	secondary vocat. cert.
maturity certificate	1158	0.1491	0.0933	0.157	0.0930	maturity certificate
missing	104	-0.7886**	0.2384	-0.7686**	0.2377	missing
Father's Social Class						
service class	863					service class
routine non-manual	1072	0.083	0.1022	0.0692	0.1019	routine non-manual
petty bourgeoisie	794	0.0825	0.1104	0.0766	0.1099	petty bourgeoisie
farmers	840	-0.1047	0.1119	-0.1285	0.1103	farmers
skilled workers	1826	0.1982*	0.0945	0.2003*	0.0943	skilled workers
non-skilled workers	2747	0.0779	0.0903	0.0751	0.0900	non-skilled workers
agricultural workers	431	0.1508	0.1356	0.1309	0.1340	agricultural workers
economic. inactive	159	0.6572**	0.1915	0.6335**	0.1907	economic. inactive
missing	131	0.1713	0.2114	0.1607	0.2117	missing

WOMEN		MODEL 4		MODEL 12		
Siblings						
no sibling	415					no sibling
one sibling	2293	0.4134**	0.1241	0.4118**	0.1239	one sibling
two siblings	2416	0.5694**	0.1238	0.5617**	0.1234	two siblings
three and more sibli.	3703	0.9041**	0.1216	0.8791**	0.1209	three and more sibli.
missing	36	0.4593	0.3924	0.4461	0.3917	missing
Size of municipality						
> 100.000 inhabitants	1478					> 100.000 inhabitants
>= 20.000 and < 100.000	2027	0.0011	0.0777	-0.0154	0.0769	>= 20.000 and < 100.000
>= 5.000 and < 20.000	2633	0.0509	0.0729	0.0726	0.0722	>= 5.000 and < 20.000
< 5.000 inhabitants	2725	0.1594*	0.0804	0.1506*	0.0752	< 5.000 inhabitants
Region						
Madrid	967					
Galicia	490	-0.2914*	0.1285	-0.1057**	0.0126	UNEMP
Asturias	248	-0.1077	0.1619	0.0184**	0.0061	TENRENT
Cantabria	204	-0.3277	0.1771	0.0186**	0.0043	DAYWORK
País Vasco	564	-0.5423**	0.1294			
Navarra	211	-0.294	0.1748			
Aragón	285	0.1038	0.1495			
Cataluña	1114	0.441**	0.0984			
Baleares	193	0.4398**	0.1743			
País Valenciano	790	0.2702**	0.1069			
Murcia	337	0.0256	0.1417			
Andalucía	1616	-0.0319	0.0927			
Extremadura	343	0.0032	0.1423			
Castilla-La Mancha	442	0.0613	0.1300			
Castilla-León	512	-0.3406**	0.1257			
La Rioja	111	0.1709	0.2251			
Canarias	436	-0.3057**	0.1305			
Intercept		-0.9596**	0.1708	-0.7114**	0.2269	
probability refer. categ.		0.28		0.33		

* statistically significant at <= 0.05   ** statistically significant at < =0.01

Variables

Cross-sectional Individual-level Variables for France/Spain (Enquête Jeunes 1992, EJ / Encuesta Sociodemográfica 1991, ESD)

1. Living Arrangement in 1991/92: at parents' home or not (IND92)
2. Number of siblings (SIBL)
3. Dwelling tenure in 1991/92 (DWELL)
4. Activity situation in 1991/92 (ACTIVEST)
5. Social class of father, EGP full version (FACLASS)
6. Educational level attained in 1991/92 (EDUC)
7. Detailed type of living arrangement in 1991/92 (LIVARR)
8. Dwelling type of the first independent household (FIRDWELL)
9. Living-arrangement for every survey year (QLAGE, YEARLEAV, PAR79-92, IND79-92)

Cross-sectional Individual-level Variables for France (EJ 1992)

1. Diversification of income: market, state and/or family (DIVERS) in 1992
2. Income level and activity situation (INCOSUM, ACTIVINC) in 1992
3. Type of resource-sharing household in 1992 (RESOUR)
4. Social dependence according to type of household (SOCIAL) in 1992

Cross-sectional Individual-level Variables for Spain (ESD 1991)

1. Change of place of residence when left home (MIGRA)

Context Variables For France and Spain (EJ 1992, ESD 1991)

1. Size of place of residence in 1991/92 (RURUBAN)
2. Region of residence in 1991/92 (REGION)

External Variables For Spain (Censo 1991, ESD 1991, Banco Hipotecario Español 1991)

1. Young men aged 20 to 29 seeking a first employment in percent of all people in this age-group by region in 1991 (UNEMP)
2. Rented and given dwellings in percent of all main residences by region in 1991 (TENRENT)
3. Average regional estimated price of a used dwelling financed by the Spanish Mortgage Bank in percent of average disposable income after tax deductions by region in 1992 (ACCES)
4. Male dayworkers in agriculture and fishing in percent of all employed men by region in 1991 (DAYWORK)
5. Consensual unions in per cent of all union by region in 1991 (COHABIT)

Bibliography

Abrossimov, C. (1995), 'La politique de l'emploi', in M. Montalembert (ed.), *La protection sociale en France.* La documentation Française, Paris, pp. 109-114.

Abrossimov, C., Gelot, D. and Roguet, B. (1993), 'Bilan de la politique de l'emploi en 1992', *Travail Et Emploi*, vol. 57, pp. 86-94.

AEL (1991), 'Anuario de Estadísticas Laborales 1991', Ministerio de Trabajo y Seguridad Social, Madrid.

AEL (1992), 'Anuario de Estadísticas Laborales 1992', Ministerio de Trabajo y Seguridad Social, Madrid.

Aguilar, M., Gaviria, M. and Laparra, M. (1995), 'La caña y el pez. Estudio sobre los salarios sociales en las Comunidades Autónomas 1989-1994', Fundación FOESSA, Madrid.

Alberdi, B. (1993), 'Una estimación del coste de la política de vivienda', *Revista Española De Financiación a La Vivienda*, vol. 24/25, pp. 59-64.

Alberdi, B. and Levenfeld, G. (1996), 'Spain', in P. Balchin (ed.), *Housing Policy in Europe*, Routledge, London/New York, pp. 170-335.

Amira, S. (1996), 'Dix ans d'indemnisation du chômage en France (1985-1995)', *Premières Informations Et Premières Synthèses*, vol. 11, pp. 223-228.

Amira, S. and Favre, D. (1996), 'Les bénéficiaires de l'allocation de solidarité spécifique', *Premières Informations Et Premières Synthèses*, vol. 10, pp. 217-221.

Balan, D. and Minni, C. (1995), 'De l'école à l'emploi. Les jeunes en mars 1994', *Receuil D'Études Sociales*, vol. 3, pp. 241-244.

Banco Hipotecario Argentaria (1992), 'Nota de Coyuntura inmobiliaria', Banco Hipotecario Argentaria, Madrid.

BANESTO (1991), 'Guía Facil. Renta '90', BANESTO, Madrid.

Barailler, C. (1997), 'Le marché du travail des jeunes. Analyse Comparative en Europe', Mémoire de DEA, GREQAM, France.

Battagliola, F., Brown, E. and Jaspard, M. (1997), 'Itinéraires de passage à l'âge adulte. Différences de sexe, différences de classe', *Sociétés Contemporaines*, vol. 25, pp. 85-103.

BEL (1994), 'Boletín de Estadísticas Laborales', Ministerio de Trabajo y Seguridad Social, Madrid.

BEL (1996), 'Boletín de Estadísticas Laborales', Ministerio de Trabajo y Seguridad Social, Madrid.

Beltrán Villalba, M. and others (1984), 'Informe sociológico sobre la juventud española 1960/82', Fundación Santa María, Madrid.

Blanc, M. and Bertrand, L. (1996), 'France', in P. Balchin (ed.), *Housing Policy in Europe*, Routledge, London/New York.

Blazévic, B., Detour, C. and Martinez, D. (1997), 'Le logement locatif de 1992 a

1996', INSEE Resultats. Consommation-Modes de Vie, vol. 93-94, INSEE, Paris.

Blöss, T. and others (1990), 'Cohabiter, décohabiter, recohabiter. Intinéraires de deux générations de femmes', *Revue Française De Sociologie*, vol. XXXI, pp. 553-572.

Blossfeld, H.-P. (ed.) (1995), 'The New Role of Women. Family Formation in Modern Societies', Westview Press, Boulder/San Francisco/Oxford.

Boelhouwer, P. and Heijden, H.V.D. (1992), 'Housing Systems in Europe: Part I. A Comparative Study of Housing Policy', Delft University Press, Delft.

Boelhouwer, P. and Heijden, H.V.D. (1993), 'Housing Policy in Seven European Countries: The Role of Politics in Housing', *Netherland Journal of Housing and the Built Environment*, vol. 8, pp. 383-404.

Bolot-Gittler, A. (1992), 'Le système d'indemnisation du chômage: évolution et caractéristiques entre 1979 et 1991', *Dossiers Statistiques Du Travail Et De L'Emploi*, vol. 84, pp. 33-80.

Bordigoni, M., Demazière, D. and Mansuy, M. (1994), 'L'insertion professionnelle à l'épreuve de la 'jeunesse'. Points de vue sur les recherches françaises', Working Paper of the Network on Transitions in Youth, Seelisberg.

Bordigoni, M. and Mansuy, M. (1997), 'Les parcours professionnels des lycéens et apprentis débutants', *Economie Et Statistique*, vol. 304-305, pp. 109-120.

Borrell, J. (1992), 'Una nueva política al paso de las necesidades', *Alfoz.*, vol. 87/88, pp. 35-39.

Bouder, A., Mansuy, M. and Werquin, P. (1995), 'Les moments de l'intervention publique sur le marché du travail en Europe?', Working paper for International Workshop "Transitions in Youth: Comparisons over Time and Across countries", Oostvoorne, The Netherlands, 22-25 September, Céreq, Marseille.

Bourdieu, P. and Passeron, J.C. (1970), 'La Reproduction', Editions de Minuit, Paris.

Bozon, M. and Villeneuve-Gokalp, C. (1995), 'L'art et la manière de quitter ses parents', *Population Et Sociétés*, vol. 297, pp. 1-4.

Bradshaw, J. and others (1993), 'Support for Children. A comparison of arrangements in fifteen countries', HMSO, London.

Breen, R. (1998), 'The persistence of class origin inequalities among school leavers in the Republic of Ireland, 1984-1993', *British Journal of Sociology*, vol. 49, pp. 275-298.

Bruckner, E., Karin Knaup and Walter Müller (1993), 'Soziale Beziehungen und Hilfeleistungen in modernen Gesellschaften', Working Paper of the MZES, Mannheimer Zentrum für Europäische Sozialforschung, Mannheim.

Buchmann, M. (1989), 'The Script of Life in Modern Society. Entry into Adulthood in a Changing World', University of Chicago Press, Chicago/London.

Cachón Rodríguez, L. (1997), 'Dispositivos para la inserción de los jóvenes en el mercado de trabajo en España (1975-1994)', *Cuadernos De Relaciones Laborales*, vol. 11, pp. 81-116.

Casal Bataller, J. (1993), 'L'emancipació familiar dels joves', Tesis doctoral, Universitat Autònoma de Barcelona, Barcelona.

Cases, L. (1995), 'De moindres hausses de loyer en 1994', INSEE Première, vol.

375, INSEE, Paris.

Castles, F.G. and Ferrera, M. (1996), 'Home Ownership and the Welfare State: Is Southern Europe Different?', *South European Society & Politics*, vol. 1, pp. 163-185.

Catala, S. (1989), 'L'utilisation des SIVP et des contrats d'adaptation:approch sectorielle', *Travail Et Emploi*, vol. 40, pp. 89-94.

Caussat, L. (1995), 'Les chemins vers l'indépendance financière', *Èconomie Et Statistique*, vol. 283-284, pp. 127-136.

Cavalli, A. and Galland, O. (eds) (1993), 'L'allongement de la jeunesse', Actes Sud, Poitiers.

Cavalli, A. and others (1984), 'Giovani oggi. Indagine Iard sulla condizione giovanile in Italia', Il Mulino, Bologna.

Charraud Ses, A. (1993), 'L'aide à l'insertion des jeunes: concilier le social et l'économique', in INSEE (ed.), *La société française. Données sociales 1993*, INSEE, Paris, pp. 138-144.

Chew, K.S.Y. (1990), 'Urban Industry and Young Nonfamily Households', in D. Myers (ed.), *Housing Demography. Linking Demographic Structure and Housing Markets*, The University of Wisconsin Press, Wisconsin, pp. 62-108.

CIS (1986), 'Condiciones de vida y trabajo en España', Centro de Investigaciones Sociológicas/Ministerio de Economía y Hacienda, Madrid.

CJB (1998), 'La problemática del trabajo y la vivienda en los jóvenes: análisis y soluciones', Working Paper, Consell de la Joventut de Barcelona, Barcelona.

Clausen, J. (1993), 'Kontinuität und Wandel in familialen Generationenbeziehungen', in Lüscher and F. Schultheis (eds), *Generationenbeziehungen in "postmodernen" Gesellschaften. Analysen zum Verhältnis von Individuum, Familie, Staat und Gesellschaft*, Universitätsverlag Konstanz, Konstanz, pp. 111-124.

Clémençon, M. and Coutrot, L. (1995), 'La relation formation-chômage. France: quelques résultats d'analyse secondaire et bilan bibliographique', *Sociologie Du Travail*, vol. 4, pp. 739-756.

CNOUS (1998), 'Chiffres-clés', August, www.Cnous.fr/chiffres.htm.

Coles, B. (1995), 'Youth and Social Policy. Youth Citizenship and Young Careers', University College London, London.

Coll Cuota, P. and Martin Jadraque, R. (1989), 'La protección de la maternidad, de la familia y de la vivienda', *Revista De Economía y Sociología Del Trabajo*, vol. 3, pp. 67-83.

Commaille, J. and Singly, F.D. (1996), 'La politique familiale', Problèmes politiques et sociaux, La documentation Française, Paris(; v. 761).

Commission of the European Communities (ed.) (1989), 'Young Europeans in 1987', ECSC-EEC-EAEC, Luxembourg.

Commission of the European Communities (ed.) (1991), 'Young Europeans in 1990', Eurobarometer, ECSC-EEC-EAEC, Luxembourg (v. 34.2).

Conde, F. (1985), 'Las relaciones personales y familiares de los jóvenes', Ministerio de Cultura/Instituto de la Juventud, Madrid.

Consejo de Universidades (1991), 'Guía de la Universidad 1991', Ministerio de Educación y Ciencia/Consejo de Universidades, Madrid.

Consejo de Universidades (1992), 'Anuario de estadística universitaria 1991', Ministerio de Educación y Ciencia/Consejo de Universidades, Madrid.

Consejo de Universidades (1993), 'Anuario de estadística universitaria 1992', Ministerio de Educación y Ciencia/Consejo de Universidades, Madrid.

Consell de la Joventut de Barcelona (1998), 'La problemática del trabajo y la vivienda en los jóvenes: análisis y soluciones', Working Paper, vol. 7 de febrero, Consell de la Joventut de Barcelona, Barcelona.

Contreras, J. (1991), 'Los grupos domésticos: estrategias de producción y reproducción', in Contreras and others (eds), *Antropología de los Pueblos de España*, Santillana, Madrid, pp. 343-380.

Coopers & Lybrand (1993), 'Manual practico para la declaracion de la renta '92', Coopers & Lybrand/BBV, Madrid.

Cortés Alcalá, L. (1995), 'La cuestión residencial. Bases para una sociología del habitar', Fundamentos, Madrid.

Crouch, C. (forthcoming), 'Western European Societies. Social Change in Contemporary Europe in an International Context'.

Cruz Cantero, P. and Santiago Gordillo, P. (1999), 'Juventud y entorno familiar', INJUVE, Madrid.

Curci, G. (1990), 'Tour de France des loyers. Les loyers dans 24 agglomerations en 1989', INSEE Première, vol. 89, INSEE, Paris.

Curci, G. and Taffin, C. (1991), 'Les écarts de loyer', *Economie Et Statistique*, vol. 240, pp. 29-36.

Delgado Diaz, J. (1989), 'Los nuevos impuestos sobre la renta y el patrimonio (1988-1989 y ejercicios anteriores no prescritos)', SIETE, Valencia.

Delgado Pérez, M. and Livi-Bacci, M. (1992), 'Fertility in Italy and Spain: The Lowest in the World', *Family Planning Perspectives*, vol. 24, pp. 162-171.

Delhoume, B. (1995), 'L'aide sociales', in M. Montalembert (ed.), *La protection sociale en France*, La documentation Française, Paris, pp. 67-74.

DEP (1995), 'Repères & références statistiques sur les enseignements et la formation. Année scolarie et universitaire 1993-1994/1994-1995', Ministère de l'éducation nationale, de l'enseignement supérieur, de la recherche et de l'insertion professionnelle/Direction de l'évaluation et de prospective, Paris.

Desplanques, G. (1994), 'Etre ou ne plus être chez ses parents', *Population Et Sociétés*, vol. 292, pp. 1-4.

Dienel, C. (1993), 'Bildungschancen und Bildungskosten-Massnahment zur Ausbildungsfoerderung in Europa als Teil der Familienpolitik', in Neubauer and others (ed.), *Zwölf Wege der Familienpolitik in der Europäischen Gemeinschaft. Eigenständige Systeme und vergleichbare Qualitäten? Studie im Auftrag des Bundesministriums für Familie und Senioren*, Kohlhammer, Stuttgart/Berlin/Köln.

Dumartin, S. (1994), 'Générations et emploi depuis 1970', *Receuil D'Études Sociales*, vol. 1, pp. 259-262.

Duncan, S. (1996), 'The Diverse Worlds of European Patriarchy', in D. García-Ramón and J. Monk (eds), *Women of the European Union. The Politics of Work and Daily Life*, Routledge, London and New York, pp. 74-110.

Dupeyroux, J.J. (1988), 'Droit de la sécurité sociale'. onzième édition, Dalloz,

Paris.
EC (1992), 'Employment in Europe 1992', Commission of the European Communities, Luxembourg.
Elzo Imaz, J. (ed.) (1994), 'Jóvenes españoles 94', Fundacíon Santa María, Madrid.
Elzo, J. (ed.) (1990), 'Jóvenes vascos 1990. Informe sociológico sobre actitudes y valores de la juventud vasca actual', Servicio Central de Publicaciones del Gobierno Vasco, Vitoria-Gasteiz.
Elzo, J.et.al. (1999), 'Jóvenes españoles 99', Fundación Santa María, Madrid.
EPA (1991), 'Encuesta de la Población Activa. Resultados detallados', vol. II. trimestre, INE, Madrid.
Eurobarometer (1993), 'Europeans and the Family', vol. 39, Commission of European Communities, Brussels.
EUROSTAT (1990), 'Family Budgets. Comparative tables: FR of Germany, Spain, France, Ireland, Italy, Netherlands', EUROSTAT, Luxembourg.
EUROSTAT (1992), 'Demographic Statistics', EUROSTAT, Luxembourg.
EUROSTAT (1995), 'Estadísticas Básicas de la Unión Europea', EUROSTAT, Luxembourg.
EUROSTAT (1997), 'Les jeunes de l'Union européenne ou les âges de transition', EUROSTAT, Luxembourg.
EURYDICE (1993), 'Die wichtigsten Systeme der Ausbildungsförderung für Hochschulstudenten in der Europäischen Gemeinschaft, Juni 1993', EURYDICE, Bruxelles.
EURYDICE (1996), 'Key Data on Education in the European Union', ECSC-EC-EAEC, Luxembourg.
Fernández Cordón, J.A. (1997), 'Youth Residential Independence and Autonomy: A Comparative Study', *Journal of Family Issues*, vol. 18, pp. 576-607.
Fernández Mellizo-Soto, M. (2000), 'Education Policy and Equality in France: a Comparison with the European Union and Its Evolution During the Socialist Years', *Journal of Education Policy*, vol. 15, pp. 11-17.
Flaquer, L. (1995), 'El modelo de familia española en el contexto europeo', in Sarasa and L. Moreno (comp), *El estado del bienestar en la Europa del sur*, CSIC/IESA, Madrid, pp. 289-312.
Flaquer, L. (2000), 'Las políticas familiares en una perspectiva comparada', Fundación La Caixa, Barcelona.
Flora, P. (1974), 'Modernisierungsforschung. Zur empirischen Analyse der gesellschaftlichen Entwicklung', Westdeutscher Verlag, Opladen.
Flórez Saborido, I. (1994), 'La contratación laboral como medida de política de empleo en España. La creciente flexibilidad en el acceso al empleo', Consejo Económico y Social, Madrid.
Forgeot, G. (1997), 'Les salaries d'embauche des jeunes: l'influence du statut au premier emploi', *Economie Et Statistique*, vol. 304-305, pp. 95-107.
Fraser, N. and Gordon, L. (1994), '"Dependency" Demystified: Inscriptions of Power in a Keyword of the Welfare State', *Social Politics*, vol. 1, pp. 4-31.
Galland, O. (1993), 'La jeunesse en France, un nouvel age de la vie ', in Cavalli and O. Galland (eds.), *L'allongement de la jeunesse*, Actes Sud, Poitiers.
Galland, O. (1995), 'Changing Family Transitions: Young People and New Ways

of Life in France', in Chrisholm, L. et al. (eds.), *Growing Up in Europe. Contemporary Horizons in Childhood and Youth Studies*, de Gruyter, Berlin/New York, pp. 133-144.

Galland, O. (1995), 'Une entrée de plus en plus tardive dans la vie adulte', *Economie Et Statistique*, vol. 283-284, pp. 33-51.

Galland, O. and Lambert, Y. (1993), 'Les jeunes ruraux', Harmattan/INRA, Paris.

Galland, O. and Oberti, M. (1996), 'Les étudiants', La Découverte, Paris.

García de Polavieja, J. (1998), 'La dualización del mercado de trabajo en España. Clase y tipo de contrato en la diferenciación de oportunidades económicas', Paper presented at the Spanish Sociological Congress of 1998, 1998.

Garrido, L. and Requena Miguel (1996), 'La emancipación de los jóvenes en España', Ministerio de Trabajo y Asuntos Sociales, Madrid.

Garrido Medina, L. (1996), 'La temporalidad.¿pacto intergeneracional oimposición?', in Consejo Económico y Social (ed.), *La duración del contrato de trabajo*, Consejo Económico y Social/Comunidad de Madrid, Madrid, pp.47-74.

Garrido Medina, L. (1997), 'La familia estatal: El control fiscal de la natalidad', in L. Garrido Medina and E. Gil Calvo (eds.), *Estrategias familiares*, Alianza, Madrid, pp.157-180.

Garrido Medina, L. (2001), 'Estructura y evolución de los sistemas formativos en la Unión Europea', in Instituto Nacional de Estadística (ed.), *Condiciones de vida en España y en Europa. Estudio basado en el Panel de Hogares de la Unión Europea (PHOGUE). Años 1994-1995*, Instituto Nacional de Estadística, Madrid, pp.79-116.

Gavira Alvarez, L. (1993), 'Segmentación del mercado de trabajo rural y desarrollo: el caso de Andalucía', Ministerio de Agricultura, Pesca y Alimentación, Madrid.

Gaye, M. (1995), 'L'exonération de cotisations patronales pour l'embouche d'un premier, d'un deuxième ou troisième salarié en 1994', Premières Synthèses, Ministère du Travail, du Dialogue Social et de la Participation/DARES, Paris (vol. 113).

Geindre, F. (1994), 'Le logement une priorité pour le XIe plan. Rapport au Premier ministre', Ministère du Logement, Paris.

Ghékiere, L. (1991), 'Marches et Politiques du Logement dans la CEE', La Documentation Française, Paris.

Glaude, M. (1991), 'L'organisation du système du quotient familial', *Economie Et Statistique*, vol. 248, pp. 51-67.

Glick, P.C. and Lin, S.-L. (1986), 'More Young Adults Are Living with Their Parents: Who Are They?', *Journal of Marriage and the Family*, vol. 48, pp. 107-112.

Goldscheider, F.K. and Goldscheider, C. (1993), 'Leaving Home Before Marriage. Ethnicity, Familism and Generational Relationships', University of Wisconsin Press, Wisconsin.

Goldscheider, F.K. and Waite, L.J. (1987), 'Nest-Leaving Patterns and the Transition to Marriage for Young Men and Women', *Journal of Marriage and the Family*, vol. 49, pp. 507-516.

Gómez Churruca, R. and Levenfeld, G. (1993), 'La accesibilidad a la vivienda en España', *Revista Española De Financiación a La Vivienda*, vol. 24/25, pp. 65-71.

Gomez, P. (1989), 'De motor de recuperación a clave de la economía sumergida', *Alfoz*, vol. 64, pp. 24-26.

Greeley, A. (1989), 'Protestant and Catholic: Is the Analogical Imagination extinct?', *American Sociological Review*, vol. 54, pp. 485-502.

Guibert-Lantoine de, C. and others (1994), 'La cohabitation adulte', *Population & Sociétés*, vol. 293, pp. 1-3.

Guide (1990), 'Guide des politiques de la jeunesse. Paysages, dispositifs, réfèerences', Syros/Alternatives, Paris.

Heath, S. and Miret, P. (1995), 'Living in and out of the parental home in Spain and Great Britain: a comparative approach', Working Paper presented at the Second European Conference for Sociology, Budapest.

Holdsworth, C. (2000), 'Leaving Home in Britain and Spain', *European Sociological Review*, vol. 16, pp.201-222.

Holdsworth, C. and Miret, P. (1997), 'Leaving Home in Britain and Spain', unpublished manuscript, Manchester.

Iacovou, M. (1998), 'Young people in Europe: Two models of household formation', *ISER Working Paper*, University of Essex, Institute for Social and Economic Research, no. 98-13, Essex.

Iglesias de Ussel, J. (1989), 'Juventud y familia', *Revista De Estudios De Juventud*, vol. 31, pp. 79-91.

INE (1995), 'Censo de Viviendas, 1991', Instituto Nacional de Estadística, Madrid.

INE (1995), 'Encuesta de Presupuestos Familiares 1990-91', vol. IV: resultados por CCAA, Instituto Nacional de Estadística, Madrid.

INE (1995), 'Encuesta sociodemográfica 1991', vol. I: principales resultados, Instituto Nacional de Estadística, Madrid.

INSEE (1992), 'Enquêtes sur l'emploi de 1990 et 1991. Résultats détaillés', Institut national de la statistique et des études économiques, Paris.

INSEE (1993), 'Annuaire Statistique de la France 1993', INSEE, Paris.

INSEE (1993), 'La société française. Données sociales 1993', Institut National de la Statistique et des Etudes Economiques, Paris.

INSEE (1994), 'Marché du travail. Séries longues', Resultats. Emploi-Revenus, vol. 305-306, INSEE, Paris.

INSEE (1996), 'Annuaire Statistique de la France 1996', INSEE, Paris.

INSS (1996), 'Guia de la Seguridad Social', Instituto Nacional de la Seguridad Social, www.inss.es.

Instituto de la Juventud (1994), 'Juventud y Consumo. Actitudes y comportamientos de los jóvenes españoles ante el consumo', Ministerio de Asuntos Sociales//Instituto de la Juventud, Madrid.

Instituto Nacional de Estadística (1993), 'Encuesta Sociodemográfica 1991', vol. II. Resultados Nacionales, INE, Madrid.

Instituto Nacional de Estadística (1993), 'Encuesta Sociodemográfica 1991. Metodología', Instituto Nacional de Estadística, Madrid.

Jallade, J.P. (1991), 'L'enseignement supérieur en Europe. Vers une évaluation comparée des premiers cycles', La Documentation Française, Paris.

Jallade, J.P., Lamoure, J. and Lamoure Rontopoulou, J. (1993), 'Tertiary Diversification in France and the Conditions of Access', in C. Gellert, *Higher Education in Europe*, Jessica Kingsley Publishers, London/Philadelphia.

Jepperson, R.L. (1991), 'Institutions, Institutional Effects and Institutionalism', in Powell and P. J. DiMaggio (eds.), *The New Institutionalism in Organizational Analysis*, The University of Chicago Press, Chicago/London, pp. 143-163.

Jones, G. (1995), 'Leaving home', Open University Press, Buckingham.

Jones, G. and Wallace, C. (1992), 'Youth, Family and Citizenship', Open University Press, Buckingham/Philadelphia.

Juès, J.P. (1996), 'L'emploi des jeunes en France', Que sais-je?, Presses Universitaires de France, Paris.

Julliot, J. (1991), 'La sécurité sociale', La Villeguerin Editions, Paris.

Jurado Guerrero, T. (1995), 'Legitimation durch Sozialpolitik? Die spanische Beschäftigungskrise und die Theorie des Wohlfahrtsstaates', *Kölner Zeitschrift Für Soziologie Und Sozialpsychologie*, vol. 47, pp. 727-752.

Jurado Guerrero, T. (1997), 'Un análisis regional de los modelos de convivencia de los jóvenes españoles. Las cuatro Españas de la emancipación familiar', *Revista De Estudios De Juventud*, vol. 39, pp. 17-36.

Jurado Guerrero, T. and Naldini, M. (1996), 'Is the South so Different? Italian and Spanish Families in Comparative Perspective', *South European Society & Politics*, vol. 1, pp. 42-66.

Kaufmann, F.X. (1990), 'Zukunft der Familie. Stabilität, Stabilitätsrisiken und Wandel der familialen Lebensformen sowie ihre gesellschaftlichen und politischen Bedingungen', Beck Verlag, München.

Kaufmann, J.-C. (1994), 'Les ménages d'une personne en Europe', *Population*, vol. 4-5, pp. 935-958.

Kiernan, K. (1986), 'Leaving home: living arrangements of young people in six West-European countries', *European Journal of Population*, vol. 2, pp. 177-184.

Kiernan, K. (1989), 'The departure of children', in Grebenik and others (eds.), *Later phases of the family cycle. Demographic aspects*, Clarendon Press, Oxford.

Leal, J. (ed.) (1992), 'Informe para una nueva política de vivienda', Ministerio de Obras Públicas y Transportes, Madrid.

Leal Maldonado, J. (1997), 'Emancipación y vivienda', in R. Vergés Escuín (ed.), *La edad de emancipación de los jóvenes*, Centre de Cultura Contemporània de Barcelona, Barcelona, pp. 113-124.

Lefranc, C. and Thave, S. (1994), 'L'évolution de l'environement familial des enfants', *Population*, vol. 6, pp. 1297-1320.

Lenoir, R. (1991), 'Politique familiale et construction sociale de la famille', *Revue Française De Science Politique*, vol. 41, pp. 781-807.

Lepsius, R.M. (1995), 'Institutionenanalyse und Institutionenpolitik ', *Kölner Zeitschrift Für Soziologie Und Sozialpsychologie*, Sonderheft.

Leridon, H. and Toulemon, L. (1995), 'France', in H.P. Blossfeld, *The New Role of Women. Family Formation in Modern Societies*, Westview, Boulder et al. pp. 77-101.

Levenfeld, G. (1990), 'Política de vivienda en Alemania, Reino Unido y Francia', *Revista Española De Financiación a La Vivienda*, vol. 12, pp. 25-36.

Levenfeld, G. (1993), 'La fiscalidad de la vivienda en España', *Revista Española De Financiación a La Vivienda*, vol. 24/25, pp. 45-52.

Levenfeld, G. (1993), 'Principales instrumentos en política de vivienda', *Revista Española De Financiación a La Vivienda*, vol. 24/25, pp. 53-58.

López Jiménez, M.A. (1987), 'Los jóvenes de Aragón. Mil y una sendas para el futuro', vol. I, II, Diputación General de Aragón, Zaragoza.

Lorente, J.R. (1986), 'La política de fomento del empleo juvenil', *Papeles De Economía Española*, vol. 26, pp. 298-310.

Luxán Serrano, M., Miret Gamundi, P. and Treviño Maruri, R. (forthcoming), 'Is the Male Provider Model Still in Place? Partnership Formation in Contemporary Spain', in J. González, T. Jurado and M. Naldini (eds), *Gender Inequalities in Southern Europe: Women, Work and Welfare in the 1990s*, Frank Cass, London.

Magnac, T. (1997), 'Les stages et l'insertion professionnelle des jeunes: une évaluation statistique', *Economie Et Statistique*, vol. 304-305, pp. 75-94.

Márquez, L.F. (1992), 'Equilibrio económico y pacto social. Una perspectiva empresarial', in S. M. Ruesga (ed.), *Economía y Trabajo*, Pirámide, Madrid.

Marry, C., Fournier-Mearelli, I. and Kieffer, A. (1995), 'Activité des jeunes femmes: héritages et transmissions', *Économie Et Statistique*, vol. 283-284, pp. 67-79.

Martín Rodríguez, M. (1996), 'Disparidades económicas regionales en España: nuevas aportaciones', *Estudios Regionales*, vol. 44, pp. 165-186.

Martín Serrano, M. and Velarde Hemida, O. (1997), 'Juventud en cifras 96', INJUVE, Madrid.

Martínez, M. and Ruiz-Castillo, J. (2001), 'The Decisions of Spanish Youth: A Cross-section Study', *Journal of Population Economics*, forthcoming.

Martínez, R. and Berney, J. (1991), 'Enquesta a la joventut de Catalunya-1990', Generalitat de Catalunya, Barcelona.

MAS (1994), 'Los jóvenes y la vivienda. Acciones en materia de acceso juvenil a la vivienda. Perspectiva', Ministerio de Asuntos Sociales, Madrid.

Masjuan, J.M., Toiano, H., Vivas, J. and Zaldivar, M. (1996),), *La inserció professional dels nous titulats universitaris*, Universitat Autònoma de Barcelon/Insitut de Ciències de l'Educació, Barcelona.

Massit-Folléa, F. and Epinette, F. (1992), 'L'Europe des universités', La documentation Française, Paris.

Mayer, K.U. (1997), 'Notes on a Comparative Political Economy of Life Courses', *Comparative Social Research*, vol. 16, pp. 203-226.

Mayer, K.U. and Müller, W. (1989), 'Individualisierung und Standardisierung im Strukturwandel der Moderne. Lebensverläufe im Wohlfahrtsstaat', in A. Weymann (ed.), *Handlungsspielräume: Untersuchung zur Individualisierung und Institutionalisierung von Lebensläufen in der Moderne*, Enke, Stuttgart, pp. 41-75.

Mayer, K.U. and Schwarz, K. (1989), 'The process of leaving the parental home: some german data', in E. Grebenik (eds), *Later phases of the family cycle.*

Demographic aspects, Clarendon Press, Oxford.

Mayer, K.U. and Wagner, M. (1989), 'Wann verlassen Kinder das Elternhaus? Hypothesen zu den Geburtsjahrgängen 1929-31, 1939-41, 1949-51', in Herlth and K. P. Strohmeier (eds), *Lebenslauf und Familienentwicklung. Mikroanalysen des Wandels familialer Lebensformen*, Leske+Budrich, Opladen, pp. 17-38.

MEC (1988), 'El sistema educativo español 1988', Ministerio de Educación y Ciencia, Madrid.

MEC (1992), 'El sistema educativo español 1991', Ministerio de Educación y Ciencia, Madrid.

MEC (1994), 'Estadística de la enseñanza en España. 1991/92. Niveles de preescolar, infantil, general básica y enseñanzas medias', Ministerio de Educación y Ciencia, Madrid.

MEN (1994), 'Géographie de l'école', vol. février, Ministère de l'éducation nationale/Direction de l'évaluation et de la prospective, Paris.

Menard, S.W. (1995), 'Applied logistic regression analysis', Sage university paper series.. Quantitative Applications in the Social Sciences, Sage, London/New Dehli(; v. 07-97).

Menniti, A. and others (1994), 'Nuovi comportamenti nuziali in Italia', Working Paper for Convegno Internazionale: Mutamenti della famiglia nei paesi occidentali. Changes in Family pattern in Western Countries, Bologna.

Meron, M. and Minni, C. (1995), 'Des études à l'emploi: plus tard et plus difficilement qu'il y a vingt ans', *Économie Et Statistique*, vol. 283-284, pp. 9-31.

Ministerio de Fomento (1992), 'Anuario estadístico 1992', Ministerio de Fomento, Madrid.

Ministerio de Fomento (1996), 'Anuario estadístico 1996', Ministerio de Fomento, Madrid.

Ministerio de Trabajo y Seguridad Social (1993), 'Anuario de Estadísticas Laborales', Ministerio de Trabajao y Seguridad Social, Madrid.

Ministerio de Trabajo y Seguridad Social (1993), 'Anuario de estadísticas laborales 1992', Ministerio de Trabajo y Seguridad Social, Madrid.

Ministerio de Trabajo y Seguridad Social (1995), 'Formación profesional ocupacional', Textos Legales, Ministerio de Trabajo y Seguridad Social, Madrid.

Ministerio de Trabajo y Seguridad Social (1996), *'Boletín De Estadísticas Laborales'*, vol. 137, Ministerio de Trabajo y Seguridad Social, Madrid.

Miret Gamundi, P. (1996), 'Nuptiality Patterns in Spain in the Eighties', Paper presented at the 1996 Annual Conference of the British Society for Population Studies. Centre for Social Sciences, University of St. Andrews, St. Andrews.

MISSOC (1992), 'Social Protection in the Member States of the Community. Situation on July 1st 1992 and evolution', Commission of the European Communities, Luxembourg.

Moncel, N. and Rose, J. (1995), 'Spécificités et déterminants de l'emploi des jeunes de 18 à 25 ans et de 26 à 29 ans: vers la fin de la transition professionnelle?', *Économie Et Statistique*, vol. 283-284, pp. 53-66.

MOPU (1987), 'Política de vivienda. Plan Cuatrienal 1984-1987. Programa Económico a Medio Plazo', Ministerio de Obras Públicas, Madrid.

Morales, L. (forthcoming), 'Political Participation: Exploring the Gender Gap in Spain', in J. González, T. Jurado and M. Naldini), *Gender Inequalities in Southern Europe: Women, Work and Welfare in the 1990s*, Frank Cass, London.

MTSS (1988), 'La política de empleo en España. Informe de base sobre instituciones, procedimientos y medidas de política de empleo', Ministerio de Trabajo y Seguridad Social/Comisión de las Comunidades Europeas, Madrid.

MTSS (1991), 'Guia laboral 1991. Fomento del empleo, formación ocupacional, prestaciones por desempleo, pensiones, inspección información, etc', Ministerio de Trabajo y Seguridad Social, Madrid.

MTSS (1992), 'La protección por desempleo. Prestación de nivel contributivo', Ministerio de Trabajo y Seguridad Social, Madrid.

Muro, J. and others (1988), 'Análisis de las condiciones de vida y trabajo en España', Ministerio de Economía y Hacienda, Madrid.

Nalidini, M. (2001), 'Evolution of Social Policy and The Institutional Definition of Family Models. The Italian and Spanish Cases in Historical and Comparative Perspective', Frank Cass, London, forthcoming.

Navarro López, M. and Mateo Rivas, M. J. (1993), 'Informe Juventud en España', Instituto de la Juventud, Madrid.

Neubauer, E. and others (1993), 'Zwölf Wege der Familienpolitik in der Europäischen Gemeinschaft. Eigenständige Systeme und vergleichbare Qualitäten? Studie im Auftrag des Bundesministriums für Familie und Senioren', Kohlhammer, Stuttgart/Berlin/Köln.

Nicole-Drancout, C. and Roulleau-Berger, L. (1995), 'L'insertion de jeunes en France', Presses Universitaries de France, Paris.

OECD (1989), 'Evolution des modes de financement de l'enseignement superieur. Rapport national: France', Working Paper, vol. avril, OECD, Paris.

OECD (1994), 'Employment Outlook 1994', OECD, Paris.

OECD (1994), 'The OECD Jobs Study. Evidence and Explanations. Labour Market Trends and Underlying Forces of Change', vol. 1, OECD, Paris.

OECD (1995), 'Education and Employment. Indicators of Education Systems', OECD, Paris.

OECD (1996), 'Employment Outlook 1996', OECD, Paris.

OECD (1996), 'Reviews of National Policies for Education. France', OECD, Paris.

Orizo, F.A. and others (1985), 'Juventud Española 1984', Fundación Santa María, Madrid.

Pablo Masa, A. de. (1976), 'La familia española en cambio', in Fundación FOESSA), *Estudios sociológicos sobre la situación social en España. 1975*, Fundación FOESSA/Euramérica, Madrid, pp. 345-404.

Parlamento Europeo (1995), 'Medidas a favor de los desempleados jóvenes en la Unión Europea. Resumen', Serie de Asuntos Sociales, Parlamento Europeo, Luxembourg(vol. E-3a).

Planas, J., Casal, J., Brullet, C. and Masjuan, J. M. (1995), 'La inserción social y profesional de las mujeres y los hombres de 31 años', Institut de Ciènies de

l'Educació/Universitat Autònoma de Barcelona, Barcelona.
Prinz, C. (1995), 'Cohabiting, Married or Single', Avebury, Aldershot.
Ragin, C. (1987), 'The Comparative Method. Moving Beyond Qualitative and Quantitative Strategies', University of California Press, Berkeley/ Los Angeles/ London.
Ragin, C. (1989), 'New Directions in Comparative Research. Divided Intellectual Labor?', in M. L. Kohn (ed.), *Cross-national Research in Sociology*, Sage, London, pp. 57-76.
Ragin, C. and Hein, J. (1993), 'The Comparative Study of Ethnicity. Methodological and Conceptual Issues', in H. Stanfield II and R. M. Dennis (eds), *Race and Ethnicity in Research Methods*, Sage, Newbury Park, pp. 254-272.
Rassat, E. (1995), 'Plus de 600000 étudiants bénéficient d'une aide au logement', *Recherches Et Prévisions*, vol. 40, pp. 57-64.
Raymond, M. (1995), 'Pauvreté, précarité, RMI', in M. Montalembert (ed.), *La protection sociale en France*, La documentation Française, Paris, pp. 37-44.
Reher, D.S. (1991), 'Marriage patterns in Spain, 1887-1930', *Journal of Family History*, vol. 16, pp. 7-30.
Reher, D.S. (1997), 'Perspectives on the Family in Spain, Past and Present', Clarendon Press, Oxford.
Requena y Díez de Revenga, M. (2001), 'Los hogares en Europa con especial referencia a España', in Instituto Nacional de Estadística (ed.), *Condiciones de vida en España y en Europa. Estudio basado en el Panel de Hogares de la Unión Europea (PHOGUE). Años 1994-1995*, Instituto Nacional de Estadística, Madrid, pp.31-78.
Requena, M. (2001), 'Los jóvenes españoles de los años noventa: formación, trabajo, convivencia', *Revista De Educación*, forthcoming.
Richter, R. (1992), 'Higher Education System. France', EUROMECUM, Stuttgart.
Rivière, J. (1996), 'La formación como ocupación y como adquisición de capital humano', in L. Garrido and M. Requena, *La emancipación de los jóvenes en España*, Ministerio de Trabajo y Asuntos Sociales/Instituto de la Juventud, Madrid.
Rodríguez, J. (1993), 'El carácter redistributivo de la política de vivienda', I. Simposio sobre igualdad y distribución de la renta y la riqueza, vol. 24-28 Mayo, Argentaria, Madrid, pp. 147-159.
Rodríguez López, J. (1994), 'El esfuerzo de acceso y política de vivienda en España', *Familia y Sociedad*, vol. 1/2, pp. 41-50.
Rossi, A.S. and Rossi, P. H. (1990), 'Of Human Bonding. Parent-Child Relations Across the Life Course', de Gruyter, New York.
Roussel, L. (1988), 'Die soziologische Bedeutung der demographischen Erschütterung in den Industrieländern der letzten zwanzig Jahre', in K. Lüscher (eds), *Die "postmoderne" Familie. Familiale Strategien und Familienpolitik in einer Übergangszeit*, Universitätsverlag Konstanz, Konstanz, pp. 39-54.
Sanchez Villar, P. (1993), 'Los precios de las viviendas en España: un comentario a las estadísticas', *Revista Española De Financiación a La Vivienda*, vol. 24/25, pp. 29-36.

Schaeferbarthold, D. (1992), 'Economic and Social Support for Students in France', *European Higher Education and Institutions: EUROMECUM*, vol. September, pp. 2-11.

Schultheis, F. (1993), 'Genealogie und Moral: Familie und Staat als Faktoren der Generationenbeziehungen', in K. Lüscher and F. Schultheis (eds), *Generationenbeziehungen in "postmodernen" Gesellschaften. Analysen zum Verhältnis von Individuum, Familie, Staat und Gesellschaft*, Universitätsverlag Konstanz, Konstanz, pp. 415-433.

Segura, J. and others (1991), 'Análisis de la contratación temporal en España', Ministerio de Trabajo y Seguridad Social, Madrid.

Serrano Secanella, P. (1997), 'La vivienda como determinante de la emancipación juvenil', in R. Vergés Escuín (ed.), *La edad de emancipación de los jóvenes*, Centre de Cultura Contemporània de Barcelona, Barcelona, pp. 91-98.

Smith, L.B. and others (1984), 'The demand for housing, household headship rates and household formation: An international analysis', *Urban Studies*, vol. 21, pp. 407-414.

Steinhilber, J. (1995), 'Frankreich: Schlanke Marianne?', in H.J. Bieling (ed.), *Arbeitslosigkeit und Wohlfahrtsstaat in Westeuropa. Neun Länder im Vergleich*, vol. 7, Institut für Politikwissenschaft des Fachbereichs Gesellschaftswissenschaften und Philosphie der Philipps-Universität Marburg, Marburg, pp. 77-106.

Stewart, G. and Stewart, J. (1988), '"Targeting" Youth or How the State Obstructs Young People's Independence', *Youth and Policy*, vol. 25, pp. 19-24.

Szydlik, M. (1995), 'Die der Beziehung zwischen erwachsenen Kindern und ihren Eltern-und umgekehrt', *Zeitschrift Für Soziologie*, vol. 24, pp. 75-94.

Taffin, C. (1991), 'Accession: l'ancien réhabilité', *Economie Et Statistique*, vol. 240, pp. 5-18.

Talego Vázquez, F. (1995), 'Los grupos domésticos jornaleros: Producción de hijos y preparación de la fuerza de trabajo. El caso de Lebrija', *Estudios Regionales*, vol. 41, pp. 205-228.

Tilly, C. (1984), 'Big Structures, Large Processes, Huge Comparisons', Sage, New York.

Toharia Cortés, L. (dir (1994), 'Empleo y paro', in M. Juárez (ed.), *V Informe sociológico sobre la situación social en España. Sociedad para todos en el año 2000*, vol. 2, Fundación FOESSA, Madrid, pp. 1277-1413.

Toharia, L. and Muro, J. (1988), 'Es elevado el salario de los jóvenes?', *Economía y Sociología Del Trabajo*, vol. 1/2, pp. 42-52.

Trilla, C. and others (1998), 'Polítiques d'Habitatge A Catalunya', in S. Giner (ed.), *La Societat catalana*, Institut d'Estadística de Catalunya, Barcelona.

Trotabas, L. and Cotteret, J.M. (1990), 'Droit fiscal', sixième, Dalloz, Paris.

Tuchszirer, C. (1993), 'Bilan de la politique de l'emploi en 1992', *Dossiers statistiques du travail et de l'emploi*, vol. 96-97, Ministère du travail, de l'emploi et de la formation professionnelle, Paris, pp. 20-31.

Tuchszirer, C., Gélot, D. and Zilberman, S. (1993), 'Les effets des aides publiques à l'emploi des jeunes, une comparaison contrat de qualification "exo-jeunes"', *Travail Et Emploi*, vol. 3, pp. 80-87.

Valenzuela Rubio, M. (dir (1994), 'La vivienda', in M. Juárez (ed.), *V Informe sociológico sobre la situación social en España. Sociedad para todos en el año 2000*, Fundación FOESSA, Madrid, pp. 1551-1734.

Valero, A. (1992), 'La prevalencia de la familia nuclear en el sistema familiar español', *Revista Internacional De Sociología,* vol. Tercera época 3, pp. 183-210.

Valiente, C. (1995), 'Family Obligations in Spain', in Millar and A. Warman, *Social Policy Papers*, vol. 23, University of Bath, Bath.

Valles, M.S. (1992), 'Hogar, familia y matrimonio', in A. de Miguel (ed.), *La sociedad española 1992-93*, Alianza Editorial, Madrid.

Valles, M.S. (1992), 'Los jóvenes y la constitución de los nuevos hogares y familias', in A. Miguel de, *La sociedad española, 1992-93*, Alianza Editiorial, Madrid.

Vaskovics, L. (1993), 'Elterliche Solidarleistungen für junge Erwachsene', in Lüscher and F. Schultheis, *Generationenbeziehungen in "postmodernen" Gesellschaften. Analysen zum Verhältnis von Individuum, Familie, Staat und Gesellschaft*, Universitätsverlag Konstanz, Konstanz, pp. 185-202.

Villac, M. (1993), 'La politique familiale. Débats autour d'une définition', *Solidarité Santé. Etudes Statistiques*, vol. 4, pp. 9-30.

Villalard, J. (1986), 'Bilan statistique du programme de travaus d'utilité collective', vol. 23-24, Ministèere des Affaires Sociales et de l'Emploi, Paris, pp. 91-102.

Villeneuve-Gokalp, C. (1990), 'Du mariage aux unions sans papiers: histoire récente des transformations conjugales', *Population*, vol. 45, pp. 265-297.

Villeneuve-Gokalp, C. (1997), 'Le départ de chez les parents: définitions d'un processus complexe', *Economie Et Statistique*, vol. 304-305, pp. 149-162.

Wagner, M. and Huinink, J. (1991), 'Neuere Trends beim Auszug aus dem Elternhaus', in G. Buttler (eds), *Acta Demographica*, Physica-Verlag, Heidelberg, pp. 39-62.

Wallace, C. (1988), 'Between the Family and the State: Young People in Transition', *Youth and Policy*, vol. 25, pp. 25-36.

Wallerstein, I. (1984), 'Household Structures and Labor-Force Fomation in the Capitalist World-Economy', in Smith, I. Wallerstein and H.D. Evers (eds.), *Households and the World Economy*, Sage, Beverly Hills/ London/ New Dehli.

Weick, S. (1993), 'Determinanten des Auszugs aus der elterlichen Wohnung', in Diekmann and S. Weick (Hg), *Der Familienzyklus als sozialer Prozeß. Bevölkerungssoziologische Untersuchungen mit den Methoden der Ereignisanalyse*, Duncker & Humblot, Berlin.

Werquin, P. (1997), '1986-1996: dix ans d'intervention publique sur le marché du travail des jeunes', *Economie Et Statistique*, vol. 304-305, pp. 121-135.

World Values Survey (1990-1993) Inglehart, Ronald. Köln: Zentralarchiv für empirische Sozialforschung; ICPSR Nr. 6160.

Yi, Z. and others (1994), 'Leaving the Parental Home: Census-based Estimates for China, Japan, South Korea, United States, France, and Sweden', *Population Studies*, vol. 48, pp. 65-80.

Young, C.M. (1989), 'The Effect of Children Returning Home on the Precision of the Timing of the Leaving-Home Stage', in Grebenik and others (eds), *Later*

phases of the family cycle. Demographis aspects, Clarendon Press, Oxford.
Zárraga, J.L. (1985), 'Informe juventud en España. La inserción de los jóvenes en la sociedad', Ministerio de Cultura/Instituto de la Juventud, Madrid.
Zárraga, J.L.d. (1989), 'Informe Juventud en España 1988', Ministerio de Asuntos Sociales/Instituto de la Juventud, Madrid.
Ziegler, R. and Schladt, D. (1993), 'Auszug aus dem Elternhaus und Hausstandsgründung', in Diekmann and S. Weick (Hg), *Der Familienzyklus als sozialer Prozeß. Bevölkerungssoziologische Untersuchungen mit den Methoden der Ereignisanalyse*, Duncker & Humblot, Berlin.

Index